THE ZEN
OF
EMPIRICAL RESEARCH

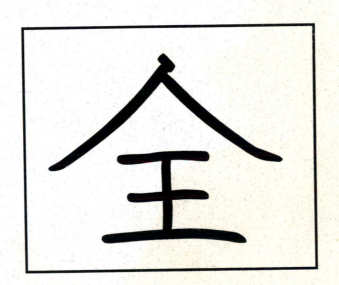

William D. Richards, Jr.

THE ZEN
OF
EMPIRICAL RESEARCH

Quantitative Methods in Communication

George A. Barnett, Editor

Persuasion: Advances Through Meta-Analysis
Mike Allen and Raymond W. Preiss, eds.

Network Models of the Diffusion of Innovations
Thomas W. Valente

The Zen of Empirical Research
William D. Richards

THE ZEN
OF
EMPIRICAL RESEARCH

William D. Richards, Jr.
Simon Fraser University

HAMPTON PRESS, INC.
CRESSKILL, NEW JERSEY

© 1998 by Hampton Press Inc.

Printed in the United States of America.

Library of Congress Catalog-in-Publication Data

Richards William D.
    The Zen of Empirical Research / William D. Richards, Jr.
        p. cm. – – (Quantitative methods in Communication)
    Includes bibliographic references and indexes.
    ISBN 1-57273-245-8
      1. Research. 2. Research – – Statistical methodsI. Richards, William.   I. Title.
II. Series.
Q180.A1R53   1998
001.4 – – dc21   98 – 43366
                                                      CIP

Hampton Press Inc.
23 Broadway
Cresskill, NJ 07626

This book is dedicated to my father who gave me the educational opportunities that he deserved but didn't have. Thanks, Dad.

CONTENTS IN BRIEF

CONTENTS IN DETAIL

II. Univariate Statistics

III. Bivariate Descriptive Statistics

V. Research approaches

Preface

Several years ago I was teaching a research methods course and the students were having trouble understanding the textbook. I started to write "notes" that explained sections of the text in an informal, conversational style. Because the students seemed to appreciate my notes, I revised what I had written and wrote several new pages each time I taught the course. It wasn't too long before the students asked why they had to buy the expensive and difficult text when my notes covered almost all the material we dealt with in the course, so the next time I taught the course I used my notes for the text. I continued to revise and expand the notes until I sent a copy to my friend Diane MacFarland who had told me she was looking for something she could use in a course she was about to teach. She said good things about it to George Barnett, the editor of this series, and he asked me if I would consider making it a "real" book. I want to thank Diane and George for the role they played in the development of this book.

I tried to write the book as if I was having a conversation with a few students. I think this is what makes this book different from many I have studied over the years. As you read it, you will hear me say things like "There are two ways to do this. If you are trying to . . . , you should take this approach . . ." I know this isn't considered "correct" academic writing, but I think it is more important that you understand what I am trying to say than that you are impressed with my proper academic sophistication.

My friend Saul Pilar suggested the title. I liked it right away, but the more I thought about it, the more right I knew it was. The title is accurate: the book *is* about the Zen of empirical research.

You may be wondering what the "Zen" of empirical research is. Zen is a different way of seeing and understanding the world. It requires the practitioner to relinquish the everyday attachment to the various demands, goals, ideas, and interpretations of events, objects, and situations. The goal is to put irrelevant details aside and go directly to the core or essence of the event.

When you work with empirical research, you also have to see and understand things in a different way than you do in day-to-day life. Here, too, the goal is to put irrelevant details aside and go to the core or essence of the event you are investigating. The two parts of research that give people the most difficulty are its dependence on precision and its use of what to most people seems like a backwards type of logic. Most of my students have a lot more trouble with these factors than they do with the mathematical part of statistics.

The precision I'm talking about here is not the precision of exact measurement, but rather the precision of the words you use to describe your research. When you are talking or writing about research, you can't use the same loose, casual style you use in day-to-day life. In order for the people who hear or read your words to understand what you are talking about, you have to choose your words carefully so that you say exactly what you mean to say, rather than something that might just as easily be interpreted to mean any of a dozen different things. This is where most of my students seem to have great difficulty. When I ask them about something they wrote on an exam, they often say "Yeah, but that is what I meant! I know that's not what I wrote, but that's what I meant." This is important because when other researchers read what you said about your work, they will assume you meant what you said and not something that you meant but didn't say.

The logic of research plays a central role in your ability to use empirical methods to answer questions about the world. The logic is the glue that makes little bits of information stick together in a way that allows you to formulate questions and use evidence to determine answers to the questions. You often will have to deal with a chain of logical steps, every one of which depends on all the ones leading up to it. The logical connections depend on correct use of logic and on clearly understood and precisely stated facts and relationships.

I hope you enjoy this book. Take your time. Think about what you are trying to say. Make sure that your words say what you mean.

WDR   richards@sfu.ca
Vancouver, British Columbia
March 23, 1998

"20 Ways to Prove Significance"
Jennifer Auten, 12/97

(To the tune of Paul Simon's "50 Ways to Leave Your Lover")

I see the problem's still inside your heads when you look at me
Isn't it easy when you think it logically?
I'd like to help you with your struggle to reject the null . . .
There must be twenty ways to prove significance.
I say it's really not my habit to intrude,
But Lord I hope my meaning won't be lost or misconstrued
But I repeat myself at the risk of being crude:

There must be twenty ways to prove significance.

Chorus

Difference 'tween the two means, Jean   A difference this large, Marge,
Is statistically significant, Kent   Ain't due to chance alone, Joan
The difference is real, Neil   Can't be no fluke, Luke
Ya gotta hear my speil: No coincidence, Vince.

Reject that null, yeah gotta reject that null

I say, it grieves me so to see you in such pain
Wish there was something I could do to make you smile again
You say you're glad I said that and
"Would you please explain about the twenty ways?"
I say, there's no reason to have to sleep on it tonight
'Cuz right here and now I can show you the light
And then you smile at me and you realize I'm probably right
There must be twenty ways to accept the null
There must be twenty ways to accept the null

Chorus

Difference 'tween the two means, Jean   Could be a fluke, Luke
Not statistically significant, Kent   Probably coincidence, Vince.
Easily due to chance alone, Joan   Those samples are odd, Todd,
Come on, hear my drone: No, you can't reject that null!

Yeah, reject that null
Yeah, reject that null
Yeah, reject that null

There must be twenty ways . . . .

I

Scientific Research

Chapter 1

Science

Research begins with a question. How many of these are also those? Why do so many of those end up in these circumstances? How often does this happen? Why does it seem to happen mainly to this type of person? etc.

Some questions can be studied empirically because they are questions about people or events or circumstances in the world that do or do not happen. Other questions can be the topic of heated debate, but they can never be resolved by looking to see what is actually the case. Other questions seem to fall partly in both categories. It is important to understand the kinds of questions that can be studied and to see how they can be framed in ways that make answers possible to find.

This book is about research—the process of asking questions about the world around you and getting answers to those questions. In particular, it's about *empirical* research—research in which the questions are about things that exist or happen, and in which the answers are obtained by somehow observing things in the world.

For purposes of this book, I'll divide "research" into three categories: *exploratory*, *descriptive*, and *explanatory*. Some people would add *evaluative* research as a fourth category, but I treat that as a combination of descriptive and explanatory research.

Some research is *exploratory* in nature, going where no one has been before. We don't know what to expect here, so we go with open eyes and ears and, we hope, minds. What kinds of issues are important to examine? How should these issues be approached? What kinds of obstacles must be overcome to do this kind of research? A few years ago I was asked to do some research on the communication networks of foster parents in British Columbia. Because I didn't know anything about foster parents or foster parenting (e.g. Where did they live? How many foster children did they have? What kinds of problems did they have to deal with? What kinds of support and assistance were available to them? Did they know one another? How did they fit into the community around them? What problems might I encounter in studying their communication patterns? What resources would be required in doing this research? Would they be willing to talk to me?) I had to begin with some exploratory research.

Once I had this background information, I was able to plan a *descriptive* study that would get at the specific kinds of information I wanted. Here my goal

was to obtain a complete and accurate *description* of events, conditions, circumstances, processes, and relationships surrounding the communication patterns of the foster parents. What were they like? What were relevant features of the interpersonal, familial, social, economic, and political contexts in which they lived? To whom did they turn for different kinds of information, for different kinds of support or assistance, etc. What kind of relationships did they have with the natural parents of their foster children? How typical were their experiences? Notice that this kind of research might tell me what was happening, but it wouldn't explain the causes of anything I saw.

To get at explanations of causal relationships between events and circumstances, a different kind of research would be more useful. When we are interested in causal relationships, we do *explanatory* research. How do the educational backgrounds of foster parents influence the way they relate to their children? Is a foster parent's success with children who come from abusive families influenced by the number and kind of relationships the parent has with other foster parents? Is the extent to which the foster parent is socially integrated related to the ability of the parent's foster children to form strong intimate ties when they become adults? Explanatory research is the most demanding kind of research, and it requires the use of special methods to identify causes and effects.

Science

The world is full of uncertainty and danger. To increase our chances of survival, we strive continuously to *understand* ourselves and our surroundings; to *predict* how people will behave and respond to our behavior; and to *control* those parts of reality that determine how our lives turn out.

Those key words—understand, predict, control—are the focus of science, which is about knowledge. (The word "science" comes from the Latin verb *scire*, which means "to know".) What makes science different from common-sense approaches to knowing about the world is that scientific explanations are subjected to empirical tests. This means that there must be evidence to support the conclusions of the explanations.

The nature of scientific inquiry

You generate knowledge about the world by systematically observing *events* and *phenomena* and by looking for *patterns* in what you observe—relations between classes of events or phenomena and other events or phenomena. Often you are not satisfied with the knowledge that a pattern or relation exists; you want explanations of why the relations and patterns are the way they are.

You perform these activities every day. I notice that people seem more likely to respond when I send them e-mail than when I send them an ordinary letter. When I want someone to do something, I'm more likely to receive cooperation when I ask them face-to-face than when I ask them over the phone or when I scribble a note. I also notice that certain themes in movies tend to make me feel unsettled for days, while others make me angry and others don't seem to do anything at all. These are examples of relationships I've noticed over time, as a result of reflecting on my own personal experience.

There are other relationships I have learned about, but not through my own experience. For example, I know that giving aspirin to a child who has measles may lead to serious medical problems. I know that you are more likely to change your attitude if you write an argument about why it would be a good thing to do than if you listen to me tell you why it would be a good thing to do. I know that taller people are often hired in preference to shorter people. I know that Canadian films are not as good as American films. And I know that we only use about 15% of our brains.

How did I learn these things, if not from my own experience? I learned about aspirin and measles on a radio program on the CBC. I learned about the power of "counter-attitudinal advocacy" in a course on interpersonal communication. I don't remember the source of the business about taller people, but it was probably a story in the newspaper. I don't really *know*

that Canadian films aren't as good, but ... , well, everyone knows they aren't, ... right?[1] And an article in *Readers' Digest* told me that "scientists have shown" that we use only 15% of our brains. If "scientists" demonstrated this, it must be true, even though the article appeared in *Readers' Digest* and not a scientific journal.

So knowledge comes from different sources: personal experience, textbooks or professors, the media, people around us, and anonymous "scientists." The "knowledge" from these different sources varies in its "hardness," in the sense that some is more dependable, more accurate, more "true." The sources vary in their credibility, and as well, any particular source will vary in the extent to which different people will believe it. In our society, people seem to rely more on knowledge that is "scientific"—knowledge that results from the use of something called the "scientific method." This book examines how the scientific method is applied in the study of communication.

Single instances vs. general patterns

A distinction is drawn between two modes of research—*idiographic* and *nomothetic-deductive*. The *idio* in "idiographic" also appears in "**idio**syncratic," which means "characteristic of thought or behavior *peculiar to an individual or group*." An idiographic study is one that explores a single person or event or situation in detail. Although the researcher doing this kind of work would learn a great deal about the idiosyncratic thoughts or behaviors of the person or situation, this information would apply only to the specific situation that was studied. Although it might give the researcher some ideas of what to look for in the wider context, it can't be used to describe the population from which the case studied was drawn.

The researcher who wants to learn something about social regularities—things that apply to people in general—must take a different approach. The nomothetic-deductive method is the one that is used

for this purpose. The *nom* in "**nom**othetic" appears in words like "auto**nom**y," "eco**nom**y," and "astro**nom**y"—all words that describe *systems of laws or principles that govern different aspects of reality*. Nomothetic research attempts to discover what those systems of laws or principles are, while idiographic research is interested in describing only a single event, person, or situation.

Since it is interested in discovering the laws or principles that govern aspects of reality, nomothetic research cannot depend on information that describes a single individual. It needs information that describes enough cases so that general patterns or relationships can be seen. Ideally, it would use information that describes all people, events, or situations. This is clearly an impossibility, so a different approach is taken. Rather than using what might be called a "brute force" strategy, in which all possible cases would be examined, we use a method that replaces the naive application of persistence with an elegant set of *logical tools*.

These logical tools are based on the relation between an entire population and a subset of that population. If the subset is chosen in the right way, you can learn about the population by studying the much smaller subset. These "subsets" are, of course, samples.

The scientific method is a four-stage process: you make *observations*; you develop a *theoretical explanation* for those observations; you *operationalize* the abstract concepts that you used in your explanation; and finally, you *verify* the explanation in a process that involves making more observations. Since the final stage often involves revising the explanations, the process is cyclic and doesn't really have an end.

Since the process requires that you observe the world around you and then use your reasoning abilities to make sense of what you see, science is a *logico-empirical* system of knowing. This means that the knowledge obtained through the use of the scientific method should be based on the actual world around you (it's empirical), and it should be consistent with your experiences. It is the fourth stage, *verification*, that makes the scientific approach so de-

---

[1] *I* think many Canadian films are *better* than American films.

pendable. Anyone can come up with an explanation for even the most bizarre situations, but these explanations can't be considered scientific until they have been tested for reasonableness, consistency, and validity.

Three Assumptions of Science

In order for the scientific approach to work, some important conditions must be met. Reality (at least the parts of it that are subjected to scientific investigation) must be well-behaved in the sense that effects have causes and the relationship between causes and their effects can be explained without reference to magical or paranormal connections, like telekinesis, psychic channeling, divine intervention, and so on. Smith (1988, p. 6) states these requirements as three fundamental assumptions:

1) *all objects of scholarly inquiry are directly or indirectly observable.*

Scientific phenomena have "empirical referents,"

I grew up just a few miles north of Windsor Ontario. I moved to California in 1971 to go to graduate school. I found, after several months, that people in California were different from the people I knew back east. I also found there to be some subtle differences in the way people seemed to relate to one another and to me. There was an apparent openness and easy familiarity—people were friendly and almost anyone would talk to you—but it seemed much more difficult to become really close to anyone.

After going through my first warm sunny winter, I decided that the reason people in California were like that was that the Environment was their Friend and they didn't need other people. In the east we had to huddle together around the fireplace in the winter and around the air conditioner in the summer. We had to run and hide from tornados, and some strong connections were forged while huddling in a corner and waiting for the "all clear" sirens to sound. This didn't happen in California, where the environment was warm and friendly—not hostile and something to be avoided, like it was back home.

Here are some personal observations of individual events, followed by an attempt to "understand" or "explain" what is going on. The explanation required some generalization from a relatively small number of specific instances and events to a much larger domain of social existence. Once I got the idea that the causal factor was the "environment," it became easy to find more and more evidence that I was on the right track. This reminds me of another piece of informal "research" I've been conducting for the last fifteen years or so.

I often had the experience of being outside when a small plane flew overhead. It seemed to me that much of the time when this happened, the shadow of the plane passed directly over me. There was a period of two or three years in which the shadow of every small plane that flew across the sky passed over me. Every one of those planes eclipsed the sun for a brief instant. Every one, without fail.

What's going on here? I suspect that I notice the planes flying overhead when they block the sun for an instant. If a plane didn't get between me and the sun, I probably would be less likely to notice it. When I do this, I am practicing a common type of selective perception. I only see the evidence that would support my belief. This is probably what was happening in the case of the "Friendly Environment," but that was a much more complex situation. It is easy to measure the number of planes that fly overhead; consider the difficulty of measuring something as abstract and socially complex as "it's easy here to meet people, but really hard to get close to anyone."

which means that their existence can be either observed or *inferred* from observation. If you are interested in an abstract concept, such as how biased the television news coverage of a particular story is, you measure (observe) the level of bias by looking for things you would see if it were biased. These things, whatever they are, will be used as *indicators* of bias. While the bias itself is abstract and not directly observable, the indicators are concrete and thus easily observed.

2) *the world we live in is structured and orderly, not chaotic and disconnected.*

All effects have causes, and any observable effect is caused by some thing or things. There is nothing spontaneous and disconnected. This doesn't necessarily mean that you will be able to determine the causes for every effect, though, because you may not know how or where to look for the connections.

3) *empirical phenomena can be explained by referring to other natural antecedent phenomena.*

This implies that all empirical phenomena are explainable. In principle, nothing is completely beyond the realm of comprehension. Furthermore, "other-worldly" or metaphysical explanations are rejected; natural phenomena can be explained by referring to other natural phenomena. You assume the world is consistent and coherent—not mysterious, disjointed, and magical.

The scientific method is one approach to knowing. Babbie compares it to others, including *tradition*, which is how we know about Canadian films, and *authority*, which is how I know about aspirin and measles (1989, pp. 7-28). In your day-to-day life, you make a number of errors as you gather knowledge. You make inaccurate observations. Since the information on which you base your conclusions is faulty, your conclusions lack validity. You overgeneralize—you see a few instances of a pattern or relationship, and you assume what you see is typical, when that may not be the case. You are guilty of selective perception—you notice an interesting pattern and you pay attention to future events or situations that

can be matched to the pattern, while you ignore anything that doesn't fit. You fill in the gaps with information that you make up on the spot. Of course you're usually not aware of doing this, because it seems so logical and appropriate that you enjoy great success in convincing yourself that it's true and accurate. You use illogical reasoning. I'm sure you've heard contradictions explained by the expression "the exception that proves the rule," which neither makes sense nor explains anything. Finally, you engage in mystification—you simply decide that some things are just beyond your ability to understand or comprehend. They are that way because that is their fate. Recently I was told that the reason a neighbor's house was broken into was that "he has bad karma."

The scientific method uses a number of tools that work to prevent the kinds of problems mentioned above. This book will introduce you to those tools so you can better understand the empirical research that you encounter as a student and so that you can make use of them in your own research.

If you wanted to characterize science, you could start with a summary of its essential qualities. Here are four of them:

1) *Science is systematic.* Science proceeds in a deliberate, orderly fashion. There are particular steps that must be taken, and they must be taken in a particular order.

2) *Science is rational.* It uses precise rules of logic. Two particular systems of logic are especially important:

a) *Induction* begins with information about specific instances and moves to a generalized inference about patterns or relationships that would explain the specific cases—from facts to theories. This form of logic is used in the development of explanations.

b) *Deduction* applies a theory to a particular case. It starts with a general statement about patterns or relationships (an explanation) and moves to conclusions about particular instances that

would be logically implied if the general statement were true. This form of logic is used in the verification of explanations. (If this explanation is true, you would expect to see X. Do you see X?)

3) *Science is cyclical and self-correcting*. Scientists begin with generalizations—conclusions about or explanations of some observed pattern in the data. If these conclusions or explanations are correct, they will be able to say that they understand the situation they are studying. So they test the generalizations against reality by making additional observations and comparing them with the predictions of the generalizations. The conclusions or explanations are revised on the basis of the result of these tests. The revised generalizations are again tested against reality by making additional observations … etc.

4) *Science is positive*. It deals with questions about what *is* and *why* it is, rather than what *ought to be*. A recent graduate student at my university wrote a thesis about assisted suicides. Who participated in the suicides and how the participants felt about what they did and what arguments they made about the correctness or appropriateness of their actions were all valid topics for scientific enquiry. Science could not, however, determine whether it is wrong to assist someone to commit suicide. This is a question of personal values and beliefs.

A Scientific Approach to Communication Research

When you study communication scientifically, you work with three processes—theory, operationalization, and observation. (If any of these are missing, you can't *do* science.) In what is often called the "Classical Scientific Method" these processes happen in this order.

You develop a *theoretical explanation* for the situation you are investigating. A theoretical explanation is a set of statements about a number of concepts and the relations between them. You might be inter-ested in the increasing divorce rate in Canadian cities. Your theoretical explanation may relate a number of concepts, such as a shift away from older traditions, increasing exposure to a variety of ethnic customs, and pressures on family structures created by the increasingly explicit content of popular media. Your theory would specify how these concepts are related to one another and how they come together to produce an increase in the divorce rate.

To connect your theory to the world you live in, you have to *operationalize* your concepts. That is, you have to create explicit links from the abstract concepts in the theory to concrete phenomena in the real world. How do you recognize a "shift from older traditions"? What are the older traditions? How do you know there is a shift away from them? How can you determine how explicit the "popular media" are? What counts as explicit? And how does this bring pressure on family structures? What is the nature of that pressure, and how can you see it in action? And so on. The links you make between the abstract and the concrete play a critical role in scientific research—the whole operation depends on their validity.

Finally you need to perform some *observations*. Everything we've done so far could take place in the library or in your study, but now it's necessary to go out into the world and collect some data on what happens there. This is the part that makes science empirical. You might think the observation part means looking or watching or listening to what happens. It does, but it also means analyzing what you see or hear. Somehow you need to establish the connection between the concrete and the abstract once again, so your results can be brought to bear on the theory you started with. One of the tools you use to do this is statistics. You'll learn something about statistics in this book—what it is about and how it is used in the study of communication.

Theory

I said above that a theory is a set of statements about a number of constructs and the relations between

them. More specifically: a *theory* is a formal statement of definitions and propositions concerning the relations among a set of constructs created for the purposes of explanation, understanding, prediction, and control of phenomena[2].

Most theories have three components: a *generative force* or motivating reason (x), a pattern of *effects* (y), and a set of *boundary conditions* (z) that specifies how and under what circumstances the generative force is likely to explain its effects (see Smith, 1988, pp. 11-12). Several years ago I did some research to investigate a theory about the relation between the way violence is portrayed in films and the effect the violent content would have on people who watched the film. The theory suggested that people who watched what was then called "sanitized violence"—violence from which the gruesome, painful, destructive, disfiguring consequences have been removed—were much more likely to see violence as a quick, efficient, and acceptable way of responding to problems than were people who saw the "unsanitized" version. Here the generative force is exposure to violent content; the effects are changes in the way people view violence as a method of dealing with problems; and the boundary condition is the extent to which the gory consequences are shown.

There are different kinds of *generative forces* in theories, leading to different forms of explanations. The simplest kind are ordinarily called "causes." A *cause* is an antecedent condition (something that happens first) that produces a consequent *effect* (something that happens later as a result of what happened earlier) over which the people involved have no control. The effect happens whether or not the person or people involved want it to; it is an unavoidable consequence of the cause. In the above example, exposure to violence and seeing or not seeing the consequences of the violence are causes.

The specific relation between the cause and the effect is often called a "mechanism," which suggests that this type of explanation may be somehow "mechanical." A theory that explains patterns by reference to uncontrollable antecedents employs

causal explanation and is called a *law*. (*ex:* Because they are naturally more aggressive and solitary, men make more assertions and give more orders than women; because they are naturally more cooperative and social, women ask more questions and make more requests than men. Men and women behave like this *because* they are men and women, not because they want to or they think they should.)

A second, more complex, type of generative force is the *rule*. A theory that explains communication patterns by reference to norms or social customs employs *rule-based explanation* and is called a *rule* of communication. Rules can take many different forms. In most countries, for example, people almost always cover certain parts of their bodies when they are in public places, even when it is warm. They do this because it is a social norm—a rule. In job interviews, people tend to perform more nonverbal actions that show deference and respect for the person giving the interview than they do in other circumstances. They do this because there is a norm (a rule) about how one behaves toward an employer. When you approach an intersection in which the traffic light is red, you stop because there is a law (a particular type of rule) that specifies what you should do in intersections. Note that it is quite possible to break these rules, although there is usually a price to be paid if you are caught.

A third type of generative force is the *reason*. A reason refers to the preexisting goals, needs, and desires of a person that explain patterns of behavior and of communication. A theory that explains patterns by reference to goals or subjective reasons for acting is called a *teleological* explanation. (*ex:* In order to avoid confusion and resulting problems, I edit my exam questions very carefully. In order to extract more warmth and caring behavior, I exaggerate the pain caused when someone "accidentally" bumps my head while putting a frying pan away.) A great deal of research energy is directed toward understanding the dynamics of communication behavior by focusing on how people's goals and their efforts to achieve them affect how they interact with one another.

---

[2] Kerlinger, 1964, p. 11

Induction (Data-to-Theory)

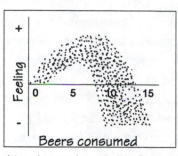

You observe how people feel after they drink different amounts of beer.

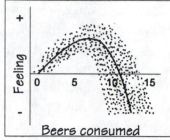

You notice there is a pattern in your data. This is an "inverted U-shaped" relationship.

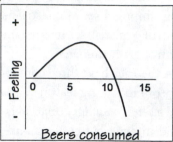

You conclude that people in general feel "better" when they drink more beer, up to a point at which more beer makes them feel worse — much worse!

Constructing Theory

There are two approaches to constructing theory. They differ in how they treat the relation between the data and the statements that comprise the theory. There has been a good deal of controversy about the conflict between these approaches.

1) When the scientist begins by making observations and then constructing a theoretical explanation that would account for the observed patterns, the logic is called *data-to-theory* and the logical method being used is *inductive*. The logical pattern is to move from the specific to the general. The data-to-theory method is sometimes called "grounded theory." This approach is useful for the

creation of theories in areas where there hasn't been much previous research. However, one weakness of this approach is that theories created in this fashion *always* match the data upon which they are based. Looking to see how well the theory "fits" the data only tells how good a job the theorist did while describing the data; the data cannot be used to test the theory. For this reason the data-to-theory approach is combined with the theory-to-data approach.

2) When the scientist begins with a theory which is tested against observed data, the logic is called *theory-to-data* and the logical process being used is *deductive*. The pattern here is to move from the general to the specific—exactly the opposite of the

Deduction (Theory-to-Data)

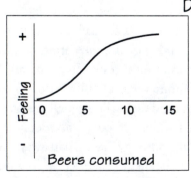

You hypothesize that drinking beer makes people feel good, and that the more beer one drinks, the better one feels.

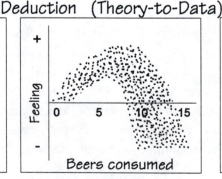

You observe how people feel after they drink different amounts of beer.

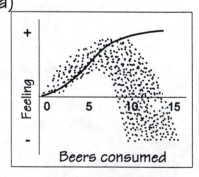

You compare your hypothesized pattern with your observed data and conclude your hypothesis needs to be revised. (After Babbie, 1989, p. 43)

inductive method. In the theory-to-data method, data are used to test the theory. A failure of the data to fit the theory is usually taken as an indication that there is something wrong with the theory, with the measurement methods (and thus with the data), with the methods being used to compare the data to the theory, or with the logic leading the researcher to expect the theory to fit the data.

While the inductive researcher is supposed to create explanations of observed data, the deductive researcher can get explanations from any source desired. In practice, the two modes of research are complimentary: the inductive approach is used in the development of theory and the deductive approach is used in the verification of theory. Used together, the two methods are much stronger than either one used separately.

Verifying Theoretical Explanations

Once you've developed your theoretical explanation, you will want to test it. Do things work the way your theory says they do? Does the theory need to be modified? At this point, the theory is nothing more than an argument based on some knowledge, some assumptions, some suppositions, and some reasoning. I could come up with a different theory that would explain the same situation, but it might be based on different concepts related in a different way, or it might have a different generative force. If you compare what the two theories say about a situation, you might see that they do not agree with one another. In any case, the next step is to test your theoretical explanation.

Right away you run into a problem. Theories are statements about relations between abstract concepts—they don't say anything about concrete reality. For example, the "uncertainty reduction theory" of social relationships says that in the early stages of a relationship, the participants will engage in certain kinds of activities aimed at reducing the uncertainty associated with not knowing one an-

other. The theory says that the relationship will not be able to develop unless this uncertainty is reduced to an acceptable level. The key concepts here are uncertainty, the uncertainty-reduction process, and the development of relationships. You can't observe these abstract concepts directly, though, so you need a way to make the theory connect with the concrete world. Here is where you use some deductive reasoning. Remember that deduction starts with a general statement relating concepts to one another (an explanation) and moves to specific conclusions about particular instances that would be logically implied if the general statement were true.

You don't test the abstract theory directly; instead, you test the specific conclusions logically implied by the theory. If the theory is true, you would expect to see particular things happen in certain situations. Because of the theory, you can make predictions about what will happen in these situations. These predictions are called *hypotheses*. Since hypotheses are predictions about specific things that may or may not happen in particular situations, they can easily be tested. Do you see what you would predict on the basis of the theory? If you do, you have obtained some evidence that supports the theory. On the other hand, if you don't see what you would predict, you know you have a problem.

Even if you do see the evidence, though, you still can't say that you have proven that the theory is true. This is because several different explanations could lead to the same conclusions. These *alternative explanations* may fit the data just as well, although they may be based on completely different generative forces and relations between phenomena. Since it is not possible to rule out all alternative explanations, it is not possible to prove the truth of a theory. However, you may be able to demonstrate that the theory is consistent with all existing evidence; it would thus be as good as if it were the one true explanation, until a situation that provokes obvious errors is encountered.

Pay careful attention to the little logical maneuver described in the above two paragraphs: Because theories are abstract, they cannot be tested directly. If

a theory is true, you should be able to see evidence of it in the concrete world you live in. Hypotheses are predictions about things that should happen in the concrete observable world. They are also logically implied by the theory—if the theory is true, the predictions made in hypotheses should also be true. This is why researchers test hypotheses when they are really interested in their theories.

Here are four criteria you may use to evaluate a theory:

1) *Empirical validity*: If a theory is a "formal statement of definitions and propositions concerning the relations among a set of constructs created for the purposes of explanation, understanding, prediction, and control," the relationships it describes ought to be seen in the data. Do the predictions implied by the theory match the data? Are the hypotheses supported by the data?

2) *Perspicuity*: A perspicuous theory is clear, lucid, readily understandable, and unambiguous. It is precisely stated. It leads to clear, unequivocal predictions. Without clear and precise definitions and predictions, it is neither possible to take the measurements needed to test the theory nor to use the data to draw conclusions about the empirical validity of the theory.

3) *Parsimony*: A parsimonious theory uses few concepts and relation; it is simple and straightforward rather than being a complex mess of many relationships tying numerous concepts together in several different ways. Because it is parsimonious, it is more likely to be internally consistent, and much easier to connect with reality. It is also more likely to lead to unambiguous and unequivocal predictions.

4) *Utility*: Does the theory, like the *USS Enterprise*, go "where no one has gone before"? Does it explain previously inexplicable phenomena? Does it present a parsimonious explanation for a set of phenomena previously thought to be unrelated? Does it have *heuristic value*—does it set the stage for further conceptual developments and empirical research? Should anyone care about the theory? Does it matter? Is it likely to have any effect on their lives?

Research Design

A number of decisions must be made when a research study is planned. These decisions concern a number of issues commonly referred to as "research design." The decisions you make here will have far-reaching implications for how the research is conducted, the nature of the data you obtain, the kinds of analysis you will be able to do, the kinds of information you will obtain about the situation under investigation, and the use to which that information may be put.

Eight of these design issues are reviewed here (in no particular order) and the implications of some combinations of these issues are examined. The presentation follows the one in Smith (1988, pp. 180-182).

1. Quantitative *vs.* Qualitative

This is probably the first distinction you would make when you consider research design. Does the research focus on quantitative issues—does it use numbers and statistics? Is it "scientific"? Does it use complicated or sophisticated approaches to measurement and analysis? Or is the focus on qualitative issues—does it focus on feelings and ideas? Does it examine narratives or stories or cultural issues? Does the data come from transcripts and documents? Is the research more "humanistic" than precise and scientific?

Many people feel this issue is important enough that they identify strongly with one approach in favor of the other. I have known people who consider quantitative research to be useless, irrelevant, weak, and wrong, while they feel qualitative research is valuable, relevant, socially important, and good. At the same time, I have known other people who consider research that doesn't have a mathematical basis to be useless and of no value. For them, the

presence of numbers is a sure sign that the research and its conclusions are valid and good. In some places there seems to be a war between the two camps. "Whose side are you on? Are you one of us or one of them?"

My own position is that Quantitative *vs.* Qualitative is a false dichotomy. These two perspectives are complementary; they are the two sides of the coin. Each one by itself is incomplete and can only give part of the picture. The prudent researcher will combine the two perspectives and produce better results. Much research is both qualitative *and* quantitative at the same time. Finally, the presence of numbers does not necessarily mean that the research is quantitative.

2. Interpretive *vs.* Functional

An increasingly popular approach to research is postmodernist deconstruction in which the "text" is analyzed and the meanings behind everything are laid bare. The interpretive approach focuses on the deeper meanings underlying events or situations. It is by its nature abstract and conceptual. In contrast, the functional approach is concerned with the study of behavior and effects. When meanings are considered here, they will be viewed as causes and effects of various communication behaviors. This research is more likely to be concrete and specific.

3. Manipulated *vs.* Observed

Researchers who want to understand the relations between phenomena may choose to introduce some kind of change to the situation so they can see what happens. The classical laboratory experiment defines one end of this continuum. It begins with random assignment, which produces two equivalent groups. One will be subjected to the changed conditions and the other will not. The other two necessary components of experiments are isolation and manipulation of an independent variable (causal factor), and subsequent measurement of a dependent variable (the effect). A study in which one group of people are shown a movie in which the gory, painful, gruesome consequences of violent acts are clearly depicted and another group are shown a version in which the consequences have been removed illustrates this approach.

The somewhat contrived experimental method may be contrasted with the naturalistic approach in which researchers observe and study processes as they take place in the course of ordinary day-to-day life, free from the artificial manipulations of the experiment. While this strategy may produce more natural or "realistic" results, it does not have the experiment's ability to identify causal relationships. With this approach, a study of the effects of exposure to the consequences of violence may produce some valuable insights, but it will at best be a correlational study that may show that people who do not see the consequences of violence may tend to behave more aggressively than those who see the consequences, but it will not be able to establish a causal link the way the experiment could.

4. Laboratory *vs.* Field

Some research is conducted in an artificial environment, all aspects of which are controlled by the researcher. Other studies take place in a natural environment where people normally are found in the course of day-to-day life. Laboratory studies are useful because the high degree of control allows the researcher to rule out possible disturbances or "contaminations" that would probably cause the results to be less reliable or valid than they otherwise would be.

Field research, on the other hand, leaves the research open to the vicissitudes of ordinary life. The researcher who wants to learn about how people in small communities behave when their houses are destroyed by a tropical storm can't answer the question with a controlled laboratory study; he has to wait for a hurricane or typhoon to develop.

The advantage of field research is that it can be used to address issues in the context in which they ordinarily occur, whereas the laboratory researcher is required to isolate the focus of inquiry from its normal context in order to prevent biasing the results. This clearly poses a dilemma: are the complexities of the field a greater threat than the certain distortions

caused by the decontextualization demanded by laboratory research?

5. Participant *vs* non-participant

The anthropologist graduate student who enrolled as a student in high school and spent a year living as a student—attending classes, hanging out in the cafeteria, participating in extra-curricular activity—all the while taking careful notes about what was done, what was said, how other students felt, and so on, was involved in an observational study as a participant. She became a student in order to gain access to knowledge of the lives of the other students. An outsider wouldn't have a chance to learn as much as the researcher who lived as one of them for a year.

In contrast is the researcher who observes the social interactions of people in a shopping mall from a vantage point at a table in the food fair. He is outside the situation under investigation and would hope to have no effect on the people he is observing. The non-participant will not be able to have the intimate knowledge of the people he is observing.

6. Overt *vs.* Unobtrusive

Students who participate in a psychological study on campus in exchange for $5.00 ("for a few minutes of your time") or for credit in Psychology 100 are aware of the fact that they are participating in someone's research project. Although they may not know the exact nature of the research, no attempt is made to hide the fact that they are being observed or measured. In contrast to the overt approach, the shoppers in the mall who are observed by the researcher sitting at a table in the food fair are not aware of being observed. An even more unobtrusive approach would be to observe the tapes produced by security cameras located high on the ceiling in many places of business. Here, the researcher is not even physically present. Unobtrusive researchers may examine any kind of evidence people may leave, including the oil spots under their cars in parking lots, the contents of their garbage cans, the litter they throw on the street, or the number of rooms in their houses that are lit up in the evening.

While overt methods may seem better for direct measurement of complex issues, the imaginative researcher may be able to devise unobtrusive ways of getting at many issues without intruding on or interrupting the natural flow of daily life in any way.

7. Cross-sectional *vs.* Longitudinal

If you were interested in changes in attitudes of students as they progress through the years of study at University, you could take measurements of a cross-section of students who are at various stages in their studies. Then you might compare students who have completed fewer than 30 credits with those who have completed 60, 90, and 120 credits. You would be approximating the process individuals go through by comparing people at various stages in their academic lives to one another.

On the other hand, you could take a longitudinal approach in which you would follow the same group of students as they progress through their studies. Where the cross-sectional method requires only one measurement at a single point in time, the longitudinal method requires a series of measurements over a much longer period of time. With the longitudinal approach, the processes and changes that are estimated by the interpolation the cross-sectional method requires are actually observed over time as they take place. The obvious drawback to the longitudinal method is that measurements must be made over long periods of time—in some cases, decades. The advantage, however, is that the longitudinal approach situates the observations in a historical context, something that is not possible with the cross-sectional method.

8. Basic *vs.* Applied

Is the research focused on purely theoretical issues with no attention given to specific applications in particular situations, or does it focus on addressing specific real problems in a pragmatic manner? Basic research, sometimes called "pure" research, is usually conducted without any direct, explicit connections to the "real" world. For example, a researcher may investigate the mathematical properties of a class of

equations without giving any consideration to what the equations describe. While this line of research may result in the discovery of unexpected mathematical properties that later turn out to be especially valuable in the analysis of important social situations, the original goal of the researcher was to explore the class of equations, not to develop solutions to social problems.

A researcher who is interested in finding a solution to a particular social problem doesn't care about discovering new mathematical properties. She is doing applied research, and she has a more immediate, concrete goal to worry about. The questions her research is trying to answer are likely to be concrete and to address specific situations or particular conditions at a single point in time.

While some applied research results in discoveries that change the way people understand the world, these kinds of results are more likely to come from basic research, where the focus of inquiry is likely to be abstract and theoretical—not tied explicitly to any particular situation or event.

Recall the distinction made between idiographic and nomothetic research on page 5. An idiographic study is one that explores a single person or event or situation in detail, while the researcher who wants to learn something about social regularities—things that apply to people in general—takes a nomothetic approach. Idiographic research is likely to be qualitative, interpretive, naturalistic, longitudinal study conducted in the natural environment where the subject of the research normally lives. An example would be the kind of study the biographer makes in preparation for a book about the early life of Charles Darwin, for example. While this research may paint a detailed picture of the book's subject, it will not explain social trends or general responses to political or economic events.

The firm that conducts a public opinion poll of attitudes toward a referendum about minority language rights in Quebec or California, on the other hand, is conducting nomothetic research, which tends to be quantitative, non-participant, overt, cross-sectional, and applied in orientation. The poll involves asking a standard set of questions to a large number of people over a short period of time by trained researchers working out of an office equipped with a bank of telephones and computer terminals. The answers to the questions are entered into the computers as the interviews are conducted. One or two days after the last interview has been completed, the results will have been analyzed, tabulated, and ready for interpretation. Patterns of attitudes and, the pollsters hope, voting trends, will be identified, although there will be no information about the attitudes of any single person.

As the book progresses, the research design issues will be referred to from time to time in order to help you see how things fit together. Various studies will be discussed in the readings, in lectures, and in tutorials. If you examine each of these in terms of the eight design issues outlined in the previous pages, you will find it easier to understand the material and to prepare various assignments and exams.

Important Terms and Concepts

abstract concept
alternative explanation
antecedent condition
applied
basic
boundary conditions
cause
causal explanation
cross-sectional
deduction vs. induction
description vs. explanation
effect
empirical
experiment
explanation
field research
functional research
generative forces
goal
grounded theory
heuristic
idiographic vs. nomothetic

interpretive research
laboratory study
law
logically implied
longitudinal
nomothetic-deductive
observable
overt
parsimony
participant observation
perspicuity
positive
rational
reason
research (exploratory, descriptive, explanatory)
rule
rule-based explanation
teleological explanation
theory
unobtrusive
utility

Chapter 2

Conceptualizing

Empirical research addresses *questions* or *hypotheses* about *relationships* between concepts or variables. The relationships may be between abstract constructs or between concrete variables . (Is this concept related to that one? What is the relation between these variables?) These questions or hypotheses usually have *theoretical support*—the researchers have reason to believe there is or is not a particular kind of relationship present, perhaps because of previous research they have done or because a theory they have studied seems relevant. They address the questions/hypotheses *empirically*, by looking for evidence that would support or refute the implications of the theory.

Concepts and Constructs

A *concept*, according to Kerlinger,[1] is a word that expresses an *abstraction* formed by *generalization from particulars*. "Prejudice" is a good example. That it is abstract is evident because it is an idea—a conception—and not a physical object or event. I'm sure you can think of several examples of prejudice, but they are only particular examples—none of them *is* prejudice. We group all the things we consider to be examples of

---

[1] 1964, p. 31.

prejudice together because they have something in common, and we are interested in that something. So we can talk about it, we give the grouping a name. The name we give the grouping is thus an abstraction formed by generalization from all the particular examples.

Although they have different meanings, the word "construct" is often used as if it were interchangeable with "concept." A construct is a concept created for a specific scientific purpose. We sometimes talk about concepts in our day-to-day lives as ordinary people. In this context, we are talking about what we would probably call "ideas." Television producers sometimes talk about a concept being turned into a program, for example. But when we are talking about research, we try to be more consciously explicit and aware of what we are doing, so we use "constructs" instead.

Something to note is that neither concepts nor constructs exist in the physical world. They are both things that we create in our minds. Although they serve a number of useful purposes—they let us share ideas and they make it easier to communicate about complicated things because they "crystallize" abstract aspects of the world around us—we have to remember that we made them up: we constructed them from nothing.

Variables

While concepts are associated with theory, variables are associated with measurement and observation. **Variables** are **empirical indicators** of constructs. Note: *The variable is not the construct*. It is something concrete that you can observe, and by its appearance you can tell whether the concept is present or absent or to what extent it is present. In a way, constructs and variables are like diseases and symptoms. When you get the flu, you have a number of experiences. You feel tired, weak, and achy. You may have nausea or other uncomfortable experiences. You may have a fever. None of these experiences are the disease. They are only *symptoms* of the disease. If you have enough of these symptoms, though, you will probably say you have the flu.

Constructs are like diseases; variables are the symptoms of constructs. You observe constructs by watching their "symptoms"—the variables that serve as their indicators. For example, the behaviors that we would say are examples of prejudice are the symptoms we would look for if we wanted to see if someone is prejudiced. Although the behaviors themselves are not prejudice, we would say that they prejudice a person who performs them.

A particularly useful way to look at variables is to see them as symbols to which values are assigned. Usually the value will be a number (GPA = 3.1) or a letter (category B). Often, it makes sense to consider a variable as representing the result of a *test* of some kind. For a given individual, the value of the variable is the individual's *score* on the test. Take, for example, the construct commonly called "intelligence." In day-to-day life, we think of intelligence as cognitive or mental ability that people have. If you want to see how much of this ability a person has, you will probably give them a test that contains questions that only someone who has the ability can answer. Because some of the questions require a higher degree of the ability than others, more intelligent people—those who have a lot of the ability—will answer more questions correctly. This test, of course, is known as the IQ test. We commonly speak of people who get high scores on this test—people with high IQs—as very intelligent. Their intelligence is the extent to which they have the cognitive or mental ability that allows them to reason and solve problems. Here, the construct is intelligence and the variable that indicates how much of this ability they have is a score on the IQ test.

Research Questions

Since the goal of empirical research is to answer a question, the first research task is to identify the question you want to answer. A good research question will be useful for a number of reasons. It will guide your efforts and help you keep your focus; it will help you decide what information you need to obtain and what methods might be appropriate to obtain that information; it will help you know how to interpret the information you do obtain, and it will help you know when you are finished.

Sometimes you may find that you have a research problem that doesn't seem to ask a question. For example, you may have a general interest in a particular line of thought. You will probably find that you can clarify your research goal and make your task more straightforward if you restate the problem in such a way that the questions implicit in the original statement become explicit. You may find that doing this is more difficult than you would expect, though, as it requires you to examine your situation and carefully analyze what it is you are trying to learn by the research. A strategy that often helps is to break off a small piece of the larger area and start with that. This will familiarize you with the particular problems you will encounter and give you an opportunity to develop ways of dealing with them.

If you are new to the area you are studying, you will probably find it most useful to do some exploratory research before you attempt to focus your questions any further. A particularly useful type of exploratory research is that which you can do in the library: see how other researches have conceptualized the problem and what research they have done, how they framed their research questions and anchored them in previous research, what theoretical perspectives they

used, what measurement and analysis methods were appropriate, what problems they encountered, etc.

The Problem Statement

Problem statements can take the form of *questions* or of *hypotheses*.

Research questions often ask for a description of something. Some examples are: *"What are the communication patterns among the people who work in this organization?" "What kind of interactions do foster parents have with the natural parents of their foster children?" "What is the non-verbal content of cigarette advertising in national magazines?"* Or they may ask for a description of a relation between two things. For example, *"Are ads that attempt to use fear of cancer and heart disease to convince people to stop smoking more or less effective than ads that take other approaches?" "How does the educational background of young parents influence the way they relate to their children?"*

A research question may be *open-ended*, in which case it leaves both the nature of the relationship to be investigated and its boundary conditions unspecified. It will then ask "what kind" of relationship, if any exists, and under what conditions it is seen. (*ex: What is the relation between how many close friends one has and how often one gets seriously ill?*) A research question may be *closed*, in which case it asks whether or not a specified type of relationship exists between two or more sets of phenomena under a particular set of boundary conditions. (*ex: Do people who have many close friends become seriously ill less often than people who have few?*) Closed questions are preferable to open-ended ones because they are more precise and it is easier to know when they have been answered unequivocally.

Hypotheses are declarative statements that predict a particular kind of relationship exists between two or more *variables* under specified conditions. For example, a body of research has led to the development of a complex theory relating several concepts, including social integration, mental health, alienation, and general well-being. Among other things, this theory says that social integration is positively related to general well-being and physical hardiness. One hypothesis implied by the theory might be: "Of the people who work in this university, those whose friends are friends of one another will experience fewer serious illnesses than will those whose friends do not know one another."

Hypotheses are derived from theory. The theory describes a *general* relationship between the concepts, while the hypothesis describes a *particular instance* of that relationship in specified circumstances. If the theory is valid, the hypothesis, which the theory logically implies, must also be valid. In the example above, the theory says that social integration is positively related to well-being and physical hardiness. If this is the case, then people whose friends are friends of one another should have fewer serious illnesses (if being "socially integrated" means that your friends are friends of one another, and if well-being and hardiness imply low levels of serious illness).

Although researchers are interested in theories, they test hypotheses (and not theories), because hypotheses talk about specific concrete phenomena which can be directly measured, while theories, on the other hand, talk about abstract concepts, which can be measured only indirectly. Theories can't be directly tested.

Hypotheses are preferable to research questions for two reasons:

1) Hypotheses delineate research problems more fully and precisely than questions. They specify the nature of suspected relationships between phenomena along with necessary boundary conditions.

2) Hypotheses are usually more exact than questions and thus more amenable to empirical testing that results in unequivocal answers.

Assessing Problem Statements

Research is like traveling. If you have to go somewhere, it is a lot easier to decide whether you should take a

plane or drive and in which direction you should travel if you know where you want to go. In fact, if you don't know where it is, you may never get there or you might not recognize it if you do. For similar reasons, you need to know the goal of your research. Here are some criteria you can use as you construct your problem statement:

1) Problem statements should be *clear* and *specific*. The question "What is the relation between Canadians and Americans?" doesn't give any indication about the type of relation the researcher is interested in? Are Canadians happier than Americans? Are Americans heavier than Canadians? Do Canadians like Americans more than Americans like Canadians? Each of these closed questions is more specific than the original open-ended one. The hypothesis "Canadians, on average, have more close friends than Americans" is even more specific.

2) Problem statements should be *empirically verifiable*. They should talk about what *is* the case, not what *ought to be* the case. The hypothesis "Canadian films are superior to American ones" would ask the researcher to settle a question of personal values or preferences empirically—something that cannot be done. In comparison, the hypotheses "Canadian films generally win more awards in international competitions" or "American films generally attract bigger audiences" are empirically testable.

3) Problem statements should be *phrased affirmatively*. It is better to say "characteristic X is related to event Y under these conditions" than "there is no relationship between characteristic X and event Y under any conditions." The former can be tested; the latter cannot. Problem statements that say there is no relationship should be avoided. For example, the hypothesis "there is no relationship between exposure to violent films and difficulty in establishing interpersonal relations" is similar to "there are no pianos in Japan" in that neither can be confirmed. You would have to examine all possible relationships between exposure to violent films and

problems in establishing interpersonal relationships. Where would you begin? How would you know whether your failure to detect a relationship (or a piano) was because you didn't look in the right place? If your hypothesis had been "People who watch many violent films tend to have more difficulty in establishing interpersonal relationships," you would have been on much firmer ground and your research would have a better chance of success.

4) Problem statements should be *stated simply*. Compound-complex sentences and double-barreled statements can lead to serious problems. The word "and" is often a danger signal. Consider this research question: "Are people who like rap music unemployed and bothered by a sense of alienation from society because they feel they have no power?" It contains at least four completely different questions: Are rap music lovers unemployed? Are they bothered by a sense of alienation from society? Does their sense of powerlessness cause them to feel alienated from society? Is their feeling of being without power the reason they are unemployed? What is the goal of the researcher who suggested this question?

Defining the Terms in Problem Statements

Problem statements contain descriptive and operative terms.

Descriptive terms represent classes of phenomena. These include constructs and variables. Problem statements with constructs are *theoretical hypotheses*, while those with variables are *research hypotheses*. (In the course of research, all constructs must be connected to variables, since it is the research hypotheses that are tested.) The variables in hypotheses fall into three classes: independent, dependent, and intervening.

- *Independent variables* are causes; *dependent variables* are effects. The value of the independent variable determines the value of the corresponding

dependent variables. Dependent variables are the classes of phenomena requiring explanation.

- *Intervening variables* are the boundary conditions that influence the relationship between independent and dependent variables. In the statement "If X, then probably Y, under condition Z," the "Z" is an intervening variable.

Operative terms clarify the relationship between the specified classes. Examples of operative terms include words and phrases such as "increasing," "decreasing," "is related to increasing," "immediately," "diminishes," etc. Operative terms may also be used to specify the type of relationship you expect to observe. Some examples are linear, curvilinear, exponential, *positive, negative, direct, inverse, inverted-U-shaped,* and *U-shaped.* For example, in the statement "viewing violent television programs and movies leads to an increase in subsequent acts of violent aggression against women," the words "leads to an increase in" are operative terms that indicate a direct or positive relationship between "viewing violent television programs" and "subsequent acts of violent aggression against women."

Conceptual Definitions

Conceptual definitions define constructs by relating them to other constructs.[2] For example, "weight" could be defined by saying that it is the "heaviness" of objects. *Operational definitions* specify the procedures for observing and measuring constructs. To say that your operational definition of intelligence is the IQ test is to say that you measure a person's intelligence by having them take the IQ test. The person's score on the IQ test, however, is not their intelligence; it is only their score on a test. We use it, though, because we believe that people who are highly intelligent will get high scores on the IQ test. So a person's IQ score is useful as an indicator of how intelligent the person is. A conceptual definition must do more than tell how the concept will be measured. For example, to say that

"intelligence is what the IQ test measures" does not define intelligence—it only tells how to measure it.

Assessing Conceptual Definitions

Here is a list of criteria you can use to judge the quality of your conceptual definitions.[3] Each criterion has an example to show how it works.

1) Conceptual definitions should denote all of the *essential qualities* of the constructs and exclude nonessential ones. They should describe the construct clearly enough so that other researchers would classify phenomena (in terms of whether or not they are occurrences of the construct) the same way as the researcher who developed the conceptual definition.

The definition "violent movies are movies in which there are scenes of kicking, stabbing, clubbing, choking, hitting, slapping, shooting, and smashing" is not a good conceptual definition because it lists many activities that are not essential and it fails to describe the essential qualities. What are the conceptual qualities that must be present before you will call something "violent"? You may want to say something like "violent movies show scenes in which one person injures, maims, or causes pain to another." This much shorter list of more abstract qualities would probably include all of the specific activities in the list above as well as many violent acts not on that list.

The specification of essential qualities is the most important part of a conceptual definition because it gives some very good clues about how the concept could be measured in a most straightforward way: look for the presence or absence of the essential qualities. For example, if you accepted the suggested definition of violent movies as those which "show scenes in which one person injures, maims, or causes pain to another" in the previous paragraph, you could determine whether or not a movie is violent, by looking to see whether it

---

[2] Kerlinger, 1964, p. 34.

[3] This section follows Smith, 1988, pp. 33-34.

contained scenes in which one person injures, maims, or causes pain to another. (But first you will have to decide what counts as injury or pain.)

2) Conceptual definitions should not be *circular*. The definition should not contain any linguistic variant of the construct being defined. This conceptual definition nicely illustrates circularity: "Negative advertising is advertising that contains statements perceived by the public to be negative." We are still left wondering what is meant by "negative."

3) Conceptual definitions should be *clear* and *precise*. Use only terms that are easily reduced to a set of primitive terms—terms with generally agreed upon meanings. Be careful here not to use terms that have more than one meaning or terms that can be interpreted in more than one way.

4) Conceptual definitions should be *complete*. They should include definitions for *all* key terms in the problem statement.

Important Terms and Concepts

abstract concepts
boundary conditions
causes
circularity
closed
concept
conceptual definitions
conceptualizing
constructs
criteria for assessing conceptual definitions
criteria for assessing problem statements
dependent variables
descriptive terms
effects
empirical
empirical research
empirically verifiable
essential qualities
explanation
exploratory research
generalization
hypotheses

independent variables
indicators
intervening variables
measurement
open-ended
operational definitions
operative terms
phrased affirmatively
positive research
problem statements
reason
relationships
research
research hypotheses
research question
scores
symptoms
theoretical hypotheses
theory
variable

Chapter 3

Operationalizing

Conceptualizing is where you define your research problem and explain the constructs and theories that are relevant. On page 18 you read that variables are used as indicators of constructs. In your conceptual definitions you explain what your constructs are by showing how they relate to other constructs. This explanation and all of the constructs it refers to are abstract—its existence is only as real and concrete as the thoughts you have while you watch a seagull soar past on a stiff breeze. To work with your constructs, you must establish a connection between them and the concrete reality in which you live. This process is called *operationalization*. Your operational definitions describe the variables you will use as indicators and the procedures you will use to observe or measure them.

The connection between conceptual and operational definitions plays a crucial role in research. Although a valid connection isn't sufficient to guarantee that the research will be valid, it is a necessary component of all valid research. The part of the conceptual definitions where you specify the essential qualities is especially relevant here because it gives some very good clues about how you can measure the concept in a straightforward way: look for the presence or absence of the essential qualities. Choose variables that are indicators of the essential qualities.

Operational Definitions

To measure a construct, you need an operational definition that specifies first, the variable you will use as an indicator of the construct, and second, the procedures you will use to measure the variable. The operational definition thus associates a variable with a construct. Creating this association—choosing a variable to be an indicator—requires you to use both your logical skills of deduction (if the construct you want to measure is, for example, intelligence, the variables you choose as indicators of intelligence must somehow actually "tap into" intelligence) and your ability to use creativity and insight to conceive of an appropriate indicator. There is no straightforward way to produce indicators for constructs; there are no standard formulas or recipes. A familiarity with the subject area and previous research that used the constructs will almost certainly be helpful. Once you have selected indicators for your constructs, you can begin to take measurements.

Measurement

There are four kinds of measurements you can take: you can sort things into categories, you can arrange them in increasing or decreasing order, you can

count them, you can measure amounts, and you can measure distances. It's important to know which kind you are doing because they use different procedures, they produce different results, and they make different things possible or impossible to do. Let's take a closer look at the four kinds of measurements.

Sorting things into categories. You might not think sorting things into categories is measurement. For example, you might sort your clothes into light and dark ones before you put them in the washing machine. Is this measurement? It would be if the fact that a person's clothes where light or dark was an indicator of an abstract construct in which you had an interest. Asking people whether they belong to the "male" or "female" category, what their occupation is, what language they speak, or whether they are single or married (or divorced, separated, cohabiting, or …) are all examples of sorting into categories.

When you are sorting things into categories, the variable tells which category whatever you are sorting has been placed into. Category 1, Category 2, or Category 3. Males or Females. Employed or Unemployed. The only distinction you can make is which category it belongs to.

When you are comparing two things in terms of the categories to which they belong, the only thing you can say about them is that they are the same (they are in the same category) or they are different (they are in different categories). You can't say anything about the *size of the difference*: you cannot tell how different they are, and you cannot say that these two are more or less different than those two.

You will want to name your categories. There are a few examples in the preceding paragraph. Here are a few more types of category names: John/Martha; Canucks/Rangers/Bruins; Dogs/Cats/Ducks. One thing to know about the names is that each category must have a unique name. Another thing to know is that the names don't have any particular meaning; they are nothing more than *labels*. If you use numbers in the names, the numbers won't have any of the properties that ordinary numbers have: you won't be able to add or subtract them and the ordering of the numbers will have no meaning. They could be re-

placed by names like Joe, Sam, and Linda or Red, Blue, and Green and no information would be lost.

Arranging things in increasing or decreasing order. When you sort things into increasing or decreasing order, you compare pairs of things like you do when you are sorting them into categories. However, when you are putting them in order, you do a slightly different kind of comparison; instead of asking if they are the same or different, you ask if the first one is smaller than, the same as, or larger than the second one. With this kind of sorting, you end up with a set of *ordered categories* where the members of any one category are different from the members of other categories in a particular way: they are either larger or smaller (less than or greater than, earlier or later, younger or older, …) than the members of other categories. Although you can say that one thing is larger or smaller than another, you still can't tell how much larger or smaller it is.

The fact that the categories are ordered makes this kind of sorting different from when you are sorting into categories on the basis of sameness or difference. The placement of a thing into a particular ordinal position, say "third largest," tells where that thing is in relation to all the other ordinal positions. The third largest position is smaller than the largest and second largest, but it is larger than the fourth and fifth largest positions. With this kind of measurement you see numbers that behave (in some ways) like numbers—"1st," "2nd," and "3rd" specify the ordinal position of the categories in a way that "Joe," "Sam," and "Linda" don't. But you still can't perform any arithmetic on them—you can't subtract "1st" from "3rd," for example—and this is why you can't tell how much larger or smaller one thing is than another.

Counting things. The third kind of measurement is when you count things. One way of measuring the size of cities, for example, is by counting how many people live there. The result of counting, like the result of sorting or ranking, is *discrete*—there are 188 people or 189 people in this village, but not 188.2 or 188.73. A hockey player is a Canuck or a Ranger, but not part Canuck and part Ranger. Mario Andretti

finished the race in 1st place or 2nd place, but not somewhere in between (1.13th place?!).

When you count things you use numbers that behave like ordinary numbers. You can add and subtract them (I have four radios and you have eight: you have four more than I do), and you can multiply and divide (you have twice as many as I do). Also, the number zero means "none," which turns out to be important.

Measuring amounts and distances is similar to counting, except you are not restricted to whole numbers. You can spend 3.00 hours a day watching television, but you could also spend 3.0001 hours a day. You may find that 19.348 percent of an issue of *The Times* is occupied by advertising. There may be 9.74 minutes between one televised murder and the next. You use measures of *distance* for locations of things in physical or conceptual space, and measures of *duration* for events located in time. Measuring amounts, distances, and durations, like counting things, uses numbers which you can add, subtract, multiply, or divide. Once again, the value "0" means "none."

Scaling

Scaling and **mapping** are ways of matching numbers or numerals to objects or events or qualities. You've seen examples of both in the preceding paragraphs. Scaling is the process of using numbers to represent phenomena in the world. It's called *scaling* because it involves use of a *scale* to measure something. Examples include bathroom scales, tape measures, "one-to-ten" ratings, batting averages, GPA, etc.

- *numerals* are symbols used as labels to indicate which category something belongs to. They are only symbols, like letters, and they have no mathematical meaning. This is the kind of mapping you do when you sort things into categories. Wayne Gretzky's "99" is an example.

- *ordinals* are numerals that can be used in arithmetical comparisons, such as "greater than," "less

than," or "equal to," but *not* in arithmetical operations, such as addition and multiplication. Ordinals take values like "1st," "2nd," and "3rd."

- *numbers*, like ordinals, are numerals that can be used in arithmetical comparisons, such as "greater than," but they can also be used in arithmetical operations, such as addition, subtraction, multiplication, and division. They have mathematical meaning—how many, how much, etc.

Variables may be **discrete** or **continuous**. A variable that can take *any* value between the lowest and highest points is *continuous*; there are an infinite (or very large) number of possible values within the range. A variable that can take a small number of specific values is *discrete*. Sand, water, income, and freedom are continuous. Family size, number of cars owned, and gender are usually considered to be discrete. Things that are *counted* or *categorized* generally result in discrete results: you speak of the *number* of people, the *number* of movies, etc. Things that are measured in terms of *quantity*, *distance*, or *magnitude* generally result in continuous results: you speak of the *length* of time that has passed, the *amount* of coffee you have consumed, the *amount* of money you have, the *height* of a building, the *brightness* of a lamp.

Discrete variables that can take on many different values over their ranges are usually treated as if they were continuous. For example, the population of cities, provinces, and countries are considered continuous. Continuous variables often involve fractions, like 3.1415987 or 2.3842665, while discrete variables almost never involve fractions.

Levels of Scaling

As the paragraphs above showed, there are different kinds of "numbers ." It's important to know which type you are dealing with. For example, what does it mean when your score on the variable *Carnumb* has a value of "7"? What sort of "seven-ness" do you have? Do you have seven cars? Have you owned six cars before this one? Does this car have a large "7"

painted on both sides so the officials in the race can identify it as yours? Is it seven feet wide? Is "7" the model number of the car, as in "Maseratti-7"? If my score on the variable *Carnumb* is "6", what is the significance of the difference between my "6" and your "7"?

To answer these questions, you need to know what level of scaling you are using. What kind of numbering system is being used for this variable—in other words, what rule are you using to map numbers to some aspect of the world around you?

Most textbooks distinguish four *levels of scaling*: **nominal**, **ordinal**, **interval**, **ratio**. As you move from nominal to ratio, the numbers in the data contain more amounts and more kinds of information about whatever it is the numbers represent.

1) With **nominal** scaling, all you are doing is *sorting* the cases into categories. Each category is associated with a numeral, which is the *name* of the category. The numerals don't mean anything; they don't imply how much or how many or how far or anything like that. No arithmetic operations can be performed on the numerals associated with categories, because they aren't numbers—they are the *names* of the categories. Data that uses nominal scaling is often called **frequency** data, because it tells how many cases there are in each category.

Comparisons: The only thing that can be said about the categories associated with two cases is that they are the *same* or they are *different*. *No arithmetic allowed.*

2) With **ordinal** scaling you *order* the cases into a set of increasing (or decreasing) categories. One comes first, another comes second, etc. You don't know how far apart one category is from the next, but you can tell how many categories come before or after the one you are looking at. Here the numerals associated with categories behave a bit like numbers—they tell the *ordinal positions* of the categories—but they still aren't ordinary numbers; they are ordinals. *No arithmetic operations can be performed on these ordinals.*

Comparisons: You can tell if one case comes before or after another case, but not how far before or after. *No arithmetic allowed.*

3) **Interval** scaling puts each case on a scale that can be likened to a ruler. Cases aren't sorted into categories; they can be anywhere on the scale (e.g. "3.14159"). Here you can look at the *distance between points* and you measure the distance in some kind of units. To do this, you subtract the number associated with one case from the number associated with a second case. Note that you are now allowing some arithmetic operations to be performed on the numbers. In fact, you can add a constant to all the numbers in a set of data or multiply all the numbers in the set by a constant without altering the information in the data. For example, to convert Fahrenheit to Celsius, you subtract 32 and multiply the result by 5/9. This doesn't change the temperatures; it just transfers them to a different scale.

Comparisons: You can tell both order and distance between points, but you can't talk about how big one value is as a fraction of another. *Subtracting one value from another is okay; multiplying and dividing are not permitted.*

4) **Ratio** scaling is the most powerful. It has everything interval scaling is, and it has a *fixed absolute zero* point. You tell both the distance between values and the relative sizes or magnitudes of values. Strangely, you can't do as many transformations of ratio data as you can on interval data. You can multiply all the values in a set of data by a constant without altering the information, but you can't add or subtract a constant. To convert your weight in pounds to grams, you multiply by 454. To convert your height in inches to centimeters, you multiply by 2.54. This doesn't change your height; it just changes the units that you using.

Comparisons: You can tell order, distance, and relative size (as a ratio) of two points. *Adding, subtracting, multiplying and dividing of values is okay.*

Comment

Some people don't consider interval scaling to be a real level of scaling. They argue that it is actually ratio scaling, but that it has been weakened or crippled by the displacement of the origin or zero value. Displacing the origin means that *numbers can't be used to indicate quantities*. Not only does it untie the quantity "none" from the numeral "0"; it also requires you to interpret all numbers only as *marks on a line*, where the only information a number carries is where that number is located in relation to the other numbers. If an interval scale can be converted to a ratio scale by a recalibration that moves the value "0" to the quantity "none", the numbers can once again be used to indicate quantity or amount.

Which Level of Scaling to Use?

The numbers from a measurement using ratio scaling contain more information than the ones from other types of measurement. They tell you that two scores are the same or not, which one is larger, how large the difference between the scores is, how large one score is as a percentage of the other, and how far the scores are away from zero (none). Because of all of this, you might think it's a good idea to always use ratio measures.

It is true that ratio scaling is the strongest of the four. In fact, it's too strong for many situations. When the thing you are measuring is a dichotomy—the person speaks English or French; the object is red or black; the person is a man or a woman—all you can do is sort the cases into categories. The form of the phenomenon matches categorical *nominal* scaling. The same is true if you are measuring something that has more than two categories. For example, who do you talk to when something is bothering you and you need to make an important decision about it? Or what kind of persuasive strategy is most effective when you are trying to convince young people not to start smoking?

If the phenomenon you want to measure is a variable trait, so that some people have more than others and you can determine who has more but not how much more they have, the form of the phenomenon matches *ordinal* scaling. Some examples of this type of concept are how uncomfortable a person becomes when someone stands too close to them in a line in the supermarket, how strongly a person feels about an opinion, and how anxious a person gets before writing a final examination in a tough course.

The form of the phenomenon matches *ratio* scaling if the phenomenon is a continuously variable trait, so that:

- the difference between two people could be anywhere between no difference at all and a very large difference;

- you can measure the sizes of the differences between pairs of people and compare the differences to one another and tell which difference is bigger and how much bigger it is; and

- it is meaningful to say that someone has none of the trait.

In other words, you should choose a level of scaling that matches the form of the phenomenon you are trying to measure. This is the *reality isomorphism* principle. "Isomorphic" is a Greek word that means "same form."

Level of Scaling

	nominal	ordinal	interval	ratio
values	names; categories	ordinal positions; relative amounts	location on a scale	amounts, sizes, quantities
example	*"Hepatitis A"* *"Jim"*	*"slightly"* *"often"*	*"Tuesday, July 3rd"* *"98.6°F"* *"11:30 PM"*	*"1.6 miles"* *"$19.95"* *"3.5 hours"*
arithmetic	none	order (>,=,<)	order (>,=,<) subtraction	order (>,=,<) subtraction division
comparison of two values — equality	*Jim is a man, Mary is a woman*	*we both like scotch a lot*	*the temperature now is the same as before*	*my pre-tax income is the same as yours*
comparison of two values — order	no	*I like scotch more than you do*	*it is warmer now than it was before*	*my pre-tax income is less than yours*
comparison of two values — size	no	no	*it is five degrees warmer now*	*you make $10,000 more than I make*
comparison of two values — ratio	no	no	no	*you make twice as much as I make*
"zero" = "none"	no	no	no	*Henry's income last year was zero*

Important Terms and Concepts

- absolute zero *vs* arbitrary zero
- amount
- arithmetical operations
- category
- continuous
- discrete categories *vs.* continuous amounts
- distance between points
- indicator
- interval scaling
- magnitude
- mapping
- mathematical relationship
- name
- nominal scaling
- none *vs.* zero
- number
- numeral
- order
- ordinal
- ordinal position
- ordinal scaling
- ratio scaling
- reality isomorphism
- scaling
- value of a variable
- variable

Chapter 4

VALIDITY AND RELIABILITY

The **validity** of a measure is *the extent to which differences in scores on the instrument reflect true differences among individuals on the characteristic the instrument is supposed to measure.* This means that different scores should reflect *only* differences in what the instrument is supposed to measure. In other words: The measure is sensitive only to what it is supposed to measure. For example, the IQ test would be valid if it measured only differences in intelligence. It shouldn't matter how tired, nervous, or hung over you are when you take the test; only your intelligence should affect your score. Of course this isn't how it works in the real world.

The **reliability** of a measure is its *consistency.* Does it give the same score on repeated measures? This may be difficult to test if the measure is reactive in any way. That is, if repeating the measure on the same people causes them to respond differently on successive attempts. If there are things like improvement due to practice, or if thinking about the questions on a questionnaire causes changes in opinions, second and subsequent measures are likely to produce different results. This doesn't mean the measure isn't reliable, though. It only means that second and subsequent applications of the measurement are effectively different kinds of events from the first one, and must be seen as different kinds of events.

If a measure is perfectly valid, it must also be reliable. If it isn't reliable, it must be giving different results from time to time. What is behind these different results? If there is anything other than actual changes in what the measure is supposed to measure, then the unreliable measure must be sensitive to something other than what it is aimed at. Thus, it cannot be perfectly valid.

If a measure is perfectly reliable, it may or may not be valid. The fact that it always gives the same results doesn't mean those results are valid. My nephew has an elastic tape measure and everything he measures is "six." He is completely consistent, but rarely are his measurements correct.

Face validity has to deal with the extent to which a measure seems to measure what it is supposed to measure. It "looks like" it ought to be measuring what it is designed to measure. It captures the full extent of the concept or construct. It measures all relevant aspects of the construct. While face validity is necessary, it is not sufficient. That is, you *must* have face validity, but you also need more.

Criterion/Pragmatic/Predictive validity all use a second measure to assess the validity of the first. Of course the second measure must be known to be valid if it is to be used as a standard.

Predictive or *pragmatic validity* is easy—does the measure make correct predictions? For example, does the GRE exam predict success in graduate school? All you have to do is wait and see. If it does, i.e. if people who get high exam scores do well in graduate school, it has predictive validity.

However, this information may be useless by the time you find out whether the prediction a measure made are accurate. What you do here is determine over a period of time whether or not a measure has predictive validity—compare what the measure predicts and the outcome over several months or years. While you are doing this, the measure is useless, because its validity is unknown. After you have some experience with a measure you will learn how accurate or consistent its predictions are.

Criterion validity is a bit more complex. If you have a second measure you know to be valid, you may be able to check to see if the first measure agrees with the second one. If it does, you have criterion validity. How do you determine whether the second measure is valid? a) face validity; b) repeated confirmation, as in predictive validity.

Construct validity is probably the most important and most complex kind of validity. It has to do with your "construct" or "concept" being a single unidimensional one, and on your measuring instrument's ability to measure the intended construct and nothing more. If the construct has several aspects or components, it will be difficult for any measure to encompass all of them in all cases. Different approaches to measuring the construct produce different results because each gets at different aspects or because each comes from a different perspective. If the construct is solid and coherent and doesn't have a range of aspects that interact with your measurement approach in this way, and if various operational definitions of the construct result in identical or similar measurements, then the construct and measurement approach together have construct validity.

Consider the construct "Canadian." What does it mean to be Canadian? I can trace my family back to Quebec in the 1640's. Does this mean that I am more

Canadian than someone whose family immigrated from Italy in 1952? I listen to CBC radio most mornings and evenings. Does this mean that I am more Canadian than someone who listens to an American radio station? A well-known difference between Canadians and Americans is that the latter own more guns than the former. I don't own a gun. Does this mean that I am more Canadian than a friend who owns several hunting rifles? I often participate in elections by working as a scrutineer. Does this mean that I am more Canadian than my neighbor who sometimes doesn't vote? I am a soft-spoken, polite, considerate person. Does this make me more Canadian than loud, arrogant, inconsiderate people who behave like Americans are thought to behave? I don't have a Canadian passport. Does this make me less Canadian than someone who does? What does it mean to "be Canadian"? Is "Canadian" one construct, or is it a large family of constructs?

Internal and **External validity** are considered most often in experimental or explanatory research in which various concepts must be operationalized and/or controlled. Internal validity refers to the *internal consistency* of the set of operational and conceptual definitions and the logical relations among them. External validity refers to the *generalizability* of the results. This will be influenced by a number of factors, including the representativeness of the sample and the "naturalness" of the research situation. Laboratory research (as in psychology experiments) is often criticized for a lack of external validity because the research situation (researchers in white lab coats, etc.) is not generalizable to everyday life. Survey studies are criticized because of problems with the samples they depend on.

Measurement Error

Measurement is not perfect. There is usually (always?) some error. Error can be classified into two types—systematic and random. *Systematic error* is what is normally called "bias." It shows up as results* consistently being distorted in the same direction.

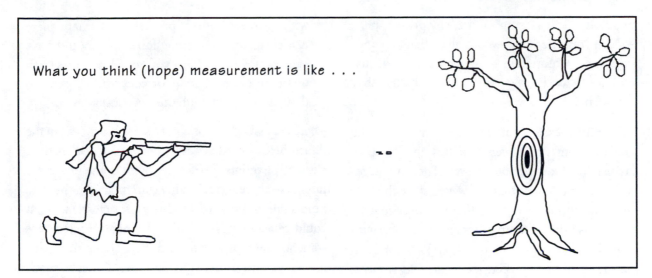

What you think (hope) measurement is like . . .

When you have systematic error you have a problem with validity.

Random error is not consistently in one direction. It varies from case to case, both in magnitude and in direction. It is what is normally call "unreliability."

We generally worry more about systematic error than random error, even though it may be possible (in some cases) to identify and compensate for systematic error. This is probably because biases tend to work differently for different subsets of individuals in the population. If they worked in the same direction and to the same extent for all cases, they would be easily compensated for.

The figure above shows how you would like measurement to work: You are clearly focused on the target construct, you know exactly what it is, and you can take precise aim and hit it every time. You

would expect to get results that look something like the ones shown in the figure below.

a) In the first case, you get consistent and accurate measurements of the bull's-eye, the construct you were aiming at. If you were measuring something like, for example, shyness, the results you would get in this case would be very close to the actual levels of shyness of the people in your study. Any deviations from the actual values would be both small and random, in the sense that they are spread in all directions.

b) In the second case, your measurement is consistent, but consistently below the center of the target. As in the first case, the errors are small, but systematically in one direction. You would say this measurement is *biased*. If you were measuring shyness and your indicator was the loudness of

 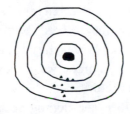 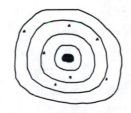 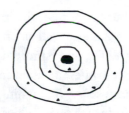

a) Reliable and Valid; both consistent and unbiased. Errors are small and not systematic.

b) Reliable but not Valid; consistent but biased. Errors are large and in one direction (systematic).

c) Valid but not Reliable; unbiased but not consistent. Errors are large and unpredictable (not biased).

d) Neither Valid nor Reliable; biased and not consistent. Errors are large but mostly in one direction (biased).

people's voices (assuming that shy people speak softly), your measures would all be biased if your measuring equipment was improperly adjusted and consistently gave readings lower than they should be.

c) In the third case, your measurements are in the general vicinity of the center of the target, but they are scattered some distance away. These measurements are not consistent. However, since they are scattered in *all* directions, there is no *systematic* bias. This is like a sample from a population with a moderate to high level of dispersion. Although no single measure is accurate, in the long run (i.e. if your sample is large enough), the average of the measurements may be reasonably close to the correct average value. In the case where you are measuring shyness by examining voice loudness as an indicator, you might obtain a result like this one if you were conducting the research in a noisy environment, which could cause erratic results like the ones shown in the third picture. Since the disturbances are not systematic, the measurements are spread all around the true value—there is unreliability, but no bias.

The reason results can be unreliable *in the short run* and still valid is that there is no bias. To get a reasonably accurate result in a case like this, all you have to do is take a large number of measurements—take a large sample. (You may recall this illustration when you read about sampling variability and the standard error of the mean in another thirty pages or so.)

d) In the fourth case, the measurements are spread out, but they are all on one side of the center of the target. The wide spread indicates a lack of consistency, while the uneven nature of the spread indicates bias. Something is pushing the results to one side of the true values; the results are *systematically biased*. If you were using loudness of voice as an indicator of shyness, you would be misled by your data which would show that people in general are more (or less) shy than they really are. This kind of distortion could be caused by a problem with the measurement procedure. Perhaps there is a cover on the microphone that should have been removed; perhaps you set a knob or switch on the amplifier to an incorrect position; perhaps there is a problem with the electrical system.

There are two other possibilities. One is shown in the figure below. In this case, there are three distinct clusters of points, as if there were somehow three targets or three modes of measurement. All the data points fall into one of the three tight clusters. What could cause this? If the measurement process were somehow tapping into three different constructs, this is what you might expect. The measurement of each individual construct may be reliable and valid, but, since there are three of them and they are mixed up together, the final result is confusing.

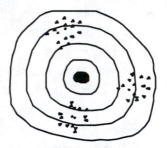

There appear to be three distinct clusters of results. This would indicate either that there are three targets or three "modes" of measurement, each producing results biased in a different direction.

You could run into a situation like this in your research if the people you are studying have different interpretations of the question you are asking. I once did some research in Alberta in which I asked people where they learned about science and science-related issues. Many of the respondents said that one of their main sources was "Nova." I have watched this science-oriented television program many times. But further questioning seemed to lead to two quite different conclusions. It wasn't until I learned that there was a major corporation in that area of the province called "Nova" that I was able to understand what was happening: there were two quite different "Novas."

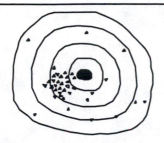

There appears to be one cluster close to the centre and a number of points spread rather erratically. This indicates two "modes" of measurement—one giving fairly accurate results and one giving unreliable ones.

The illustration above shows a different pattern. Here, there is a tight cluster of points near the center of the target and a number of widely-scattered points around the periphery. A result like this could happen if only some of your respondents were affected by the construct or if there were two constructs—one for which the measurement produces reliable, accurate results and the other for which the measurement procedure gives only a rough approximation.

Both of these last two cases illustrate problems with *construct validity*. There are more than one construct, and they are being confounded—mixed up by the researcher, who thinks there is only one. Construct validity is probably the most difficult issue to deal with when you are studying abstract constructs. The best way to deal with it is to use an approach called "multiple methods, multiple measures." To do this, you use several approaches to measurement, where each uses different methods or comes at the construct from a different direction. If the various approaches produce results that agree with one another, you can feel more confident that you in fact have only one construct. If they disagree, the validity of the construct would be called into question. However, it doesn't necessarily mean that you have multiple constructs—you may simply have problems with your measurement procedures.

The picture below shows what may be happening when you are having problems with construct validity. The hunter trying to shoot at the target is the researcher trying to measure a construct. As you can see, there are three targets/ constructs, and the hunter is looking at them through a mirror, which causes distortions and makes it difficult to aim properly. The mirror in the picture represents the operational and conceptual definitions the researcher is using to guide the study. The difficulty is that the hunter/ researcher thinks the situation is like the one on page 31, where there is one target and the measurement process is direct and simple.

In a study of the effects of watching lots of violent films and TV programs, for example, the researchers might be attempting to measure increases in the amount of aggressive behavior performed by a large group of young men in some specified social setting. If they understand "aggressive behavior" as overt physical belligerence and assault, their measurements

What measurement of abstract constructs is REALLY like . . . .

will miss both explicit verbal aggression and more subtle forms of implicit or indirect aggression that are manifested by excluding others from conversation or from participating in social activities. A different group of researchers might have a different conceptual understanding of aggression and might thus tap into a different set of behaviors, resulting in measurements that disagree with those of the first team.

A more complete conceptualization of the construct would result in a more complex measurement procedure that produced more consistent results. The bad news is that most measurement is probably more like the situation shown on page 33 than the one on page 31.

Important Terms and Concepts

accuracy
bias
conceptual definition
consistency
construct validity
criterion validity
external validity
face validity
generalizability
internal consistency
internal validity
multidimensional constructs
multiple methods, multiple measures
precision
predictive/criterion validity
random error
reliability
systematic error
unidimensional construct
validity

Things to think about .....

What is the difference between validity and reliability?

Why do you need both validity and reliability?

Why is construct validity more difficult to assess than the other types of validity?

Explain the pictures of the target shooter on pages 31 and 33. What are they trying to show you about measurement?

Why is measurement of abstract constructs more difficult than measurement of concrete variables?

What is the difference between random error and systematic error?

Chapter 5

Sampling

Remember the distinction between *idiographic* and *nomothetic-deductive* modes of research? Nomothetic research attempts to discover the systems of laws or principles which govern various aspects of reality, while idiographic research is interested in describing only a single event, person, or situation.

Since it is interested in discovering the laws or principles that govern aspects of reality, nomothetic research needs information that describes enough cases so that general patterns or relationships can be seen. It uses information that describes *a subset of the population*—a sample. The samples you construct by randomly choosing members from a population are the kind you can use most easily to understand patterns and relationships in the population.

The aim of sampling is to get enough information about a manageable subset of the population you are interested in to make some reasonable inferences about the characteristics of the population. It has been said that researchers have three characteristics that lead them to use samples: they are cheap, lazy, and late. They have to minimize their expenses because they have a limited amount of money; they don't want to do more work than is necessary; and they are working under pressing deadlines that don't really give them enough time to do the job. Imagine that you were given the job of determining how much time the typical person spends on the Internet. Even if you have $100,000.00 to cover expenses and four months to do the work, you couldn't possibly ask everyone who uses the Internet how much time they spend using it. The population of users is just too big and too geographically spread out. So you will have to settle for a sample of the members of that population and hope that it is possible to make some valid inferences about the population on the basis of the information you obtain from your sample.

A *population* is the total set of individuals that meet a specified set of criteria. If you are interested in the relation between university students' grades and the size of debt they have built up with student loans, your population would be all students in universities

Studying a sample to learn about the population is a lot like when trying to pick a flavor of ice cream, you ask for a spoonful (a sample) of "that one in the back corner" so you can see what it tastes like. When you are using a sample in a research project, you have the same hopes that you do when choosing ice cream — that the sample gives you reasonably accurate information about the population it comes from, and that collecting information from the sample doesn't damage or ruin the population.

around the world. You are more likely to be interested in students in universities in your country, though, because different countries have different student loan systems that require different repayment schedules which is probably something you do not wish to deal with. In addition, you probably are more interested in full-time students who have not yet been employed long enough to build up substantial financial reserves. Your population is thus not "university students," but rather "full-time university students who live in your country and who borrow money to finance their education."

Once you have defined your population, you are ready to decide how to draw a sample that will represent it. In order to know that the sample is representative, you need to know who (or what) is in the population. If you have a list of all the members, your task is made easier. In real life, though, it is likely that there will not be a list of all the members of the population. For example, there is no list of all the residents of the cities of Vancouver, Topeka, or Inverness. It is easy, though, to obtain telephone directories for these cities. If you use the telephone directory to draw the sample, only people whose phone numbers are listed will have a chance of being included. The list you use to draw your sample is called a *sampling frame*. Ideally, the sampling frame should include everyone in the population, but in practice it won't.

The quality of your sample will depend in part on the completeness of the sampling frame. You should do everything you can to determine how the sampling frame is likely to be incomplete and to address the gaps by means of whatever resources might be available. If you can't find ways to include the cases missed by your sampling frame, you should consider the implications of the missing cases. What do they have in common with one another? Very wealthy people tend to have unlisted phone numbers, so they tend not to be in the phone book. At the other end of the financial scale are those who do not appear in the book because they don't have a fixed place of residence or if they do, can't afford a telephone. So a sample drawn from a telephone book will tend to exclude the very wealthy and the very poor. If you

can't find a way to give these people a chance to be included, you should consider the possibility of redefining your population.

Sample Designs

The primary goal of using a sample is to be able to generalize to the population from which it was drawn. Of course you can only do this if the sample is an unbiased and reasonably accurate representation of the population. Your sample will be representative if an analysis of your sample produces results similar to what you would get if you performed the analysis on the entire population. Since you are not likely to have the resources it would take to check the representativeness of your sample by doing the same analysis on the whole population, it would be useful to see what approaches have been developed to ensure that your sample is likely to be representative to begin with.

There are several different kinds of sampling methods, each of which has its own strengths and weaknesses. The most important thing about a sample is whether or not you know the probability of being included in the sample for each and every member of the sampling frame; in other words, whether you have a probability sample or a non-probability samples.

Non-probability samples

If you can *not* specify the probability that any given individual will be in the sample (p_i = ?), you have a *non-probability* sample. Some combinations of individuals may be more likely to be selected than others. Some individuals may have absolutely no chance of being selected. Since you don't know which members of the population have a chance to be included in your sample, you won't know whether or not your sample accurately represents the population. This means you won't be able to generalize your results to the population. In fact, there is no way to tell what population (if any) a non-probability sample represents.

At this point you might be wondering why anyone would use a non-probability sample if they are so poor at representing populations. The main reason is that they are cheap and easy. When you are developing a questionnaire to be used in a survey or you want to tryout some special interviewing techniques, you may have no desire to make inferences to the population. In situations like this, it is quite likely that a non-probability sample will adequately address your needs.

Three non-probability sample designs are used most frequently.

Accidental or *convenience samples*. If you take whoever comes along or whoever is easily accessible, you will have an accidental or convenience sample: a sample selected without the aid of formal selection procedures. This kind of sample is easy to do, but it has no external validity. *Convenience samples do not accurately represent the population from which they are drawn.*

Purposive samples. In these "handpicked" samples, the researcher decides who will be included as "typical" or "representative." Since the decision to choose or not choose an individual for the sample depends on the researcher's subjective judgement, it isn't possible to predict the probability that any given member of the population will be selected, which means that the link between the sample and the population it is supposed to represent is, at best, tenuous. This method is most often used for situations in which small samples are needed, and in which there is no desire to generalize to the population. An example is the television advertising campaign which attempts to use a "representative" mix of people — young and old, male and female, blue collar and white collar, white and yellow and red and brown and black-skinned, etc., and to do all this with only ten or twelve people. *Purposive samples do not accurately represent the population from which they are drawn.*

Quota or *proportionate sample*. If you try to select a sample that is as similar to the population as possible, in terms of the relative proportions of the population that are made up of various types of people, you will probably use a quota or proportionate sample. For example, if 23 percent of the population are single men, 40 percent have brown eyes, and 19 percent drive blue cars, then 23 percent of the sample will be single men, 40 percent will have brown eyes, and 19 percent will drive blue cars, etc.

Although the sample's proportions may match the population's on a number of characteristics, the sample is *not likely to be representative of the population* for two reasons:

1) individuals are chosen by the same methods used to choose purposive samples; within the assigned quotas, there are no guidelines to indicate which people should be chosen, and you might as well be doing a convenience sample.

2) it is not possible to match a population on all relevant characteristics, especially when those characteristics and their proportions in the population have not been identified.

Although they are sometimes called "representative" samples, quota or proportionate samples *aren't representative*. A much better way is to use random sampling methods, which, among other things, automatically produce valid proportionate samples.

Probability samples

A sample in which the probability of being included in the sample is known for each and every member of the population is a probability sample. This is the single feature that clearly distinguishes them from non-probability methods. *Only with probability samples can you make valid generalization to the population from which they are drawn.* There are several types:

Simple random samples. If you build your sample by randomly choosing members of the population, you will have drawn a simple random sample. This kind of sample has two essential characteristics: *equal probability* and *independence*.

1) *Equal probability*. All members of the sampling frame have an equal chance of being selected. In mathematical terms,

$$p_i = p_j = n/N$$

which means that the probability that any particular person will be selected (p_i) is the same as the probability that any other person will be selected (p_j), and this probability is equal to the number of people in the sample (n) divided by the number of people in the sampling frame (N).

2) *Independence*. The fact that one member is selected has no effect on any other member's chance of being selected.

Equal probability and independence are important issues and you should make sure you understand what they are. They are the factors that make simple random samples representative of their populations. In a simple random sample, all combinations of population members are equally likely. The chance of any individual being selected is equal to the *sampling ratio*, which is the sample size (n) divided by the population size (N).

One way of randomly choosing a random sample is to list all the members of the population and number them from 1 to N. Then get N identical balls, number them from 1 to N, put them in a large bin that has a lid and can be rolled around to mix up the balls. Then open the lid and remove one ball. Close the lid; roll the bin around; and remove another ball. Continue doing this until you have the desired number of balls. Use the numbers on the balls you removed from the bin to reference the list of population members and see who has been selected for your sample.

The problems you are likely to encounter when you attempt to do this include the following.

- The population is so large that it is not practical to get enough balls to do this.

- There are so many balls that the bin is too big to roll around; it is very difficult to mix up the balls after each drawing.

- You may know the name of the people selected to be in your sample, but you won't be able to get in touch with many of them because they have moved, changed their telephone numbers, decided they don't want to participate, or died. In other words, you do not have access to many members of the population.

- You can't get a list of all the members of the population.

It is easy to avoid the use of a large bin of numbered balls with variations on this method and thus reduce the cost or increase the practicality of the procedure, but these variations don't address the last two problems on the list.

The simple random sample is the ideal against which all other probability samples must be judged. Its strengths include its simplicity, lack of bias, and relatively straightforward math. The main weakness of this method is that it requires that you have a list of all the members of the population and that you are able to get access to any members who may be chosen. Because there are many research situations in which such a list doesn't exist or isn't available—situations in which you thus can't randomly select a sample from the population—systematic methods were developed.

Systematic samples. If you are able to line up all members of your population and move down the line one member at a time, you can draw a systematic sample by taking every k^{th} member (for example, every tenth member) of the population. If the first member selected is chosen randomly, your sample becomes a *systematic sample with a random start*, which, although much easier to do, is almost as valuable as a simple random sample. Although many combinations of members are not possible with this method, the characteristics of equal probability and, *to an extent*, independence, are still present. Thus,

$$p_i = p_j = 1/k$$

which is equivalent to simple random sampling.

This method has two potential weakness. The first one is that it requires that there be a way to line up all

members of the population so you can count them off and choose every k^{th} one. This is not always possible. The second potential weakness is that the members of the population may be organized in some sort of cyclical or periodical fashion so that every, say, tenth member is different from the others in a systematic way. For example, there may be ten houses in each block, and the houses on the corner lots are likely to be bigger or more expensive than the others. If you are taking every tenth house ($k = 10$) in the neighborhood and you happen to get the ones on the corner lots, your sample will not represent the population as a whole. In this case, you should pick every eleventh house ($k = 11$), which will eliminate the periodicity of the population as a biasing factor.

Stratified random sample.   If you divide your population into a number of strata (sub-populations), where each stratum is internally homogeneous with respect to the characteristic being studied, and you take a random sample from each stratum. For example, you may be interested in people who live in your city who use the Internet on a regular basis. You may have reason to believe that people who use it recreationally may have attitudes that differ from those of people who use it in connection with their job. So you might decide to stratify the population on this basis and draw a random sample from each group.

A stratified random sample will be more *efficient* than a simple random sample when the population can be divided into a small number of strata such that the strata differ from one another in terms of variables related to the issue being studied, and the members of any given stratum are relatively similar to one another in terms of these variables.

You will have a *proportionate stratified sample* if the sampling ratio is the same for all strata. This means that the sample you draw from a stratum that has more members should be larger than the sample you draw from a stratum that has fewer members. If, for example, you knew that 10,000 people in your city use the Internet and 7,000 of those do so as part of their jobs, you would want to draw a larger sample from the stratum that contains people who use the Internet at work and a smaller one from the stratum

that contains people who use it recreationally. If you wanted a total sample of 100 people, you would take 70 from the first stratum and 30 from the second. A proportionate random stratified sample is equivalent to a simple random sample, in terms of its ability to represent the population.

Stratified random sampling does not have to be proportionate. If some strata have more variance than others, for example, you might choose to represent them with larger samples or with samples that have larger sampling ratios. Because some people may have higher or lower chances of being included in the sample depending on which stratum they belong to, this method is called *disproportionate* stratified sampling. The math needed to do statistics here is more complex than for proportionate stratified samples.

Cluster samples.   This is a sample in which *clusters* of people are sampled. You take either all the members of a given cluster or none of the members. For example, you could sample university students by doing a cluster sample of courses. You would choose courses randomly; then take everyone in each chosen course. This method is probably the best one to use if you want to study the attitudes of elementary school children in grades 1 to 3. It is extremely disruptive to take a small number of children from a class of 25 or 30. They feel like they are receiving special treatment and the children not selected are likely to be very curious about what is going on or unhappy because they weren't selected or both curious and unhappy.

In a larger study you might do a *multi-stage cluster sample*. You might randomly select a number of school districts. From each district you might randomly select a number of schools. From each school you randomly select the classes of students who are interviewed.

Cluster samples are less efficient than simple random samples or stratified random samples; there is more variability from sample to sample with cluster samples; and the math needed to do statistics with cluster samples is more complex than the math for simple random and systematic samples. Like disproportionate stratified samples, cluster samples are not likely to have equal probability.

Comments

If you want to draw a probability sample, you will have to know the probability of being included in the sample for every person in the population. This is what differentiates probability samples from non-probability samples. Note that the probabilities will all be the same only for simple random samples, systematic samples, and proportionate stratified samples. In disproportionate stratified sampling and cluster sampling, some people may have higher or lower chances of being included than others.

Probability samples are usually more representative (i.e. they have higher external validity) than non-probability samples because there is less bias. For simple random samples, systematic samples with a random start, and proportionate stratified random sampling, the random selection of individuals guarantees that there will be no bias in the sample, provided that the sample is large enough for the level of variance in the population.

An important thing to be aware of is that the efficiency of a sample of a given size is a function of *only one thing* — the degree of heterogeneity or the variance of the population from which it is drawn. The size of the population generally doesn't matter.

Probability samples are better than non-probability ones because you can estimate the accuracy of the sample; that is, you can estimate the level of confidence you can have that your sample statistics differ from the population parameters by no more than a given level of error. Because you can do this, you can generalize to the population from which the sample was drawn. You cannot do this with non-probability sampling methods.

Important Terms and Concepts

census
a sample that includes the entire population

confidence intervals
the range of values within which a population parameter is estimated to lie. When a newspaper article says that the results show that 23% of the population supports the Prime Minister and that these results are within 3 percent 19 times out of 20, the confidence interval is from 20% to 26% — from (23% − 3%) to (23% + 3%), or in other words, 23% ± 3%. The width of a confidence interval is determined by the standard error of the statistic used to estimate the parameter and the desired confidence level. SEE ALSO: *standard error*

confidence levels
the estimated probability that a population parameter lies within a given confidence interval. The confidence level in the example above is 95% (19 times out of 20).

efficiency
the degree of confidence and level of accuracy that a sample of a given size is able to provide. A more efficient sample is one that provides greater accuracy and/or confidence than another one of the same size.

equal probability
for certain kinds of samples (e.g. simple random samples, systematic samples), the probability of being selected to be in the sample is the same for all members of the population ($p_i = p_j$). SEE ALSO: *random selection*

homogeneity
the extent to which the members of a population (or sample) are similar to one another.

heterogeneity
the extent to which the members of a population (or sample) are different from one another. The greater the heterogeneity, the more sampling variability there will be, and the larger the sample must be for a given level of confidence. SEE ALSO: *sampling variability*

independence

the fact that one person was selected has no effect on any other person's chance of being selected. SEE ALSO: *random selection*

non-probability samples

a type of sample in which you cannot specify the probability that any given individual will be in the sample ($p_i = ?$). Some combinations of individuals may be more likely to be selected than others, and the fact that one individual is selected may have an effect on the chances of others. These samples are generally *not* representative.

parameter

a summary description of a particular aspect of the entire population. Example: the mean age of citizens in the country.

probability sample

a type of sample in which, for every member of the population, the chance of being included in the sample is known. These are the only kind of sample that can be used with inferential statistics to make valid generalizations, because they are generally the only kind of sample that is truly representative of the population.

proportionate sampling

selecting elements for your sample so the number of each type of element is proportional to their relative frequency in the population. Because they are usually non-probability samples, proportionate samples are generally *not* representative.

(*note*— don't confuse "proportionate samples" with "proportionate stratified samples.")

population

the entire set of individuals, events, units with specified characteristics. Examples: citizens of California; students; adults; men.

random selection

a process in which members are drawn from a population where each member of the population has the same chance of being selected as all other members, and where the selection of one person has no influence on anyone else's chances of being selected. SEE ALSO: *equal probability; independence*

representativeness

the extent to which a sample has the same distribution of characteristics as the population from which it was selected. A representative sample is necessary if you want to make statements or conclusions about the population with any degree of confidence. Non-probability samples are generally *not* representative.

sampling frame

the list (or quasi-list) of units comprising a population from which a sample is to be selected. If the sample is to be representative of the population, the sampling frame should include all members of the population.

sample

the subset of the population from which data is collected and used as a basis for making statements about the entire population.

sampling distribution

The distribution of the values of a statistic for the set of all possible samples of a given size is a sampling distribution. Certain characteristics of the sampling distribution allow the calculation of things like confidence intervals or levels. Probability samples are generally required for these calculations and estimates to be made. The *sampling distribution of sample means* would contain a list of the means of all possible samples of a given size. The *sampling distribution of differences between means* would contain a list of the differences between the means of all possible pairs of samples of a given size.

sampling ratio

the proportion of a population taken into the sample: sampling ratio = n/N

sampling unit

the smallest element or set of elements considered for selection in a sample. In a simple random sample, the sampling unit is the individual. In a cluster sample, the sampling unit will be a cluster of individuals.

sampling variability

if more than one sample were taken from a population, each would have a slightly different value

for a given statistic. The differences between statistics of multiple samples drawn from a population is *sampling variability*. The more heterogeneous the population is, the greater the sampling variability for a given sample size. SEE ALSO: *statistical significance*

social significance

"Social significance" is not a technical term. A difference that is socially significant is one that is important to people or one that has some important social implications. Some statistically significant differences have little or no social significance. A difference that could be explained as being due to sampling variability, however, should not be considered to be either statistically or socially significant.

stratum

a subset of a sample. To be useful, a stratum must be comprised of individuals that are homogeneous in a way that is relevant to the study being conducted.

statistic

a summary description of a particular aspect of a sample. Example: the mean age of people in the sample. Statistics are used to describe samples and to estimate population parameters.

standard error

the standard deviation of a sampling distribution; a measure of the amount of sampling variability. Also called **sampling error**. The standard deviation of the sampling distribution of sample means is known as the *standard error of the mean* (SEM), and the standard deviation of the sampling distribution of differences between sample means is known as the *standard error of the difference between means* (SEDBM). SEE ALSO: *sampling variability*

statistical significance

If you take two samples and compare their statistics, you will almost certainly see some difference, even if they come from the same population. This is sampling variability. If the difference between two samples is large enough, you would conclude that the samples could not have come from the same population. You would then say that the difference is *statistically significant*. There is always a probability level associated with tests of statistical significance. It is the probability that the difference could be due to sampling variability alone. Common *significance levels* are the probabilities ".05" and ".01". Statistical significance is *only* an issue when you have data from samples and are interested in the populations from which the samples were drawn.

unit of analysis

the smallest unit or individual that is considered when the data are analyzed. Usually our sampling unit will be the individual person, although we may use advertisements, movies, episodes of television programs, conversations, organizations, families, etc.

Symbols

N the number of individuals in the population

n the number of individuals in a sample

p_i the probability that the ith individual will be in the sample

---

Things to think about .....

When you go to Baskin Robbins and ask for a spoonful of "that one in the back corner" to see what it tastes like, you hope the sample gives you reasonably accurate information about the ice cream in that container. Under what conditions would your sample give you *incorrect* information about "that one in the back corner"? Do you think the same thing could happen when you use a sample in a research project?

What could you do to reduce the likelihood of this problem?

What is the difference between a socially significant difference and a statistically significant one?

II

Univariate Statistics

Chapter 6

U NIVARIATE DESCRIPTIVE STATISTICS

"Statistics" is four things:

- an academic subject or discipline. There is a Department of Statistics in many universities. You may take a course called Statistics 101.

- a set of methods used to process and interpret quantitative data. Most of this "processing" and "interpretation" involves doing things that allow you to see patterns in the data.

- collections of data gathered with the methods described above.

- a set of figures that summarize a set of data. More precisely, statistics are figures that summarize *samples*, while parameters summarize populations.

In this book I'm going to ignore the first and third types of "statistics." I'll spend most of my time on the second type — the methods used to interpret quantitative data.

Descriptive and Inferential Statistics

On page 35 you read about sampling — what it is and why you do it. You know that samples are different from the population, and you know something about the relation between samples and their populations. It won't surprise you to learn that the statistical methods used for samples are different from the ones used for populations. The methods used for samples are known as *descriptive* statistics, while the ones used for populations are known as *inferential* statistics.

Descriptive statistics are simple. Their task is to *describe* the data in a sample. You are probably already familiar with some kinds of descriptive statistics; the quantity commonly known as "the average" is the most familiar one. When you calculate the average of the ages of a group of people, you are doing descriptive statistics: you are summarizing the data you have.

Inferential statistics are more complicated. Where you would use descriptive statistics to summarize the data from your sample, you don't have data from the population, so you have to make logical inferences about it. This is where inferential statistics are used. Their task is to help you make *inferences* about the population based on the information you have about your sample. While the math is a little bit more complicated here than it is for descriptive statistics, it is the logic involved that most people find confusing when they first learn inferential statistics.

I'll begin with the simplest kind of descriptive statistics — the ones that describe only one variable

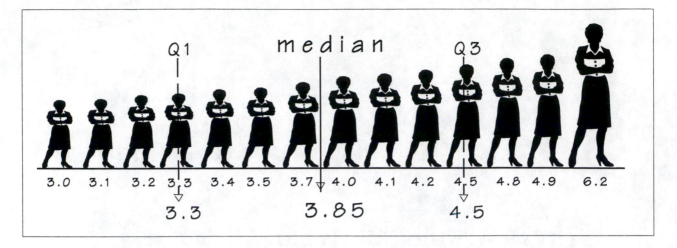

Descriptive Statistics

Descriptive statistics are tools you use to summarize your data in an effective and meaningful way. They are used to pull information about important aspects of your data out of the pile of numbers and to make it visible in a useful way.

On page 23 you read that variables are either discrete (also called *categorical* because they are used to sort things into categories) or continuous. The methods used for discrete variables are generally different from the ones used for continuous variables. Whether a variable is discrete or continuous turns out to have important implications for what you can do with it and how you use it. These implications will be discussed in the following pages.

There are two classes of univariate descriptive statistics: measures of **central tendency** and measures of **dispersion**.

Central tendency gets at the "typical" or "most common" value in a set of values. *Dispersion* tells how much spread or how much scattering around the central value there is. You use different measures of central tendency and dispersion for data scaled at different levels. The main reason for this is that different types of scaling produce different kinds of

at a time. Then I'll move to the kind that describe differences or relationships. These use two variables at a time. After I've laid the groundwork, I'll venture into the area of inferential statistics.

"numbers," and they vary in the extent to which they allow you to perform arithmetical operations (addition, multiplication, etc.) on them.

Central Tendency

Because different kinds of numbers represent different aspects of reality, you need to use different measures of central tendency for different levels of scaling. Remember that nominal data sorts cases into categories and only tells which category each case belongs to; with nominal data you can only tell whether two cases are in the same category or in different categories. Ordinal data tells you more; it orders cases from low to high. With ordinal data you can tell whether one value is higher than another, but you can't tell how much higher it may be. With interval data you can not only do everything that you do with nominal and ordinal data; you can also determine the size of the difference between two values. With interval scaling, the numbers you get behave like real numbers — you can add and subtract values. Ratio scaling goes one step further because the scale is anchored by an absolute zero value. These differences mean that you have to match your analytic approach to your data.

The **mode** is *the most common category or value* in the data. If more women are named Linda than any other name, Linda is the modal value of women's names. The mode is the only measure of central tendency that can be used with nominal data. It is a

discrete measure, and cannot be used with continuous interval or ratio data without first grouping the data into discrete categorical ranges. For example, if you wanted to get the mode of the height of students at your university, you would have to group their heights into categories by rounding, say, to the nearest inch. This would make height a discrete variable.

- The mode is not influenced by extreme values.

- The mode is sensitive only to the most frequently occurring score; it is insensitive to all other scores.

- The mode is of little value for non-categorical (e.g., continuous) data; it is used almost exclusively for discrete variables.

The **median** is *the value at the midpoint of a rank-ordered list of all the values* in a set of data. If you have a large group of people line up in order from shortest to tallest, the height of the person in the middle of the line will be the median of the group's height.

Half the values are above the median and half are below the median. If there are an odd number of scores, the median will be the center point in the rank-ordered list of points. If there are an even number of scores, the median will be the mean of the two centermost points. *Note that the median is not the midpoint of the range* (the difference between the highest and lowest values).

If you split the list of values into the half below the median and the half above the median (a "median split"), you could find the middle value of each half. These values (marked "Q1" and "Q3" on the drawing on page 46), together with the median, divide the list of values into four parts called "*quartiles*," each of which contains 25% of all the cases in your data. The median is sometimes referred to as the "second quartile."

Because the only thing it needs from your data is the order of the values, the median can be used for all types of scaling except nominal.

- The median can be used for discrete or continuous variables.

- The median is not influenced by extreme values.

- The median is sensitive *only* to the value of the middle point or points; it is *not* sensitive to the values of all other points.

The **mean** is *the arithmetic average of a set of values*. It is calculated by dividing the sum of all the values by the number of values. Because the calculation of the mean requires addition, it can only be used with interval or ratio data. Since every value in a set of data affects the mean, the mean uses more of the information in the data than the median does. Extreme values have a disproportionately large effect on the mean.

With the mean we see the first mathematical equation and symbols for this course. The symbol for the mean of a sample is $\bar{X}$ (pronounced "x-bar"). The symbol for the mean of a population is μ (the lower-

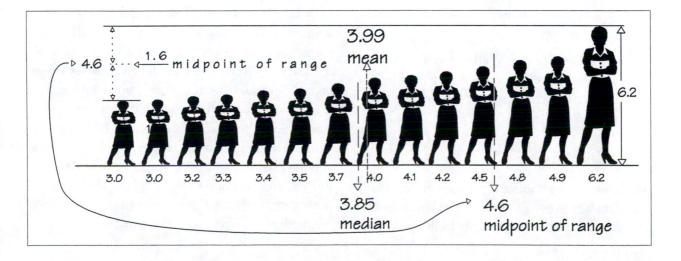

case Greek letter "mu"). In the formula below, $\bar{X}$ is the mean of all the values for the variable X in a set of data.

The symbol $\sum$ is a Greek uppercase sigma — about as close as you can get in Greek to the letter "S" (as in "sum"). It means "add up all the things that follow." In the equation below, it means add together the scores of all the people on the variable X:

$$\sum_{i=1}^{n} X_i = X_1 + X_2 + X_3 + \ldots + X_n$$

The part to the left of the equal sign in the equation is read as "the sum of X-sub-i; i goes from 1 to n."

To calculate the mean of a list of numbers, you add them all together and divide the result by how many there are. In other words,

$$mean = \bar{X} = \frac{\sum X_i}{n}$$

So the mean of the numbers 2, 3, 4, 5, 6 would be:

$$\frac{2+3+4+5+6}{5}$$

- The mean requires interval or ratio data.

- The mean is the preferred measure for interval or ratio data.

- The mean is generally not used for discrete variables.

- The mean is sensitive to **all** scores in a sample (every number in the data affects the mean), which makes it a more "powerful" measure than the median or mode.

- The mean's sensitivity to all scores also makes it sensitive to extreme values, which is why the median is used when there are extreme values.

Dispersion

Something you will notice if you look at almost any set of data is that not all observations have the same score on any variable. People differ from one another in terms of their attitudes, their beliefs, or their behaviors. Magazines differ from one another in terms of their content, their format, their cost, and how often they are published. The goal of most research is to describe or explain the variability in the data.

The simplest thing you can do with your data is measure *the amount of variability* in the scores of your variables. When you do this, you will be measuring *dispersion*. Dispersion tells how scattered or spread out the values are. The less spread out the values are, the more concentrated or clustered they will be, and the more likely it is that there will be a "most common" or "typical" or "central" value. Also, the less dispersion there is, the more you can learn about the whole set of values by knowing its central value.

For *nominal* data, the only kind of comparison you can do with a pair of values is to see whether they are the same or different. You can only use a measure of dispersion that looks at the extent to which the values in the data are the same as or different from one another. The measure of dispersion that does this is the information-theoretic measure of **uncertainty**.

If all the cases in your data have the same value — if they all occupy the same nominal category — there is no uncertainty about what the typical value is. For example, if all dogs were named Spot, the most common name for a dog (the *modal* name) would be Spot. In fact, you would have little doubt (uncertainty) about what the name of the next dog you saw would be. If each case is the sole occupant of its category, there is maximum uncertainty of what the typical value is. For example, if every dog had a different, unique name, there would be no "typical" dog's name; you would be completely uncertain about what the next dog's name would be. If half of all dogs were named Spot and the rest were named Rover, you would have more uncertainty than if they were all named Spot, but less than if they all had different names. The measure of uncertainty in your data tells you the extent to which the values in your data are different from or equal to one another. This measure is not commonly used, mainly because people don't often calculate dispersion for nominal data.

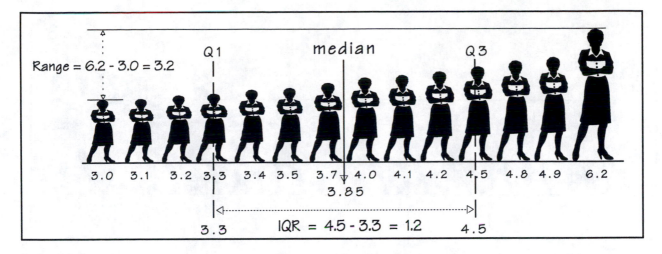

Range = 6.2 - 3.0 = 3.2

Q1   median   Q3

3.0 3.1 3.2 3.3 3.4 3.5 3.7 4.0 4.1 4.2 4.5 4.8 4.9 6.2

3.85

3.3   IQR = 4.5 - 3.3 = 1.2   4.5

The simplest measure of dispersion for numerical data is the **range** — the difference between the highest and lowest values, as you can see in the drawing on the next page. Because the difference is a distance, the range can only be calculated on interval or ratio data. The range is determined by only two values — the lowest and the highest — the two most extreme values in the data. As you can see from the drawing above, the range is strongly influenced by extreme values. If the tallest woman is included, the range is 3.2. If she were excluded from the data, the range would drop to 4.9 - 3.0 = 1.9. *Because of this dependence on the two most unusual values, the range doesn't tell much about the data.* It tells nothing, for example, about how far from the center typical values lie.

The **interquartile range** (**IQR**) can be used for ordinal, interval, or ratio data. It is the difference between the first and third quartiles in the data. If you remove the top 25% and the bottom 25% of all cases and then calculate the range of the remaining cases, you will get the IQR. While the IQR is more valuable than the range because it is not influenced as much by extreme values, it is more difficult to calculate, as it requires the data points to be rank ordered. The figure above illustrates the IQR in relation to the median. You would say either "The IQR is 1.2" or, more likely,   "Half of the sample have heights between 3.3 and 4.5."

Neither the range or the interquartile range take all of the values in your data into account. The range is determined by the two most extreme values and the

IQR is determined by the lowest and highest values in the middle 50% of your data. There are two measures of dispersion that take every value in your data into consideration. For nominal data, you can use the information-theoretic measure of uncertainty. For continuous (i.e. interval or ratio) data, you would use variance or its very close relative, standard deviation.

Variance

All measures of dispersion are assessments of what you might call "variability" or "variety" — the extent to which values in your data differ from one another. *Variance* is a particularly useful measure of variety or variability for interval- or ratio-scaled data. It is probably the most important statistical concept, and it is used in a very wide range of situations.

The variance of a set of numbers is based on the distance between each value and the mean of all the values. It starts with *deviation scores*. The deviation score for an individual is the difference between the individual's score and the mean. It is written like this:

$$d_i = X_i - \bar{X}$$

where "d_i" is the deviation score for the ith individual, and "X_i" is the ith individual's value (i.e., the score for person number i).

If an individual's score is higher than the mean, the deviation score will be positive; if it is lower than the

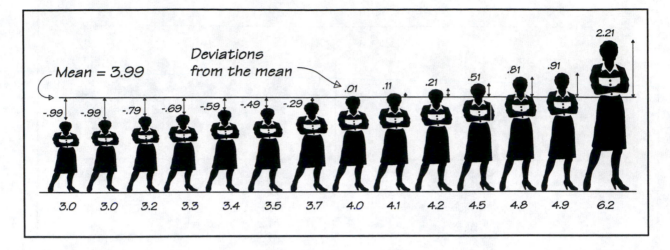

mean, the deviation score will be negative, as in the drawing above. It might seem to make sense to calculate the mean of the deviation scores. There is a problem with this, though, because the sum of the deviation scores is *always* zero (*why does this happen?*), so the mean of the deviation scores will also always be zero.

Sometimes people speak of the "*average deviation*" or the "*mean absolute deviation*," which is the mean of the **absolute values** of the deviation scores. (The "absolute value" means that you ignore minus signs and treat all scores as if they were positive numbers.)

It turns out that there is a better way of dealing with negative deviation scores. If you square a negative number, the result becomes positive. So, if you square the deviation scores, the results will always be positive. The sum of the squared deviation scores is called the *sum of squares* (SS). The SS is the first step in the calculation of variance, and it is something you will see in a variety of situations in the coming chapters.

$$SS = \sum d_i^2$$

The **variance** is the sum of squares divided by the number of scores that went into the sum. In other words, it is the *mean* of the *squared* deviation scores. This is why variance is sometimes called by the more descriptive name **mean square**. Note that this name tells you how to calculate the variance (*if you can remember what it is you have to square!*).

The symbol for a population's variance is σ^2. The letter in the symbol is a lowercase Greek sigma. Here is the equation for a *population's* variance:

$$\sigma^2 = \frac{\sum D_i^2}{N}$$

In the equation, the "D_i" is deviation scores — the differences between the individual scores and the population's mean. "N" is the number of cases. (The "D" and "N" are uppercase because they are *population* values, not sample values.)

The symbol for the variance of a sample is "s^2." When you calculate the variance for a *sample*, the size of the sample is transformed into a value called **degrees of freedom**. The degrees of freedom for a sample of size n is $n - 1$, so you divide by **(n-1)** instead of **N**. *This correction makes the variance of a sample a better estimate of the population's variance.* (This issue is discussed in more detail on page 53.) So the equation for a *sample's* variance is:

$$s^2 = \frac{\sum d_i^2}{n - 1}$$

Standard Deviation

The *standard deviation* is the square root of the variance. It is sometimes called the **root mean square**, because it is the square *root* of the *mean* of the *squared* deviation scores. The standard deviation is

the most commonly used measure of dispersion for interval or ratio level data.

While the *variance* is a measure of the overall amount of variability or spread around the mean, the *standard deviation* is a measure of the typical deviation from the mean. Like the variance and the mean, the standard deviation is sensitive to **all** scores. The symbol for a sample's standard deviation is a lowercase "*s*". The symbol for population standard deviation is a lowercase Greek sigma: σ. The equation for a sample's standard deviation is:

$$s = \sqrt{\frac{\sum d_i^2}{n-1}}$$

Standard Scores (or "z-scores")

If an individual person's score is converted so it tells how far from the mean the person is, it will become a relative score that will let you know how this person compares to the rest of the sample. The most common way of doing this is to calculate a *standard score*. The word "standard" in "standard score" is the same one as in "standard deviation." This is not a coincidence. To calculate standard scores, you divide the individual's deviation score (the difference between the individual's score and the mean) by the standard deviation. The equation to calculate an individual's standard score is:

$$z_i = \frac{x_i - \bar{x}}{s}$$

The subscript *i* tells which person you are doing this for. x_i is person *i*'s score on the variable. The *s* in the denominator is the standard deviation. If the standard deviation is 2, the mean is 5, and your score is 7, your z-score would be

$$\frac{(7-5)}{2} = \frac{2}{2} = 1.0$$

If your score was 4, your z-score would be

$$\frac{(4-5)}{2} = \frac{-1}{2} = -0.5$$

A positive z-score means that you are above the mean; a negative z-score means that you are below the mean.

A person's z-score tells how far away from the mean that person's score is, in terms of standard deviations. If your z-score is 1.0, you are one standard deviation above the mean. If your z-score is −3.5, you are three and a half standard deviations below the mean.

If you know the mean and standard deviation and you want to convert z-scores back into raw scores, you can use this equation:

$$x_i = (z_i \times s) + \bar{x}$$

Just multiply the z-score by the standard deviation and add the result to the mean. Here are a few examples:

Mean	Std. Dev.	Raw Score	z- score
10	2	6	-2.0
10	2	13	1.5
10	5	12	0.4

The table below summarizes which measures of central tendency and dispersion are used for different levels of scaling.

Level of Scaling	discrete or continuous	central tendency	dispersion
nominal	discrete	mode	uncertainty
ordinal	discrete	median	IQR
interval	continuous	median or mean	std. dev. or IQR
ratio	continuous	median or mean	std. dev. or IQR

Calculating Standard Deviation

An alternative name for standard deviation, "root mean square," tells how to calculate it: the standard deviation is the square *root* of the *mean* of the *squared* deviation scores. The deviation score (d_i) is the difference between the individual's score (X_i) and the mean ($\bar{X}$).

So the equation for standard deviation is:

$$S.D. = \sqrt{\frac{\sum d_i^2}{n-1}}$$

$$= \sqrt{\frac{\sum (X_i - \bar{X})^2}{n-1}}$$

$$= \sqrt{\frac{(X_1 - \bar{X})^2 + (X_2 - \bar{X})^2 + \ldots + (X_n - \bar{X})^2}{n-1}}$$

The above equation shows the additions, subtractions, and multiplications you have to do to calculate the standard deviation. This is the equation you first saw on page 51. The only good things that you can say about this equation are first, that it works; and second, that you can remember it if you can remember "root mean square." *(Don't forget that it is the deviation scores that get squared!)* The bad thing about it is that it involves a *lot* of work. You have to calculate the mean, then you have to subtract the mean from every value on the list. Then you have to square the differences and add them up. Finally, you divide by *n - 1* and take the square root.

Here is a different form of the equation, called the "computational form" because it is much easier to use. It is easier because you don't have to calculate the mean or the deviation scores:

$$S.D. = \sqrt{\frac{\sum X_i^2 - (\sum X_i)^2 / n}{n-1}}$$

1) First, calculate the sum of the squares of the original scores: $\sum X_i^2$

2) Then calculate the sum of the original scores, square it, and divide the result by *n*, the sample size: $(\sum X_i)^2 / n$

3) Now subtract the result of step 2 from the first sum;

4) Divide the result of step 3 by your sample size minus 1;

5) ...and take the square root. *Voila!*

The result is exactly the same as if you calculated the mean, the deviation scores, the squares of the deviation scores, the sum of the squares .... With the new method, you do a *lot* less work. You only need to add up all the scores for one total and then add up the squares of the scores for the second total. The rest is easy. The table below shows a comparison of the amount of work you have to do with the two methods for samples containing 7 and 50 cases.

	original method		computational form	
	n = 7	n = 50	n = 7	n = 50
additions	27	150	14	100
subtractions	8	51	2	2
multiplications	7	50	8	50
divisions	1	1	2	2
square roots	1	1	1	1
total	44	253	27	155

The numbers in the last line of this table actually underestimate the difference in the amount of work. This is because the original method usually requires working with messy numbers — numbers involving decimals like 27.3841, 4.2938, etc. These numbers result from subtracting the mean from the original scores to calculate deviation scores. When you square

the deviation scores, the numbers get even messier, increasing the amount of time it takes to do the work, increasing the probability that you will make mistakes, and requiring more rounding, which introduces rounding errors. In comparison, almost all of the numbers you use with the computational form are whole numbers. It's easy to see that the computational form is the one you would want to use: It takes less work, you will probably make fewer mistakes, and there is less rounding error.

Sample or Population?

The equation for a *population's* variance and standard deviation are:

$$\sigma^2 = \frac{\sum D_i^2}{N} \quad \text{and} \quad \sigma = \sqrt{\frac{\sum D_i^2}{N}}$$

In the equation, the "D_i" is deviation scores — the differences between the individual scores and the population's mean. The "N" is the population's size. The "D" and "N" are uppercase because they are *population* values, not sample values.

To calculate σ for a population, you need to calculate the sum of the squares of the deviation scores for *all* members of the population. Since most social research is interested large populations — in which getting data from all members is either impossible or impractical — you will rarely find yourself trying to *calculate* σ. Instead, you will most likely be using data from a sample to *estimate* σ.

Remember that a *sample* is a subset of a population, chosen in such a way that what you learn about the sample can be generalized to the population. Because sample statistics are used as the basis for estimates of population parameters, there may be some adjustments made to the equations used for the corresponding population parameters. For standard deviation and variance, you use *n-1* instead of *n* in the denominator, which produces a slightly larger result. The difference will be more significant for smaller samples than for larger ones. In general, a larger

standard deviation or variance will produce a more conservative conclusion from any statistical decisions you might make. Since small samples provide results that are less stable than those from larger ones, this conservative modification is a desirable thing to do.

The equations for a *sample's* variance and standard deviation are:

$$s^2 = \frac{\sum d_i^2}{n-1} \quad \text{and} \quad s = \sqrt{\frac{\sum d_i^2}{n-1}}$$

The Uses of the Standard Deviation

Standard deviations are used for several purposes, sometimes to give information directly, and sometimes in the calculation of another statistical measure. Here are three important uses of the standard deviation:

● The standard deviation is the most common measure of dispersion when the data is scaled at the interval or ratio level. Here you are describing the extent to which the elements in a sample are spread out from one another — in particular, *how far the typical value is from the mean*. If you think about this, you will realize that knowing the standard deviation allows you to know how good an estimate of central tendency the mean is.

For example, for a course with 50 students, if the mean score on the final exam is 75 and the standard deviation is 0.5, you will know that most scores are pretty close to 75. (In fact, about 95% of all the scores will be between 74 and 76.) In this case, the mean, is a very good indicator of the "typical" score.

In contrast, if the mean is 75 and the standard deviation is 28.0, you don't really know what the "typical" score is. There might not even be any scores between 70 and 80. It turns out that you would be safe in estimating that 95% of all scores are between 25 and 125, but this is a pretty big range. Generally, you would want a more precise estimate than that.

- The sample standard deviation, when it is calculated with $(n-1)$ in the denominator, is used as an estimate of the population's standard deviation, which tells you how much variety or heterogeneity there is in the population.

- When you combine the mean with the standard deviation in the calculation of z-scores (for a normally distributed variable), you can tell where an individual is in the distribution relative to the other members. For example, if your z-score is 2.52, you are above 97.5% of everyone else in the sample. If your z-score is 1.0, about 16% of the other people are above you.

  One benefit of using z-scores is that it allows you to compare variables that have different means and standard deviations. Remember that the z-score is also known as the *standard score*.

When you transform a person's raw score (the original value) into a z-score, you standardize it by converting it to a scale where the mean is zero and the units are marked off in standard deviations. Starting from the mean and going up, you have 0, 1, 2, and so on. These numbers mean "0, 1, 2, etc. standard deviations above the mean." Once you have standardized your scores by computing z-scores, you can compare a person's score on one variable to their score on another variable (or to someone else's score on another variable).

The computational formula for standard deviation

If you are curious, here is a demonstration of the basis for the computational formula for standard deviation. Compare the original and computational versions. Note that the only difference between the two equations is the numerators:

original equation	computational equation
$s = \sqrt{\dfrac{\sum d_i^2}{n-1}}$	$s = \sqrt{\dfrac{\sum x_i^2 - (\sum x_i)^2/n}{n-1}}$

Consider the numerator of the original formula:

$$\sum d_i^2$$

Since d_i, the deviation score, is $x_i - \bar{x}$, you could rewrite the numerator like this:

$$\sum (x_i - \bar{x})^2$$

which is:

$$\sum (x_i - \bar{x})(x_i - \bar{x})$$

If you multiply the terms in the product, you get:

$$\sum (x_i x_i - x_i \bar{x} - x_i \bar{x} + \bar{x}\bar{x})$$

which you can simplify as:

$$\sum (x_i^2 - 2x_i \bar{x} + \bar{x}^2)$$

You can break it up into three sums:

$$\sum x_i^2 - \sum 2x_i \bar{x} + \sum \bar{x}^2$$

Since $\bar{x}$, the mean, is $\dfrac{\sum x_i}{n}$, you can rewrite the above sum as:

$$\sum x_i^2 - \sum 2x_i \left(\frac{\sum x_i}{n}\right) + \sum \left(\frac{\sum x_i}{n}\right)^2$$

which simplifies to:

$$\sum x_i^2 - 2\sum x_i \left(\frac{\sum x_i}{n}\right) + \frac{(\sum x_i)^2}{n}$$

and then to:

$$\sum x_i^2 - 2\frac{\sum x_i \sum x_i}{n} + \frac{(\sum x_i)^2}{n}$$

which gives:

$$\sum x_i^2 - 2\frac{(\sum x_i)^2}{n} + \frac{(\sum x_i)^2}{n}$$

and, at last, we have:

$$\sum x_i^2 - \frac{(\sum x_i)^2}{n}$$

. . . which is the numerator of the computational formula!

As a bonus, here is a simpler computational version:

$$s = \sqrt{\frac{\sum x_i^2 - n\bar{x}^2}{n-1}}$$

How to calculate standard deviation with the original method

$$s = \sqrt{\frac{\sum d_i^2}{n-1}}$$

(1) X_i	d_i	d_i^2
(2) 8	(5) 2	(6) 4
6	0	0
4	2	4
5	1	1
6	0	0
5	1	1
4	2	4
8	2	4
7	1	1
8	2	4
4	2	4
5	1	1
8	2	4
7	1	1
6	0	0
5	1	1
5	1	1
6	0	0
8	2	4
5	1	1

1. Make three columns, like the ones on the right, headed "X_i," "d_i," and "d_i^2"

2. Write the values of the variable in the first column, and count them to see how many there are. (*ex: n = 20*)

3. Add all the values in the first column to get a total. (*ex: total = 120*)

4. Divide the total by the number there are to get the mean. (*ex: mean = 120/20 = 6.0*)

5. Subtract the mean from each value in the first column and write the results in the second column.

6. Square each value in the second column and write the result in the third column.

7. Add all the values in the third column to get a total. This is the "sum of squares". (*ex: total SS = 40*)

8. Divide the sum of squares by $n - 1$ to get the variance. (*ex: variance = 2.1052632*)

9. Take the square root of the variance to get the standard deviation. (*ex: std. dev. = 1.4509525*)

Sums: (3) 120   0   (7) 40

(2) n = 20

(4) Mean = 120/20 = 6.0

(8) variance = 40/19 = 2.105263158 ≈ 2.105

(9) std. dev. = $\sqrt{\text{variance}}$ = 1.4509525 ≈ 1.451

How to calculate standard deviation with the computational method

$$s = \sqrt{\frac{\sum x_i^2 - (\sum x_i)^2/n}{n-1}}$$

(1) X_i		X_i^2
(2) 8	(4)	64
6		36
4		16
5		25
6		36
5		25
4		16
8		64
7		49
8		64
4		16
5		25
8		64
7		49
6		36
5		25
5		25
6		36
8		64
5		25

Sums: (3) 120 (5) 760

1. Make two columns, headed "X_i" and "X_i^2"

2. Write the values of the variable in the first column, and count them to see how many there are. (ex: n = 20)

3. Add all the values in the column to get a total. (ex: total = 120)

4. Square each value in the first column and write the result in the second column.

5. Add all the values in the second column to get a total. (ex: total = 760)

6. Square the first total. (ex: 120 × 120 = 14,400)

7. Divide the value you obtained in step 6 by the sample size. (ex: 14,400 / 20 = 720)

8. Subtract the result of step 7 from the result of step 5. The difference is the sum of squares (SS). (ex: 760 - 720 = 40)

9. Divide the sum of squares by (n-1) to get the variance. (ex: 40 / 19 = 2.1052632)

10. Take the square root of the variance to get the standard deviation. (ex: std. dev. = 1.4509525)

(6) 120 × 120 = 14400

(7) 14400 ÷ 20 = 720

(8) 760 − 720 = 40

(9) variance 40/19 = 2.105263158 (2.105)

(10) std. dev. = $\sqrt{}$ variance = 1.4509525 (1.451)

Important Terms and Concepts

average deviation
central tendency
computational formula
degrees of freedom
descriptive statistics
deviation scores
dispersion
extreme value
inferential statistics
information-theoretic uncertainty
interquartile range (IQR)
mean absolute deviation
mean
mean square
median
midpoint of range
modal value
mode
range
root mean square
standard scores
standard deviation
statistics
sum of squares (SS)
variability or spread around the mean
variance
z-score

Things to think about .....

Add one more observation with the value of 9 to the data on page 55 and see what it does to the results, using the calculation method on page 55. You will have to calculate a new sum for the first column, a new mean, new deviation scores, new squared deviation scores, etc. It's a *lot* of work! The new sum in the first column will be $120 + 9 = 129$. The new n will be 21 instead of 20.

What is the new mean?

What is the new sum of squares?

What is the new variance?

Do the same thing with the data on page 56 and see what it does to the results, using the calculation method on page 56.

What is the new mean?

What is the new sum of squares?

What is the new variance?

Which method do you prefer?

Which result is likely to be more accurate? Why?

Examples of data and mean & standard deviation:

3 sets of data	$\bar{x}$	s	$\sum x$	$\sum x^2$
7, 28, 12, 17, 23, 13, 0, 16, 25, 7, 25, 15, 13, 9, 2, 4	13.50	8.5557	216.0	4014.0
95, 79, 83, 61, 85, 59, 52, 54, 95, 79, 74, 91, 83, 84, 94, 64	77.00	14.6924	1232.0	98102.
41, 31, 36, 42, 47, 49, 38, 45, 46, 31, 37, 48, 35, 32, 43, 39	40.00	6.05530	640.	26150.

Notes

Chapter 7

DISTRIBUTIONS

The measures of central tendency and dispersion provide a very concise way of summarizing the data in a sample. The chart below, for example, summarizes a little over a thousand numbers (365 daily high temperatures for three cities) as it shows the mean daily maximum temperature for Vancouver, Montréal, and Regina. You can see that Montréal, and Regina are, on average, cooler than Vancouver. Although the mean daily maximum temperature in Vancouver is 13.5°C (56.3°F) and only 11°C (51.8°F) in Regina, you may want to know more about the data before you decide which city has a more pleasant climate. You may want to know the mean low daily temperature as well as the mean highs.

The chart on the right shows both the mean daily high and low temperatures. You can see that the mean daily low temperature in Vancouver is 6°C, while both Montréal and Regina are considerably colder, at 1.2°C and -3.8°C, respectively.

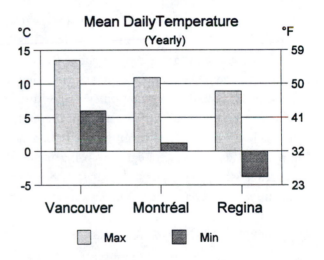

With this additional information, you would probably still conclude that both Montréal and Regina are chilly places. It's not just that their high temperatures are lower than Vancouver's, but their low temperatures are lower as well. If you had more information though, you might draw a very different conclusion. The chart on the top of the next page shows the same data for the same three cities broken down into four seasonal periods. Here, you can see that Vancouver is warmer than the other two cities in

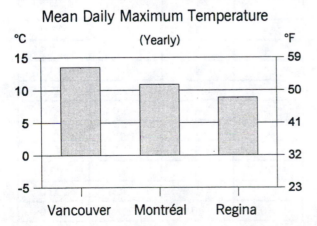

the winter, and cooler in the summer. In the spring and fall it is just a degree or two warmer. From this chart you would conclude that the climate in Vancouver is milder than in the other two cities.

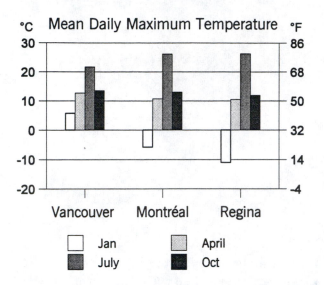

°C Mean Daily Maximum Temperature °F

Vancouver   Montréal   Regina

☐ Jan ☐ April
■ July ■ Oct

The chart below shows the range between the mean high and low temperatures for the three cities in the same four times of the year. Now you can get a more complete and accurate picture of how the cities compare. You can see that the biggest difference is in the winter, where Vancouver's mean *minimum* temperature is above the freezing point and the other two cities' mean *maximum* temperatures are several degrees below freezing. The summers are hotter in Montréal and Regina, but in Regina there is a greater range between the mean highs and mean lows. Spring and fall in Vancouver are a few degrees warmer. The

climate of Regina appears to be generally more extreme. This pattern is what you might expect if you were to look on a map and see that Vancouver is on the west coast where the Pacific Ocean and the Japan Current have significant moderating effects. Regina is in the middle of vast open prairies and the weather in Montreal is buffered by the Great lakes.

These charts summarize the data and attempt to present it in a way that you can see its main features in a glance. Because they summarize the data, they do not show all the details; instead, they show only main patterns or trends in the data. A more complete representation might show weekly or even daily high and low temperatures. This would allow you to extract even more information. For example, how many times a year does the temperature goes above 30 and how often does it goes below zero? To do this, you would examine the entire *distribution* of values.

If you are working with discrete/categorical data, the distribution for a variable will show how many times each value occurred. Since such a distribution describes the *frequency* of occurrence of each value, it is often called a *frequency distribution*. The example below shows the distribution of grades in CMNS 540, a course about fish communication methods. For a given row in the table, the first column contains the value of the variable; the second is the number of times that value appeared in the data; the third column is what percent of all cases have this value; and

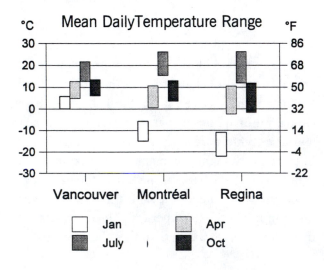

°C Mean DailyTemperature Range °F

Vancouver   Montréal   Regina

☐ Jan ☐ Apr
■ July ■ Oct

Frequency distribution of Grades CMNS 540			
Grade	Freq.	%	Cum %
A+	1	2.5	2.5
A	2	5.0	7.5
A-	3	7.5	15.0
B+	5	12.5	27.5
B	4	10.0	37.5
B-	7	17.5	55.0
C+	6	15.0	70.0
C	4	10.0	80.0
C-	5	12.5	92.5
D	2	5.0	97.5
F	1	2.5	100.0
Total	40	100.0	100.0

the last column is the cumulative percentage, counting down from the top (what percent of cases appear in this row or any of the rows above this one).

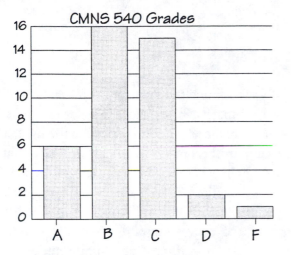

The charts on this side of the page are *histograms*. They provide graphic representations of the data that appears in the table on the previous page. The histogram makes it possible to see the *shape* of the distribution of scores. In this case, the majority of scores are concentrated in the middle of the range, with fewer scores being at either end of the range. Both histograms show the same data. The one below shows a finer breakdown of grades than the one above. You can see that the finer breakdown provides a better picture of the shape of the distribution.

The dashed line rising from the bottom left to the top right of the histogram shows the *cumulative percentage*. In bell-shaped distributions — ones in

which most of the cases are concentrated in the middle of the range — the cumulative percentage line is shaped like a stretched-out "S". The point at which the cumulative percentage line crosses the 50% mark is the median.

When you are using categorical variables, your histograms will most likely resemble the above examples. If you have a continuous variable, though, and if your sample is large, you can break the range down into a larger number of "bins," as in the figures below. If there are enough bins to give a relatively smooth histogram, you might just draw the outline of the distribution instead of the bins. Because they are usually curved lines, these outlines are called "curves."

The two distributions below show the cumulative percentages. The one on the top is very close to being a perfect *normal* distribution, while the one on the bottom is positively skewed or skewed to the right. This is the type of distribution you are likely to see when you examine the distribution of things like wealth, salary, education, and so on. A small percentage of people have larger amounts of the commodity, while the majority of people have smaller amounts.

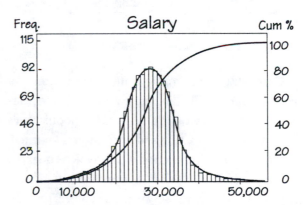

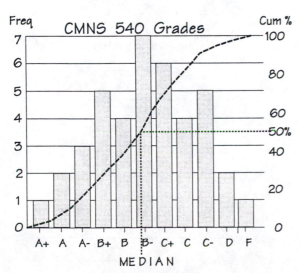

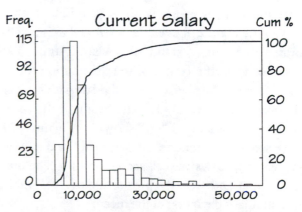

The Normal Distribution

The shape of a sample's histogram or distribution is usually similar to the shape of the distribution of the population from which the sample was drawn. The most important kind of shape for distributions is the one shown below — the *normal distribution*. It is also called "bell-shaped" because it looks like the cross section of a bell. Most phenomena that vary randomly have normal distributions.

The normal curve is a theoretical probability curve that has a particular shape. About 68% of the area under the curve is within one standard deviation of the mean; about 95% is within two standard deviations, and a little more than 99% is within three standard deviations. (The exact numbers for 95% and 99% are 1.96 and 2.58 standard deviations.)

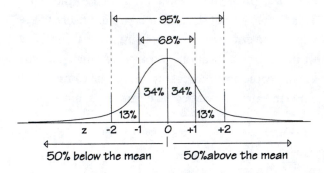

Cases drawn randomly from a population in a random sample will "distribute about" the population's mean — they will be close to the population's mean. If the population's distribution is normal, about 68% of randomly chosen cases will be no more than one standard deviation away from the mean (they will have z-scores between -1.0 and 1.0). About 95% will have z-scores between -2.0 and 2.0.

In the picture above, the horizontal axis is calibrated in terms of standard deviation units. The distance from the center of the distribution to the mean is zero. The point one standard deviation above the mean is marked "+1." The height of the curve over the point labeled "+1" shows how many cases have scores one standard deviation above the mean (how many cases have z-scores of 1.0). The area between -1 and +1 is the proportion of cases within one standard deviation of the mean.

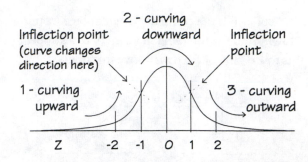

If you examine the shape of the normal curve, you will see that it can be divided into three sections. Starting from the left end and moving to the right, it curves upward, becoming increasingly steep until you get to the point where $z = -1.0$, and it starts to bend in the other direction. This continues until you reach the point where $z = 1.0$ and it once again switches direction and curves outward, eventually sloping down toward the horizontal line. Note that the points where the curvature switches direction (the "inflection points") are located at -1.0 and 1.0.

Not all distributions are normal. The drawing below shows some of the kinds of things you might see. There are three types of distortion to notice. The

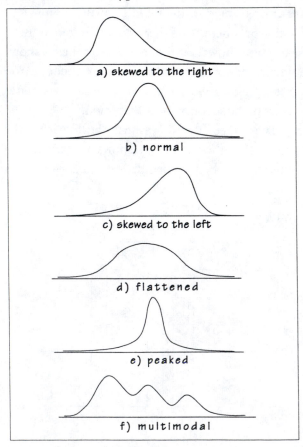

first includes distributions a) and c) — the ones *skewed* to the left and right. Distribution a) might resemble the distribution of family incomes. There are a few people with very low incomes, then the great majority with low to moderate incomes, and finally a small number with high and very high incomes. There are few people near Bill Gates, who is way up at the highest part of the range. The extent to which a distribution is distorted in this way is measured by a quantity called *skewness*.

Distributions d) and e) show a different kind of variation. Neither shows any skewness, but they both look quite different from b), the normal distribution. The one in d) is rather flattened with a wide peak, while the one in e) is quite narrow, with a thin pointy peak. The statistic that measures this kind of distortion is *kurtosis*. Distribution f) on the bottom is a *multimodal* distribution — one in which there is more than one peak. In this one, you can see that there are three values that occur more often than the others, so this one has three modal values. It is possible that this distribution represents cases drawn from three more-or-less distinct populations.

Three "real" normal distributions are shown below. As you can see, they are not smooth curves like the ones in the previous examples. The one in the top (g) is the smoothest of the three, but it has 20,000 data

points spread over about 400 different possible values. The one in the middle (h) has 1,000 data points spread over the same 400 values, while the one on the bottom (i) has 1,000 data points spread over about 140 different values. Notice how rough the bottom one is, compared to the one on the top. Yet you can still see the overall shape of the distribution.

The drawing below shows the upper half of a normal distribution. It shows the percentage of all cases that fall between the mean ($z = 0$) and $z=0.5$, $z=1.0, \ldots z=3.0$.

For example, 43.3% of all cases fall between the

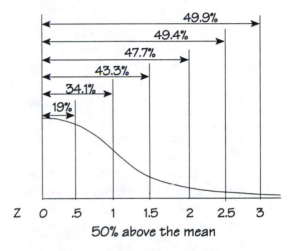

mean and $z = 1.5$. (In other words, 43.3% of cases are between the mean and 1.5 standard deviations above the mean.) A table showing what percent of cases fall between the mean and other areas appears on the next page. It is called the "Table of areas under the normal curve." It is the most important — and the most basic — of all statistical tables. (A much more complete version of this table is Table 1 in Appendix A, Tables.)

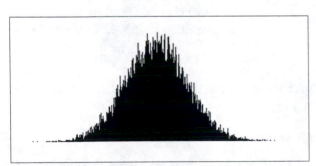

g) a large real random distribution

h) small random distribution

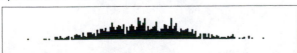

i) a smaller random distribution

Table 1: Areas under the normal curve

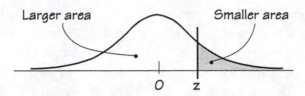

z	z to mean	smaller area	larger area		z	z to mean	smaller area	larger area
0.00	0.0000	0.5000	0.5000		2.00	0.4772	0.0228	0.9772
0.10	0.0398	0.4602	0.5398		2.10	0.4821	0.0179	0.9821
0.20	0.0793	0.4207	0.5793		2.20	0.4861	0.0139	0.9861
0.30	0.1179	0.3821	0.6179		2.30	0.4893	0.0107	0.9893
0.40	0.1554	0.3446	0.6554		2.40	0.4918	0.0082	0.9918
0.50	0.1915	0.3085	0.6915		2.50	0.4938	0.0062	0.9938
0.60	0.2257	0.2743	0.7257		2.60	0.4953	0.0047	0.9953
0.70	0.2580	0.2420	0.7580		2.70	0.4965	0.0035	0.9965
0.80	0.2881	0.2119	0.7881		2.80	0.4974	0.0026	0.9974
0.90	0.3159	0.1841	0.8159		2.90	0.4981	0.0019	0.9981
1.00	0.3413	0.1587	0.8413		3.00	0.4987	0.0013	0.9987
1.10	0.3643	0.1357	0.8643		3.10	0.4990	0.0010	0.9990
1.20	0.3849	0.1151	0.8849		3.20	0.4993	0.0007	0.9993
1.30	0.4032	0.0968	0.9032		3.30	0.4995	0.0005	0.9995
1.40	0.4192	0.0808	0.9192		3.40	0.4997	0.0003	0.9997
1.50	0.4332	0.0668	0.9332		3.50	0.4998	0.0002	0.9998
1.60	0.4452	0.0548	0.9452		3.60	0.49984	0.00016	0.99984
1.70	0.4554	0.0446	0.9554		3.70	0.49989	0.00011	0.99989
1.80	0.4641	0.0359	0.9641		3.80	0.49993	0.00007	0.99993
1.90	0.4713	0.0287	0.9713		3.90	0.49995	0.00005	0.99995
2.00	0.4772	0.0228	0.9772		4.00	0.49997	0.00003	0.99997

To see what proportion of cases fall between the mean and a particular value:

▸ Translate the value into a z-score. To do this, subtract the mean from the value and divide the result by the standard deviation.

▸ Look for the z-score under the column labeled "z" (if your z-score is negative, ignore the minus sign). The number in the column to the right of the z-score ("z to mean") is the proportion of cases that fall between the mean and your value.

To see what proportion of cases fall above a particular value:

▸ Translate the value into a z-score.

▸ If the value is positive, look in the column labeled "Smaller area." If the value is negative, look in the column labeled "Larger area." The number in the appropriate column is the proportion of cases that fall above your value.

Examples

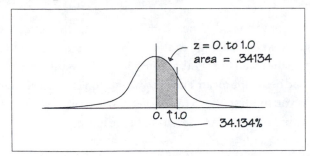

z	z to mean	smaller area	larger area
0.00	0.0000	0.5000	0.5000
:	:	:	:
0.80	0.2881	0.2119	0.7881
0.90	0.3159	0.1841	0.8159
1.00	0.3413	0.1587	0.8413
1.10	0.3643	0.1357	0.8643

1. What percent of cases lie between the mean and one standard deviation above the mean?

This picture shows the area between the mean ($z = 0.0$) and $z = 1.0$. You can see in the "z to mean"column of the table that this area is .34134 of the total area under the normal curve. This means that in a normal distribution, 34.134% of all cases have z-scores between 0.0 and 1.0.

Part of the table areas under the normal curve is shown on the left. The z-score and the corresponding area from z to the mean for this example are circled on the table and shown in the drawing below.

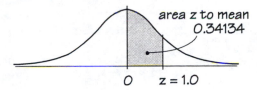

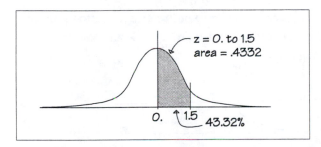

z	z to mean	smaller area	larger area
0.00	0.0000	0.5000	0.5000
:	:	:	:
1.40	0.4192	0.0808	0.9192
1.50	0.4332	0.0668	0.9332
1.60	0.4452	0.0548	0.9452

2. What percent of cases lie between the mean and 1.5 standard deviations above the mean?

This picture shows the area between the mean ($z = 0.0$) and $z = 1.5$. You can see on the table that this area is .4332 of the total area under the normal curve. In a normal distribution, 43.32% of all cases have z-scores between 0.0 and 1.5

The z-score and the corresponding area from z to the mean for this example are circled on the table and shown in the drawing below.

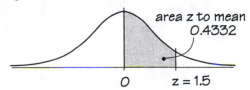

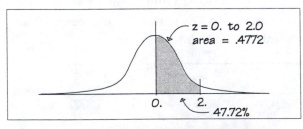

z	z to mean	smaller area	larger area
0.00	0.0000	0.5000	0.5000
:	:	:	:
1.90	0.4713	0.0287	0.9713
2.00	0.4772	0.0228	0.9772

3. What percent of cases lie between the mean and 2.0 standard deviations above the mean?

This picture shows the area between the mean ($z = 0.0$) and $z = 2.0$. You can see in the table that this area is .4772 of the total area under the normal curve. In a normal distribution, 47.72% of all cases have z-scores between 0.0 and 2.0.

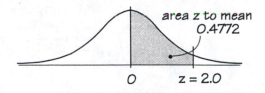

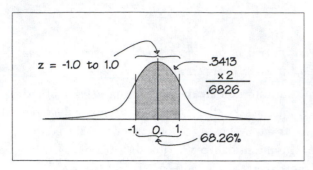

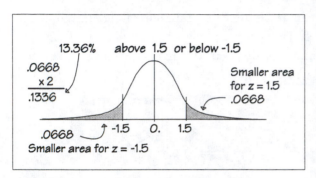

z	z to mean	smaller area	larger area
0.00	0.0000	0.5000	0.5000
0.10	0.0398	0.4602	0.5398
:	:	:	:
1.40	0.4192	0.0808	0.9192
1.50	0.4332	0.0668	0.9332
1.60	0.4452	0.0548	0.9452

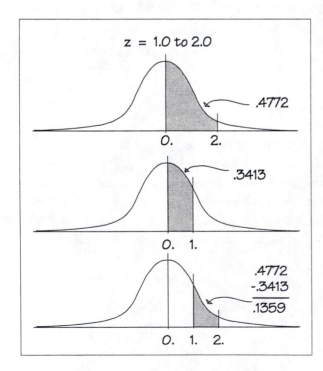

4. What percent of cases are within one standard deviation of the mean?

First you convert the distance from the mean to a z-score. One standard deviation gives $z = 1$. Then look to see the area from the mean to $z = 1.0$, and get .3413. You want both above and below the mean, and the distribution is symmetrical, so you multiply .3413 by 2 to get .6826, or 68.26% of cases within one standard deviation of the mean.

5. What percent of cases are more than one and a half standard deviations away from the mean?

Do the right half of the distribution first. You want the ones above $z = 1.5$, so you use the table to get the "smaller area" for $z = 1.5$, which is .0688. You also want the area below -1.5, which is the same as the area above $z = 1.5$, so you multiply .0668 by 2 and find that 13.36% are more than one and a half standard deviations away from the mean.

The z-score and the corresponding area from z to the mean for this example are circled on the table and shown in the drawing below.

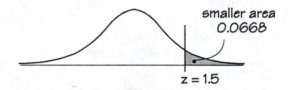

6. What percent of cases are more than one and less than two standard deviations above the mean?

First convert the distances to z-scores. This is easy: 1.0 and 2.0. Then look for both of these on the table to get the areas. From the mean to $z = 2.0$ is .4772; from the mean to $z = 1.0$ is .3413. Subtract the second from the first (.4772 - .3413 = .1359) to see that 13.59% of cases are between one and two standard deviations above the mean.

z	z to mean	smaller area	larger area
0.00	0.0000	0.5000	0.5000
:	:	:	:
0.90	0.3159	0.1841	0.8159
1.00	0.3413	0.1587	0.8413
1.10	0.3643	0.1357	0.8643
:	:	:	:
1.90	0.4713	0.0287	0.9713
2.00	0.4772	0.0228	0.9772

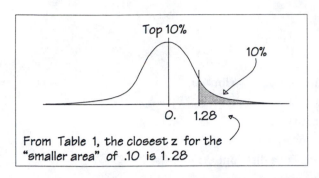

From Table 1, the closest z for the "smaller area" of .10 is 1.28

z	z to mean	smaller area	larger area
0.00	0.0000	0.5000	0.5000
:	:	:	:
1.26	0.3962	0.1038	0.8962
1.27	0.3980	0.1020	0.8980
1.28	0.3997	0.1003	0.8997
1.29	0.4015	0.0985	0.9015
1.30	0.4032	0.0968	0.9032

entry closest to .1000

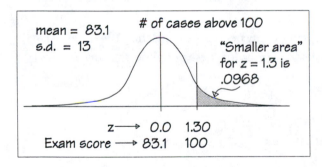

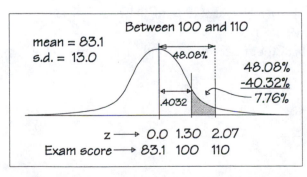

7. *If you want the top ten percent of scores, how far above the mean do you have to go?*

This time you start with the area (10%) and need the z-score that corresponds to it. The z-score will divide the normal curve into two sections; the smaller will be the top 10% and the larger will be the other 90%. So look for the number in the "smaller area" column closest to 0.10 and you see 1.28 is the best. You need to be at least 1.28 standard deviations above the mean to be in the top 10%.

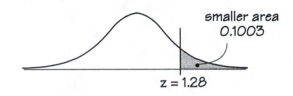

8. *If the scores on the IQ test are normally distributed with a mean of 100 and standard deviation of 10, how high an IQ do you need to be in the top ten percent?*

Do as #7, then translate the z-score back into an IQ score. For IQ, the standard deviation is 10 and the mean is 100, so $z = 1.28$ would be 1.28 x 10 = 12.8 (rounded to 13) points above the mean, or 100 + 13 = 113. Thus, if your IQ score is 113 or above, you are in the top ten percent.

9. *If the mean exam score is 83.1, the standard deviation is 13, the sample size is 600, how many people have scores above 100?*

First, calculate the z-score. It would be 100 - 83.1 = 16.9, and then 16.9 / 13 = 1.3. The "smaller area" for $z = 1.3$ is 0.0968 or 9.68%. Finally, 9.68% of 600 is 58.08 which rounds to 58 people.

10. *If the mean is 83.1, standard deviation is 13, sample size is 600, how many people have scores between 100 and 110?*

First, calculate the z-scores as in the example above. For raw scores of 100 and 110, the z-scores will be 1.30 and 2.07. The area for $z = 1.3$ is .4032; the area for $z = 2.07$ is .4808, so to find the area between 100 and 110, subtract 40.32% from 48.08% to get 7.76%. To find out how many people, multiply 7.76% by 600 to get 46.56, which rounds to 47 people.

Important Terms and Concepts

areas under normal curve
bell-shaped curve
bins
cumulative percentage
distribution
frequency distribution
histogram
inflection points
kurtosis
the larger area

multimodal distribution
normal distribution
normal curve
proportion
shape of a distribution
skewness
the smaller area
standard scores
z-scores

Things to think about .....

General Foods conducts a market research study of fast food eating habits. They take a random sample of 500 people, one of which was you. The mean number of times people in the sample ate at MacDonalds in 1991 was 87. The variance was 169. Assume the distribution is normal, and that the frequency of visits to MacDonalds is not subject to seasonal variations, and that you went to MacDonalds 74 times.

a. What is your z- score? _____
b. Show where you are on the curve below.

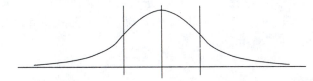

c. How many people went more often than you?
(shade the area for these people in the curve below)

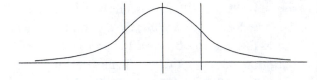

d. What percent of people went less often than you?
(shade the area for those people in the curve below)

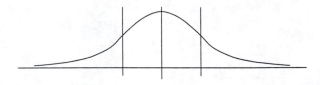

e. How many people went less than 104 times a year?
(shade the area for these people in the curve below)

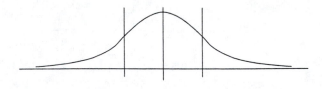

f. How many people went between 100 and 104 times a year?
(shade the area for these people in the curve below)

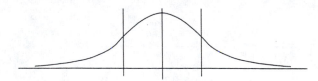

Chapter 8

THE NORMAL CURVE AND SAMPLES: SAMPLING DISTRIBUTIONS

A picture of an ideal normal distribution is shown below. The horizontal axis is calibrated in *z*-scores—in terms of standard deviation units. The *z*-score of the mean is zero. The point one standard deviation above the mean is marked "+1".

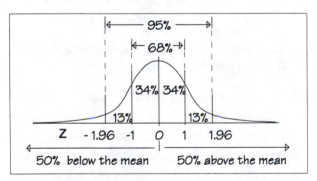

The height of the curve over the point labeled "+1" shows how many cases have scores one standard deviation above the mean (how many people have *z*-scores of 1.0).

The area between **-1** and **+1** is the proportion of cases within one standard deviation of the mean. For normally-distributed variables, 68% of all scores are within one standard deviation of the mean; 95% are within 1.96 standard deviations, and more than 99%

(99.7%, to be exact) are within three standard deviations.

The relation between standard deviation and the areas under the normal curve turns out to be of great value when you want to generalize from a sample to a population.

This takes us into the area of **inferential statistics**, where we use information about a *sample* to make inferences about the *population*. It's almost like magic, where we use information about a small number of people to learn about a much larger population. This is probably the most amazing and valuable analytic tool you will ever encounter.

There are two kinds of estimates you can make about a population on the basis of a sample drawn from the population:

- First, you can use sample statistics, like the mean and standard deviation, to estimate the corresponding population parameters.

- Second, you can use knowledge about some of the properties of random samples to say how accurate your sample mean is as an estimate of the population's mean, and to tell how much confidence you can place in that assessment of accuracy.

It's easy to estimate the mean and standard deviation of a population:

- Your best estimate of the population's mean is simply the sample's mean.

- To estimate the population's standard deviation, all you have to do is calculate the standard deviation of the sample, using "(n-1)" in the denominator instead of "n".

Assessing the accuracy of those estimates and how much confidence you can place in them is a bit more complicated. To understand how this procedure works, you have to understand **sampling distributions**.

Sampling Distributions

Imagine you are going to do a study of Australian undergraduates (this is an international text). You can't afford to collect data from all of them, though, so you do a sample. Because of the higher cost of tuition and books, you are short on money, so your sample includes only two dozen (24) students, chosen *randomly* from the millions of undergraduates in the country down under. Your results show that the mean age of students in your sample is 24. You conclude that, since the sample mean is the best estimator of the population mean, the mean age of Australian undergraduates is 24.

But then you learn that someone else did the same study, and they got a mean age of 25.

The difference between that result and yours makes you curious. You ask some friends, and you find two dozen more studies that used the same procedures and same types of samples. When you plot the results along with yours, this is what you see:

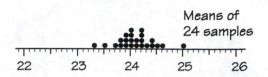

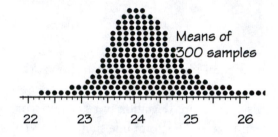

Upon further investigation, you learn that three hundred people did the same study. Even more strange than that, they all followed the same procedures and asked the same questions and constructed their samples in the same way. You manage to get the results of all three hundred studies. Now you have a distribution of three hundred sample means. This is the beginning of a *sampling distribution* of sample means. If you managed to somehow take *all possible* samples of 24 Australian undergraduates, selected at random, you would have the complete sampling distribution for this variable and this sample size.

If you were able to do this, you would notice two things that turn out to be extremely important:

- First, *the mean of the sampling distribution is the same as the population's mean.*

- Second, about 68% of all sample means fall within one standard deviation of the population mean; 95% fall within two standard deviations; and about 99% fall within three standard deviations.

You would probably suspect (correctly!) that the means of these random samples are *normally distributed*. Therefore, if you can find a way to calculate the standard deviation of the sampling distribution, you will know how certain you can be that your sample mean is within a given distance of the population's mean.

There are three important things to know about sampling distributions of sample means. If this were a statistics course taught in the Math department, you

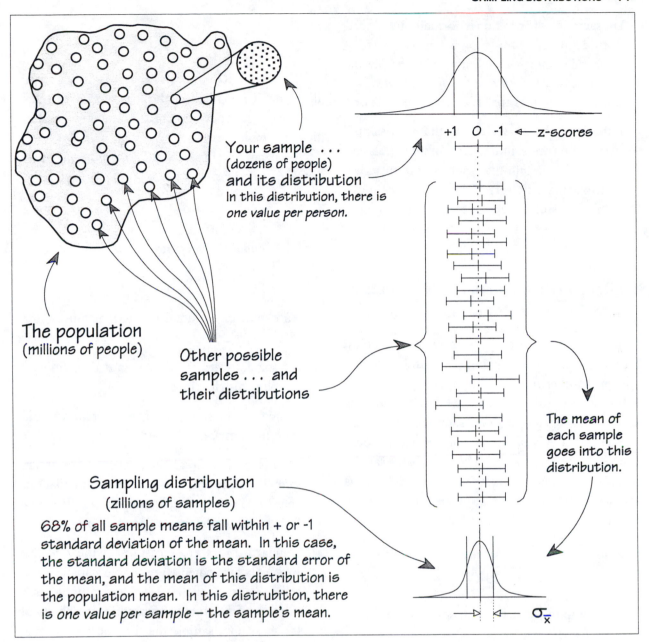

+1 O -1 ←—z-scores

Your sample . . .
(dozens of people)
and its distribution
In this distribution, there is
one value per person.

The population
(millions of people)

Other possible
samples . . . and
their distributions

The mean of
each sample
goes into this
distribution.

Sampling distribution
(zillions of samples)

68% of all sample means fall within + or -1
standard deviation of the mean. In this case,
the standard deviation is the standard error of
the mean, and the mean of this distribution is
the population mean. In this distrubition, there
is one value per sample — the sample's mean.

$\sigma_{\bar{x}}$

might have to be able to prove that these things are true, but we'll just have faith in the honesty of the mathematicians and believe it when they tell us:

1. The mean of the sampling distribution is the same as the mean of the parent population.

2. The standard deviation of the sampling distribution of sample means is related to the standard deviation of the population the samples come from. It can be calculated by dividing the standard deviation of the parent population by the

square root of your sample size:

$$\sigma_{\bar{x}} = \frac{\sigma}{\sqrt{n}}$$

"But," you say, "we don't know the standard deviation of the population! How can we do this?" I say "Ah hah! You know the standard deviation of your sample, and you might remember that you can use this as an estimate of the population's standard deviation."

3. The sampling distribution is normally distributed when the parent population is normally distributed, and is approximately normal *even when the parent population isn't normally distributed*—as long as the samples are large (n = 30 or more).

You can be about 68% certain that your sample mean lies within one standard error of the population mean, and 95% certain that your sample mean lies within two standard errors of the population mean. (Does "these results are accurate to within 4% nineteen times out of twenty … " sound familiar?)

Standard Errors: Standard Deviations of Sampling Distributions

The drawing on the next page shows several samples. You will notice that their means all differ slightly from one another and from the population mean. On the bottom of the drawing is a small distribution. This one shows the means of all the samples. If it had the means from *all possible samples* of this size, it would be a "*sampling distribution.*" The mean of the sample means is obtained by adding all the sample means together and dividing the result by the number of samples, which in the diagram is 29, like this:

$$\frac{Mean_1 + Mean_2 + Mean_3 + \ldots + Mean_{29}}{29}$$

The sampling distribution has a *mean* and a *standard deviation*.

● The mean of the sampling distribution is the same as the population mean.

● The standard deviation of the sampling distribution is called a *standard error*. The standard deviation of the sampling distribution in the example above is the *standard error of the mean* because the sampling distribution in the example is the distribution of means of samples.

The symbol for standard error of the mean tells you a lot about what it is:

$$\sigma_{\bar{x}}$$

The Greek "σ" indicates that it is the standard deviation of a population; the subscript $\bar{x}$ tells that it is the standard deviation of the sampling distribution of sample means.

There are also the *standard error of the difference between two means*:

$$\sigma_{\bar{x}_1 - \bar{x}_2}$$

and the *standard error of proportions*:

$$\sigma_{\bar{p}}$$

Here are some important things to remember about standard errors:

● All standard errors are standard deviations of sampling distributions.

● Standard errors are *population parameters* and must therefore be estimated.

● The populations described by standard errors are sampling distributions—*theoretical* populations comprised of all possible samples of a given size from your sample's parent population.

● Standard errors are measures of the *sampling variability* associated with sample statistics. The standard error of the mean, for example, is a measure of the amount of sampling variability of the mean of a sample the size you are working with. In other words, they are measures of how reliable the sample statistic is as a measure of a population parameter.

A common misunderstanding of the standard error of the mean is that it is the "standard deviation of the mean." This is only partly correct. The standard error of the mean is the standard deviation of the sampling distribution of sample means. In other words, it is the standard deviation of the list of means from all possible samples of a given size drawn from a single population.

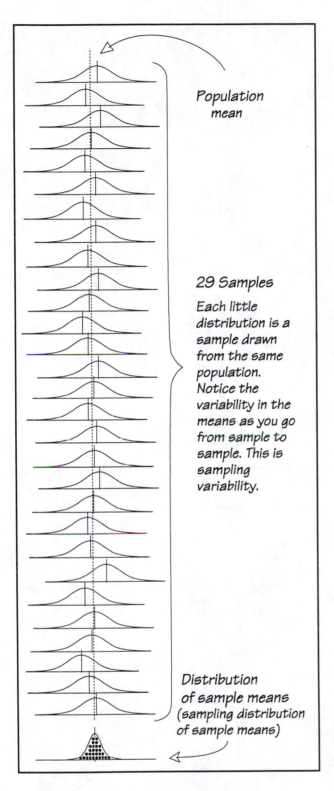

Population mean

29 Samples

Each little distribution is a sample drawn from the same population. Notice the variability in the means as you go from sample to sample. This is sampling variability.

Distribution of sample means *(sampling distribution of sample means)*

Well, if sample means are normally distributed about the population mean, then 68% of sample means are within one standard deviation of the population mean, therefore there is a 68% chance that your sample's mean is within one standard deviation of the population mean. In other words, you can be 68% certain that the difference between your sample's mean and the population's mean is no more than one standard deviation. *Remember that the "standard deviation" here is the standard deviation of the sampling distribution—the standard error of the mean.*

Here is an example. Say you have a sample of 49 randomly-chosen university students, and you know each student's height, accurate to within a tenth of a millimeter. You could easily calculate the mean and standard deviation of the 49 numbers in your sample. Let's say the mean turns out to be 190cm and the standard deviation (calculated with "n-1" in the denominator!) is 35cm. Your best guess for the mean height of all students would be 190cm. But how close to the true population mean would your sample's mean be?

The standard error of the mean (SEM) is

$$\frac{s}{\sqrt{n}}$$

which for you is

$$\frac{35}{\sqrt{49}} \quad \text{or } 5 \text{ cm.}$$

This tells you that the means of about 95% of all random samples of 49 students will be within two standard errors (10 cm) of the true population mean. In other words, there is a 95% probability that your sample mean is off by no more than 10cm. In still other words, you can be 95% certain that the population's mean height is between 180cm and 200cm.

An application

How would you know how certain you could be that your sample mean is a certain distance from the population mean?

Important Terms and Concepts

estimating population parameters

normal distribution

population parameters vs. sample statistics

random samples

sampling distribution

sampling distribution of sample means

sampling variability

standard errors

    standard error of the mean

    standard error of the proportion

    standard error of the difference between means

Chapter 9

Inferential statistics: From samples to populations

It is easy to measure sample *statistics*—just take a sample and calculate its mean or standard deviation, etc. The number you get for the sample statistic summarize the values in the sample. This is *descriptive* statistics.

Inferential statistics is the tool that lets us use information about a sample to make some inferences about the population.

In particular, *we use information about sample statistics to make estimates of population parameters.*

This technique is based on four assumptions:

- Sample data are selected randomly from a well-defined population.

- The characteristics of each random sample drawn from the population are related to the true population parameters.

- Multiple random samples drawn from a population yield sample statistics that cluster around the population parameters in predictable ways.

- We can calculate the sampling error associated with a sample statistic, and we can estimate how far a given sample statistic is likely to be from the true population parameters.

The key to inferential statistics is the *sampling distribution*, a distribution that would result from drawing all possible samples of a given size, measuring a summary statistic for each sample, and examining how the values from the set of samples are distributed.

Descriptive statistics are used to **summarize** data from samples, while **inferential statistics** are used to make estimates about a population, based on the sample data you have. In a sense, inferential statistics is a leap into the unknown, but it is based on a knowledge of the relation between samples and populations.

The shape of a sample's histogram or distribution is usually similar to the shape of the population from which the sample was drawn. The most important kind of shape for distributions is the one we call the "normal distribution". It is also called "bell-shaped" because it looks somewhat like the cross section of a bell. Most phenomena that vary randomly have normal distributions. If these distributions aren't normal, they may be a variation on the normal distribution. Perhaps one "tail" is longer than the

other or the top of the bell is narrow and pointy or wide and flattish. Distributions may also have more than one main "hump"—these would be called "bimodal" or "multimodal"—or they may be flat and rectangular. (See the picture on page 62.)

The normal curve is a theoretical probability curve that has a particular shape. About 68% of all scores are within one standard deviation of the mean; about 95% are within two standard deviations, and a little over 99% are within three standard deviations. (The exact numbers for 95% and 99% are 1.96 and 2.58 standard deviations.)

If a number of random samples are drawn from a population, the means of the samples will "distribute about" the population's mean—they will be close to the population's mean. If a very large number of samples were to be drawn, we could study the distribution of the large set of sample means. This is called a **sampling distribution of sample means**. Sampling distributions of means are normal. The standard deviation of a sampling distribution of means is called the **standard error of the mean** or **SEM**. The standard error of the mean is a very important concept.

A sampling distribution of sample means has a mean equal to that of the parent population. It has a standard deviation that is related to the standard deviation of the parent population. This standard deviation is the **SEM**, and it is calculated by dividing the population's standard deviation by the square root of the sample's size:

$$S.E.M. = \sigma_{\bar{x}} = \frac{Population\ S.D.}{\sqrt{sample\ size}} = \frac{\sigma}{\sqrt{n}} \approx \frac{s}{\sqrt{n}}$$

Because the sampling distribution of means is normal, we know that about 68% of all sample means are within one standard deviation of the population mean. We also know that 95% are within ± 1.96 standard deviations and 99% are within ± 2.58 standard deviations of the population mean. Keep in mind that the "standard deviation" here is the standard deviation of the sampling distribution—the standard error of the mean.

When I say "I'm 95% certain that these results are off by no more than ± 1.96 standard deviations," the "95%" is my **confidence level**—the level of certainty I have; and the ± 1.96 standard deviations is my **confidence interval**—the size of error I must accept at that level of confidence.

Standard errors are *estimates of dispersion or spread for a special kind of population—the population of all possible samples of a given size.* In less mathematical terms, they are measures of sampling variability—the variability from sample to sample.

A large standard error means that there is a lot of variability among samples— that the results of multiple samples drawn from a population are quite different from one another—and that estimates of the population based on the sample are not very reliable. A high standard error means that the sample's mean is likely to be quite different from the population's mean.

Only two factors go into the standard error of the mean—the population's standard deviation and the sample size. You can see that if you increase the sample size or reduce the population standard deviation, you will get a smaller standard error. Conversely, if you reduce the sample size or increase the population standard deviation, you will get a larger standard error.

A standard error generally has associated with it a *level of confidence.* The more homogeneous the population from which the sample is drawn, the smaller the sampling variability, and the more confidence you can place in an estimate at a given level of accuracy. With less homogeneous populations, you have more sampling variability, and thus less confidence for the same level of accuracy—unless you make the sample bigger. Bigger samples have smaller sampling variability, so you can have more confidence and expect more accuracy.

The standard error of the mean is used to determine how close to the true population mean you can expect your sample mean to be, and how much confidence you can place in that expectation.

Standard Errors

Sampling variability is the variability from sample to sample. Because the members of each sample are randomly chosen from the population, if you take several samples from a population and look at the summary statistics (e.g. mean and standard deviation) for each one, you will see that there is some variability from sample to sample.

Standard errors are methods of quantifying this variability and using what is known about it to form estimates of how accurate you can expect your sample to be and how much confidence you can place on estimates of population parameters based on the sample.

You already know how to measure the variability in a list of numbers—calculate the standard deviation of the numbers in the list. This is exactly what standard errors are.

I will deal with three kinds of standard errors in this text:

- Standard Error of the Mean

- Standard Error of Proportions

- Standard Error of Difference Between Means.

The basic symbol for all standard errors is a lower-case Greek sigma (σ). This is used because all standard errors are population standard deviations, and σ is the symbol for standard deviation of a population. Keep in mind, though, that the populations described by standard errors are not ordinary populations; they are sampling distributions, which are theoretical populations composed of all possible samples of a given size drawn from an ordinary everyday garden variety population.

The rest of the symbol for standard errors is the part that tells you what kind of sampling distribution they describe. This is always done with a subscript which is the symbol of a sample statistic.

$\sigma_{\bar{x}}$ —The **standard error of the mean** is the most commonly used standard error. It is a measure of the variability in the **means** of samples. Specifically, it is the standard deviation of the set of means you would get if you took all possible random samples of a given size from a population and calculated the mean of each one. It is defined as:

$$\sigma_{\bar{x}} = \frac{\sigma}{\sqrt{n}}$$

and estimated as:

$$\sigma_{\bar{x}} = \frac{s}{\sqrt{n}}$$

In plain English, the standard error of the mean is the standard deviation of the population from which the samples were drawn (σ) divided by the square root of the sample size. Because you don't have the population's standard deviation, you estimate it with the sample standard deviation, s (calculated with "n-1" in the denominator).

The standard error of the mean is used to estimate how closely a sample's mean can estimate the corresponding population's mean, and how much confidence you can have in the estimate.

$\sigma_{\bar{p}}$—The **standard error of proportions** is used when you want to know how accurately your sample data represents the corresponding proportions in a population. Say 42% of your sample likes statistics and 58% don't. You want to know if this proportion can be generalized to the whole population at large. The standard error of the proportion is defined and calculated as:

$$\sigma_{\bar{p}} = \sqrt{\frac{pq}{n}}$$

The p and q are the proportions of the sample who respond in the two ways. Because there are only two things that could happen (e.g. people like statistics or they don't), the sum of p and q must be **1.0**.

$\sigma_{\bar{x}_1 - \bar{x}_2}$—The **standard error of the difference between means** (SEDBM) is used to determine the likelihood that two samples with different means could have come from the same population. In other

words, could the difference between the two means be due to chance (i.e. to sampling variability)?

The standard error of the difference between means is defined as:

$$\sigma_{\bar{x}_1 - \bar{x}_2} = \sqrt{\frac{\sigma_1^2}{n_1} + \frac{\sigma_2^2}{n_2}}$$

and estimated as:

$$\sigma_{\bar{x}_1 - \bar{x}_2} = \sqrt{\frac{s_1^2}{n_1} + \frac{s_2^2}{n_2}}$$

Note once again that you use the standard deviations of the two samples to estimate the standard deviations of the populations.

The three standard errors described above are measures of the amount of sampling variability you would expect when you work with a random sample. Remember that sampling variability is the variability in results from sample to sample when you take more than one sample from a population. Because each sample contains different people, you would expect each one to give different results.

The amount of sampling variability is a function of the *homogeneity* of the population from which the sample is drawn and the *size* of the sample. To reduce the amount of sampling variability, you would either make your sample larger or increase the homogeneity of the population by stratifying or by defining a new population which is a subset of the original one.

Important Terms and Concepts

assumptions behind inferential statistics

confidence interval

confidence level

estimation versus calculation

homogeneity of population

how to minimize sampling variability

inferential statistics

the impact of sample size

tradeoff between accuracy and confidence

sampling distributions
- of sample means
- of proportions
- of differences between sample means

sampling variability

standard error as measure of sampling variability

standard error as SD of sampling distribution

standard error of the mean

standard error of the difference between means

standard error of the proportion

Chapter 10

Univariate inferential statistics

There are two kinds of questions you can ask about the relation between the mean of a sample and the mean of the population the sample comes from:

- Based on the sample's mean, what is the population's mean likely to be? The goal here is to generalize from a sample to a population. The procedure you use here is called "*estimating a confidence interval.*"

- Based on the sample's mean, what are the chances that it came from a population whose mean you already know? The goal here is to determine whether *this* sample comes from *that* population. The procedure you use here is called a "*z-test of a single mean.*"

Estimating Confidence Intervals

The goal here is to generalize from one sample to a population. You want to estimate the mean of a population, so you take a sample and look at its mean. If you want to use the sample mean to estimate the population mean, you ought to have some measure of how good your sample mean is as a measure of

the population mean. This measure will be based on how much variability there is from sample to sample. If there is little sampling variability, your sample will be a good estimate of the population. On the other hand, if samples vary widely from one to the next, your sample will be of little use.

It would be good to know how much confidence you can place in your estimate and how accurate you can expect your estimate to be (i.e., I'm 95% certain that I am off by no more than 2 inches).

What you would be doing is *estimating the chances that sample* is weird — one composed of odd people who are quite different from the population at large; one whose mean differs appreciably from the population's mean. If there is little sampling variability, the chances of getting an odd sample will be small. If there is a lot of variability from sample to sample, the chances will be much higher.

There are three ways to determine how much variability there would be from sample to sample:

1. Take all possible samples the same size as your sample and calculate the mean of each one. Make a list of these means. You now have the "*sampling distribution of sample means*" for your population. Calculate the standard deviation of

the numbers on this list. This will tell you how much variability there is from sample to sample and from the individual samples to the mean of all samples. *[The only problem is that it is not possible to take all possible samples.]*

2. Take a very large number of samples (thousands) the same size as your sample and calculate the mean of each. Make a list of these means. Calculate the standard deviation of the numbers on this list. Use this standard deviation as an estimate of the result you would get if you could look at all possible samples. *[While this is possible, it will be **extremely** time-consuming and expensive.]*

3. Estimate the standard error of the mean, using the standard deviation of your sample and the square root of the sample's size. *[This is actually quite easy to do and it requires only a few seconds of work.]*

You can use the fact that random things have normal distributions. A random sample is a random thing, so a distribution of random samples will be a normal distribution, and a distribution of the means of random samples (*the sampling distribution of sample means*) will be a normal distribution.

There are three important things to know about the sampling distribution of sample means:

A. THIS DISTRIBUTION IS NORMAL;

B. ITS MEAN IS THE SAME AS THE POPULATION MEAN;

C. ITS STANDARD DEVIATION IS THE *STANDARD ERROR OF THE MEAN*.

Remember that if you have a normal distribution, you know that 68% of all cases fall within one standard deviation of the mean and about 95% of all cases fall within 1.96 standard deviations of the mean. If you take one thing at random, you can be 95% certain that it falls within 1.96 standard deviations of the mean. Your random sample is the one thing you take at random, so you can be 95% certain that its mean

falls within 1.96 standard deviations of the population's mean.

> **Important Notes:**
>
> 1) The "standard deviation" you use here is the standard error of the mean, NOT THE SAMPLE'S STANDARD DEVIATION!
>
> 2) The "population" here is NOT THE POPULATION YOUR SAMPLE COMES FROM; it is the sampling distribution of sample means — the total set (the population) of means of all possible samples the same size drawn from the same population your original sample comes from.

How to do it:

1. Calculate the mean ($\bar{x}$) and standard deviation (*s*) of your sample.

2. Estimate the *standard error of the mean* (SEM):

$$\sigma_{\bar{x}} = \frac{s}{\sqrt{n}}$$

3. You can be 68% certain that your sample's mean is within one standard error of the population mean. You can be 95% certain that your sample's mean is within 1.96 standard errors of the population mean.

Example 1:

Say you want to know how many speeding tickets the average professor has received. Say you have taken a random sample of 100 professors, and that the mean number of tickets for the ones in your sample is 12 and the standard deviation is 3. What is the mean number of tickets for all professors?

Your best guess will be the same as the mean of your sample, which is 12. But how good an estimate is this? How close to the correct value is it likely to be? How certain of that are you?

You can use the standard error of the mean to calculate a confidence estimate. Calculate the standard error as follows:

$$SEM = \frac{3}{\sqrt{100}} = \frac{3}{10} = 0.300$$

(Notice that the sample's mean does not affect the standard error of the mean.)

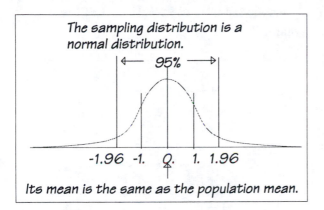

The sampling distribution is a normal distribution.

Its mean is the same as the population mean.

Let's see what you know. Since you are interested in the population's mean, and since you are going to use your sample's mean to estimate it, you will use what you know about the sampling distribution of sample means.

1. You know that sampling distributions are normally distributed.

2. You know that the mean of the sampling distribution is the same as the population's mean.

3. You know that the standard deviation of the sampling distribution is the *standard error of the mean*, and that you can estimate it (which was done up above), and that your estimate is 0.300.

4. Because the sampling distribution is normal, you know that about 95% of all sample means will be within ±1.96 standard errors (SEM) of the mean (the population's mean!).

5. Therefore, you can be 95% certain that your sample mean, which is 12, will be within ±1.96 standard errors (SEM) of the population's mean. In other words, you can be 95% certain that the difference between your sample's mean and the population's mean is no larger than 1.96 × SEM (1.96 × 0.300 = .588). Or, you can be 95% certain

that the population mean is neither lower than 12 - .588 nor higher than 12 + .588. In plain English, you can be 95% certain that the population mean is between 11.412 and 12.588.

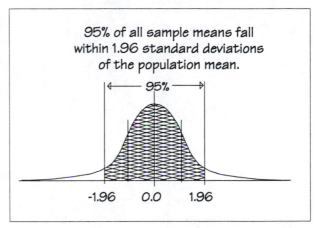

95% of all sample means fall within 1.96 standard deviations of the population mean.

So, when you use the mean of your sample of 100 professors to estimate the population mean, you are 95% certain that you are no more than .588 tickets away from the true population mean.

Example 2:
Let's say you didn't need 95% certainty — 92% is good enough for you.

1. Because you are starting with a level of confidence (92%), you need to translate the percentage into a z- score. You can use the table of areas under the normal curve to do this. Because the table only tells you about one half of the distribution, you would divide .92 by 2, and get .46. Look for the entry on the table closest to .46, and you will find .45993, which is the area for a z-score of 1.75. This says that about 46% of all values are between the mean and 1.75 standard errors *above* the mean. Another 46% will be between the mean and 1.75 standard errors *below* the mean. You can thus be 92% certain that your sample mean is no more than 1.75 standard errors away from the population mean.

2. Now multiply the z-score by the standard error to get the actual number of speeding tickets. The

standard error of the mean was calculated for example #1 and is 0.3. In other words, you can be 92% certain that the population mean lies between

$$12 \pm (1.75 \times .3)$$

or

$$12 \pm .525$$

or

$$12 - .525 \text{ and } 12 + .525$$

or

$$11.475 \text{ and } 12.525$$

The normal curve below shows the area corresponding to a z-score of plus or minus 1.75. This area accounts for 92% of the area under the curve, with 46% on each side of the mean.

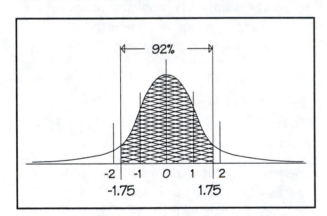

If you wanted to be 68% certain, you would be interested in the area between plus and minus one standard error. This would mean that you are 68% certain that your sample mean differs from the population mean by no more than 1.0 × .3, or that the population mean is between 11.7 and 12.3 speeding tickets.

Example 3:

The previous example started with the *level of confidence* you wanted to have (92%). You could start with the *level of accuracy* instead.

Say you wanted to be accurate to within one half of a speeding ticket. You would then follow these steps:

1. Compute the z-score that 0.5 speeding tickets would be. To do this, divide 0.5 by the standard error of the mean. Since the standard error of the mean is 0.3, you would get a z-score of 0.5/0.3, which is 1.667. (You can see that this will give you a smaller area under the normal curve than the previous example of 92%, since 1.667 is smaller than 1.75.)

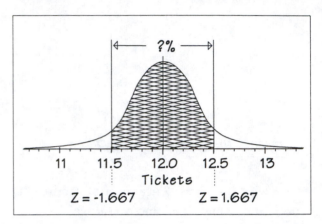

2. Look the z-score up on the table of areas under the normal curve. You find that the value of z closest to 1.667 is 1.67, with a corresponding area of .4525. Since this is for one side of the distribution, you have to multiply the area by 2, and you get .9050, which is pretty close to 90%. So you can be about 90% certain that your sample mean is off by no more than ½ of a speeding ticket.

Z-test of a Single Mean

If you know the mean of a sample and want to know if the sample could be from a population with a different mean, you would use a *"z-test of a single mean."*

The International Teleprompter Training Institute (ITTI) runs a highly profitable school that claims to produce newscasters who can read Teleprompters faster and with fewer errors than all other similar training programs. They claim that graduates of their program can read Teleprompters at a rate of 225 words per minute with no errors.

Imagine that you have been asked by the Federal Truth In Advertising Commission to test the accu-

racy of the claims of the ITTI. You begin your assessment by administering a test to a sample of 36 graduates of the ITTI program. Your results show that the mean error-free maximum reading speed is 211 words per minute with a standard deviation of 25 words. The question you must now answer is this: Could you get a sample with a mean reading speed of 211 words per minute from a population with a mean speed of 225 words per minute?

You know there will be some sampling variability associated with your measurement and that your sample mean will probably be different from the population mean even if the ITTI claims are correct, so the difference between your sample mean of 211 and the ITTI claimed population mean of 225 *could* be due to sampling variability. But you also know that the ITTI has been suspected of shady business practices in the past and you feel that their advertised rate of 225 words per minute may be inaccurate.

So you have two competing explanations for the discrepancy between the two means. The first is that the difference is due to sampling variability. The second is that the difference is due to the fact that your sample, with a mean of 211, did not come from a population with a mean of 225. In other words, graduates of the ITTI program can not read the Teleprompter without errors at a rate of 225 words per minute.

These competing explanations are called *hypotheses*. The first one is the *null hypothesis*; it says that the population mean is 225 and that the reason your sample mean is different from this is due to sampling variability. The second one is called the *alternate hypothesis*; it says that the mean of the population from which the sample was drawn is not 225 and that this is why your sample mean is different from the claimed 225 words per minute. These hypotheses would be written like this:

$$H_{\varnothing}: \mu = 225$$

$$H_{ALT}: \mu \neq 225$$

To perform the test, you calculate the difference between the sample mean and the hypothesized population mean and then you decide if that difference is so large that it couldn't be due to sampling variability. The difference is 211 - 225 = -14. This is the easy part.

The question now becomes "How likely are you to get a difference this large due to sampling variability?" Since the standard error of the mean is a measure of the sampling variability associated with a sample mean, it will play a key role in answering this question.

$$\sigma_{\bar{x}} = \frac{s}{\sqrt{n}} = \frac{25}{\sqrt{36}} = \frac{25}{6} = 4.1667$$

Now you go back to what you know about the sampling distribution of the sample mean:

- It is normally distributed.

- Its mean is the population mean.

- Its standard deviation is the standard error of the mean.

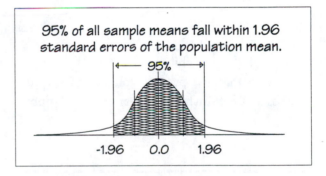

95% of all sample means fall within 1.96 standard errors of the population mean.

Because the sampling distribution is normally distributed, you would expect 95% of all sample means to be within 1.96 standard errors of the population mean. To see the distance between your sample mean and the hypothesized population mean in standard errors, you calculate a z-score by dividing the difference between the means by the standard error of the mean:

$$z = \frac{\bar{x} - \mu}{\sigma_{\bar{x}}} = \frac{211 - 225}{4.1667} = \frac{-14}{4.1667} = -3.360$$

Your sample mean is 3.36 standard errors away from the hypothesized population mean. You know that less than 5% of samples will have means more than 1.96 standard errors away from the population's mean, so you can reject the null hypothesis.

A more complicated approach uses the table of areas under the normal curve. You can see that less than one tenth of one percent of samples drawn from a population would have means more than 3.35 standard errors away from the population mean. 0.04% would be more than 3.35 standard errors above the population mean; another 0.04% would be more than 3.35 standard errors below the population mean.

z	z to mean	smaller area	larger area
0.00	0.0000	0.5000	0.5000
:	:	:	:
3.20	0.4993	0.0007	0.9993
3.30	0.4995	0.0005	0.9995
3.35	0.4996	0.0004	0.9996
3.40	0.4997	0.0003	0.9997

Ordinarily, if the probability that the null hypothesis is true is less than five percent, you "reject" the null hypothesis. What you have just seen is that the proba-bility of getting a difference between the sample mean and the population mean as large as the one you have in this data — i.e. the probability that the null hypothesis ($H_{\emptyset}$: μ = 225) is true — is less than 0.08%.

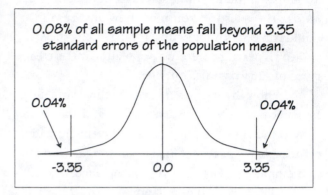

0.08% of all sample means fall beyond 3.35 standard errors of the population mean.

0.04%   0.04%

-3.35   0.0   3.35

Because of sampling variability, you would expect a sample's mean to be different from the population's mean. But a difference as large as the one in this example would be so unlikely that you would find it hard to believe that this difference is due to sampling variability. You would therefore reject the null hypothesis that says the population mean is 225. This leaves you with the alternate explanation which says that the ITTI claim that its graduates can read at 225 error-free words per minute is erroneous. The mean of the population from which this sample was drawn is not 225.

Important Terms and Concepts

accurate of estimate
alternate hypothesis
area under the normal curve
competing explanation
confidence of estimate's accuracy
confidence intervals/estimates
estimation of population mean
estimation of *standard error of the mean* (SEM)
generalization from a sample to a population
larger area
normal distribution

null hypothesis
random samples are random things
random things normally distributed
sampling distribution
smaller area
standard error of the mean
standard error
standard deviation of sampling distribution
z-score for a mean
z-test for a single mean

Bivariate Statistics

Chapter 11

CROSSTABULATION

Crosstabulation is the approach you use to summarize the distribution of cases when you have a pair of discrete (categorical) variables. Say we have a new experimental wonder drug that is supposed to help people perform complex cognitive tasks, like take statistics exams. Suppose I divide a class of 80 students randomly into two groups, and I give the people in one group a pill that contains the drug and the people in the other group get a pill that looks and tastes exactly the same, but it contains nothing. I'm careful not to let anyone know whether they get the drug or the fake. Then I look to see what kind of grades they receive.

I know that half of the 80 students received the pill containing the drug and half received the fake pill. Let's say I find that 50 students pass the test and 30 fail. If I tabulate these results I get the following two tables, one for each variable:

Table 1. Drug use

	count	percent
drug	40	50%
no drug	40	50%
total	80	100%

Table 2. Performance

	count	percent
pass	50	62.5%
fail	30	37.5%
total	80	100%

But this doesn't tell us anything about the relation between taking the drug and performance on the test. In order to see the relationship, we need a different kind of table. We need a table that shows how many of the people who took the drug passed and how many of the people who did not take the drug passed. We also want to see how many of the people who failed did or did not take the drug. Since this table tabulates one variable against the other, the process of making one is called "*cross tabulation*," and the table is called a "crosstab."

Table 3 on the next page is an example of a crosstabulation table. The information contained in Table 1 appears in the "totals" row at the bottom of Table 3. The information contained in Table 2 appears in the "totals" column of Table 3. The "total" row and column contain what is known as *the marginals*—the frequencies (50, 30, 40, 40) and percents (62.5%,

37.5%, 50%, 50%) that describe the two variables by themselves. The marginals don't tell us anything about the relation between the variables.

The four numbers inside the heavy square (30, 20, 10, 20) contain the information we are interested in. But these numbers are just the *counts* or *frequencies* -- they only tell how many people fall into each *cell* of the table.

Table 3. Drug use × Performance

		Drug use		
		drug	no drug	totals
Performance	pass	30	20	50 62.5%
	fail	10	20	30 37.5%
	total	40 50.0%	40 50.0%	80 100.0%

For example, 30 people took the drug and passed, ten people took the drug and failed. Table 4 has added *row percents* -- what percent of the people in the row took the drug or did not take the drug. With these numbers you can see that 60% of the people who passed took the drug, 40% of the people who passed did not take the drug, 33.3% of the people who failed took the drug, and 66.7% of the people who failed did not take the drug.

Table 4. Drug use × Performance

row% col%		**Drug use**		
		drug	no drug	totals
Performance	pass	30 60.0%	20 40.0%	50 62.5%
	fail	10 33.3%	20 66.7%	30 37.5%
	total	40 50.0%	40 50.0%	80 100.0%

Table 5 shows the *column percents*—the percentage of people in the columns who passed or failed the exam. For example, 75% of the people who took the drug passed and 25% of the people who took the drug failed.

It looks like most of the people (75%) who took the drug passed, while only half of the people (50%) who took the fake pill passed. Alternatively, we can see that most (60%) of the people who passed took the drug, while only a third (33.3%) of the people who failed took the drug.

Table 5. Drug use × Performance

count row% col%		**Drug use**		
		drug	no drug	totals
Performance	pass	30 60.0% **75.0%**	20 40.0% **50.0%**	50 62.5%
	fail	10 33.3% **25.0%**	20 66.7% **50.0%**	30 37.5%
	total	40 50.0%	40 50.0%	80 100.0%

How to Read a Crosstabulation

There are a lot of numbers in a crosstabulation. In the body of the table each cell has three numbers: a count, a row percent, and a column percent. The count tells how many cases fall into this cell. The row percent tells what percent of this row's cases are found in this cell. The column percent tells what percent of this column' cases are found in this cell. Which percentages do you compare when you are reading one of these tables?

There are two ways to read the table. Which one you use depends on whether the independent variable determines which row or which column a case is in. If the independent variable's values are associated with rows, you should use "**percentage across, compare down.**" This means that you use the **row**

percentages (percentage *across*), and you do comparisons *between the rows* (compare *down*) of a single column. In Table 6 below, you could compare the finding that:

a) 60% of people who passed took the drug. (30 is 60% of the 50 who passed.)

with the finding that:

b) 33% of the people who failed took the drug. (10 is 33% of the 30 who failed.)

Table 6. Drug use × Performance

count row% col%	drug	no drug	totals
pass	30 **60.0%** 75.0%	20 40.0% 50.0%	50 62.5%
fail	10 **33.3%** 25.0%	20 66.7% 50.0%	30 37.5%
total	40 50.0%	40 50.0%	80 100.0%

Performance

As the illustration below shows, you are actually comparing one row in the table with another row when you do percentage across, compare down.

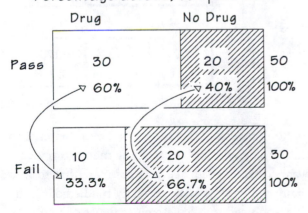

Percentage across, compare down

If the independent variable's values are associated with columns, you should use "**percentage down, compare across.**" Here you use the **column** percent-

ages (percentage *down*), and do comparisons *between the columns* (compare *across*) of a single row. In Table 7 you see that 75% of people who took the drug passed, while only 50% of the people who did not take the drug passed.

Table 7. Drug use × Performance

count row% col%	drug	no drug	totals
pass	30 60.0% **75.0%**	20 40.0% **50.0%**	50 62.5%
fail	10 33.3% 25.0%	20 66.7% 50.0%	30 37.5%
total	40 50.0%	40 50.0%	80 100.0%

Performance

As the illustration below shows, you are actually comparing one column in the table with another column when you do percentage down, compare across.

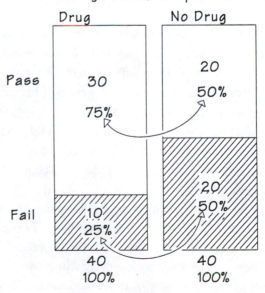

Percentage down, compare across

Note that all comparisons use percentages, and not the counts. Remember that if you use row percentages, you compare numbers up and down; if you

use column percentages, you compare numbers to the left and right.

Here are a couple of examples:

Example 1. You decide to do a study of the accuracy of the weather forecast aired on your favorite radio station every morning at 7:45, so you make a point to listen every morning and record whether the forecast is for a sunny day or a cloudy day. That evening, just before you go to bed, you record whether the day was actually sunny or cloudy. At the end of the year you tabulate the results and get the following table:

Table 8

count % of total	sunny	cloudy	total
Predicted	192 52.60%	173 47.40%	365 100.0%
	sunny	cloudy	total
Actual	189 51.78%	176 48.22%	365 100.0%

It looks like your weather station was quite reliable—it predicted 192 sunny days, and there were 189. It seems that the predictions were wrong only three times. Since you were lucky enough to have made a record of each day's prediction and each day's actual weather, though, you can make a table that shows the relation between each prediction and each outcome. The crosstabulation that does this comparison is Table 9.

Now your weather station doesn't seem so reliable. It was cloudy on 80 of the 192 days that were supposed to be sunny, and it was sunny on 77 of the 173 days that were supposed to be cloudy. Altogether, the prediction was wrong 157 times and correct 208 times. The overall success rate was only

$$208 \div 365 = .569863 = 57.00\%$$

Your weather station's predictions were correct about

11 times every 20 days.

Table 9

	Actual		
count	sunny	cloudy	total
Predicted sunny	112	80	192
Predicted cloudy	77	96	173
total	189	176	365

You might want to know if the station is more likely to be correct when it predicts sun or when it predicts clouds. To do this, you would need two success rates—one for sunny predictions and one for cloudy predictions. Table 10 shows that predictions of sun were correct 58.33% of the time and that predictions of clouds were correct 55.49% of the time. You should have a little bit more faith in predictions of sun than in predictions of clouds. Here you are using *row percentages*.

Table 10

	Actual		
count row%	sunny	cloudy	total
Predicted sunny	112 58.33%	80 41.67%	192 100.0%
Predicted cloudy	77 44.51%	96 55.49%	173 100.0%

But it turns out that the news is even better than this. You could look to see how many sunny days were correctly predicted and compare that to how many cloudy days were correctly predicted. To do this, you need to calculate percentages of sunny (or cloudy) *days*, rather than percentages of sunny (or cloudy) *predictions*. Table 11 shows that sunny days are more accurately predicted (59.25%) than cloudy

days (54.55%). Note that this table uses *column percentages*.

Table 11

count **col%**	**Actual**	
Predicted	sunny	cloudy
sunny	112 59.25%	80 45.65%
cloudy	77 40.75%	96 54.55%
total	189 100.0%	176 100.0%

Rather than using four separate tables, you can combine all the information into a single crosstabulation as shown below.

Table 12

count row% col%	**Actual**		
Predicted	sunny	cloudy	total
sunny	112 58.33% 59.25%	80 41.67% 45.65%	192 100.0% 52.60%
cloudy	77 44.51% 40.75%	96 55.49% 54.55%	173 100.0% 47.40%
total	189 51.78% 100.0%	176 48.22% 100.0%	365 100.0%

Example 2. You've been listening to recent media coverage of the effects of violent content in television programs and movies. You decide to see whether Canadian programming is more or less violent than American programming. You manage to convince several friends to help you with this project. Each person watches a single channel every evening from 8:00 to 11:00. At 9:00, 10:00, and 11:00, the number of murders shown in the previous hour is recorded. You are careful to make sure that each program is counted only once when it is broadcast on more than one channel at the same time. At the end of this phase of your study, you have data for 368 hours of television programming. The data goes into the crosstabulation in Table 13.

Here you have assigned each hour of programming to one of three levels of violence: low (0 to 5 murders), moderate (6 to 10 murders), or high (more than 10 murders). Each hour of programming is also categorized according to the country that produced it (Canada or the U.S.).

Table 13

count row% col%	**Number of murders per hour**			
Country	0 - 5	6 - 10	more	total
Cdn.	77 40.10% 62.10%	50 26.04% 46.30%	65 33.85% 47.79%	192 52.17%
USA	47 26.71% 37.90%	58 32.96% 53.70%	71 40.34% 52.21%	176 47.83%
total	124 33.70%	108 29.35%	136 36.96%	368 100.0%

How to interpret the table

There are four ways to interpret Table 13. Only the last two give you information about the relation between the level of violence and the country of origin.

a. **Focus on the marginals**—the numbers and percentages in the column and row labeled "Total."

1) A little over half (52.17%) of the hours of programming were Canadian and the rest (47.83%) were American.

2) One third (33.7%) of the hours fell into the "low violence" category; slightly fewer hours (29.35%) were "medium violence;" the rest (36.96%) were "high violence."

This approach summarizes the distribution of the two variables—country of origin and level of violence—but it takes each one separately, with no reference to the other.

b. Focus on the individual cell counts. 77 Canadian hours were "low violence;" 50 Canadian hours were "medium;" 65 Canadian hours were "high;" 47 American hours were "low;" 58 American hours were "medium;" and 71 American hours were "high." This approach summarizes the raw data, but it says nothing about the variables or the relation between them.

c. Focus on the row percentages. This approach is also known as "percentage across, compare down," because you compare the row percentages in each row with the corresponding ones in the other row(s). In this case, you would say that:

1) 40.10% of Canadian hours were low violence, compared to only 26.71% of American hours;

2) American programming (32.96%) was more likely to be moderately violent than Canadian programming (26.04%); and

3) 40.34% of American hours were high violence, compared to only 33.85% of Canadian hours.

In other words, American programming is more likely than Canadian programming to be moderately or highly violent, while Canadian programming is more likely to be classified as "low violence."

d. Focus on the column percentages. This approach is known as "percentage down, compare across," because you compare the column percentages in each column with the corresponding ones in the other column(s):

1) 62.10% of the low violence hours were Canadian, compared to 46.30% of moderate violence and 47.79% of high violence hours.

2) only 37.90% of low violence hours were American, compared to 53.70% of moderate violence and 52.21% of high violence hours.

In other words, low-violence programming tends to be Canadian, while moderate or high-violence programming is more likely to be American.

For the data in this table, the percentage across, compare down approach is the most appropriate because the rows are associated with different values of the independent variable (country). You can tell the country of origin is the independent variable because the country of origin could determine how violent a program is (Americans are more violent than Canadians, so American programming tends to be more violent than Canadian programming), but making the program more or less violent wouldn't change the country from Canadian to the USA or from the USA to Canada.

Important Terms and Concepts

column percentage
counts
crosstabulation
frequencies
marginal frequencies
marginal percentages
marginals
percentage down, compare across
percentage across, compare down
row percentage

Chapter 12

Strength of Relationships: Discrete

Descriptive statistics are tools you use to summarize your data. They are used to pull information about important aspects of your data out of the pile of numbers and to make it visible in a useful way. In other words, the goal of statistics is to reduce a large, unwieldy mass of information about numerous individuals to a parsimonious, manageable description of the set of people in general. This is *data reduction*. The idea is that information about patterns is more valuable than information about single cases. For example, if your data shows that most of the people (75%) who have started to smoke cigarettes within the last year are between the ages of 9 and 17, the information you have is more useful than a long list of the initials of the people who started to smoke with the age of each person written next to their initials. That the 127th person on the list is 16 years old only tells you about the 127th person — it doesn't tell you anything about the general pattern.

Measures of strength of association

When you have two variables and want to know how strongly one is related to the other, you use a measure of the strength of association. There are several such measures, a few of which are described in the chapters in this section of the book. These measures differ from one another in a number of ways that determine how appropriate they are for use with your data, how they are used, and what they tell you about the relationship being measured.

Level of scaling

The kind of information your data contains depends to a large extent on the level of scaling you used. With nominal scaling, the only thing you can say about two cases is whether they are the same or different. With ordinal scaling you can say that one is larger than, the same as, or smaller than the other. With interval or ratio scaling, you can also say how large the difference between two values is. These different kinds of information are reflected in how the various measures of relationships are calculated and interpreted. Also, since there is more information in ordinal data than in nominal data, measures for ordinal data tell you more about the relationship than measures for nominal data. Similarly, measures for interval or ratio data tell you more than measures for ordinal data.

Symmetric *vs.* asymmetric measures

For symmetric measures, no distinction is made between independent and dependent variables. With these measures, you can switch the two variables and

it doesn't make any difference: you get the same result. For asymmetric measures, you have to decide which are the independent and dependent variables before you do the analysis. If you switch the variables and do the calculations again, you are likely to get a different result.

"Standard" *vs.* "nonstandard" measures

Some measures have three characteristics that make them both more informative and easier to interpret:

- When the two variables are not related to one another, the measure of association has the value 0.00.

- The value of the measure has an upper limit of 1.00 and, when the relationship can have direction, a lower limit of -1.00. Both of these extreme values indicate the relationship is perfect in the sense that if you know the value of one variable, you also know the value of the other one.

- The value of the measure is proportional, in one way or another, to the degree of association of the two variables. This means that the measure can be interpreted in terms of the degree to which the value of one variable depends on the value of the other.

A measure that meets these criteria tells you more about the strength of the connection between your variables than one that doesn't. In Chapters 13 and 16 you will see covariance and chi-square, measures that do not meet the last two of the criteria. Because of this, these measures don't actually tell you how strong the connection between the variables is — you don't have an absolute measure of the strength of the relationship. You can't, for example, compare two covariances or two chi-squares and say that one indicates a stronger relation than the other.

Nominal Data

If you have two nominal variables and you want to know how strong the relationship between them is, you should use lambda (λ). This measure is based on your ability to correctly guess or predict the value of one variable when you know the value of the other one. The only thing considered here is whether your guess is correct or incorrect; direction or size of errors are not meaningful for nominal data.

Imagine that you have a binary variable and you know the frequencies (how many cases fall into each category), and you are asked what the value will be for the next case I pick. If you guess randomly, you would expect to be wrong half of the time. A better strategy would be to guess the modal value — the one with the highest frequency.

For example, say the variable is whether or not a person smokes cigarettes. 2200 people are asked whether they smoke and 924 say they do while the other 1276 say they don't (Table 1). The percentages are thus 42% and 58%. If you had to predict whether a person selected from the group is a smoker, you would be more likely to be correct if you guessed the modal response "no" than if you guessed "yes." In fact, if you had to predict the answer for all 2200 people, you would be correct 58% of the time if you

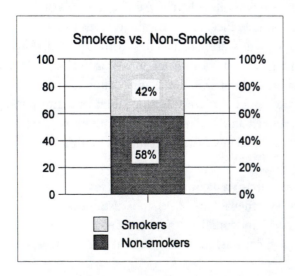

Table 1. Smoking

Smokers	924	42%
Non-smokers	1276	58%
Total	2200	100%

always guessed "no." While you'd be wrong 924 times, this would be the best you could do without additional information.

Even though you would be wrong 42% of the time with this strategy, you would still be doing better than if you had guessed randomly, predicting "yes" half of the time and "no" half of the time. In this case, knowing the frequencies of the two responses and always guessing the modal response allows you to reduce the number of errors of prediction from 1100, which you would expect with random guessing, to 924. The *proportionate reduction of error* (PRE) is:

$$\frac{1100 - 924}{1100} = \frac{176}{1100} = .16 = 16\%$$

Now say there is a second binary variable that is related to the first one. The first variable is smoking (y/n) and the second is whether or not the person has a university degree (y/n). Assume that overall, 81% of those with degrees do not smoke and 65% of those without degrees do (Table 2).

Now suppose you know the educational status of a person and have to predict whether or not that person smokes. If the person has a degree you would guess "non-smoker," since 81% of those with degrees do not smoke. On the other hand, if the person doesn't have a degree you would guess "smoker," because 65% of those without degrees are smokers. If you had to make predictions for all 2200 people (half with degrees and half without) and you used this strategy, you would be correct 81% of the time for those with degrees and 65% of the time for those without degrees. In other words, you would make 209 errors for those with degrees and 385 errors for those without degrees — 594 errors altogether. This is 330

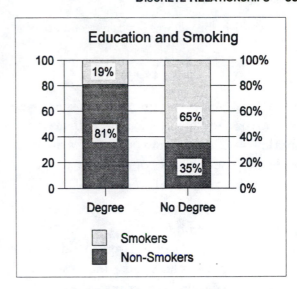

fewer than if your guesses were based only on the smoking variable.

Because you know the relation between having a degree and smoking, knowing the value of one variable (degree) allows you to make a considerable improvement in your chance of correctly predicting the value of the other variable (smoking). This is a reduction from 924 errors to 594 errors, which gives a proportionate reduction of error of:

$$\frac{924 - 594}{924} = \frac{330}{924} = .357 = 35.7\%$$

This is *lambda*, the reduction in errors expressed as a proportion of how many you would have made if you only had information about smoking.

If having a degree were not related to smoking, the data would look like the numbers shown in Table 3. In this case, your best guess — both for people with degrees and people without degrees — would be that they are non-smokers. You would be wrong 924 times, the same as if you used only the data on smok-

Table 2. Education and Smoking

	Degree	No Degree	Total
Smokers	**209**	715	924
Non-smokers	891	**385**	1276
Total	1100	1100	2200

Table 3. Education and Smoking

	Degree	No Degree	Total
Smokers	462	462	924
Non-smokers	638	638	1276
Total	1100	1100	2200

ing. In this case, the value of lambda would be

$$\frac{924 - 924}{924} = \frac{0}{924} = 0.0 = 0.0\%$$

On the other hand, if all people with degrees were non-smokers and all other people were smokers, you would know whether or not a person was a smoker as soon as you knew whether or not the person had a degree. In this case, lambda would be 100%.

How to calculate lambda

The method described here will work for situations in which your variables have more than two values. First, calculate the number of errors you would make if you only had data for the dependent variable. To do this, look at the Totals for the dependent variable and find the frequency of the modal value — the one that has the highest frequency (**1276** in Table 4). Subtract this number from the number of cases. The result (2200 - 1276 = **924**) is the number of errors you would make if you use the most efficient strategy with the data from the dependent variable.

Table 4. Education and Smoking

	Degree	No Degree	Total
Smokers	209	715	924
Non-smokers	891	385	1276
Total	1100	1100	2200

Next, take each value of the independent variable separately. In the table above, take people with degrees and then people without degrees. For each value, find the highest frequency and subtract it from the total in its column. In the table above, this would be 1100 - 891 = **209** and 1100 - 715 = **385**. Add the results of the subtractions together to get the number of errors you would make when you take the second variable into consideration: 209 + 385 = **594**. Finally, subtract this number from the original number of errors to get the reduction and divide the reduction by the original number of errors:

$$\frac{924 - 594}{924} = \frac{330}{924} = .357 = 35.7\%$$

Lambda is not *symmetrical*. You may get a different value if you start with the number of errors with the other variable. For example, you could have started with the Education variable, which would lead to 1100 errors, regardless of which value you guessed. When you add the Smoking variable, the number of errors is reduced to 594, which gives you:

$$\frac{1100 - 594}{1100} = \frac{506}{1100} = .460 = 46.0\%$$

For a more in-depth discussion of lambda and related measures, you might want to look at Freeman (1968) or Johnson (1988).

Yule's Q

A more straightforward measure of association for nominal data is Yule's Q. It uses an approach that is the basis for several other measures, some of which are described later in this chapter. Imagine that I were to interview ten people, five of whom had used this book for a course in research methods and five who had used a book by a different author. In the interview I asked them a single question about how they feel about statistics: "Do you feel anxious when you know you will be asked to explain what the numbers in a statistical table mean?" They were asked to answer by choosing one of "yes" or "no." I put the results of the interviews in a simple table:

		Which book?	
		Mine	Other
Are you anxious?	Yes	0	5
	No	5	0

You can see from this table that my publisher should be very happy about this book. Everyone who used it said they would not be anxious when confronted with a statistical task, while everyone who didn't use this book said they would be anxious. This

illustrates a perfect relationship. The picture could not be more clear. The author of the other book hears about these results and decides to do more research. This author repeats the same study with ten other people, five who used her book and five who used my book. Here are the results:

Which book?

		Hers	Mine
Are you anxious?	Yes	2	3
	No	3	2

This time you get a different picture. From this data you can see that most of the students who used her book say they would not be anxious and most of the students who used mine said they would be anxious. The relationship isn't as clear as the previous one, and it goes in the opposite direction, as far as my book is concerned.

My publisher hears about this second study and asks me to do a definitive study that will give a clear statement about the value of my book. I ask a friend for some advice and he suggests that it might not have been this book that was the causal factor in my study. He thinks the results may be due to the fact that I had played relaxing harp music in the background when I taught the course that used this book. The students in the other course had to listen to rap music, the favorite of the instructor. So I decided to do a study in which I interviewed only people who didn't have any background music, removing the effects of this factor. Here are the results:

Which book?

		Mine	Hers
Are you anxious?	Yes	5	0
	No	0	5

Now you see that there is again a perfect relationship — one that shows precisely the opposite of the first one.

The difference between the three situations can be described in terms of *concordant* and *discordant* pairs. In the first study, the people who used my book (+) said they would not be anxious (–), while those who did not use my book (–) said they would be anxious (+). All pairs were discordant and the relation between using my book and being anxious was a perfect negative one. In the third example, all the pairs were concordant: everyone who used my book (+) said they would be anxious (+); those who did not use my book (–) said they would not be anxious (–). This describes a perfect positive relationship between using my book and being anxious.

How to calculate Yule's Q
You need two numbers: the number of concordant pairs and the number of discordant pairs. Start by setting up your crosstabulation so the "+" column is on the left and the "+" row is on the top like this:

Variable 1

		Yes (+)	No (–)	Total
Variable 2	Yes (+)	a	b	$a+b$
	No (–)	c	d	$c+d$
	Total	$a+c$	$b+d$	$a+b+c+d$

The number of concordant pairs is given by the number in the "++" cell times the number in the "– –" cell ($a \times d$); the number of discordant pairs is the number in the "+–" cell times the number in the "–+" cell ($b \times c$). Now you are set to calculate Q:

$$Q = \frac{(ad) - (bc)}{(ad) + (bc)}$$

You can see that if all the cells are concordant, there will be no cases falling in the "+–" or the "–+" cells and the product $b \times c$ will be zero. The value of Q will thus be ad/ad which is 1.00. This is a perfect positive association. If the cases are spread evenly throughout the four cells of the table, the two cross-products, ($a \times d$) and ($b \times c$), will be equal and the value of Q will be zero.

One thing to be aware of is that it is possible to get a value of +1.0 for Q when some cases fall into one of the "+−" or the "−+" cells. Consider the table below. The hypothetical data in this table show that no women and most men say they are afraid to purchase feminine hygiene products in a neighborhood drug store.

Sex

		Men	Women	Total
Afraid	Yes	67	0	67
	No	30	94	124
	Total	97	94	191

For this data, the value of Q will be:

$$Q = \frac{(ad) - (bc)}{(ad) + (bc)}$$

$$= \frac{(67 \times 94) - (0 \times 30)}{(67 \times 94) + (0 \times 30)}$$

$$= \frac{(67 \times 94)}{(67 \times 94)}$$

$$= 1.0$$

This is a *conditionally perfect* association. If you know that the person is a woman, you know she will not be afraid. If the person is a man, you can only guess that he probably will (but may easily not) be afraid. Because of this kind of possibility, you should always examine a crosstabulation of your data.

Like lambda, Q also has a PRE interpretation. The proportional reduction in errors made predicting the value of one variable when you know the value of the other one turns out to be Q. When Q is 1.00 or -1.00, you can eliminate all errors. When it is between these values, you can eliminate fewer of the errors. In general, the larger the proportion of cases that fall in one diagonal, the higher the value of Q will be. If the variables are independent, the proportion of cases falling on one diagonal will be roughly equal to the number on the other diagonal.

Johnson (1988, p. 142) suggests that the scale below can be used to interpret Yule's Q:

Value of Q			Appropriate phrase
.70	to	1.00	Very strong positive association
.50	to	.69	Substantial positive association
.30	to	.49	Moderate positive association
.10	to	.29	Low positive association
.01	to	.09	Negligible positive association
	.00		No association
-.01	to	-.09	Negligible negative association
-.10	to	-.29	Low negative association
-.30	to	-.49	Moderate negative association
-.50	to	-.69	Substantial negative association
-.70	to	-1.00	Very strong negative association

Pearson's Phi Coefficient

An improvement on Yule's Q is its close relative, Pearson's phi (ϕ), defined by the following equation:

$$\phi = \frac{(ad) - (bc)}{\sqrt{(a+b)(c+d)(a+c)(b+d)}}$$

Variable 1

		(+)	(−)
Variable 2	(+)	a	b
	(−)	c	d

As you can see, the numerator is the same as the one for Q, but the denominator is a bit more complicated, requiring you to multiply the marginal totals together and take the square root of the product.

Like Q, phi is a *symmetric* measure with a PRE interpretation, and ϕ will be zero when there is no relationship between the variables. In addition, ϕ is a *standard* measure — it *only* gives a value of 1.00 or -1.00 when the relationship is perfect, while Q can also give these extreme values in relationships that are conditionally perfect. For example, while the value of Q for the table on the left of this page is 1.00, the value

of ϕ is 0.7236. In order to obtain a ϕ of 1.00 or -1.00, *all* of the cases must fall in one of the diagonals of the table.

The PRE interpretation of Pearson's ϕ is more useful than the one for Yule's Q. Here are eleven sets of data that show one reason why this is so. Notice how the value of Q rises quickly as you go from the first to the sixth one. By the time ϕ reaches .50, Q is already up to .80. By the time the relationship is strong enough to give a ϕ of .70, there is little more room for Q to vary — it is up to .94. This reduces the usefulness of Q when you are trying to tell the difference between strong or very strong relationships. The numbers in the tables below are hypothetical answers from eleven different groups of people who were asked whether they owned a computer.

		men	women	Q	ϕ	ϕ^2
1	Yes	20	20	0.000	0.00	0.00
	No	20	20			
2	Yes	22	18	0.198	0.10	0.01
	No	18	22			
3	Yes	24	16	0.385	0.20	0.04
	No	16	24			
4	Yes	26	14	0.551	0.30	0.09
	No	14	26			
5	Yes	28	12	0.690	0.40	0.16
	No	12	28			
6	Yes	30	10	0.800	0.50	0.25
	No	10	30			
7	Yes	32	8	0.882	0.60	0.36
	No	8	32			
8	Yes	34	6	0.940	0.70	0.49
	No	6	34			
9	Yes	36	4	0.976	0.80	0.64
	No	4	36			
10	Yes	38	2	0.995	0.90	0.81
	No	2	38			
11	Yes	40	0	1.000	1.00	1.00
	No	0	40			

An extremely valuable property of ϕ^2 is another reason ϕ has a more useful PRE interpretation. If you square the value of ϕ, you get a measure of the proportion of the variability in the dependent variable that is "accounted for" or explained by its association with the independent variable. In the first row of the table on the left you can see that whether a person is a man or woman tells you nothing about whether the person owns a computer — both are equally likely to own one. As you move down in the table you see that more and more of the variability in owning a computer is associated with the variability in sex — more and more men are in the "yes" row and more women in the "no" row. ϕ^2 tells you what proportion of the variability in computer ownership is statistically accounted for by the differences in sex.

Because ϕ^2 is a proportion, it provides a measure of the absolute strength of the relationship that makes it possible to directly compare the strengths of different relationships to one another. A relationship in which ϕ^2 is .80 is twice as strong as one in which ϕ^2 is .40 and four times as strong as one in which ϕ^2 is .20. You can't do this with Yule's Q or with ϕ.

Ordinal Data

With ordinal data you have more information to work with. In addition to whether or not a pair of values are the same, you have know which one is larger than the other. This additional information can be taken into consideration when you assess the strength of the relationship. There are several measures you could use for ordinal data, including the Spearman rank correlation (sometimes also called "Spearman's rho"), the Kendall rank correlation coefficient (τ or tau), and the gamma measure of Proportionate Reduction of Error. While Spearman's rho is probably the one you are most likely to encounter, I'll begin with gamma because it is simpler.

Goodman and Kruskal's Gamma

Gamma is an extension of Yule's Q that can handle variables that have more than two values. (For dicho-

tomous variables, the two measures give you the same result.) If you have a pair of positively related variables and you look at the scores of two people on the variables, you would expect that the person whose score on one variable is higher than the other person's score would also have a higher score on the other variable. The example below shows that Molly enjoys watching movies and reading books more than George. The arrows indicate the direction of higher values. You can see that they are both pointed in the same direction; the pattern is consistent with a positive relationship between the variables.

	Enjoys movies	Enjoys books
Molly	↑ very much	↑ moderately
George	somewhat	slightly

Here is a different picture: Tom enjoys movies more than George, but he likes books less. This data is not consistent with a positive relation between the variables:

	Enjoys movies	Enjoys books
George	↑ somewhat	↑ slightly
Tom	moderately	not at all

How to calculate gamma

Gamma is the proportion of paired comparisons that fits this pattern. You will need to calculate the number of concordant and discordant pairs – ones that go in the same direction and ones that go in opposite directions.

An example is shown here, using hypothetical data on how nervous musicians say they are before performing and how emotionally intense their performance is rated by music critics. To calculate the number of concordant and discordant pairs, make an ordinary crosstabulation table with one row for each value of one variable and one column for each value of the other variable. Don't bother with the percentages; you won't need them for gamma. Put the column for the lowest value on the left and the

one for the highest value on the right. Put the row with the lowest value on the top and the highest on the bottom. Your table will look something like this:

Table 5. Nervousness and Intensity

	Emotional intensity ratings		
	High	Moderate	Low
How nervous High	70	30	20
Moderate	40	80	50
Low	10	40	90

To get the number of pairs having the *same* direction of ranking on the two variables, multiply the frequency of each cell by the sum of the frequencies of all cells below and to the right of it in the table. Add up all these products. For this table you would get:

$$70(80 + 50 + 40 + 90) = 18200$$
$$30(50 + 90) = 4200$$
$$40(40 + 90) = 5200$$
$$80(90) = \underline{7200}$$
$$34800$$

To get the number of discordant pairs, multiply the frequency of each cell by the sum of the frequencies of all cells appearing below and to the left of it in the table. Add all these products together. For this table you would get:

$$20(40 + 80 + 10 + 40) = 3400$$
$$30(10 + 40) = 1500$$
$$50(10 + 40) = 2500$$
$$80(10) = \underline{800}$$
$$8200$$

The rest of calculating gamma is similar to calculating Yule's Q:, subtract the number of discordant pairs from the number of concordant pairs and divide the result by the sum of the number of concordant and discordant pairs:

$$gamma = \frac{concordant\ pairs\ -\ discordant\ pairs}{concordant\ pairs\ +\ discordant\ pairs}$$

$$= \frac{34800 - 8200}{34800 + 8200} = \frac{26600}{43000} = 0.6186$$

A gamma of .6186 means that almost 62% more of the pairs examined had the same ranking rather than the opposite ranking. Gamma has a PRE interpretation: if, for each pair of people who have different levels of nervousness you always guess that the one who is more nervous will be judged as playing with more intensity, you will make 62% fewer errors than if you randomly guess differences on intensity.

Lambda for the same data is either .269 or .296, depending on whether you use the row marginals or the column marginals to calculate the original number of errors. In either case, it is much lower than gamma. The reason for this is that gamma uses more of the information in the data than lambda does. Lambda works mainly with the modal values in rows (or columns) and is "blind" to much of the information contained in the data. Gamma, on the other hand, uses information about the relative ordinal positions of all the values in the data matrix. It is thus able to "see" more of the relationship between the variables.

How to interpret gamma

If gamma is positive, you know the relation between the variables is positive. A negative gamma indicates a negative association. If all pairs have the same ranking, you will get a gamma of 1.0; if all pairs have the opposite ranking, gamma will be - 1.0. These are the upper and lower limits of Gamma. The closer to 1.0 or -1.0 a gamma is, the stronger the relationship between the variables. A gamma of 0 means the number of pairs that have the same sign is equal to the number that have opposite signs. In other words, there is no relation between the variables. In several ways, Gamma is like a correlation coefficient.

If you have several ordinal variables, you can make a correlation matrix of the gammas for all pairs of variables. In a study of communication patterns,

several dozen people rated every conversation they had for several days in terms of the urgency of the content, the level of intimacy, how much laughter there was, and how focused the conversation was. All four aspects were rated on a scale that included "very little," "slight," "moderate," "considerable," and "very much." Gamma was calculated for all pairs of variables with the following result:

Table 6. Gamma correlation matrix

	intimacy	laughter	focused
urgency	0.100	-0.189	0.482
intimacy	—	0.488	0.047
laughter		—	-0.332
focused			—

The strongest relationships in this matrix can best be described as moderate: more intimacy was associated with a higher amount of laughter (0.488), greater urgency was associated with a higher degree of focus (0.482), and the more focused the interaction was, the less laughter there was (-0.332). On the basis of these results, you might say that there were two dimensions along which these interactions varied: how close the participants were (intimacy/laughter) and the extent to which the conversation was of pressing importance (urgency/focused). There is almost no relationship between intimacy and urgency or intimacy and focus; there is a weak negative relation between laughter and urgency/focus.

Problems with gamma

There are two problems with gamma. The first is that you can get a gamma of 1.0 or -1.0 for data that does not have a perfect relationship, as the tables on the top of the next page show. For both tables, gamma is 1.00.

The second problem is due to the fact that gamma is based on a comparison of how cases differ on one variable with the way they differ on the other variable. Note that this says nothing about cases that differ on the first variable but not on the second one. You

might call these cases *ties*. The problem is that gamma ignores the ties. While the pairs in which the direction of rankings are the same indicate a positive relationship between the variables and the pairs in which the direction of rankings are the opposite indicate a negative relationship, ties are an indication that there is no relationship between the variable. Since gamma ignores the ties, the result it produces may overestimate the strength of the relationship between the variables (Johnston, 1988, p. 153).

Variable Two

	High	Med	Low
High	10	50	0
Med	0	10	80
Low	0	0	10

(Variable One)

Variable Two

	High	Med	Low
High	10	50	30
Med	0	0	30
Low	0	0	90

(Variable One)

Somer's *d*

To address the weakness of gamma caused by the fact that it only includes pairs that show there is a relationship between the variables, you might make a simple change to the way you calculate the measure. Instead of:

$$gamma = \frac{concordant\ pairs - discordant\ pairs}{concordant\ pairs + discordant\ pairs}$$

you might use:

$$\frac{concordant\ pairs - discordant\ pairs}{concordant\ pairs + discordant\ pairs + tied\ pairs}$$

Making this change gives you Somers' *d* instead of gamma. The only difference in calculating the two is that you include a count of the tied pairs in the denominator for *d*. To count the tied pairs, multiply the number of cases in each cell by the sum of the numbers to its right. Do this for all cells that have another cell to their right, except for the ones in the bottom row. With the data in Table 5 on page 100 (repeated below), you would get this:

$$70(30 + 20) = 3500$$
$$30(20) = 600$$
$$40(80 + 50) = 5200$$
$$80(50) = \underline{4000}$$
$$13300$$

	High	Moderate	Low
High	70	30	20
Moderate	40	80	50
Low	10	40	90

When you add the number of tied pairs into the equation for gamma, you get the following:

$$d = \frac{same\ pairs - opposite\ pairs}{same\ pairs + opposite\ pairs + tied\ pairs}$$

$$= \frac{34800 - 8200}{34800 + 8200 + 13300} = \frac{26600}{56300} = 0.4725$$

For comparison, the gamma for this data was 0.6186, a much higher estimate. The main strength of Somers' *d* is that it is a more conservative measure of association — and probably more accurate, since it uses more of the information contained in your data. In comparison to gamma, the main drawback is that Somers' *d* does not have a PRE interpretation. Johnson (1988, p. 142, 154) suggests that the scale on page 98 can also be used to interpret Somers' *d*.

Spearman's rho

Like gamma and Somers' *d*, Spearman's rho (ρ or r_s), sometimes called "the Spearman rank-order

correlation," requires both variables to be measured at least on ordinal scales so that whatever is being measured can be arranged into rank-ordered sequence. With this measure, there will be a perfect relationship if the object having the highest score on one variable also has the highest score on the other variable; the one having the second-highest score on one variable has the second-highest score on the other variable, and so on. Spearman's rho uses the differences in rankings as an indication of the extent to which the two sets agree or disagree.

While gamma and d both work well when the variables have a small number of possible values, Spearman's rho (r_s) works better when the variables can have a much wider range of values. The reason for this will be evident shortly.

To calculate r_s, you begin by ordering the scores on each variable from lowest to highest. Then you assign the ordinal position in the ranked lists to the corresponding scores. Next, calculate the difference between the ranks of each person's scores on the two variables (**d**) and then the squares of those differences.

The example shown below uses the scores 16 students (A, B, ... P) received on two midterm exams in a statistics course. The table shows the exam scores

and their ranks, the differences between the ranks, and the squared differences.

For a check on your ranking and subtractions, you can add the differences together. The sum should be zero as it is in the table above.

At this point you are ready to calculate r_s.

Here is the equation for r_s and the calculations for the data from the example above:

$$r_s = 1 - \frac{6\sum d_i^2}{n^3 - n}$$

$$= 1 - \frac{6 \times 212}{16^3 - 16}$$

$$= 1 - \frac{1272}{4080}$$

$$= .6882$$

This result shows that there is a moderately high relationship between the scores on the two exams. Students who did well on the first midterm tended to do well on the second one too. You can see by looking at the data that some students did considerably better on the second exam (students C and J), while others saw their performance drop quite a bit (students (students M and O), but the rankings of most students changed little or not at all.

The method you used with the equation above was the easy way to calculate r_s. If you were willing to do a bit more work, you could have calculated the ordinary Pearson's r (Chapter 13) of the numbers in the "rank" columns of the table, rather than working with the squared differences between the ranks. You would get almost the same result that you get with the squared d's. I calculated Pearson's r of the ranks and found a correlation of .688235294, which is pretty close to .688235294. The reason this works is that Spearman's rho is essentially the Pearson's r of the ranks of the values of the data. If you want to see a proof of this, have a look at Seigel (1956, p 209-210).

With some important restrictions, Spearman's rho can be interpreted and used almost in the same way as the Pearson correlation, which you will see in the next chapter. A limiting factor for r_s is that it is affected by

ID	Exam 1	rank	Exam 2	rank	d	d²
A	21	1	46	2	-1	1
B	26	2	40	1	1	1
C	33	3	60	10	-7	49
D	38	4	49	4	0	0
E	39	5	53	6	-1	1
F	42	6	47	3	3	9
G	43	7	55	7	0	0
H	45	8	61	11	-3	9
I	48	9	58	9	0	0
J	49	10	70	15	-5	25
K	50	11	65	13	-2	4
L	52	12	64	12	0	0
M	54	13	52	5	8	64
N	59	14	67	14	0	0
O	61	15	57	8	7	49
P	64	16	76	16	0	0
					0	212

ties. You are likely to see data in which more than one case has the same score on one of the variables. This will be especially likely to happen when your variables have a small number of possible values and you have a large number of cases. (This is why r_s is better for situations in which your variables have a wide range of possible values.) When you see tied scores, the ranks of the tied scores should be set to the average of the ranks they would have received had they not been tied. When there are few ties, r_s will be very close to the value you would get with Pearson's r. If there are many ties, the divergence between r_s and Pearson's r will be larger. Siegel (1956, p. 206-210) discusses a method for taking the ties into account and producing a corrected result. Because this correction is rather complex and its effect is small, it isn't discussed here.

Summary

The table on page 106 summarizes and compares the measures of strength of association described in this chapter. When you are choosing a method of analysis, you should carefully examine several key issues, including level of scaling, number of values, and type of relationship.

Level of scaling. For nominal data, in which the only comparison you can make of two values is whether or not they are the same, your choice is limited to lambda, Yule's Q, or chi-squared (discussed in chapter 16), all measures that don't need information about the order of values or the size of the differences between them. For ordinal data, you can also use measures that consider the ordering or ranking of values — gamma, Somers' d, and Spearman's rho. With interval or ratio scaling, measures of association can take advantage of the additional information about the size of the differences between values in your data.

As is the case with univariate measures of central tendency and dispersion, any measure that can be used with one of the lower levels of scaling can also be used with the higher ones. This means that you can use lambda and Yule's Q for ordinal and interval data

and gamma or Somers' d for interval or ratio data, although you may have to reduce the number of categories in the ordinal data or convert the continuous interval data to discrete categorical data. Since this conversion from higher to lower levels of scaling requires you to throw away some of the information originally contained in the data, you will probably prefer to use the stronger measures instead.

The number of values. Lambda, Yule's Q, gamma, Somers' d, and chi-squared all work best with data in the form of a crosstabulation table. This means that for these measures, your variables shouldn't have a large number of different values. Any more than ten values for each variable will result in large tables that are difficult to interpret. Having tables with fewer rows and columns, though, means that you are very likely to have several cases falling into each cell of the table. This will cause problems for Spearman's rho, which requires you to rank order the data points for the two variables as the first step of analysis. The calculations for rho are made more complex when you have to deal with the ties that you have when several cases have the same value for a variable. This measure works better when the number of cases is not much larger than the number of different values a variable can take.

The type of relationship. For nominal data, relationships between variables are present or absent; strong, moderate, or weak. For ordinal data, it is also possible for relationships to have direction. If larger values of one variable are associated with larger values of the other one, the relationship is positive. If larger values of one are associated with smaller values of the other, the relationship is negative. Neither of these can happen with nominal data where "larger" and "smaller" have no meaning.

A further complicating factor with ordinal or interval/ratio data is that relationships may be positive in the low end of the range of one variable and negative in the high end of the range. An example is shown in the table below where the number of movies watched is cross tabulated against the number of books read.

This is a curvilinear relationship. People who watch few movies tend to read few books. The more movies people watch, the more books they tend to read, up to a point where further increases in movies tends to be associated with a decrease in book reading. People who watch the most movies tend to read even fewer books than those who watch the fewest movies. None of the measures of association for ordinal data described in this chapter work when you have curvilinear associations between your variables.

The following table shows a more linear relationship between the number of books and the number of magazines read per month. Here you can see that people who read more books also tend to read more magazines, and that this pattern continues over the range of both variables. Note that lambda, the measure that ignores the order of values, is the same as for the previous example. However, both gamma and Somers' d look quite different.

Movies per month

	0-1	2-4	5-8	9-16	17+
0-1	9	4	1	3	17
2-3	11	5	2	6	5
4-6	7	17	5	19	2
7-8	3	8	11	6	3
9+	2	4	3	2	0

Books per month

lambda (rows):	0.2050
lambda (cols):	0.2380
gamma:	-0.1180
Somers' d:	-0.0980

Magazines per month

	0-1	2-3	4-6	7-8	9+
0-1	17	9	4	3	1
2-3	5	11	5	6	2
4-6	2	7	17	19	5
7-8	3	3	8	6	11
9+	0	2	4	2	3

Books per month

lambda (rows):	0.2050
lambda (cols):	0.2380
gamma:	0.4950
Somers' d:	0.4120

Measures of strength of bivariate association

Measure	discrete or continuous	minimum level of scaling	PRE	Symmetric	Range	Limitations
lambda	discrete	nominal	yes	no	0.0 to 1.0	few values
Yule's Q	discrete	nominal	yes	yes	-1.0 to 1.0	frequencies only, dichotomous, can be misleading
Pearson's ϕ	discrete	nominal	yes	yes	-1.0 to 1.0	frequencies only, dichotomous
chi squared	discrete	nominal	no	yes	0.0 to ?	expected < 5 in no more than 20% of cells, few values
gamma	discrete	ordinal	yes	yes	-1.0 to 1.0	frequencies only, few values, linear relationships only
Somers' d	discrete	ordinal	no	no	-1.0 to 1.0	frequencies only, few values, linear relationships only
Spearman's rho	discrete	ordinal	no	yes	-1.0 to 1.0	ranks with few ties, linear relationships only
Pearson's r	continuous	interval	yes	yes	-1.0 to 1.0	linear relationships
covariance	continuous	interval	no	yes	?	linear relationships

Important Terms and Concepts

concordant pairs
conditionally perfect association
conservative measure
correlation matrix
cross-product
data reduction
discordant pairs
Goodman and Kruskal's gamma
lambda
negative relationship

perfect association
positive relationship
proportional reduction of error
rank-order correlation
Somers' d
Spearman's rho
strength of a relationship
symmetric/asymmetric measure
tied pairs
Yule's Q

Chapter 13

STRENGTH OF RELATIONSHIPS: CONTINUOUS DATA

"Variance" is a technical word for "variability." It is a measure of spread about the mean. Variance is the mean of the squared deviations from the mean:

$$s^2 = \frac{\sum (x_i - \bar{x})^2}{n} = \frac{\sum d_x^2}{n}$$

Q: Why square the deviations?

A: If you just add the deviations up without squaring them, the total will always be zero, and this won't tell you anything at all. Squaring them removes the minus signs, among other things.

To get the *standard deviation*, you take the *square root of the variance*. This compensates for the fact that you squared the deviations before adding them up.

If you are talking about how many cups of coffee per day people consume, the standard deviation is in units of cups-per-day. So if the mean is 5 cups per day, the standard deviation is 2 cups, and the distribution is normal, 68% of everyone drinks between 3 and 7 cups per day.

If you also have age as a variable and you find that the standard deviation of age is 5 years, you will have a problem if you want to compare age with coffee consumption. For one thing, the measures of spread (standard deviation) for the two variables are in different units. For coffee, the units are cups of coffee per day. For age, the units are years of life. How do you compare cups of coffee per day to years of life?

I'm going to make two changes to the equation for variance. The first change allows you to get a measure of how much of the variance in one variable is shared by another variable, or, in other words, how closely associated or tied together are the two variables. The second change will get rid of the units the variables are measured in (cups, years, whatever) by changing the original units into standardized units. This change will make it possible to use the measure of shared variance to compare the strength of the relationship between different pairs of variables.

The First Change: Covariance

If you want to measure how the two variables vary together—"covariance"—you do a simple change to

the equation for variance. Instead of calculating the mean of the *squared* deviation scores like this:

$$var_x = \frac{\sum (x_i - \bar{x})^2}{n} = \frac{\sum d_x^2}{n} = \frac{\sum d_x d_x}{n}$$

you calculate the mean of the *cross-products* of the deviation scores. That is, instead of multiplying each deviation score by itself, you multiply it by the corresponding deviation score of the second variable:

$$cov_{xy} = \frac{\sum (x_i - \bar{x})(y_i - \bar{y})}{n} = \frac{\sum d_x d_y}{n}$$

Look closely at the equation for variance and compare it with the one for covariance. The only difference is that variance multiplies each deviation score by itself, while covariance multiplies the deviation score on the *first* variable by the corresponding deviation score of the *second* variable. Everything else is the same.

One consequence of combining the two variables' deviation scores like this is that the sum of the products may be either negative or positive.

If the first variable is *below* the mean whenever the second one is *also* below the mean, both deviation scores will be negative, and the product of the two will be positive. If the first variable is *above* the mean

whenever the second one is also above the mean, both deviation scores will be positive, and the product of the two will be positive. The sum of the products will thus be positive, which means the covariance will be positive. An example of this kind of situation is shown in the drawing on the left.

On the other hand, if the first variable is *below* the mean when the second one is *above* the mean, or the first variable is *above* the mean when the second one is *below* the mean, the products of the deviation scores will be negative, and the covariance will be negative, as you can see in the drawing below.

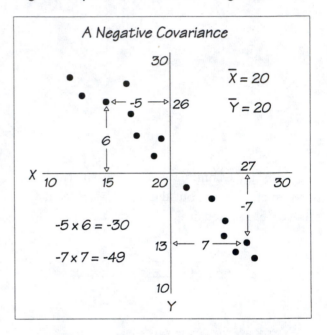

A positive covariance means that the two variables co-vary (vary together) in a positive way: when one is high, so is the other; when one is low, so is the other. A negative covariance means that the variables co-vary in a negative or inverse way: when one variable is high, the other one is low; when one is low, the other is high. For any given pair of variables measured in a particular way, the larger the covariance is, the stronger the relationship between the variables is.

An example:

Imagine that you are a toy dealer doing some market research on various toys. This time you are particularly interested in xylophones and yo-yo's. You want to see whether there is a relationship between the

number of xylophones and the number of yo-yo's a typical child owns. You happen to be studying covariance in a statistics course you are taking, and you see this as an opportunity to put your new knowledge to some good use.

You decide to count the number of xylophones and yo-yo's owned by each child in your neighborhood and to call the variables "X" (number of xylophones) and "Y" (number of yo-yo's), and to calculate the covariance of the two variables.

Here is the equation for covariance:

$$cov_{xy} = \frac{\sum d_x d_y}{n}$$

In this equation, d_x and d_y are deviation scores for the two variables. The data and all relevant calculations are summarized in the table below.

i	X	d_x	Y	d_y	$d_x d_y$
1	2	-3.4	1	-4.9	16.660
2	2	-3.4	3	-2.9	9.860
3	3	-2.4	6	.1	-.240
4	4	-1.4	5	-.9	1.260
5	5	-.4	3	-2.9	1.160
6	6	.6	8	2.1	1.260
7	7	1.6	6	.1	.160
8	7	1.6	10	4.1	6.560
9	8	2.6	8	2.1	5.460
10	10	4.6	9	3.1	14.260
Tot	54	0.0	59	0.0	56.40

$$\bar{x} = 5.4 \qquad \bar{y} = 5.9 \qquad n = 10$$

$$\sum d_x d_y = 56.40$$

$$cov_{xy} = \frac{\sum d_x d_y}{n} = \frac{56.40}{10} = 5.640$$

The covariance is 5.640, which indicates that there is a positive relationship between the two variables. The more xylophones a child in your neighborhood owns, the more yo-yo's the child is likely to own. You could compare this covariance with one calculated with the same variables next year and see whether the relationship between the two variables has become stronger or weaker, but you couldn't use it to compare the relationship between xylophone and yo-yo ownership with the one between age and coffee consumption. The covariance doesn't tell you how strong the relationship is in terms of how many of the children in the neighborhood fit the pattern nor in terms of how many more yo-yo's a child with three xylophones is likely to have than a child with only one or two.

An easier way to calculate covariance

Instead of using this formula for covariance,

$$cov_{xy} = \frac{\sum d_x d_y}{n}$$

you could use this one:

$$cov_{xy} = \frac{\sum xy - \frac{\sum x \sum y}{n}}{n}$$

The advantage of this *computational* form of the equation is that you do not have to calculate sample means and deviation scores first. It takes less work, there is less rounding error, and you are more likely to get the correct answer. Try it with the data shown in the table on the left and see how it compares. Compare the above equation with the computational formula for variance and make note of the differences and similarities of the two:

$$var_x = \frac{\sum x^2 - \frac{(\sum x)^2}{n}}{n}$$

The Second Change: Correlation

The units you use to measure amount of coffee consumed and the person's age are easy to understand—cups and years. But covariance is measured in strange units. If you used covariance to assess the relation between age and number of cups of coffee consumed per day, you would multiply each person's deviation score for amount of coffee (*cups*) by the person's deviation score for age (*years*). The covariance units for this example would be something like "cup-years"—a strange unit indeed. Think about the units you'd be using in the xylophone & yo-yo example.

If you had another variable that might be related to coffee consumption, say height, you could calculate the covariance of the relation between height and cups of coffee per day. But you could not compare this to the covariance of coffee and age to see which relationship is stronger, because the second covariance would be in units of "cup-inches" or "cup-centimeters" which are not comparable to "cup-years." This is the first problem with covariance.

The second problem with covariance is that it is strongly influenced by the variance of the variables you are working with. A variable whose values are spread far away from the mean will have large deviation scores, while one whose values are clustered closely around the mean will have small deviation scores. This means that you will be likely to get larger covariances when your variables have higher levels of dispersion than when the dispersion is low, regardless of the strength of the relationship between the variables. In other words, the covariance may, to an extent, be a function of the dispersion of your variables as much as a measure of the strength of the relationship between the variables. You can eliminate this problem if you can standardize your variables so they always have the same level of dispersion. This turns out to be an easy thing to do.

If you turn both height and number of cups into standard scores (z-scores), the resulting variables will both have means of 0.0 and standard deviations of 1.0. Z-scores are in units of "standard deviations," and they can be compared to one another, unlike the original variables. You standardize your variables (convert deviation scores to z-scores) by dividing by the standard deviation.

So you make a modification to covariance. Instead of using the sum of the cross-products of the *deviation* scores, you use the sum of the crossproducts of the *z-scores*. While using deviation scores centers your data and removes the effect of the mean (by subtracting it from each value), converting the deviation scores to z-scores removes the effects of the original units of measurement and the degree of dispersion of the variable. You change from

$$\frac{\sum d_{x_i} d_{y_i}}{n} \quad \text{to} \quad \frac{\sum z_{x_i} z_{y_i}}{n}$$

You could achieve the same result by dividing the covariance by the product of the standard deviations of the variables. This does the same as converting the deviation scores to z-scores:

$$\frac{cov_{xy}}{s_x s_y} = \frac{\dfrac{\sum d_x d_y}{n}}{s_x s_y} = \frac{\sum d_x d_y}{n s_x s_y}$$

but . . .

$$\frac{\sum d_x d_y}{n s_x s_y} = \frac{\sum \dfrac{d_x}{s_x} \dfrac{d_y}{s_y}}{n} = \frac{\sum z_x z_y}{n}$$

Changing from deviation scores to z-scores produces an important result. The value you get now is the *Pearson product-moment correlation coefficient*, more commonly known as the "correlation." The correlation can have values between -1.0 and 1.0. If the correlation is 1.0, the two variables are perfectly correlated with one another. They are in effect interchangeable, for when you know the value of one, you also know the value of the other. If the correlation is -1.0, they are perfectly correlated, but the relationship is negative—when one is high, the other is low. If the correlation is 0.0, there is no relationship at all between the two variables; knowing the value of one tells you nothing about the value of the other.

You can compare any correlation with any other correlation, for they are all in the same units. The correlation coefficient is one of the most commonly used descriptive statistics. It is relatively easy to calculate, and it describes the relationship in a very concise and economical way.

Why correlation is better than covariance

• Because correlation removes the effect of the variance of the variables, it provides a standardized measure of the strength of the relationship, making it possible to compare any correlation to any other correlation and see which is stronger. This is an *absolute* measure of the strength of the relationship. You cannot do this with covariance.

• Because correlation replaces the original units in which the variables were measured with standard deviations, you don't have to deal with the strange hybrid units that covariance produces.

• Because the value of *r* is bounded by -1.0 and 1.0, it provides an *absolute* measure of the strength of the relationship. Furthermore, the squared correlation (r^2) is a measure of how much of the variance in one variable is explained by the other variable. This measure, *the coefficient of determina-*

tion, ranges from 0.0 to 1.0. You cannot do this with covariance.

Calculating *r*

Say you have a group of ten people. For each of them you know how many magazines they subscribe to (X) and how many books they purchase per month (Y). The data for this example is plotted on the right. You would like to know if the people who subscribe to a lot of magazines also purchase a lot of books. This is an appropriate situation to illustrate the use of the correlation. Three ways to calculate *r* are demonstrated below. The first is the definitional formula based on *z*-scores, the second uses deviation scores, and the third is the computational formula.

1) *r* based on *z*-scores

The Pearson product moment correlation coefficient is defined as

$$r_{xy} = \frac{\sum z_x z_y}{n}$$

In this equation, z_x and z_y are z-scores for the two variables *x* and *y*; *n* is the sample size. While this is the simplest complete definition of the correlation, it

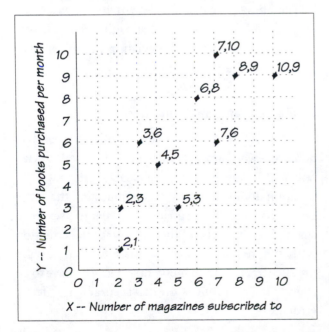

X -- Number of magazines subscribed to

Important Notes:

When calculating correlations, it doesn't matter if you use *n* or (*n-1*), as long as you are consistent. If you use (*n-1*) anywhere, you must use it everywhere.

1. When using the computational formula, keep life simple—*don't use (n-1) in either the numerator or the denominator.*

2. When using the formula based on deviation scores, if you use (*n-1*) to calculate the standard deviations in the denominator, you must also use (*n-1*) in the denominator. If you use *n* to calculate the standard deviation, you must also use *n* in the denominator.

3. When using the formula based on z-scores, if you use (*n-1*) to calculate the standard deviations for the z-scores, you must also use (*n-1*) in the denominator. If you use *n* to calculate the standard deviation, you must also use *n* in the denominator.

is probably the most difficult one to use, because it uses z-scores, each of which involves a subtraction and a division. First you calculate the means, then the deviation scores and the standard deviations. Next you divide the deviation scores by the standard deviations to get the z-scores which you multiply to get the cross-products in the last column. The sum of the cross-products goes in the numerator of the equation for r. As you can see in the example here, it is difficult to do these calculations without introducing rounding errors.

i	X	d_x	z_x	Y	d_y	z_y	$z_x z_y$
1	2	-3.4	-1.340	1	-4.9	-1.767	2.367
2	2	-3.4	-1.340	3	-2.9	-1.046	1.401
3	3	-2.4	-.946	6	.1	.036	-.034
4	4	-1.4	-.552	5	-.9	-.325	.179
5	5	-.4	-.158	3	-2.9	-1.046	.165
6	6	.6	.236	8	2.1	.757	.179
7	7	1.6	.630	6	.1	.036	.022
8	7	1.6	.63	10	4.1	1.478	.932
9	8	2.6	1.025	8	2.1	.757	.776
10	10	4.6	1.813	9	3.1	1.118	2.026
Tot	54	0.0		59	0.0		8.014

$\bar{x} = 5.4$ $s_x = 2.5377$ $\bar{y} = 5.9$ $s_y = 2.7731$ $n = 10$

$$r_{xy} = \frac{\sum z_x z_y}{n} = \frac{8.014}{10} = .8014$$

2) r based on deviation scores

The formula below is a bit more complicated than the one that uses z-scores, but it is a lot easier to use. With this method you use deviation scores instead.

$$r_{xy} = \frac{\sum d_x d_y}{n s_x s_y} = \frac{cov_{xy}}{s_x s_y}$$

Here, d_x, d_y, s_x, and s_y are deviation scores and standard deviations for the two variables. This approach and the one that uses z-scores should give you the same answer. This one is easier to calculate than the one with z-scores, but it is still a lot of work and prone to errors because it needs deviation scores.

i	X	d_x	Y	d_y	$d_x d_y$
1	2	-3.4	1	-4.9	16.660
2	2	-3.4	3	-2.9	9.860
3	3	-2.4	6	.1	-.240
4	4	-1.4	5	-.9	1.260
5	5	-.4	3	-2.9	1.160
6	6	.6	8	2.1	1.260
7	7	1.6	6	.1	.160
8	7	1.6	10	4.1	6.560
9	8	2.6	8	2.1	5.460
10	10	4.6	9	3.1	14.260
Tot	54	0.0	59	0.0	56.40

$\bar{x} = 5.4$ $s_x = 2.5377$ $\bar{y} = 5.9$ $s_y = 2.7731$ $n = 10$

$$r_{xy} = \frac{56.40}{10 \times 2.5377 \times 2.7731} = .8014$$

The above calculations show that it is easier to work with deviation scores than with z-scores if you already have the standard deviations. You can see, though, that the result is the same.

3) the computational equation for r

A computational form of the equation for correlation, somewhat similar to the one for standard deviation, makes it even easier to calculate r. Although the equation looks a lot more complicated than the original one, you will find it *much* easier to use. Once again, the advantage of the computational equation is that it requires fewer calculations that usually produce fractions and messy numbers that have to be rounded. The result is greater accuracy and fewer errors.

Here is the computational equation for r:

$$r_{xy} = \frac{n\sum xy - \sum x \sum y}{\sqrt{n\sum x^2 - (\sum x)^2} \; \sqrt{n\sum y^2 - (\sum y)^2}}$$

Besides the raw data, this equation requires five sums which are fairly easy to calculate. If your raw data values are whole numbers, there will be no fractions in any of these sums making this an easy task to complete:

$\sum x$ — the sum of the x values

$\sum y$ — the sum of the y values

$\sum x^2$ — the sum of the squared x values

$\sum y^2$ — the sum of the squared y values

$\sum xy$ — the sum of the cross-products of the x and y values

i	X	X^2	Y	Y^2	XY
1	2	4	1	1	2
2	2	4	3	9	6
3	3	9	6	36	18
4	4	16	5	25	20
5	5	25	3	9	15
6	6	36	8	64	48
7	7	49	6	36	42
8	7	49	10	100	70
9	8	64	8	64	64
10	10	100	9	81	90
Tot	54	356	59	425	375

$$r_{xy} = \frac{(10 \times 375) - (54 \times 59)}{\sqrt{(10 \times 356) - 54^2} \times \sqrt{(10 \times 425) - 59^2}} = .8014$$

Compare the numbers in the above table with the ones for the first two methods for calculating r. Note that the numbers used with this method are all whole

numbers up to the point where you plug them in the equation.

I once asked a class of 35 students to calculate correlations with the data in the examples here using the first method. I counted 26 different answers. Most of the differences were due to differences in the way the students rounded the intermediate values in their calculations. Even after receiving careful instructions on rounding procedures, their results deviated from the correct answer by as much as ten percent. In contrast, almost all students who use the computational formula get very close to the correct answer. For them, most differences are either the result of overzealous rounding of the final answer or the product of arithmetic errors.

A Gallery of Correlations

On the next page are scatterplots for data with correlations ranging from 0.0 to 0.999 so you can get an idea of what various correlations look like. In each of these plots, both variables are normally distributed and have the same variance and mean. The only thing that differs from plot to plot is the correlation between the variables.

If you cover the text on the bottom of the scatterplots, you probably will have difficulty seeing any difference between the ones for correlations of 0.0, 0.15, and 0.3. With a correlation of 0.4, the pattern in the scatterplot is noticeable but certainly not something to write home about. The r^2 values tell you that these correlations account for 0%, 2.25%, 9%, and 16% of the variance. The scatterplot for $r = .4$ shows you how little 16% of the variance is.

A gallery of correlations

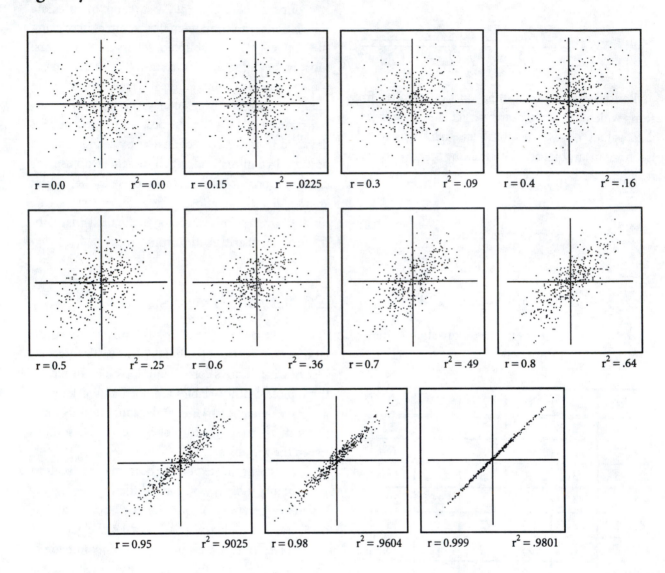

r = 0.0 r² = 0.0	r = 0.15 r² = .0225	r = 0.3 r² = .09	r = 0.4 r² = .16
r = 0.5 r² = .25	r = 0.6 r² = .36	r = 0.7 r² = .49	r = 0.8 r² = .64
r = 0.95 r² = .9025	r = 0.98 r² = .9604	r = 0.999 r² = .9801	

Important Terms and Concepts

coefficient of determination
computational equation
correlation
covariance
cross-products
deviation scores
negative relationship

Pearson's *r*
positive relationship
r^2
standard scores
variance
z-scores

Chapter 14

REGRESSION

Recent studies seem to indicate that the number of broken windows there are in a neighborhood is related to the amount of property crime (vandalism, theft, etc) in the area. Let's also say that we can measure property crime and get a single number that tells how much crime there is in an area. If we want to convince building owners to repair their windows, we need to convince them that doing so will reduce crime. You convince the Department of Justice to study this issue and to hire you to test the relationship in a national study.

Somehow you collect data in 1,000 neighborhoods across the country. You count the number of broken windows and you study local police records of property crime. Some have many broken windows; some have few or none. Similarly, some have many crimes reported and some have few or none. You make a scatterplot of your data and it looks something like the one on the right.

The Regression Line

The vertical axis is the amount of crime, as measured by the "p-crime" scale. The horizontal axis is the number of broken windows — "breaks." The diagonal line drawn through the data points is the *regression line*; it shows a summary description of the relationship between the two variables. Because the relationship is treated as a *linear* one, the line is *straight*.

The first thing to notice in the example is that *the regression line does not go through the origin* (the origin is the point at which both **x** and **y** equal 0.00). In fact, the lowest level of crime measured was "**a**" on the plot — 2.0. This is because there is some crime even when there are no broken windows. The point where the regression line intercepts the vertical axis, the value of **y** when **x** = 0, is the ***intercept***. Sometimes the intercept will be 0.00, which means the regression line goes through the origin. Usually, however, this will not be the case.

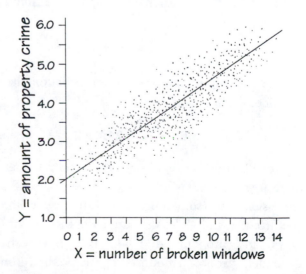

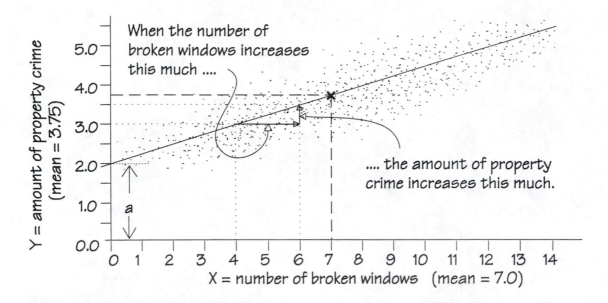

The second thing to notice in the example is that *the line goes through a point at the means of both variables* (7.0 broken windows and 3.75 on the crime scale). The third thing to notice is that, in this example, *the line slopes upwards*. The more broken windows, the higher the level of crime. In fact, when the number of broken windows goes up by **2**, the amount of crime goes up by **0.5**.(If the correlation between the variables is positive, the line will slope upwards. If it is negative, the line will slope downwards.) If you know the size of change in one variable that is associated with a given change in the other, you can calculate the **slope** of the line by dividing the change in the dependent variable (**y**) by the corresponding change in the independent variable (**x**). In the example above, the slope would be:

$$b = \frac{0.5}{2.0} = 0.25$$

The **regression equation** — the equation that describes the line — is:

$$\hat{Y} = bX + a = 0.25X + 2.0$$

where "**a**" is the intercept — the level of crime when there are no broken windows, "**b**" is the slope of the regression line (sometimes called the "regression coefficient"), and "**X**" is the number of broken windows. "$\hat{Y}$" (pronounced "Y-hat") is the level of the dependent variable, amount of crime, predicted on the basis of the value of the independent variable, number of broken windows.

Residuals

The data points are not all on the line, so the line does not completely describe the relationship between the two variables. Some areas have more crime than others, and some are more or less sensitive to the number of broken windows than others. The "errors" between where the data points are and where the regression equation would predict them to be (errors of prediction) are called *residuals* or *unexplained variation*. These "errors" are what would be left over if the effect of the number of broken windows were to be "statistically removed." They are variations in the dependent variable that are not accounted for by the independent variable.

Although the data points are not actually on the line, you can see that the line does seem to reasonably

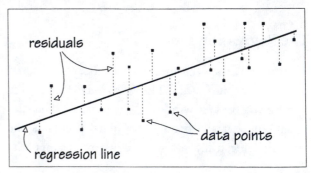

describe the overall relation between level of crime and broken windows. Also, if you know how many broken windows there are in an area, you can make a reasonably accurate estimate of that area's level of property crime. Thus, you have explained some of the variation in crime by knowing the number of broken windows. The *variance explained* by the relationship is the difference between the total variance and the unexplained variance.

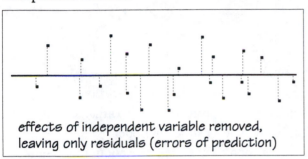

effects of independent variable removed, leaving only residuals (errors of prediction)

Explained Variance

The variance of a variable is a measure of the extent to which values are spread about the mean. The more spread out the values are, the higher the variance is. You will remember that the variance is calculated as the mean of the squared deviation scores ("mean square"):

$$var = s^2 = \frac{\sum (Y_i - \bar{Y})^2}{n}$$

If an area's level of crime and the number of broken windows were not related to one another, the best you could do if you were trying to predict the level of crime would be to guess the overall mean — 3.75.

With the regression analysis, you can see that the more broken windows there are, the more crime there is. In fact, you can calculate your best guess for level of

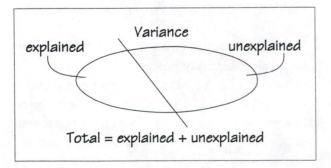

Variance
explained   unexplained

Total = explained + unexplained

crime in any area, based on the number of broken windows by plugging the number of broken windows into the regression equation:

$$\hat{Y} = 0.25\,X + 2.0$$

Now you are on the track to explaining some of the variance in the amount of crime; with the regression equation you can make better estimates for the level of crime than you could above, when the only reasonable guess you could make was the mean. For each value of the independent variable, X (number of broken windows), you can calculate an estimate for the dependent variable, $\hat{Y}$ (the level of crime).

The variance of these predictions, part of the variance in the original variable, can be calculated as:

$$s^2_{predicted} = \frac{\sum (\hat{Y} - \bar{Y})^2}{n}$$

You can also see that this is just a general trend, since some areas with *fewer* broken windows have *higher* levels of crime. So the regression line describes the general trend but not the individual cases. In other words, it only explains part of the variability (variance) in levels of crime. In fact, if you divide the variance of the predictions by the original variance, you will see that:

$$r^2 = \frac{variance\ of\ predictions}{total\ variance} = \frac{s^2_{\hat{y}}}{s^2_y}$$

You can also calculate the variance of the residuals, the variance *not* explained by the regression line, as follows:

$$s^2_{residual} = \frac{\sum (Y - \hat{Y})^2}{n} = (1 - r^2)\,s^2$$

Now you can add the variance of the predictions to the variance of the residuals, and the result will be the original variance:

$$s^2_{predicted} + s^2_{residual} = s^2$$

Correlation and Residuals

If you divide the explained variance by the total variance, you get a measure of the *proportionate reduction of error,* an index of how strong or "clean" is the relationship between the two variables. It turns out that this measure of strength of relationship will be the same as the familiar *coefficient of determination,* r^2. Regression analysis usually computes both the values of r and r^2, because r can be negative or positive, and it tells the direction of the relationship. If the correlation between the variables is negative, the line will slope downwards instead of upwards as it does in the example on the previous pages.

The scatterplots below show data where the correlations are 0.6 and 0.95. Notice that the data points in the plot with the higher correlation are much closer to the regression line. This illustrates the *direct relationship* between the correlation and the residuals:

> The closer the correlation is to 0.0, the larger the residuals will be. Alternatively, the closer the correlation is to 1.0 or -1.0, the smaller the residuals will be. This shows that stronger correlations explain more of the variability (variance) in the data.

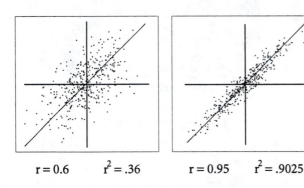

r = 0.6 r^2 = .36   r = 0.95 r^2 = .9025

Since r^2 tells you the fraction of the variance that is accounted for, $1 - r^2$ will tell you the fraction of the variance that is *not* explained by the relationship. You may encounter the term *coefficient of alienation,* which is a measure of the extent to which your variables are *not* related to one another.

$$\text{coefficient of alienation} = \sqrt{1 - r^2}$$

The stronger the relationship between your variables, the smaller the coefficient of alienation you will get. For a perfect relationship in which $r = 1.0$, the coefficient of alienation will be zero.

The correlation between the two variables comes into play in one other way. If you know the correlation and the standard deviations (s_x and s_y), you can calculate the slope of the regression line:

$$\text{slope} = b_{y.x} = r_{xy} \frac{s_y}{s_x}$$

The subscript, $y.x$, indicates that the variable y is the dependent variable — the one whose value will be predicted on the basis of the value of the other one. If you switch the position of the variables, you will almost always get a different slope.

If you don't have the correlation and standard deviations, you might use the computational equation for the slope:

$$b_{y.x} = \frac{cov_{x,y}}{s_x^2} = \frac{n\sum xy - (\sum x)(\sum y)}{n\sum x^2 - (\sum x)^2}$$

If you also know the means of the two variables, you can calculate the intercept:

$$\text{intercept} = a = \bar{Y} - b\bar{X}$$

Once you have the slope and intercept, you have the regression equation:

$$\hat{Y} = bX + a$$

Since level of crime is the dependent variable (Y) and the number of broken windows is the independent variable (X), your regression equation becomes:

$$\hat{Y} = .5X + 2.0$$

You are probably wondering why anyone would want to calculate a regression equation. The answer is that it allows you to predict the value of one variable if you know the other. Let's say you did the study on crime and broken windows and found the regression equation above. If your data came from a representa-

tive sample of the region, you would be able to tell people how much their crime levels would decline if they repaired a given number of broken windows.

Multiple Regression

It is possible to do a regression that includes several independent variables. If you include variables like "level of unemployment," "amount of drug addiction," and "good living conditions," you will probably be able to explain more of the variance in level of crime than you can when you only look at how many broken windows there are. The regression equation for this kind of analysis looks something like this:

$$\hat{Y} = a + b_1X_1 + b_2X_2 + b_3X_3 + b_4X_4 + e$$

Here, as before, a is the intercept, X_1 is the number of broken windows, X_2 is the level of unemployment, X_3 is the amount of drug addiction, and X_4 is how good the living conditions are. e is the *residual error*, or unexplained variance. This one equation shows how the four independent variables go together to influence the level of crime.

Linear *vs* Curvilinear Regression

The examples and discussion in this chapter have all used **linear** regression. It is called "linear" regression because the regression equation describes a *straight line*. The slope of the line does not change. In other words, the sensitivity of the dependent variable to a change in the independent variable remains constant over the entire range of values.

Many of the relationships you will encounter are not linear. You may have experienced the non-linear relationship shown in the drawing above. It's obvious that a straight line couldn't possibly provide a useful summary of the relationship between these variables. This is the biggest weakness of linear regression: it cannot describe non-linear relationships. If the regression line needs to be curved to better match the data, you would use *curvilinear regression* instead.

Example

Here are scores on a mid-term exam (X) and a final exam (Y) for 16 students in a course on statistics:

i	X	Y
1	69.74	57.33
2	92.11	76.00
3	61.84	55.33
4	84.21	80.00
5	61.84	70.00
6	72.37	77.00
7	68.42	48.00
8	64.47	60.00
9	80.26	58.67
10	78.95	58.67
11	85.53	92.00
12	76.32	63.33
13	52.63	54.00
14	88.16	82.67
15	75.00	80.67
16	73.68	86.00

$$\bar{x} = 74.095 \quad s_x = 10.399$$
$$\bar{y} = 68.729 \quad s_y = 12.967$$
$$n = 16$$

For this data, $r = .5977$ and the slope of the regression line is:

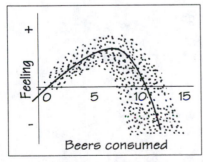

A scatterplot of some data with a non-linear regression line

$$slope = b = r_{xy}\frac{S_y}{S_x} = .5977 \times \frac{12.967}{10.399} = .7452$$

The intercept is:

$$a = \bar{Y} - b\bar{X}$$

$$= 68.729 - .7452 \times 74.095 = 13.511$$

The regression equation is:

$$\hat{Y} = bX + a = .7452\,X + 13.511$$

The fact that the intercept is 13.511 means that you would expect a student who received a score of 0.0 on the mid-term exam to receive a score of 13.511 on the final exam. The positive slope indicates that the higher a student's score on the mid-term was, the higher you would expect the student's score on the final exam to be.

The drawings on the right shows the regression line superimposed on a scatterplot of the data. You will notice that the data points do not fall directly on the regression line. Since the correlation is .5977, the score on the mid-term exam explains only 35.72% of the variance in the final exam scores. If r were closer to 1.0, the data points would be closer to the regression line, which would allow more precise predictions of Y (final exam scores), given the value of X (mid-term exam scores).

The top drawing has been enlarged so you can see the data points more clearly; it does not show the intercept.

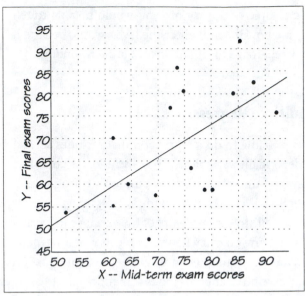

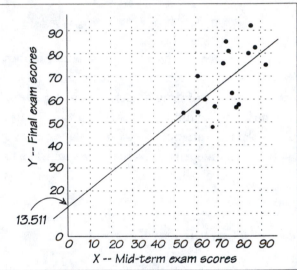

Important Terms and Concepts

coefficient of alienation
coefficient of determination
correlation
covariance
cross-products of deviation scores
cross-products of z-scores
curvilinear regression
direct or positive relationship
explained variance

indirect or inverse
intercept
multiple regression
Pearson's r
proportionate reduction of error
r-squared
regression
regression line
regression equation
residuals
slope of the regression line
unexplained variance

IV

Hypothesis testing

Chapter 15

Statistical Significance

The idea of generalizing from a sample to a population was taken up in chapter 8, where the concept of a *sampling distribution* was introduced and discussed. You may recall the discussion in chapter 9, where the properties of a sampling distribution were used to make some inferences about the relation between the mean of a random sample and the mean of the population from which the sample was drawn. A key idea in this process was the *standard error of the mean* — the standard deviation of the sampling distribution of sample means. You probably remember also that the standard error is a measure of the amount of *sampling variability* — the extent to which samples differ from one another.

In order to use a sample's mean as an estimate of the population's mean, you need to know how close to the population your sample mean is likely to be. You know that your sample's mean is probably not exactly the same as the population's mean, and you know that you will get different means if you take different samples. To determine how close to the population's mean your sample mean is likely to be, you get an estimate of how much variability there would be from one sample to the next: the standard error of the mean. You combine this with your knowledge that the means of random samples drawn from the same population are normally distributed;

that 95% of all sample means will be within 1.96 standard errors of the true population mean. This lets you answer questions like "How close to the population mean is my sample mean likely to be?" and "What are the chances that my sample came from a population with a mean of 125?"

Sampling Variability . . . or Not?

You take a similar approach when you have two variables. If the data in your sample seems to indicate that the variables are related to one another, you will want to know if that relationship is present in the population. Perhaps it isn't. Perhaps it appears to be present in your sample data because you got an odd sample. A different sample might not show the same relationship. In other words, perhaps the apparent relationship is due to sampling variability. The question you will have about your sample data is "What are the chances that the relationship I see in my sample are due to sampling variability?"

This chapter introduces the concept of *statistical significance*, one of the most important tools you will encounter in your studies of statistics. Statistical significance is an issue whenever you have data from a sample and want to generalize to the population the

sample represents. The reason it becomes an issue is something you can't avoid when you use a sample: *sampling variability*.

When, as a researcher, you are interested in some aspect of a population, you start by drawing a representative sample and making the appropriate measurements. Then you examine the data and get a tentative answer to the question you had about the population. But this answer is based solely on the sample. So now you have to determine whether you can generalize from the sample to the population. If the men *in your sample* know more about political issues and less about scientific events than the women *in your sample*, can you conclude that men *in general* know more about political issues and less about scientific events than women *in general*? The basic question you are asking here is whether the pattern you see in the sample is a reflection of a similar pattern in the population or simply a product of sampling variability.

It may help to think of the situation of a person in court on charges of committing a crime. It is the job of the judge and jury to decide whether the evidence is so convincing that the person's claim of innocence cannot be accepted. Remember that the justice system is based on the assumption that the defendant is presumed to be innocent, and that the person is considered innocent until proven guilty.

The Null Hypothesis

With inferential bivariate statistics, you work with two variables. They are assumed to be independent of one another ("innocent"), until there is enough evidence to convince you that this assumption is not consistent with the data. The assumption that the variables are not related to one another is called the *null hypothesis*, and is written as "$H_\emptyset$."

The null hypothesis has two parts:

● The first part is always stated explicitly. It always says "the variables are not related," although it usually doesn't use those exact words.

● The second part is almost never stated explicitly. It always says "the apparent relationship between the variables is nothing more than a product of sampling variability."

If the null hypothesis is true, the pattern you see in the data is due to sampling variability. If the null hypothesis is false, the pattern you see in the data is there because your sample comes from a population in which there is a similar relationship between the same variables.

It is your job as researcher to determine whether the pattern you see could be due to sampling variability. If you conclude that sampling variability could *not* be the cause of the pattern you see, you reject the null hypothesis and declare that the pattern is "statistically significant." If, on the other hand, you conclude that the pattern you see in your data *could* be due to sampling variability, you "fail to reject" the null hypothesis, and you declare that sampling variability is a reasonable cause of the apparent pattern. If you suspect that the sampling distribution and the standard error would be important tools in making this determination, you are right. (Remember that standard errors are measures of sampling variability!)

While the specific steps you take will depend on the kind of variables you have, the basic logic does not change. You start by developing a measure of the size of the pattern you see. The "pattern" you are measuring will usually be a difference between two things. It may be as simple as the difference between two sample means, or it may be something a bit more complicated, such as the difference between what you see in your data and what you would expect to see if the null hypothesis were true. With the aid of a standard error (or something very much like a standard error), you compare the difference to the sampling distribution.

You want to know if this difference is big enough to convince you that the null hypothesis couldn't be true — if this difference is so big that it couldn't be due to sampling variability. So you would like to know how likely you are to get a difference this large if you drew a random sample from a population in which there is no difference. In other words, how

likely you are to get a difference this large when the null hypothesis is true.

Let's take a chance

Ordinarily a 95% confidence level is accepted, which means that you are willing to take a 5% chance of making an error. What kind of error might you make? Actually, there are two types, called "Type I" and "Type II." (Aren't statisticians imaginative?)

You commit a Type I error *if you reject a true null hypothesis* — that is, if you conclude that the difference in your data indicates a real difference in the population, when in fact there is none (i.e., when the difference in your sample data was due to sampling variability).

On the other hand, you commit a Type II error *if you fail to reject a false null hypothesis* — that is, if you conclude that the difference in your data is due to sampling variability when, in fact, the reason you saw the difference in your data is because your sample came from a population in which the same pattern was present.

In simpler words, you make a Type I error when you incorrectly say "there is a difference." This is like convicting an innocent person for a crime he didn't commit. You make a Type II error when you incorrectly say "there is no difference." This is like releasing a guilty criminal by mistakenly finding him innocent. Because statistics (like the justice system) is conservative, you generally worry more about making a Type I error than about making a Type II error. This is why you always test the null hypothesis.

Testing the Null Hypothesis

There are many ways to test a null hypothesis. The one you use will depend on the kind of variables you have (continuous or discrete, dichotomous/trichotomous/etc.), and how large your sample is.

In every case, you compare a measure of the difference in your data to a sampling distribution. The question you ask is always "what is the probability of getting a difference this large when the null hypothesis is true?" To answer this question, you use special tables that were constructed to describe sampling distributions in which the null hypothesis is true. For each of these tables, you can quickly determine how large a difference you would expect to see in only one percent of samples, in five percent of samples, in ten percent of samples, etc. This makes it easy to tell the likelihood of a difference as large as the one you have.

The standard "rule of thumb" is that a difference so large that it would be seen in less than five percent of samples is large enough that it cannot be explained as due to sampling variability. In other words, if the probability of getting a difference this large is less than five percent ("$p < .05$"), you can reject the null hypothesis as a reasonable explanation for what you see.

Critical values

If you look at the table appropriate for the data you are examining, you can easily tell how large a difference you need to see before you would reject the null hypothesis. Before you do the actual analysis with your data, you go to the table and determine the size of the difference that is the *critical value*. If the difference in your data is smaller than the critical value, it means that the probability of getting a difference this large when $H_{\emptyset}$ is true is greater than five percent, so you fail to reject the null hypothesis. If the difference is larger than the critical value, it means that the probability of getting a difference this large when $H_{\emptyset}$ is true is less than five percent, so you reject the null hypothesis.

As you know, sampling distributions are theoretical distributions. There are so many possible samples from even relatively small populations that it is essentially impossible to construct an actual sampling distribution. Mathematicians have studied a variety of sampling distributions and you have access to their efforts in the form of a series of tables. You are already familiar with the most important of these, the table of areas under the normal curve. There are three other tables of "critical values" used in this book. (All of these tables are in Appendix B.)

- If you have a pair of *categorical* variables, you use Table 2, Critical Values of Chi Squared.[1]

- If you have one categorical variable that sorts cases into *two groups* and one *continuous* variable, and each group has *30 or more cases*, you use Table 1, Areas Under the Normal Curve and you perform a *z*-test for the difference between means.

- If there are two groups and one or both have *fewer than 30 cases*, you use Table 3, Critical Values of *t* and you perform a *t*-test for the difference between means.

- If there are *more than two groups*, you use Table 4, Critical Values of F and you perform an analysis of variance.

- If you have two *continuous* variables or two *ordinal* variables, you use Table 6, Critical Values of *r* and you perform a *t*-test for the significance of *r* or *rho*.

In all cases, if your measure of the size of the difference is larger than the appropriate entry in the table of critical values, you can reject the null hypothesis.

If you reject the null hypothesis . . .

When you reject $H_\emptyset$, you are saying that you conclude the difference is not due to sampling variability. Since you have rejected the null hypothesis, you must accept the alternative — the *alternate hypothesis* — which says that the difference between samples is due to a real difference in the population; the difference is just too large for sampling variability to be the cause. Most researchers are happy when they are able to reject the null hypothesis because it means that they have found a significant pattern (one that matters) in their data.

If you talk to researchers when they are in a thoughtful frame of mind, you might get them to talk about the bias against "negative findings." A negative finding is one in which the researcher fails to reject the null hypothesis — one in which the researcher concluded that the pattern in the data could well have been due to sampling variability. The bias against negative findings becomes apparent when you look at the published research reports in scholarly journals. It is unusual for a research report that contains only negative findings to be published. It's as if studies that result in negative findings are considered to be less informative or less important than those that result in statistically significant differences.

The next three chapters examine ways of testing null hypotheses. Chapter 16 presents the chi squared test that you use when you have a pair of categorical variables. Other tests for significance of the relationship between nominal and ordinal variables are described in Chapter 17. In Chapter 18 you will see the *z*-test for the difference between means — the test you use when you have one continuous variable and one categorical variable that divides your sample into two groups. Chapter 19 looks at tests you use when your samples are too small for the *z*-test or when you have more than two groups to be compared.

Important Terms and Concepts

alternate hypothesis

critical value

fail to reject the null hypothesis

negative finding

null hypothesis

reject the null hypothesis

sampling distribution

sampling variability

standard error

statistical significance

Type I error

Type II error

---

[1] "Chi," the Greek letter "χ," sounds like "ky" in "sky."

Chapter 16

CHI-SQUARED

Chapter 11 began with a discussion of some research on a new experimental wonder drug that is supposed to help people perform complex cognitive tasks, like take statistics exams. In that study, I divided a class of 80 students randomly into two groups, and I gave the people in one group a pill that contains the drug and the people in the other group a pill contained nothing, although it looked and tasted exactly the same. The table below (Table 5 on page 88) shows that most of the people (75%) who took the drug passed, while only half of the people (50%) who took the fake pill passed.

Drug use × Performance

count row% col%	Drug use		
	drug	no drug	totals
pass	30 60.0% **75.0%**	20 40.0% **50.0%**	50 62.5%
fail	10 33.3% **25.0%**	20 66.7% **50.0%**	30 37.5%
total	40 50.0%	40 50.0%	80 100.0%

Performance

It appears to be the case that the variables— taking or not taking the drug and passing or failing the statistics exam—are related to one another. But this could be a result of sampling variability. You will remember from Chapter 14 that the null hypothesis says that the variables are *not* related to one another. This is the hypothesis you must test. If you reject the null hypothesis, you will be left with the alternate, which says that the variables *are* related to one another.

Observed vs Expected

To test the null hypothesis, you compare what you see in your data with what you would expect to see if taking the drug has no effect passing or failing the test. It is this difference—the difference between what you *observe* in your data and what you would *expect* if the null hypothesis were true—that you are interested in.

Even if the row variable has no effect on the column variable, sampling variability will cause the observed numbers in the table to be somewhat different from what the null hypothesis would lead you to expect. However, if the row variable is related to the column variable, the differences between the observed and expected values will be larger.

You want to know *how large* is the difference between observed and expected, and you want to know whether or not a difference that large could be due to sampling variability. If the difference could be due to sampling variability, you would say that the row variable is not related to the column variable; that the drug has no effect. If the difference is so big that it couldn't be due to sampling variability, you would reject the null hypothesis and say that the row variable is related to the column variable; that taking or not taking the drug is related to passing or failing the exam—that the two variables are related; they are *not independent*. You want to determine whether or not the variables are independent.

observed	drug	no drug
pass	30	20
fail	10	20

How to Calculate the Expected Values

There are two ways to calculate the expecteds. For both, you need to add a few more numbers to the table. The marginal counts and percentages, often called "the marginals," have been added to the table below. You can see that 62.5% of all people passed the test and 50% took the drug.

The first way to calculate the expecteds uses the marginal percentages. If the drug had no effect, you would expect people who didn't take the drug to do just as well on the exam as the people who did take it. Since overall 62.5% passed, you would expect 62.5% of the people who took the drug to pass. Now, 62.5%

observed	drug	no drug	totals
pass	30	20	50 / 62.5%
fail	10	20	30 / 37.5%
total	40 / 50%	40 / 50%	80 / 100%

of 40 people is 25. You would also expect 62.5% of the people who didn't take the drug to pass. So you'd expect 25 drugged people and 25 non-drugged people to pass. Since there are 40 people in each condition, you would expect the rest, which is 40 - 25 = 15, to fail. Now you can fill in the expected values, which has been done in the table below.

expected	drug	no drug	totals
pass	25	25	50 / 62.5%
fail	= 15	15	30 / 37.5%
total	40 / 50%	40 / 50%	80 / 100%

The second method of calculating the expecteds is a bit more straightforward and is likely to result in slightly more accurate results because it reduces rounding error. To calculate the expecteds for the top left cell, multiply the number of cases in the top row by the number in the left column and divide the result by the total number in the table. Do the same for the rest of the table, each time multiplying the number of cases in the cell's column by the number in the cell's row and dividing the result by the table's total.

expected	drug	no drug	totals
pass	$\frac{50 \times 40}{80} = 25$	25	50
fail	15	15	30
total	40	40	80

Calculating Chi-squared

In the table below there are two numbers in each cell—the observed and the expected. This lets you see what is happening with the data. Looking in the "drug" column, you see there are 5 more people than

expected in the "pass" row and 5 people fewer than expected in the "fail" row. Looking in the "no drug" column, you see there are 5 fewer people than expected in the "pass" row and 5 more than expected in the "fail" row.

observed [expected]	drug	no drug	totals
pass	30 [25]	20 [25]	50 62.5%
fail	10 [15]	20 [15]	30 37.5%
total	40 50%	40 50%	80 100%

If you add up all the differences, you get an astounding number:

$$diff = \sum (obs - exp) = 5 + (-5) + 5 + (-5) = 0$$

A familiar problem: the positives exactly balance the negatives. We use a familiar solution: square the differences. This gives a different result: 100. But it turns out that just summing the squared differences isn't enough. To account for the fact that some columns or rows may have more than their even share of people, you divide each squared difference by the expected value for that cell. So the formula now looks like this:

$$diff = \sum \frac{(o - e)^2}{e} = \chi^2$$

The numbers for this equation are shown in the table below.

$\frac{(o-e)^2}{e}$	drug	no drug	totals
pass	$\frac{(30-25)^2}{25}$	$\frac{(20-25)^2}{25}$	50 62.5%
fail	$\frac{(10-15)^2}{15}$	$\frac{(20-15)^2}{15}$	30 37.5%
total	40 50%	40 50%	80 100%

The sum of the squared differences divided by expecteds is the overall measure of the difference between what is observed in the data and what you would expect to see if the null hypothesis is true. This measure is called "χ^2" or *chi-squared*.

With the data are plugged into the equation, you get this:

$$\frac{(30-25)^2}{25} + \frac{(20-25)^2}{25} + \frac{(10-15)^2}{15} + \frac{(20-15)^2}{15} =$$

$$\frac{(5)^2}{25} + \frac{(-5)^2}{25} + \frac{(-5)^2}{15} + \frac{(5)^2}{15} = 5.33\overline{3}$$

Each cell contributes something to the total value. For example, you expected 25 people in the "drug-pass" cell but you see 30 people there. The difference is 5. You square the difference and divide by the expected and get 25/25 = 1.0, which is that cell's contribution to chi-squared. The bigger the difference between observed and expected, the bigger the cell's contribution will be.

When you add the results from all the cells together, you get the final value for chi-square: 5.333.

How Big *Is* the Difference?

Now you need to know how to interpret a chi-square of 5.333. Is it a big one or a little one?

The expected frequencies are generally based on the assumption that the row variable is independent of the column variable. You may recognize that this assumption is the null hypothesis. Even if this assumption is true—if the row variable is independent of the column variable, and thus the expected frequencies accurately describe the population— there will still almost certainly be differences between the expected and observed values, although the differences aren't likely to be large. These differences, of course, are due to sampling variability. If, on the other hand, the row variable is *not* independent of the column variable, the expected frequencies will *not* describe the population you are studying, and the differences between observed and expected values will be larger. When you try to interpret the value you

get for chi-squared, you are trying to determine whether the differences are so small that they could be due to sampling variability, or whether they are so large that you cannot accept the expected values as a reasonable description of the population.

The more rows and columns you have, the bigger the overall value is likely to be, so it seems that the number of rows and columns should somehow be taken into account. It is. You calculate what are called *degrees of freedom* by multiplying the number of rows minus one times the number of columns minus one:

$$\begin{aligned} df &= (rows - 1) \times (cols - 1) \\ &= (2 - 1) \times (2 - 1) = 1 \end{aligned}$$

Now look up the value you get for *df* on Table 3, "Critical values of chi-square," a piece of which appears below. In the ***df*** column you find your value, which, for the above example, is "1." This will tell you which row of the table you will be using. Now move to the right across the columns until you find the first value that is larger than 5.3333, the result you got for chi-square. Since 5.3333 is larger than 3.841 and smaller than 5.412, you fall in between the **.05** and the **.02** columns.

df = 1, so use this row

Critical values of chi-squared

df	Probability				
	.1	**.05**	**.02**	**.01**	**.005**
1	2.706	3.841	5.412	6.635	7.879
2	4.605	5.991	7.824	9.210	10.597
3	6.251	7.815	9.837	11.345	12.838
4	7.779	9.488	11.668	13.277	14.860
5	9.236	11.070	13.388	15.086	16.750

When the expected frequencies are an accurate description of reality, i.e., when the null hypothesis is true, the probability of getting a difference between observed and expected as large as the one you see here (5.3333) is between .02 and .05 (2% and 5%). In other words, the probability of getting observed values that differ from the expected values as much as the ones in the example is between 2% and 5%. This is smaller than 5%, which is the ordinary cutoff point, so you would say that the apparent relation between taking the drug and doing well on the exam is not due to sampling variability; taking the drug *is* related to performance on the exam. This relationship is *statistically significant at* $p < 0.05$.

Something you have to remember here is that it isn't enough to calculate chi-square and look it up on the table. Doing this only tells you whether or not you can reject the null hypothesis—whether or not the row variable is related to the column variable. It does not tell you whether taking the drug improves or harms performance on the exam. To see which is the case, you have to perform either percentage across, compare down or percentage down, compare across to know what the relationship is.

Summary of the Procedure

These are the steps you follow to do a chi-squared test to determine whether or not a pair of categorical variables are related to one another:

- Your null hypothesis states that the row variable is independent of the column variable.
- The alternate hypothesis states that the row variable is not independent of the column variable.
- Calculate the expecteds, which are the numbers you would expect to see if the null hypothesis is true.
- Subtract each expected from the corresponding observed count.
- Square each difference and divide it by the expected for that cell.
- Add the results of the last step together. The number you get is chi-squared.
- Calculate degrees of freedom as (rows - 1) × (cols - 1) and use it to select a row in Table 3.
- Scan to the right in the row until you find the first number that is higher than your value of chi-squared. Read the probability in the top of this column and the one in the column to the left.

- The probability of getting a value of chi-square as large as the one you got is between these two probabilities. If this probability is less than .05, you can reject the null hypothesis and conclude that the row and column variables are not independent of one another.

A Canadian example

A referendum is held in Quebec. The question the voters will be asked is "Do you want to separate from the rest of Canada?" The government wants to know how people intend to vote so they can develop the appropriate advertising strategy. They ask a public opinion firm to do a poll. Voting intentions of a random sample of 4,000 voters are tabulated according to whether the voter is a Francophone (French speaker) or an Anglophone (English speaker), and whether the planned vote is "yes" or "no." The results are shown in the table above right.

Since the independent variable is Language (the variable that determines which row the person is in), it is appropriate to compare the *rows* in this table. That means "compare down," which is always combined with "percentage across." So, the correct way to read this table is: 64.7% of Francophones voted "yes," while only 44.9% of Anglophones voted "yes." You could also say "Francophones were more likely to vote yes (64.7%) than Anglophones (44.9%)."

count row% col%	Vote		totals
	yes	no	
French	1320 **64.7%** 60.0%	720 35.3% 40.0%	2040 51.0%
English	880 **44.9%** 40.0%	1080 55.1% 60.0%	1960 49.0%
total	2200 55.0%	1800 45.0%	4000 100.0%

The results of the poll seem to indicate that there is a clear relationship between the language a person speaks and how they intend to vote in the referendum. If you want to know whether this relationship is "real" or whether it could be due to sampling variability, you would perform a chi-square test.

The table below shows the observed values, the expected values, and the difference between the two in each cell.

obs exp obs-exp	Vote		totals
	yes	no	
French	1320 *1122* 198	720 *918* 198	2040 51.0%
English	880 *1078* 198	1080 *882* 198	1960 49.0%
total	2200 55.0%	1800 45.0%	4000 100.0%

To calculate chi-squared, it's necessary to square the difference between observed and expected, and then to divide by the expected. The table below shows the difference between observed and expected, the expected values, and the result of dividing the squared difference by the expected.

obs-exp exp (o-e)²/ exp	Vote		totals
	yes	no	
French	198 *1122* 34.94	198 *918* 42.71	2040 51.0%
English	198 *1078* 36.37	198 *882* 44.45	1960 49.0%
total	2200 55.0%	1800 45.0%	4000 100.0%

The sum of the results of the squaring and dividing is shown here:

$$34.94 + 42.71 + 36.37 + 44.45 = 158.52$$

There is one degree of freedom for this cross-tabulation, so you look at the first row in the table of critical values of chi-square. You see that the value you got, 158.52, is much larger than the largest value in the first row, 10.828, so you would conclude that the probability of getting a difference (between observed and expected) this large is much less than 0.001. You must reject the null hypothesis, which says that there is no relation between language and voting intention.

In other words, knowing whether the person is an Anglophone or a Francophone tells you a lot about how the person plans to vote in the referendum, and this pattern is not likely to be due to sampling variability. Francophones are more likely to vote yes (64.7%) than Anglophones (44.9%), so advertising should be directed at the Francophones.

An American example

A referendum is held in California to determine whether English should be made the official language. Voting intentions of a random sample of 2,000 voters are tabulated according to whether the first language of the voter was Spanish or English, and whether the stated choice was "yes," "refused to answer," or "no." The results are shown in the table below.

	count row% col%	**Language** Spanish	 English	totals
Vote	yes	478 48.58% 38.70%	506 51.42% 39.72%	984 39.22%
	refused	215 42.24% 17.41%	294 57.76% 23.08%	509 20.29%
	no	542 53.35% **43.89%**	474 46.65% **37.21%**	1016 40.49%
	total	1235 49.22%	1274 50.78%	2509 100.0%

Since the independent variable is language (the variable that determines which column the person is in), it is appropriate to compare the *columns* in this table. That means "compare across," which is always combined with "percentage down." So, the correct way to read this table is:

- 43.89% of Spanish speakers say they will vote "no," compared to only 37.21% of English speakers.
- Furthermore, 17.41% of Spanish speakers refused to answer, compared to 23.08% of English speakers.
- Almost the same proportions of both linguistic groups (38.7% for Spanish and 39.72% for English) said they would vote "yes."

You could also say "speakers of Spanish are more likely to vote "no" (53.14%) than speakers of English (48.37%), while English-speaking respondents were more likely to refuse to answer (17.41%) compared to Spanish-speaking respondents."

As you can see, this table is more complicated to interpret than the one for the Canadian example because there are three rows instead of two. It would be fair to say that there are two findings in this table. First, more Spanish-speaking respondents intend to vote against the proposition; second, more English speaking individuals refused to answer the question. It is easy to understand the first finding, but the second one leads to another research question: why do more English-speaking individuals refuse to answer this question?

The results of the poll seem to indicate that there is a relationship between the language a person speaks and both how they intend to vote in the referendum and whether they are willing to answer the question.

If you want to know whether this apparent relationship reflects a pattern in the population or could simply be due to sampling variability, you would perform a chi-square test.

The following table shows the observed values, the expected values, and the difference between the two in each cell.

To calculate chi-squared, it's necessary to square the difference between observed and expected, and

obs *exp* **obs-exp**	Language		totals
	Spanish	English	
	542	**474**	**1016**
yes	*500.10*	*515.90*	40.49%
	41.90	**-41.90**	
refused	**215**	**294**	**509**
	250.54	*258.46*	20.29%
	-35.54	**35.54**	
no	**478**	**506**	**984**
	484.35	*499.65*	39.22%
	-6.35	**6.35**	
total	**1235**	**1274**	**2509**
	49.22%	50.78%	100.0%

Vote (row label)

then to divide by the expected. The table below shows the difference between observed and expected, the squared difference, and the result of dividing by the expected. The sum of the results of the squaring and dividing is shown here:

$$3.511 + 3.403 + 5.041 + 4.887 + 0.083 + 0.081 = 16.259$$

Because this table has three rows and two columns, there are two degrees of freedom for this crosstabulation. Therefore, you look at the *second* row in the table of critical values of chi-square. The value you got, 16.259, is to the right of the largest entry in the row—10.597, so you would conclude that

obs *exp* **(o-e)²/e**	Language		totals
	Spanish	English	
	542	**474**	**1016**
yes	*500.10*	*515.90*	40.49%
	3.511	**3.403**	
refused	**215**	**294**	**509**
	250.54	*258.46*	20.29%
	5.041	**4.887**	
no	**478**	**506**	**984**
	484.35	*499.65*	39.22%
	0.083	**0.081**	
total	**1235**	**1274**	**2509**
	49.22%	50.78%	100.0%

Vote (row label)

the probability of getting a difference (between observed and expected) this large is less than 0.005, which is one half of one percent. In other words, if there is no relationship between the language a person speaks and how the person responds to the question about voting intentions, the probability of getting a difference this large is less than 0.005%.

Critical values of chi-squared

df	Probability				
	.1	.05	.02	.01	.005
1	2.706	3.841	5.412	6.635	7.879
2	4.605	5.991	7.824	9.210	10.597
3	6.251	7.815	9.837	11.345	12.838
4	7.779	9.488	11.668	13.277	14.860
5	9.236	11.070	13.388	15.086	16.750
6	10.645	12.592	15.033	16.812	18.548
7	12.017	14.067	16.622	18.475	20.278
8	13.362	15.507	18.168	20.090	21.955

Because the probability of getting a chi-square this large is less than 0.5%, you would reject the null hypothesis, which says that there is no relation between language and stated voting intention.

Percentage down, compare across tells you that speakers of Spanish are more likely to vote "no" (43.89%) than speakers of English (37.21%) and English-speaking respondents were more likely to refuse to answer (17.41%) than Spanish-speaking respondents. As you can see by looking at the lower table on the left, the largest contributions to chi-squared come from the "refused to answer" row, since the largest numbers for (o-e)²/e (5.041 and 4.887) are in this row. Whether the respondent refused to answer the question or not accounts for more of chi-squared than whether the respondent intended to vote "yes" or "no." If you wanted to, you could combine the "yes" and "no" responses into a single row and create a new table that would compare those who answered with those who did not answer, in terms of language spoken. This would give you a better understanding of the data.

Important Terms and Concepts

cell's contribution to chi-squared

Chi-squared—χ^2

counts

column percents

critical value of chi square

cross tabulation

degrees of freedom

expected values

frequencies

independence of row and column variables

marginals

marginal percentages

observed and expected

percentage across, compare down

percentage down, compare across

row percents

Things to think about .....

The expecteds are calculated on the basis of a certain assumption. What is that assumption ordinarily called? (i.e. what is the ordinary name of that assumption?)

Why does it make sense to make this assumption when you are calculating the expecteds?

Chapter 17

Z-TEST FOR DIFFERENCES BETWEEN MEANS

The situation: You are hired by a market research company to find out whether men drink more or less coffee than women. So you get a sample of adults from the city you live in and you record their sex and how much coffee they drink in a typical day. To compare the men to the women, you calculate the mean amount of coffee consumed per day by men and the mean amount consumed by women. When you compare the two, you see they are not the same: the mean for men was 4.1 and the mean for women was 3.85 cups.

You want to know whether:

a) the difference between the two is so small that it could be due to sampling variability, which would mean that the men *in your sample* may drink more than the women *in your sample*, but that men and women *in general* drink the same amount of coffee. This is the *null hypothesis* — the hypothesis that there is no real difference in the population, that the difference you see between the means is due to sampling variability.

Or, could it be the case that . . .

b) the difference is so large that it is extremely unlikely that you would get a differ-ence this large between men and women unless men *in general* drink more coffee than women *in general*. This is the *alternate* or *research hypothesis*, the hypothesis that the difference you see between your means is due to a differ-ence between men and women *in general*, and not to sampling variability.

In other words, can you generalize your findings to the population represented by your sample, or must you conclude that they could be due to sam-pling variability? In still other words, *is the difference statistically significant?*

Hypotheses about Differences

Working with hypotheses is a bit like working with the legal system. When someone is accused of a crime and goes on trial, it is assumed that the person is innocent until proven guilty. The lawyer for the defense argues that the defendant is innocent and the lawyer for the prosecution argues that the defendant is guilty. The point of the trial is to determine which of these arguments is correct. This is done by examin-ing the evidence brought before the court to see if it is consistent with the claim of innocence. If it is found that the evidence isn't consistent with the claim of

innocence, that claim is rejected and the person is convicted.

When you are comparing the means of two groups, you can have two kinds of hypotheses.

The first is called the **Null Hypothesis**. The null hypothesis generally says "there is no difference" or "there is nothing happening here" or "there is no relation between what group you are in and your score on the variable." This hypothesis is like the defendant's claim of innocence. If the null hypothesis is true, any differences you see between the means must be due to sampling variability. This is like the defendant's explanation for how the evidence doesn't prove his guilt; he says "it proves nothing; it's just a coincidence."

In the example used in the opening paragraph of

this chapter, the null hypothesis would be "in general, men and women drink the same amount of coffee" or "*there is no difference* between how much coffee men and women drink" or, formally, "$\mu_m = \mu_f$" Any difference you see between sample means proves nothing; it's due to sampling variability (it's just a coincidence).

The symbol for the null hypothesis is $H_\emptyset$. That's an "H" with a subscript of "∅." The "∅" is the "null" or "nothing" symbol.

The second kind of hypothesis is the **Alternate** or **Research Hypothesis**. The alternate hypothesis generally says "there is a difference" or "there is something happening" or "there is a relation between what group you are in and your score on the variable." The alternate hypothesis is like the prosecutor's

---

1. *re: statistically significant differences*

- *"The difference between the two means is statistically significant."*
- "The difference is real."
- "A difference this large couldn't be due to chance alone."
- "A difference this large couldn't be due to sampling variability."
- "A difference this large couldn't be just a fluke or a coincidence."
- "The samples couldn't have come from the same population."
- "The probability of getting a difference this large when the samples come from the same population is so small that we can't believe they came from the same population."
- "The probability of getting a difference this large when the samples come from the same population is so small that we must reject the null hypothesis."
- "We reject the null hypothesis."
- "p < .05" (or "p < .01")

These are ways of saying that the samples are so different that you must assume the populations they came from are also different. In this case, men and women in general don't drink the same amount of coffee. The "p" in the last line is the probability of getting a difference this large or larger due to sampling variability alone.

2. *re: differences that aren't statistically significant*

- *"The difference between means is not statistically significant."*
- "This difference could easily be due to chance alone."
- "This difference could easily be due to sampling variability alone."
- "This difference could just be a fluke or a coincidence."
- "We got a difference because we just happened to get odd samples."
- "There's no reason to think the samples didn't come from the same population."
- "We could easily get a difference this small if we were drawing samples from the same population."
- "The probability of getting a difference this large when the samples come from the same population is so high that we can easily believe they came from the same population."
- "The probability of getting a difference this large when the samples come from the same population is so high that we can't reject the null hypothesis."
- "There really is no difference between these samples."
- "We *fail to reject* the null hypothesis."
- "p > .05" (or "p < .1")

These are ways of saying that the difference between the samples is so small that you must assume they come from the same population.

argument that the defendant is guilty and that the evidence is not "just a coincidence"; it is not consistent with the claim of innocence and it shows that the defendant's claim of innocence is untrue.

If the null hypothesis is false, the alternate hypothesis must be true. So, if the null hypothesis, which says "there is no difference" is found to be false, it must be the case that there is a difference.

In the example above, the alternate hypothesis would be "men and women *do not* drink the same amount of coffee" or "*there is a difference* between how much coffee men and women drink" or "sex is related to coffee consumption." You would say that differences between sample means are due to differences between the samples' populations.

The symbol for the alternate hypothesis is H_{ALT}. That's an "H" with a subscript of "ALT." It's called the "alternate" hypothesis because it is the alternative to the null hypothesis. If the null hypothesis is false, then whatever is left over (the alternate) must be true.

The contest is between two competing explanations for the differences between sample means: 1) sampling variability, or 2) differences between the samples' parent populations. The null hypothesis always blames the difference on sampling variability. The alternate hypothesis says that sampling variability is not the cause of the difference: the difference between the sample means is due to a "real" difference between population means.

The mean amounts of coffee in the sample for men and women in the example at the beginning of this chapter were 4.10 and 3.85 cups. The difference is 4.10 - 3.85 = 0.25, or one fourth of a cup. You want to know if this difference is big enough to convince you that men and women in general don't drink the same amount. You thus want to know if the null hypothesis could be true — if a difference this big could be due to sampling variability. In other words, you want to know if this difference is just a coincidence (you just happened to get a pair of samples in which the men drank more than the women). So you would like to know how likely you are to get a difference this large if you draw pairs of random samples from a single population.

To test the null hypothesis, you ask the question: "What are the chances of getting a difference as big as the one you have if the null hypothesis is true?" If the chances are less than 5%, you conclude that the null hypothesis isn't a reasonable explanation for your results, and you reject it. In doing this you are saying that you conclude the difference is not due to sampling variability. Since you have rejected the null hypothesis, you must accept the alternative — the alternate hypothesis — which says that the difference between samples is due to a real difference between two populations.

With the coffee example, you assess the chances that a difference between the means of two samples drawn from a single population could be as large as the difference you found between the means in your sample data. If this probability is less than 5%, you will say that you reject the null hypothesis as a reasonable explanation for the difference; the difference is just too large for sampling variability to be the cause.

You could draw pairs of random samples from a population and record the difference between the means of each pair. An examination of this list of differences would give you an idea of how much variability there is from one pair to another. If you took all possible pairs, you would have the *sampling distribution of differences between sample means*. Like many other sampling distributions, this one is a normal distribution. Its mean is zero (0.00), and its standard deviation is the *standard error of the difference between sample means* (SEDBM), $\sigma_{\bar{x}_1 - \bar{x}_2}$. About 95% of pairs of samples randomly drawn from the same population will have differences which fall between -1.96 and 1.96 SEDBM.

You can use this information to determine how likely it is that your two samples (men and women) came from the same population (as far as coffee consumption is concerned). If the difference between their means, which you calculated up above to be 0.25 cups, is less than 1.96 standard errors, you would conclude that the difference is so small that it could be a result of sampling variability. If the difference is greater than 1.96 standard errors, you would conclude that it is too big to be due to sampling

variability, and must be due to differences between the two populations (men and women).

Let's say you have computed the SEDBM, and let's say that it is 0.10. If you compare your observed difference of 0.25 cups to the SEDBM, you get a z of 0.25/0.10 = 2.50. This puts you in the region *outside* ±1.96, so you know that fewer than 5% of all differences between pairs of random samples drawn from the same population would be larger than this. In other words, a difference between means as large as this one would happen less than 5% of the time if you were drawing pairs of samples from a single population.

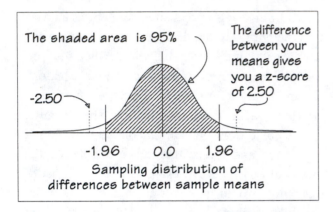

You can say, with 95% confidence, that these results show that men and women do not drink the same amount of coffee. The words you would use would probably be these:

"The mean coffee consumption of men and women in my samples were 4.1 and 3.85, respectively. This difference is statistically significant, with p < .05."

You can see, however, that the z of 2.5 is not in the region outside ±2.58, so you know that more than 1% of all differences (between pairs of samples drawn randomly from a single population) are larger than this, which means that your confidence level would be between 95% and 99%.

You have just performed a "z-test" for the difference between two means. With a z-test, you are asking whether the difference between two means is small enough that it could be due to sampling vari-

ability or whether it is so large that sampling variability isn't an adequate explanation.

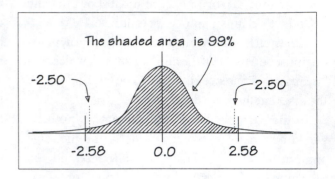

One or two tails?

There are two kinds of z-tests: *one-tailed* and *two-tailed*. If your research question is:

"Do men and women drink the same amount of coffee?"

you would take a different approach than you would take if it is either:

"Do men drink more coffee than women?"

or

"Do women drink more coffee than men?"

The difference is that the first question doesn't specify the *direction* of the difference; it only asks if the two groups drink the same amount or a different amount. The second and third questions specify the direction of the difference: men drink more, or men drink less.

When you don't have any reason to expect one group's mean to be higher than the other's (when you just expect them to be different, but you don't know which will be higher) you should use an *undirected* hypothesis. An example of an undirected hypothesis for men and women and coffee consumption is:

"The mean coffee consumption of men is not the same as that of women" or "$\mu_m \neq \mu_f$"

The corresponding null hypothesis is:

"The mean coffee consumption of men is the same as the mean consumption of women" or "$\mu_m = \mu_f$"

The research hypothesis says "there is a difference," but doesn't say what direction the difference will go. The null hypothesis says "there is no difference."

Whenever you have a theoretical or conceptual reason to expect one group's mean to be higher than the other group's mean, you should use a *directed* hypothesis. An example for coffee consumption would be "The mean coffee consumption of men is *higher* than the mean coffee consumption of women" or "$\mu_m > \mu_f$." The corresponding null hypothesis is "The mean coffee consumption of men is *not higher* than that of women" or "$\mu_m \leq \mu_f$."

(Note that the null hypothesis here is *not* "The mean coffee consumption of men is *lower* than that of women." Why? Because if the mean for men is "not higher" than the mean for women, it could be either *the same as* or *lower than* the mean for women.)

The direction — or lack thereof — will be reflected in how you decide whether or not a difference is significant.

The two following pictures show the difference between how you use the normal curve for a one-tailed and a two-tailed test. In both drawings the *un*shaded part is the *critical region*. If z falls into this area, you would conclude that the difference between the means is too large to be due solely to sampling variability.

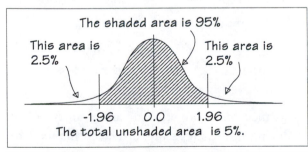

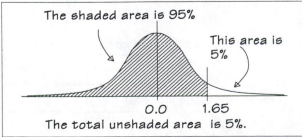

In the upper drawing, the critical value of z, the value of z beyond which the difference is significant, is ± 1.96, which means that z must be below -1.96 *or* above 1.96 to be in the unshaded area. The z-test you would do here is a "two-tailed" test because the critical region includes the parts at *both ends* of the distribution. In the lower drawing, the critical value is 1.65 and the unshaded area is on the right side, which means that z has to be above 1.65 to be in the critical region. Here you would do a "one-tailed" test because the critical region includes the part at *only one end* of the distribution.

Undirected hypotheses

For the undirected hypothesis that says "there is a difference between the two means," the difference, which is calculated by subtracting the second mean from the first one, may be either positive or negative and still be relevant. With the coffee example, if the alternate hypothesis is "men do not drink the same amount of coffee as women," you are asking "is there a difference between how much the men drink and how much the women drink?" The answer is "no" if they drink the same amount and "yes" if either the men drink more or the women drink more.

Directed hypotheses

For the directed hypothesis the direction of the difference does matter. For the hypothesis that says "the first mean is larger than the second one," the only condition that really matters is that subtracting the second mean from the first results in a positive value. For the coffee example, if the alternate hypothesis is "men drink more coffee than women," you are asking "do the men drink more than the women?" The answer is "no" if they drink the same amount as the women *or if the women drink more.*

Common critical values of z

If you are using the 95% confidence level, for a 2-tailed test you need a z below -1.96 or above 1.96 before you say the difference is significant. For a 1-tailed test, you need a z greater than 1.65. If you are

using a 99% confidence level and a 2-tailed test, you need a z below -2.58 or above 2.58. For a 1-tailed test you need a z above 2.33. The table below summarizes these numbers. It's a good idea to memorize these four critical values of z.

Common Critical Values of z

confidence	1-tailed	2-tailed
95%	1.65	± 1.96
99%	2.33	± 2.58

Examples

The situation: You do a study of study methods of university students and you want to compare the men with the women. You get a random sample of 120 students. For each student you have the following information: age, sex, number of credits completed, preferred study method, time spent studying per week, CGPA, and GPA. The variables are coded as follows:

- **Age**: years, accurate to two places to the right of the decimal.

- **Sex**: Male or Female.

- **Number of credits**: the actual number of credits completed.

- **Preferred study method**: Method A (solitary study in library), Method B (study in pub with friends), Method C (solitary study at home with TV on), or Method D (study in groups in empty classrooms).

- **Time spent studying per week**: the mean of the number of minutes spent studying in each of the last four weeks.

- **CGPA and GPA**: between 0.00 and 4.33 on the standard four-point GPA scale.

You want to determine the following:

1. **Are men more efficient than women?** (Efficiency is the ratio of grades to time spent studying. Someone who studies a short period of time and gets high grades is more efficient than someone who studies a long period of time and gets the same or lower grades.)

Here you will compute the means of the two groups and the difference between the means. You will then determine whether:

a) the difference between the samples is so small that it could be due to sampling variability, which would mean that the men *in your sample* may be more efficient than the women *in your sample*, but that men and women *in general* are equally efficient. This is the *null hypothesis* — the hypothesis that there is no real difference in the population, that the difference you see between the samples is due to sampling variability.

Or, could it be the case that . . .

b) it is extremely unlikely that you would get a difference this large between your samples unless men *in general* are more efficient than women *in general*. This is the *alternate* or *research hypothesis* — the hypothesis that the difference you see between your samples is due to a real difference between the populations, and not to sampling variability.

Here are your hypotheses:

$H_\emptyset$: men are not more efficient than women. (The mean efficiency scores of men are less than or equal to those of women.)

H_{ALT}: men are more efficient than women. (The mean efficiency scores of men are higher than those of women.)

Efficiency scores	men	women
mean	1.18	1.06
standard deviation	.45	.31
n	65	55

2. Is there a difference in the grades (CGPA) of older and younger students? ("Older" students are students older than 23. "Younger" students are students up to 23 years old.)

Here you will compute the means of the two groups and the difference between the means. You will then determine whether:

a) the difference between the sample means is so small that it could be due to sampling variability, which would mean that the older students *in your sample* may get higher (or lower) grades than the younger students *in your sample*, but that there is no difference between the grades of older and younger students *in general*. This is the *null hypothesis* — the hypothesis that there is no real difference in the population, that the difference you see due to sampling variability. Or, could it be that . .

b) it is unlikely that you would get a difference this large between your samples unless older students *in general* get higher (or lower) grades than younger students *in general*. This is the *alternate* or *research hypothesis* -- the hypothesis that the difference you see between the samples is due to a real difference between the populations, and not to sampling variability.

$H_{\emptyset}$: there is no difference between the grades of older and younger students. (The mean grades of older students are the same as those of younger students.)

H_{ALT}: the grades of older students are not the same as the grades of younger students. (The mean grades of older students are higher than or lower than those of younger students.)

CGPA	older	younger
mean	3.30	3.08
standard deviation	0.80	0.35
n	60	60

3. Do more experienced students (students who have completed more than 60 credits) get higher grades (CGPA) than less experienced students?

Here you will compute the means of the two groups and the difference between the means. You will then determine whether:

a) the difference between the samples is so small that it could be due to sampling variability, which would mean that more experienced students *in your sample* may get higher grades than less experienced students *in your sample*, but more experienced students *in general* do not have higher grades than less experienced students. The hypothesis that the difference you see in your sample is due to sampling variability and does not reflect a difference in the population is the *null hypothesis*. Or, could it be the case that . . .

b) it is unlikely you would get a difference this large between your samples unless more experienced students *in general* get higher grades than less experienced students *in general*. This is the *alternate* or *research hypothesis* — the hypothesis that the difference you see between your samples reflects a real difference between the populations and is not due to sampling variability.

$H_{\emptyset}$: the grades of more experienced students are not higher than the grades of less experienced students. (The mean grades of less experienced students are not lower than those of more experienced students.)

H_{ALT}: the grades of more experienced students are higher than the grades of less experienced students. (The mean grades of less experienced students are lower than those of more experienced students.)

CGPA	more exp'd	less exp'd
mean	2.91	3.37
standard deviation	0.51	0.72
n	65	55

Procedure

In all three cases you are asking whether you can generalize your findings to the population represented by your samples, or whether you must conclude that they could be due to sampling variability. In other words, *are the differences statistically significant?*

You do this assessment by comparing the differences between the sample means to the *sampling distribution of differences between sample means*, which is a normal distribution whose mean is zero (0.00), and whose standard deviation is $\sigma_{\bar{x}_1 - \bar{x}_2}$ (the standard error of the difference between sample means, SEDBM).

You estimate this standard error as follows:

$$\sigma_{\bar{x}_1 - \bar{x}_2} = \sqrt{\frac{s_1^2}{n_1} + \frac{s_2^2}{n_2}}$$

Here are the important pieces of information for the three examples:

Ex #	tails	$x_1 - x_2$	$\sigma_{\bar{x}_1 - \bar{x}_2}$	z
1	1	0.12	0.0697	1.7209
2	2	0.22	0.1127	1.951
3	1	0.46	0.1159	3.9698

1. Are men more efficient than women?

$H_\emptyset$: men are not more efficient than women

"$\mu_{men} \leq \mu_{women}$"

H_{ALT}: men are more efficient than women

"$\mu_{men} > \mu_{women}$"

Because the hypotheses contain reference to the direction of the difference, this one involves a 1-tailed test. Only 5% of the area lies to the right of 1.65 (the critical value of z). The difference is calculated by subtracting the mean efficiency of women from the mean efficiency of men. If H_{ALT} is true, this will result in a difference greater than zero. In a population where men are not more efficient than women, only 5% of differences between pairs of random samples will have z larger than 1.65.

Since the difference you see in the example has a z larger than 1.65, the null hypothesis (that the difference is due to sampling variability) is rejected. Differences this large are not likely to be due to sampling variability.

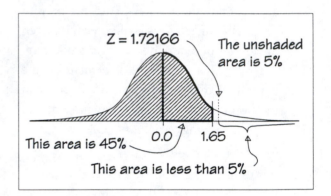

$$z = \frac{\bar{x}_{men} - \bar{x}_{women}}{SEDBM} = \frac{1.18 - 1.06}{.0697} = 1.72166$$

2. Is there a difference in the grades (CGPA) of older and younger students?

$H_\emptyset$: there is no difference between the grades of older and younger students.

"$\mu_{older} = \mu_{younger}$"

H_{ALT}: the grades of older students are not the same as the grades of younger students.

"$\mu_{older} \neq \mu_{younger}$"

The hypotheses here are not directed, so this example involves a 2-tailed test. The difference could be either positive or negative. For a confidence level of 95%, the critical value is ±1.96, so if z is larger than 1.96 or smaller than -1.96, you would reject the null hypothesis.

The z you get for this data is 1.951, which falls between the mean and the critical value. Although 1.951 is pretty close to 1.96, it is smaller, so you cannot reject the null hypothesis. Differences as large as this one are likely to be seen more than 5% of the time when the samples come from the same population, so you cannot reject sampling variability as the cause of the difference. You must conclude that the data are not inconsistent with the explanation that there is no difference between the grades of older and younger students.

samples drawn randomly from the same population. This is so seldom that you cannot consider sampling variability as the cause of the difference. The null hypothesis is strongly rejected, and the conclusion is clearly that the grades of more experienced students (in general) are higher than those of less experienced ones (in general).

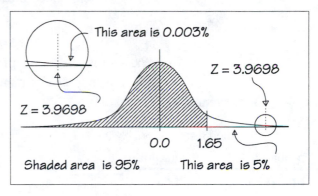

$$z = \frac{\bar{x}_{more} - \bar{x}_{less}}{SEDBM} = \frac{3.37 - 2.91}{.1159} = 3.9698$$

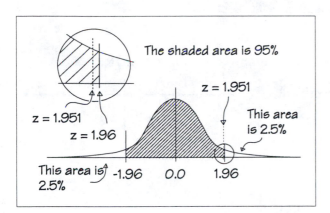

$$z = \frac{\bar{x}_{older} - \bar{x}_{younger}}{SEDBM} = \frac{3.3 - 3.08}{.1127} = 1.951$$

3. Do more experienced students get higher grades (CGPA) than less experienced students?

$H_\emptyset$: the grades of more experienced students are not higher than the grades of less experienced students.

"$\mu_{more\ experienced} \leq \mu_{less\ experienced}$"

H_{ALT}: the grades of more experienced students are higher than the grades of less experienced students.

"$\mu_{more\ experienced} > \mu_{less\ experienced}$"

The hypotheses here are directed, so a 1-tailed test is appropriate. The critical value is 1.65. The z you get for the data is 3.9698, which falls a long way beyond the critical value. Differences as large as this one would be seen about three times in 100,000 pairs of

Z-test for difference between means

1) Select a confidence level (90%, 95%, 99%, . . .)

↓

2) Calculate means, difference between means, standard deviations, standard error of the difference between means, and z-score of difference

↓

3) 1 - tailed or 2 - tailed ?

Does the question ask about the direction of the difference, or does it merely ask about the existence of a difference?

existence of difference   _direction_ of difference

2-tailed test

probability		critical value
.10	(90%)	± 1.65
.05	(95%)	±1.96
.01	(99%)	±2.58

4) Determine critical value of z

1-tailed test

probability		critical value
.10	(90%)	1.30
.05	(95%)	1.65
.01	(99%)	2.33

5) Compare _z to critical value_

If z is closer to 0.0 than the critical value, fail to reject the null hypothesis. The difference is not statistically significant; it could be due to sampling variability

If z is farther from 0.0 than the critical value, reject the null hypothesis. The difference is statistically significant; it is probably not due to sampling variability.

Important Terms and Concepts

alternate or research hypothesis
critical region
critical value
directed hypothesis
fail to reject the null hypothesis
null hypothesis
one-tailed test
reject the null hypothesis

sampling distribution of differences between sample means
standard error of the difference between sample means
statistically significant difference
$\sigma_{\bar{x}_1 - \bar{x}_2}$
two-tailed test
Type I error
Type II error
undirected hypothesis

Chapter 18

TESTS FOR CORRELATIONS

Significance of Pearson's r

You are a researcher investigating the relation between smoking and illness. From a random sample of 100 people, you have collected data on the number of cigarettes a person smokes per day and how many days of major or minor illness the person experiences in a year. You grind the data through the equation for Pearson's r and find a correlation of .38 between cigarettes per day and days of illness per year. You think this is important, but you have to determine whether the correlation you got could be due to sampling variability, while in the population represented by your sample, there is in fact no relation between smoking and illness.

If you have read Chapter 17, this probably sounds familiar to you. You see a pattern in your data that comes from a sample, and you want to know if that pattern describes the population or if it could be due to sampling variability. In other words, could the apparent pattern be the result of an odd sample? To answer this question, you need a method to determine whether the correlation for your sample is significantly different from zero.

The null and alternate hypotheses will be as follows:

$H_\emptyset$: the population r is zero

H_{ALT}: the population r is not zero

Because these hypotheses don't say anything about the direction of the difference between the sample and population correlations, they are not directed. The null hypothesis will be rejected if the sample correlation is large enough, regardless of its sign. These hypotheses call for a two-tailed test.

The approach you take here is similar to the one you took with the z-test for a single mean (pages 81-83). There is, however, a problem that has to be addressed first: the sampling distribution of Pearson's r isn't normal. In fact, it doesn't resemble any of the nicely behaved and well-understood sampling distributions that are available. It turns out, though, that the sampling distribution of the following transformation of r is normal with a variance of n - 2:

$$\frac{r}{\sqrt{1 - r^2}}$$

If you add the variance to the equation, you get a most useful number that you can use in a test of significance:

$$t = r \sqrt{(n - 2) / (1 - r^2)}$$

Under the null hypothesis which says that the population r is zero, this number distributes as t with $df = n - 2$. You can thus use Table 2 in Appendix B to evaluate it. If t is larger than the critical value, you reject the null hypothesis; if it is smaller, you fail to reject the null.

With the data from the example, you get the following:

$$t = r\sqrt{(n - 2)/(1 - r^2)}$$
$$= .38\sqrt{(100 - 2)/(1 - .38^2)}$$
$$= .38\sqrt{98/.867}$$
$$= 4.040$$

You look up this value on Table 2 with 98 degrees of freedom ($df = n - 2$) and see that it is larger than the highest value in the closest row of the table, 3.390. This indicates that the probability of getting a correlation as high as .38 for a sample taken from a population in which the correlation is zero is less than .001. In other words, the probability of getting a correlation this large when the null hypothesis is true is less than one in a thousand—so small that you reject the null hypothesis.

df	Level of significance for two-tailed test			
	.05	.01	.005	.001
80	1.990	2.639	2.887	3.416
90	1.987	2.632	2.878	3.402
100	1.984	2.626	2.871	3.390
110	1.982	2.621	2.865	3.381

You would conclude that there *is* a relation between smoking and illness in the population, that your correlation of .38 cannot be explained by sampling variability, and that the population correlation is not zero. You would say that your sample correlation of .38 is "statistically significant" or that it is "significantly greater than zero."

How to do it: To perform a t-test for the significance of a correlation, you:

1) note that you will be doing a 2-tailed test;

2) select your level of confidence (which will determine which column of the table you should use);

3) compute the degrees of freedom, to see which row of the table you should use ($df = n - 2$) ;

4) determine what the critical value of t will be with the aid of the table of critical values of t;

5) calculate t: $\quad t = r\sqrt{(n - 2)/(1 - r^2)}$

6) compare your value of t to the critical value determined in step 4. If your value is larger than the critical value, you reject the null hypothesis; if it isn't, you fail to reject..

Difference Between Two rs

Like most researchers, you are excited by the results of the test that allowed you to reject the null hypothesis. Since your ordinary day-to-day life is boring in comparison to your life as a researcher, you decide to take your research on smoking and illness one step further. If you are a fan of Emeril the TV chef, you might say "let's kick it up a notch!" So you add a second variable to the picture: sex. You collect data from another sample, using the same method in the previous study, except you also ask your respondents to indicate their sex. Now you calculate separate correlations for men and women.

Correlation between smoking and illness

	Males	Females
r	0.45	0.24
n	95	90

On the basis of your sample data, it appears to be the case that the correlation between smoking and illness is stronger for men than it is for women. The question you need to ask is whether this difference could be due to sampling variability or not. In other words, is it possible that there is no difference between men and women in general, in terms of the association between smoking and illness? What is the

probability of getting a difference as large as the one you see when there is no difference between men and women in general?

Your hypotheses would be:

$$H_\emptyset: \; r_1 = r_2$$

$$H_{ALT}: \; r_1 \neq r_2$$

Because they refer only to the existence of a difference and not the direction of a difference, you would do a two-tailed test. The 95% significance level will be used for the example.

The problem with the sampling distribution of r were mentioned above. A different transformation of r is used here: *Fisher's r to Z*. Each of your correlations must be converted according to:

$$Z = \frac{1}{2} \ln \left[\frac{1 + r}{1 - r} \right]$$

To make things a bit easier, I have included a table of Fisher's r to Z as Table 5 in Appendix B. This table is easy to use. Just find your r value and read the value of Z to its right. If your correlation is negative, ignore the sign when using Table 5, and put a minus sign in front of the value of Z you get from the table. The values of Z for the correlations in the example are shown below.

Correlation between smoking and illness

	Males	Females
r	0.45	0.24
n	95	90
Z	0.485	0.245

*Note that the Z you get from Table 5 is **not** an ordinary z-score. It is **not** a standard score (a measure of how far a score is away from a mean). It can only be used for correlations.*

Two qualities of Z produced by Fisher's transformation are particularly useful here. First, unlike the sampling distribution of Pearson's r, the shape of the distribution produced by Z is *not* affected by the

population correlation. Second, Z is so close to being normal that it can be treated as if it were normal with very little loss of accuracy.[1] The *standard error of Z* is:

$$\sigma_Z = \frac{1}{\sqrt{n - 3}}$$

To test the significance of the difference between a pair of correlations, you convert them to Zs and test the significance of the difference between the Zs. To do this, you use the *standard error of the difference between two Zs*,

$$\sigma_{Z_1 - Z_2} = \sqrt{\frac{1}{n_1 - 3} + \frac{1}{n_2 - 3}}$$

the same way you use the standard error of the difference between two means in a z-test for the difference between means. That is, you divide the difference between two Zs by the standard error of the difference:

$$z = \frac{Z_1 - Z_2}{\sigma_{Z_1 - Z_2}}$$

For the data in the example, the standard error is:

$$\sigma_{Z_1 - Z_2} = \sqrt{\frac{1}{n_1 - 3} + \frac{1}{n_2 - 3}}$$

$$= \sqrt{\frac{1}{92} + \frac{1}{87}}$$

$$= 0.1495$$

and, finally, z is:

$$z = \frac{Z_1 - Z_2}{\sigma_{Z_1 - Z_2}} = \frac{0.485 - 0.245}{.1495} = 1.605$$

For a two-tailed z-test at 95% confidence, the critical value of z is 1.96 (see page 136). Because the obtained value, 1.605, is smaller than the critical

---

[1] McNemar, 1969, p.157.

value, you fail to reject the null hypothesis. In other words, the difference between the sample correlations is so small that it could easily be due to sampling variability alone. It is easily possible to get a difference as large as the one you see here when you draw a pair of samples from a single population. Your evidence isn't strong enough to convince you that men in general differ from women in general in terms of the association between smoking and illness.

How to do it: To perform a z-test for the differences between two correlations, you:

1) decide whether you should do a 1- or 2-tailed test;

2) select your level of confidence;

3) determine what the critical value of z will be with the aid of Table 1 (areas under the normal curve);

4) use Table 5 to transform r to Z;

5) compute the difference between your Zs;

6) compute the standard error of the difference between two Zs:

$$\sigma_{Z_1 - Z_2} = \sqrt{\frac{1}{n_1 - 3} + \frac{1}{n_2 - 3}}$$

7) divide the difference by the standard error, which gives you a z for the difference:

$$z = \frac{Z_1 - Z_2}{\sigma_{Z_1 - Z_2}}$$

8) look on the table to see if your value of z is larger than the critical value determined by your level of confidence.

Significance of Spearman's *rho*

You are interested in the television viewing habits of university students. You are working with a theory that leads you to expect that people will prefer to watch programs that are more visually complex than those that present a simpler visual image.

Visual complexity is a combination of several factors including the number of objects visible in a typical image, the rate at which objects are moving, the number of camera angles used, the extent to which the camera itself is moving rather than remaining static, the amount and number of bright colors visible at any given time, and the degree of contrast between objects visible on the screen.

You randomly choose a week in February to collect your data. You examine the Neilson rating statistics for television programs regularly broadcasted by the major networks (excluding movies, news, and weather reports) between the hours of 7 PM and 11 PM. From the audience statistics for the chosen week you identify the 30 programs with the largest audiences and rank them in increasing order. Then you have several carefully trained judges rate the visual complexity of these 30 programs.

You now have two variables—the rank of the programs in terms of audience size and the visual complexity ratings provided by the trained judges. Because these are ordinal variables, the appropriate measure of the strength of their association is Spearman's rho (r_s). You calculate r_s for your data and obtain a correlation of 0.367.

You think this finding supports your theory, but you have to determine whether the correlation could be due to sampling variability, while in the population represented by your sample, there is in fact no relation between visual complexity and viewing preference. To answer this question, you perform a t-test to determine whether the correlation for your sample is significantly different from zero. In fact, the test you use here is exactly the same one that you would use for Pearson's r.

The null and alternate hypotheses are:

$H_{\emptyset}$: the population r_s is zero

H_{ALT}: the population r_s is not zero

Because they are not directed hypotheses, you will use a two-tailed test. The procedures are the same as

for Pearson's *r*. You use the same equations, the same tables, and the same method of interpreting your results.

$$t = r \sqrt{(n-2) / (1-r^2)}$$

$$= .367 \sqrt{(30-2)/(1-.367^2)}$$

$$= .367 \sqrt{28 / .865}$$

$$= 2.088$$

From Table 2, you see that the critical value of *t* is 2.048 at the 95% level of confidence and with 28 degrees of freedom. The value you obtained, 2.088, is larger than the critical value, so you can reject the null hypothesis. In plain english, the probability of getting a value of *t* (and thus of r_s) this large when $H_\emptyset$ is true is less than 5%. In other words, it's very unlikely that you would get a correlation as high as the one you got unless people prefer to watch programs that are more visually complex than those that present a simpler visual image.

	Level of significance for two-tailed test			
df	.05	.01	.005	.001
25	2.060	2.787	3.078	3.725
26	2.056	2.779	3.067	3.707
27	2.052	2.771	3.057	3.690
28	2.048	2.763	3.047	3.674
29	2.045	2.756	3.038	3.659
30	2.042	2.750	3.030	3.646

How to do it: To perform a *t*-test for the significance of a rho, follow the steps for Pearson's *r* on page 146.

Difference Between Two *rho*s

Once again, your good luck with your data spurs you on to greater efforts. Thinking that data on television viewing in the middle of February might be influenced by the dismal weather at that time of the year, you decide to repeat the same measurements in August to see if your finding holds for the middle of the summer as well as the middle of the winter.

	February	August
n	30	30
r_s	0.365	0.115

Your hypotheses would be:

$$H_\emptyset: \ rho_{feb} = rho_{aug}$$

$$H_{ALT}: \ rho_{feb} \neq rho_{aug}$$

The procedure you use here is the same as the one you would use to test the significance of the difference between two Pearson *r*'s. Because the hypotheses are not directed, a two-tailed test is appropriate. For the 95% confidence level, the critical value of *z* is ±1.96. With Table 5 (*r* to *Z*) you convert 0.365 and 0.115 to 0.383 and 0.116. The standard error of the difference between two *Z*s is:

$$\sigma_{Z_1-Z_2} = \sqrt{\frac{1}{n_1-3} + \frac{1}{n_2-3}}$$

$$= \sqrt{\frac{1}{30-3} + \frac{1}{30-3}}$$

$$= 0.2722$$

Now divide the difference by the standard error, which gives you a *z* for the difference:

$$z = \frac{Z_1 - Z_2}{\sigma_{Z_1-Z_2}}$$

$$= \frac{0.383 - 0.116}{.2722}$$

$$= 0.9809$$

Because the obtained *z*, 0.9809, is smaller than the critical value, you fail to reject the null hypothesis. The difference you see between the two Spearman rhos could easily be due to sampling variability. Your

findings do not demonstrate that the strength of the association between viewing preference and visual complexity varies from February to August.

How to do it: To perform a z-test for the difference between two *rhos*, follow the steps for the difference between two Pearson's r on page 148.

Important Terms and Concepts

Fisher's r to Z transformation

Pearson's r

Spearman's *rho*

standard error of the difference between two Zs

standard error of Z

t-test for the significance of a correlation

z-test for the difference between two correlations

Chapter 19

Mᴏʀᴇ ᴍᴇᴀɴ ᴅɪꜰꜰᴇʀᴇɴᴄᴇꜱ: *z, t,* ᴀɴᴅ *F*

Critical Ratios

If you find that the mean age of the males in a random sample of students was 23.6 and the mean age of females was 22.1, you might want to determine whether it would be fair to conclude that, in general, male students are older than female students. To do this, you would use the *z*-test for the difference between two means with which you are now familiar. You use a *z*-test when you have the means of two samples and you want to know whether the difference could be due to sampling variability. The test uses a standard error to determine how large the difference between the means is:

$$size = z = \frac{difference\ between\ means}{standard\ error\ of\ the\ difference\ between\ means} = \frac{\bar{x}_1 - \bar{x}_2}{\sigma_{\bar{x}_1 - \bar{x}_2}}$$

This kind of procedure — dividing a statistic by the standard error of the statistic — is at the center of many of the tests you use to make inferences about populations. The fraction you get when you perform this division is sometimes called the *critical ratio*. It's

a *ratio* because it involves a division; it's the *critical ratio* because it's the value you compare with the critical value to determine whether you should reject the null hypothesis.

$$\frac{statistic}{standard\ error\ of\ the\ statistic}$$

The *z*-test compares the difference between two means to the standard error of the difference between two means to give you a measure of how large the difference is. If it is large enough, you conclude that it can not be explained by sampling variability alone; that it is a "real" difference that reflects differences between the populations from which the samples were drawn.

If you found a correlation of .35 between amount of coffee consumed and age for male students in your sample and a correlation of .21 for female students, you might want to know whether you can conclude that, in general, the correlation between coffee consumption and age is stronger for males than for females. You convert the *r*s into *Z*s and divide the difference by the appropriate standard error:

$$size = z = \frac{\text{difference between two Zs}}{\begin{array}{c}\text{standard error of the}\\\text{difference between two Zs}\end{array}} = \frac{Z_1 - Z_2}{\sigma_{z_1 - z_2}}$$

In a way similar to the *z*-test, you could compare the difference between the transformed correlations to the standard error of the difference between the transformed correlation to determine whether the difference could be due to sampling variability, or whether it is so large that it must be a reflection of a "real" difference between the correlations in the population.

Variance Accounted for

In general, you are interested in knowing how your variables are related to one another. If they are completely unrelated, you have a set of unrelated bits of information, and your data doesn't help explain or understand anything. If the variables are related to one another, you may be able to develop an understanding of what is happening. If you know the value of one variable, you may be able to predict the value of the other one or at least narrow down the range of possibilities. The PRE (proportionate reduction of error) approach used by lambda, Yule's Q, and gamma takes precisely this approach (Chapter 12). For interval or ratio scaled data, you use a closely related approach that examines the amount of variance shared by a pair of variables. When you know that two variables overlap in terms of their variance, you say that one variable *accounts for* some of the variance in the other variable. You also say that you have *explained* some of the variance in one of the variables. The stronger the association between the variables, the more variance will be accounted for by the relationship.

One of the particularly nice things about Pearson's *r* is that it tells how much of the variability in one variable is accounted for by variability in the other one. The way you do this is simple: square the correlation. If the correlation is .6, the variance accounted for is .6 × .6 = .36, or 36%. (You will encounter the term "r-squared" from time to time in statistics. It generally means "the amount of variance accounted for.")

For example, if you are able to show that the number of courses completed in a university degree program is correlated with a greater sense of accomplishment and of making progress to achieving one's goals, you would say that the number of courses completed at least partly *explains* having a sense of accomplishment or making progress toward one's goals. If the correlation is .7, you would say that the number of courses completed explains or accounts for 49% (.7 × .7) of the variance in having a sense of accomplishment. Researchers often say "$r^2 = .49$"

"Variance explained" and "variance accounted for" are abstract terms. If you have 49% variance accounted for, you can *not* say "49 times out of a hundred, people who have completed a certain number of courses feel a sense of accomplishment." Instead, you say that you have accounted for about half of the variance in having a sense of accomplishment when you determine how many courses the person has taken.

Whenever you compare two variables, you are interested in knowing how much of the variance is accounted for and how much is not. The variance not accounted for is called *error variance, random variance,* and *residual variance.* They are all the same thing. The name "random variance" suggests that the variance not accounted for is *spread evenly in all directions*; that it is *unbiased.* Calling it "error variance" suggests that your explanatory model is *incomplete*; your predictions of one variable based on the value of another are *imperfect*; your prediction makes *errors.* Calling it "residual variance" suggests that it is *what is left over* after you consider what you know about the relationship in your data.

$$ratio = \frac{statistic}{\begin{array}{c}standard\ error\ of\ the\ statistic\end{array}} = \frac{accounted\ for}{unaccounted\ for} = \frac{biased}{random} = \frac{between\ groups}{within\ groups} = \frac{explained}{error}$$

The critical ratio is the ratio of *variance-accounted-for* to *variance-not-accounted-for*. It is sometimes described as the ratio of biased to random variance. If you can account for more of the variance than you can't account for, the ratio will be larger than 1.0. If the amount of variance you can not explain is larger than the amount you can explain, the ratio will be smaller than 1.0. In the *z*-test for differences between means, the ratio gives you a value for *z*. In ANOVA, which you will see later in this chapter, it is the ratio of "between-groups" variance to "within-groups" variance.

z-test for Difference Between Means

The *z*-test is used to determine whether two population means are different, based on data from two samples. It is used when both of the samples have *30 or more* scores. As you can see from the equations in the box below, the *z*-test uses a critical ratio that compares observed differences (differences you see between the means) with an estimate of expected differences (differences you would expect to see between means due to sampling variability).

The numerator tells how big the difference between the two groups is; the denominator is the standard error of the difference between means, $\sigma_{\bar{x}_1-\bar{x}_2}$, an estimate of how much variation you would expect to see if you draw many pairs of samples and calculated the difference for each pair. Some pairs of samples would give larger differences, while other pairs of samples would give smaller differences. This variation in the size of differences is due to sampling variability, an *unavoidable side effect of working with samples*. It is sometimes described as "random error," "random variation," or "*error*." If the population is normally distributed and if your samples are randomly selected, this variation will be "unbiased" or *random*. It will be the variance that is *not accounted for*.

How to do it: To perform a *z*-test for the differences between means, you:

1) decide whether you should do a 1- or 2-tailed test;

2) select your level of confidence (which will determine which column of the table you should use);

3) compute the difference between your sample means;

4) divide the difference by the standard error of the difference between means ($\sigma_{\bar{x}_1-\bar{x}_2}$), which gives you a *z* for the difference;

5) look on the table to see if your value of *z* is larger than the critical value determined by your level of confidence. For 95% confidence and a 2-tailed test, the critical value is ±1.96.

Requirements: The *z*-test requires one categorical independent variable (the one that sorts cases into groups), and one continuous dependent variable (the one used to calculate the means that are compared). Also, the *z*-test requires samples that contain at least 30 cases apiece. If your samples aren't this big, you should use a *t*-test instead.

t-test for Difference Between Two Means

The *t*-test is used to determine whether two population means are different, based on data from two samples. It is used in place of the *z*-test when one or both of the samples have fewer than 30 scores. Like the *z*-test, it also uses a critical ratio that compares the observed difference between two samples and an estimate of chance differences (differences expected due to sampling variability).

As in the calculation of *z*, the numerator in the calculation of *t* is the difference between the two means. As in *z*, the denominator is an estimate of sampling variability, but the one used here is a ver-

$$z = \frac{observed\ differences}{expected\ differences} = \frac{\bar{x}_1-\bar{x}_2}{\sigma_{\bar{x}_1-\bar{x}_2}} = \frac{accounted\ for}{unaccounted\ for} = \frac{biased}{random} = \frac{explained}{error} \qquad \sigma_{\bar{x}_1-\bar{x}_2} = \sqrt{\frac{s_1^2}{n_1}+\frac{s_2^2}{n_2}}$$

$$t = \frac{\bar{x}_1 - \bar{x}_2}{SE_{\bar{x}_1 - \bar{x}_2}} = \frac{explained}{error} = \frac{accounted\ for}{unaccounted\ for} = \frac{biased}{random} \qquad SE_{\bar{x}_1 - \bar{x}_2} = \sqrt{\left(\frac{\Sigma d_1^2 + \Sigma d_2^2}{n_1 + n_2 - 2}\right)\left(\frac{n_1 + n_2}{n_1 n_2}\right)}$$

sion of the standard error of the difference between two means that contains a correction for small sample sizes. Its symbol in the equation in the box at the top of the page is $SE_{\bar{x}_1 - \bar{x}_2}$.

Note the $\Sigma d_1^2 + \Sigma d_2^2$ in the equation. Σd_1^2 is the sum of the squared deviation scores in the first sample and Σd_2^2 is the sum of the squared deviation scores from the second sample. (Remember the "sum of the squares" from the calculation of standard deviation?) Also, n_1 and n_2 are the sizes of the two samples.

The *t*-test, like chi-squared and many other tests, uses *degrees of freedom*. This number is based either on the number of people in a category (in some cases, in a sample) or on the number of categories of people. Degrees of freedom for ANOVA and the *t*-test use both the number of people and the number of categories. You'll see more about degrees of freedom in the next eight to ten pages.

While the *z*-test uses the table of areas under the normal curve (Table 1) to determine the critical value, the *t*-test uses the table of critical values of *t* (Table 2), part of which is shown on the right. This table needs two values — the level of confidence you want to have and degrees of freedom (abbreviated "*df*") which is determined by the sizes of your samples:

$$df = n_1 + n_2 - 2$$

How to do it: to perform a *t*-test of the difference between two means, you follow a series of steps that are very much like the ones you do to perform a *z*-test:

1) decide whether you should do a 1- or 2-tailed test;

2) select your level of confidence (which will determine which column of the table you should use);

3) compute the degrees of freedom (which will determine which row of the table you should use);

4) determine what the critical value of *t* will be with the aid of the table of critical values of *t*;

5) compute the difference between your sample means;

6) compute the corrected estimate of the standard error of the difference between means ($SE_{\bar{x}_1 - \bar{x}_2}$);

7) calculate *t*: divide the difference by the corrected estimate of the standard error of the difference between means ($SE_{\bar{x}_1 - \bar{x}_2}$);

8) compare your value of *t* to the critical value determined in step 4. If your value is larger than the critical value, you reject the null hypothesis; if it isn't, you fail to reject..

Requirements: The *t*-test requires one categorical independent variable that sorts cases into groups, and one continuous dependent variable used to calculate the means that are compared. Also, the *t*-test can be used for small samples, those that contain 30 or fewer cases.

Example

Random samples of students studying statistics or history at your university were taken. The mean age of the students enrolled in a second-year statistics course is 20.4 and the mean age of students enrolled in a second-year history course is 23.8. There were 25 students in both groups. Could this difference in ages be due to sampling variability, or is it more likely that history students in general tend to be older than statistics students at your university? Here is the relevant information:

	mean	std. dev.	n
statistics	20.4	2.47	25
history	23.8	3.62	25

Because you want to compare the means of two groups of students, and your samples have fewer than 30 members, a *t*-test is appropriate.

1) Because your research question asks whether history students are older than statistics students, you would do a *one-tailed* test and your hypotheses would be directed:

$$H_{\emptyset}: \overline{age}_{Hist} \leq \overline{age}_{Stat}$$

$$H_{Alt}: \overline{age}_{Hist} > \overline{age}_{Stat}$$

2) A 95% level of confidence is acceptable.

3) Degrees of freedom:

$$df = n_1 + n_2 - 2 = 25 + 25 - 2 = 48$$

4) Use the confidence level and the *df* to find the critical value of *t*.

df	Level of significance for one-tailed test				
	.10	.05	.025	.01	.005
	Level of significance for two-tailed test				
	.2	.1	.05	.02	.01
:	:	:	:	:	:
10	1.372	1.812	2.228	2.764	3.169
20	1.325	1.725	2.086	2.528	2.845
25	1.316	1.708	2.060	2.485	2.787
30	1.310	1.697	2.042	2.457	2.750
40	1.303	1.684	2.021	2.423	2.704
50	1.299	1.676	2.009	2.403	2.678
60	1.296	1.671	2.000	2.390	2.660

The critical value is 1.676. If the value you calculate for *t* is larger than 1.676, you reject $H_{\emptyset}$; if it isn't larger, you fail to reject.

5) The difference between the means is

$$23.8 - 20.4 = 3.4.$$

6) You need to divide the difference by the adjusted standard error ($SE_{\overline{x}_1 - \overline{x}_2}$), which requires the sum of the squared deviation scores. You can get these from standard deviations if you square them (to get variance) and multiply by n-1 (the denomina-

tor used in calculation of variance). Doing this gives you the following sums of squares:

	statistics	history
std. dev. (s)	2.470	3.620
variance (s^2)	6.101	13.104
Σd^2	146.422	314.506

This allows you to calculate $SE_{\overline{x}_1 - \overline{x}_2}$:

$$SE_{\overline{x}_1 - \overline{x}_2} = \sqrt{\left(\frac{\Sigma d_1^2 + \Sigma d_2^2}{n_1 + n_2 - 2}\right)\left(\frac{n_1 + n_2}{n_1 n_2}\right)}$$

$$= \sqrt{\left(\frac{146.422 + 314.506}{25 + 25 - 2}\right)\left(\frac{25 + 25}{25 \times 25}\right)}$$

$$= 0.876$$

7) Calculate *t*:

$$t = \frac{\overline{x}_1 - \overline{x}_2}{SE_{\overline{x}_1 - \overline{x}_2}} = \frac{3.4}{0.876} = 3.881$$

8) Now compare your value of *t* with the critical value in the table. You see that your value of *t*, 3.881, is considerably larger than the critical value, 1.676, so you can reject the null hypothesis. In fact, your value of *t* is so large that you can say that the difference between the means is significant at $p < 0.005$.

Beyond *t* and *z*...

Both the *z*-test and the *t*-test are used to tell whether a difference between a *pair* of means could be due to sampling variability. They both work when the independent variable has *two values* — when you have *two groups*. If your independent variable has more than two values (if you have more than two groups), you have to use another test known as Analysis of Variance, or ANOVA.

$$\text{ratio} = \frac{\text{accounted for}}{\text{unaccounted for}} = \frac{\text{biased}}{\text{random}} = \frac{\text{between groups}}{\text{within groups}} = \frac{\text{explained}}{\text{error}} = F$$

ANOVA — Analysis of Variance

ANOVA allows you to determine whether the variable that determines which group people are in (the independent variable) is related to the value of a second variable for which you calculate means (the dependent variable). In effect, ANOVA tests the size of the differences among the means of two or more groups. The independent variable is the one you use to sort cases into groups; it must be a discrete or categorical variable. (ex: married/single/divorced, etc.) As in the *z* or *t* tests for differences between means, the dependent variable is continuous (ex: age, income, GPA, score on aggression scale, amount of coffee consumed, etc.).

The logic here is similar to that of the *z* test, where you compare differences between means to overall differences (variances). Here you compare the differences you see *between groups* to the differences *within groups*. If there is more variability between groups than within groups (if the members of one group are more different from the members of other groups than from one another) you say that the independent variable is related to the dependent variable.

For example, you might compare the ages of students majoring in Communication with those of students majoring in Psychology and Business. If the between-groups variance is larger than the within-groups variance, that is, if the differences between the ages of Communication students and Psychology students, or between Communication students and Business students are larger than the differences between Communication students and other Communication students, you would conclude that area of study is related to age.

For ANOVA, you calculate an *F*-ratio instead of a *z*, as shown in the box on the bottom of the page. For example, you have been hearing that teenage women are continuing to take up cigarette smoking at higher rates than other groups. You might get a large sample of teenage men and women and compare the two groups in terms of their smoking habits. If you find that the *F*-ratio is large — that the differences between men and women are generally larger than the differences between women and women or between men and men, you would say that sex is related to smoking. Since there are only two groups in this example, you could have used a *z*-test. If you had, you would have obtained the same results, because the two methods are equivalent when there are two groups.

The calculations for ANOVA are more complicated than those for the *z*-test between means. Don't worry, though, because people almost always have a computer do all the work. You use ANOVA because it allows you to use an independent variable that divides the population into *more than two* categories (e.g. youth/adult/ middle/old), or to include a second independent variable, such as highest degree earned. The *z*-test only works for two groups (an independent variable that has only two values).

ANOVA has degrees of freedom associated with both the numerator and denominator of the *F*-ratio. The degrees of freedom for the numerator (df_n) is the number of sample groups (*k*) minus 1. It is also called the *between-groups df*. The degrees of freedom for the denominator (df_d) is the total number of cases in all groups (N) minus the number of groups. It is also called the *within-groups df*.

$$F = \frac{s_b^2}{s_w^2} = \frac{\text{between groups variance}}{\text{within groups variance}} = \frac{\text{explained}}{\text{error}} = \frac{\text{biased}}{\text{random}} = \frac{\text{accounted for}}{\text{unaccounted for}}$$

ANOVA in Detail

ANOVA allows you to test the size of a difference between the means of two or more groups. The independent variable is the one you use to sort people into groups; it must be a discrete or categorical variable (ex: female/male, drugs/no drugs, married/single, etc.). As in the *z* test for differences between means, the dependent variable is continuous (ex: age, income, GPA, score on aggression scale, amount of coffee consumed, etc.).

The logic here is similar to the logic of the *z* test for differences between means. There you compared differences between means to overall differences (variances). Here you compare the differences you see within groups to the differences between groups. If there is more variability between groups than within groups, you say that the independent variable is related to the dependent variable (the one whose variance you are calculating).

For example, you have been hearing that teenage women are continuing to take up cigarette smoking at higher rates than other groups. You might get a large sample of teenage men and women and compare the two groups in terms of their smoking habits. If you find that the differences between men and women are generally larger than the differences between women and women or between men and men, you would say that gender is related to smoking. You could do the same comparison with a test of proportions of two groups or with a test of differences between means, but ANOVA would let you add a second independent variable, such as age, while the other tests only work for one independent variable that divides the people into two groups.

The comparison you often make takes the form of a ratio of variance accounted for to variance not accounted for. It is sometimes described as the ratio of biased to random variance. In ANOVA it is the ratio of between-groups variance to within-groups variance.

Sources or types of variance

There are four sources or types of variance:

1. *Population variance.* This is the variance of a total population or universe of elements. In general, it is not possible to calculate the population variance, because you do not have access to all the elements in the population.

2. *Sampling variance.* A special class of sampling variances are *standard errors.* I also use the less formal term "sampling variability". This is the variance of statistics computed from samples. For example, the standard error of the mean is the variance of the set of means of all samples from a population. In fact, since it describes the entire set of all possible means drawn from a population, the standard error of the mean is a type of population variance. You calculate estimates of sampling variances, and you use them to make inferences about the relation between a sample and its parent population ("based on this sample, you can say that you are 95% certain that the population mean is between 98 and 102"), or between the populations associated with two samples ("the difference between the means of these two samples is so large that you must conclude they didn't come from the same population").

3. *Systematic variance.* This is variance in measures due to some known or unknown influences that "cause" the scores to lean in one direction more than another. For example, men tend to be heavier than women. This is systematic variance. Sex explains part of the variance in weight. This factor divides the population into two classes or groups. In this case, the systematic variance — the overall difference between men and women in terms of height or weight — is called *between-groups* variance.

4. *Error variance.* This is the fluctuation or varying of measures due to chance. It is 'random' variance. It is the variance left over in a set of measures after all known sources of systematic variance have been removed from the measures. In the example given above, if you subtracted the between-groups variance from the total variance of your measurements, what would be left would be error variance.

In this case the error variance would also be called *within-groups* variance.

The goal of analysis of variance is to break down the total variance in a set of measures into systematic and error variance, to compare the two variances to each other, and to determine whether there is enough systematic variance to conclude that the difference between the means of the groups is "real" and not due to "chance".

The theoretical relation between total, between-groups, and within-groups variance is simple:

$$V_t = V_b + V_w$$

If you take a set of measures of a variable for two groups and calculate the three variances in the equation, you will find that $V_b + V_w$ will not precisely equal V_t. The reason is that variances are not perfectly "additive." However, the sums of squares (SS) used in the calculation of variances are additive. In other words:

$$SS_t = SS_b + SS_w$$

You can try this to convince yourself. You need three sums of squares. Here is how . . .

ANOVA: an eight-step plan

1. To calculate Ss_w, (within-groups sum of squares), you take the groups one at a time. You calculate the sum of squares for each group. To do this, you subtract the mean of the first group from each of the scores of the group, which gives you deviation scores. Square the deviation scores and add them together. This will give you the sum of squares for the group. Do the same for the other groups. Finally, add the SS for all the groups together, which gives you SS_w.

$$SS_w = SS_1 + SS_2 + \ldots$$

or

$$SS_w = \sum (x_{i,1} - \bar{x}_1)^2 + \sum (x_{i,2} - \bar{x}_2)^2 + \ldots$$

Calculation of means and SS for ANOVA				
	Males		Females	
i	x_i	d_i^2	x_i	d_i^2
1	18	1	12	9
2	11	36	6	9
3	20	9	10	1
4	22	25	9	0
5	15	4	8	1
6	18	1	11	4
7	16	1	10	1
8	15	4	8	1
9	22	25	9	0
10	13	16	7	4
totals	170	122	90	30

	Males	Females	Total
$\bar{x}$	17.0	9.0	13.0
SS_w	122.0	30.0	152.0

$$SS_w = SS_1 + SS_2$$
$$= 122.0 + 30.0$$
$$= 152.0$$

2. To calculate the between-groups sum of squares, SS_b, you subtract the grand mean from each group's mean to get deviation scores. Square each of these deviation scores, multiply each one by the number of people in its group, and add the results together:

$$SS_b = n_1 (\bar{x}_1 - \bar{X}_T)^2 + n_2 (\bar{x}_2 - \bar{X}_T)^2$$
$$= 10 (17 - 13)^2 + 10 (9 - 13)^2$$
$$= 10 (4)^2 + 10 (-4)^2$$
$$= 160 + 160$$
$$= 320$$

3. To calculate the total sum of squares, SS_t, you need the deviation of each score from the grand mean. This means you calculate the overall mean of all your scores. Subtract this mean from each score, square the difference, and add the results together. Effectively, you treat your data as if you have only one group of cases and are calculating the variance.

$$SS_t = \sum (X_i - \bar{X_t})^2 \quad where \quad \bar{X_t} = \sum \frac{X_i}{n}$$

4. Calculate the *degrees of freedom (df)*:

• The between-groups *df* is the number of groups minus one. If you have *k* groups, the between-groups *df* is given by:

$$df_{bet} = k - 1$$
$$= 2 - 1 = 1$$

• The within-groups df is the number of people minus the number of groups. If you have *n* people and *k* groups, the within-groups df is given by:

$$df_w = n - k$$
$$= 20 - 2 = 18$$

• Write the degrees of freedom and the sums of squares in the summary table.

Summary ANOVA table

Source of variance	SS	*df*	MS
Between-groups	320	1	
Within-groups	152	18	

5. Use the table of critical values of *F* to determine your critical value of *F*. You begin by choosing a row and a column. The column is determined by the numerator in the *F* ratio, the between-groups MS, which has **1** degree of freedom. The row is determined by the denominator, the within-groups MS, which has **18** degrees of freedom.

Numerator degrees of freedom			(p = .05 p = .01)		
	1	2	3	4	5
16	4.49	3.63	3.24	3.01	2.85
	8.53	6.23	5.29	4.77	4.44
17	4.45	3.59	3.20	2.96	2.81
	8.40	6.11	5.18	4.67	4.34
18	4.41	3.55	3.16	2.93	2.77
	8.29	6.01	5.09	4.58	4.25
19	4.38	3.52	3.13	2.90	2.74
	8.18	5.93	5.01	4.50	4.17
20	4.35	3.49	3.10	2.87	2.71

For a significance level of .05, the critical value of *F* is 4.41; for a significance level of .01, it is 8.29. If the value you obtain for *F* is larger than the critical value, you reject the null hypothesis, which says that the independent variable is not related to the dependent variable.

6. In each row of the table, you now calculate a variance. In an ANOVA table, the variance is called "MS," as in "mean square." To do this, divide each row's SS by its *df*. The results have been filled in the summary table below.

Summary ANOVA table

Source of variance	SS	*df*	MS
Between-groups	320	1	320
Within-groups	152	18	8.444

7. Finally, calculate the *F* ratio by dividing the between-groups variance by the within-groups variance:

$$F = \frac{320}{8.444} = 37.897$$

You have now obtained all the information you need for an *F*-test which is the test of significance you use with ANOVA. Your degrees of freedom are 1, 18 and the value of *F* is 37.897.

8. The last step is to compare the *F* value you obtained, 37.897, to the critical value of 4.41. You can see that your *F* is much larger than 4.41. In fact, it is much larger than the critical value for the 99% confidence level, which is 8.29. You would thus conclude that $p < .01$ and you would reject the null hypothesis.

Summary

The three tests described in this chapter are used to determine whether the differences between means is significant. When you have two means and the sample sizes are greater than or equal to 30, use a *z*-test. When you have two means and the sample sizes are smaller than 30, use a *t*-test. When you have more than two means, use ANOVA.

All three tests use critical ratios — they require you to calculate the difference between means and divide that difference by a measure of sampling variability. For the *z*-test, you divide by the standard error of the difference between means. For the *t*-test, you divide by an adjusted standard error that takes the sample sizes into account. For the *F*-test, you divide the differences between groups, measured by the between-groups variance (also known as the between-groups mean square), by the differences within groups, measured by the within-groups variance (also known as the within-groups mean square).

The *t*-test uses degrees of freedom, calculated as the total number of cases minus 2. The *F*-test also uses degrees of freedom, one based on the number of means (k-1), and the other based on the number of cases minus the number of groups ($n - k$).

Important Terms and Concepts

between-groups mean square (MS_b)

between-groups sum of squares (SS_b)

biased variance

critical value

critical ratio

degrees of freedom

denominator degrees of freedom

error variance

numerator degrees of freedom

random variance

sum of squares (SS)

systematic variance

variance accounted for

within-groups mean square (MS_w)

within-groups sum of squares (S_{sw})

V

Research approaches

五

Chapter 20

EXPERIMENTS

There are several approaches to the structure or "design" of research. This text considers four that are used in the study of human behavior: experiments, survey research, field research, and unobtrusive research.

Experiments are the most highly controlled of the four. They tend to be used more by researchers with a background in psychology or social psychology. Survey methods tend to be used by researchers who take a more sociological approach, while field and unobtrusive methods are favored by those doing anthropological work. Because of the multi disciplinary nature of communication research, it uses all four approaches.

The Stereotypical Laboratory Experiment

You have probably heard about the results of laboratory experiments if you've ever heard a news report of a new drug that was subjected to a "double blind" test. You may have been a participant in a laboratory experiment if you ever wandered too close to the psychology department in a university. You have probably seen a movie in which a scientist—perhaps a "mad scientist"—poured chemicals from beakers into test tubes and then administered the contents to an unsuspecting subject. Something strange probably

happened to the recipient, and, of course, the scientist wore a white lab coat. These are all versions of the classical laboratory experiment.

Experiments are a particular kind of research involving the measurement of the consequences of an action. If you want to know whether the way you dress has an influence on the extent to which people believe you, you might try wearing different kinds of clothing and observing people's responses to what you say. This is an experiment, but it isn't a laboratory experiment. If you want to know whether one brand of yeast makes the bread rise faster than another brand of yeast, you might make two batches of bread dough, each with one of the two brands. Then you would take note of what happened over the next hour or two. This is an experiment, and it is more controlled than the first one, but it still isn't a laboratory experiment.

In a laboratory experiment, you would control as many of the things that could interfere with the results as you could. If you wanted to turn the first example described above into a laboratory experiment, you would want to standardize the situation in which you observe people's responses to what you say so that the only thing that varied from one time to the next was what you wore. In other words, the experiment would always take place in the same setting, you would always say the same things, you would assess

the extent to which they believe you in the same way, the people you spoke to would always approach their interaction with you from the same perspective or with the same purpose in mind, and so on. There would never be any disturbances that could distract the people you were interacting with. The easiest way to control all of these factors is to conduct the experiment in a special room from which the potential disturbances have been removed—a "laboratory."

You can probably see how conducting the research in your specially-prepared room will eliminate many potential disturbances, but you may still be wondering about how you can control for all the things that make each person unique. One strategy that some researchers attempt to use is called "matching." Subjects are paired with people very similar to themselves—same age, same sex, same education, etc. Then one member of each pair sees you wearing ratty old comfortable hanging-out clothes and the other sees you wearing more formal attire.

An easier and much more effective approach is to *randomly assign* subjects to conditions. In the same way that random selection makes your sample representative and eliminates bias, randomly assigning subjects to conditions automatically matches the groups much more completely than the laborious strategy of matching subjects in pairs. For one thing, random assignment controls for all possible kinds of differences between people, while the matched pairs strategy only controls for the differences you are able to observe, and only when you are able to find appropriate matches for all of your subjects.

I'll begin with *pre-experimental* designs. None of these are actually experiments because they are all missing one or more of the important logical components that give experiments their explanatory power.

Not-quite Experiments

Experiments are about causal relations. While I was typing this page, something strange happened to my computer. I got what is called a "GPF"—a General Protection Fault. When that happens, a little window opens on my screen and tells me I can "Ignore" the problem or "Close." If I select Close, the system shuts down the program I was using (WordPerfect) and I lose anything I haven't saved. If I select Ignore, everything may go back to normal, or I may get another GPF. In any case, I am likely to lose some work. Because GPFs interrupt my work and force me to do things twice, I want to avoid them. I have a motivation for determining their causes. The last time it happened, I was trying to make a graphical figure bigger, so I might assume that making the figure bigger was the cause of the GPF. When I get WordPerfect started up again, I might try to make the same figure bigger to see if I could repeat the GPF. This is an informal "not-quite" experiment—it doesn't have everything that needs to be there for it to be an experiment.

You could represent this kind of design like this:

One-Shot Case Study

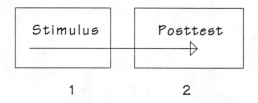

The main weakness of the One-Shot case study is that you don't know whether it was what you did (the *stimulus*) or something else that caused what you saw in the *Posttest*. Furthermore, you have nothing to compare the results of your measurement with. This leads to an improved design, called the One-group Pretest-Posttest design:

One-Group Pretest-Posttest

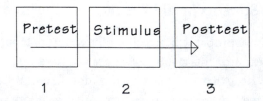

With this approach, you take a measurement before you apply the stimulus (the *Pretest*) as well as one afterwards. Although this design lets you determine whether or not there has been a change between the results of the two measurements, you still can't tell whether the change was due to the stimulus. To get

any information about that, you need to add a second group, a group that doesn't receive the stimulus. This is the purpose of the *Control Group*—group A in the drawing below.

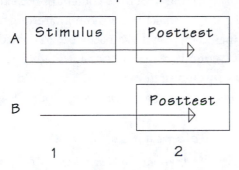

While the Static-Group design lets you compare the cases that were exposed to the stimulus with those that weren't, you still can't rule out the possibility that something else caused any differences you saw. Perhaps the two groups were different to begin with.

Two-group Designs

So far you have seen the three minimum components of what is sometimes called the "classical experiment":

- *random assignment* of subjects to one of two conditions;

- the subjects in one condition are treated differently from those in the other condition;

- measurements or observations are made after the subjects have been exposed to the treatments.

There are two variables associated with experiments. The goal of experimental research is to determine what effect the *independent variable* has on the *dependent variable*. The independent variable is controlled by determining which condition the subject is assigned to. In the example above, your style of dress is the independent variable. The dependent variable is what you measure or observe; it is what you expect to be affected by the independent variable. In the example above, this is the extent to which the subjects believe what you say. The inde-

pendent variable is the *cause* and the dependent variable is the *effect*. The design of this experiment is represented schematically here:

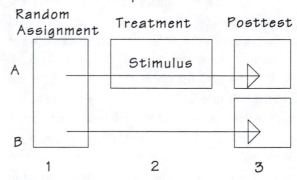

Because this experiment has measurement only after the treatments, it is called a *two-group posttest only* design. It is the simplest complete experimental design. There are numerous variations on this theme. Probably the most common one is to add a *pretest* measurement:

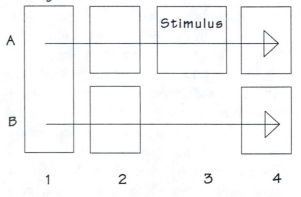

This design, called a *two-group, pretest-posttest* design, adds a test to see if the two groups were the same before the treatment. The pretest is a check on the validity of the random assignment to conditions. While randomly assigning individuals to conditions *should* make the two groups comparable, there is a possibility that they may turn out to be different (think sampling variability). One goal of the pretest is to determine whether or not this has happened. The pretest has another, equally important, goal, which is

to allow you to perform before-and-after comparisons on the subjects in your experiment.

Without the pretest, the only thing you can do to measure the effect of the treatment is to compare the measurements of the control group to those of the experimental group. Generally, this comparison will take the form of a *z*-test for the difference between two means. There will almost certainly be some variability among the individuals in each group before the treatment. This variability will be reflected in the posttest results, and will partially obscure any differences you may see between the two groups.

With the pretest, however, you can calculate a *change score* for each individual in the experiment. This will allow you to compare the mean change of the people in the experimental group to the mean change of those in the control group. Having the pretest measures allows you to subtract off any differences among the individuals in the two groups.

To see how this works, consider the following situation: Say you wanted to see what effect drinking a cup of coffee would have on people's ability to understand complicated instructions. Say you know that drinking a cup of coffee will improve someone's score on a comprehension test by five points. Say you have randomly divided twelve people into two groups of six, and that their scores on the posttest were 60, 66, 69, 72, 75, 80 and 65, 71, 74, 77, 80, 85. You will see that the difference between the means of the two sets of scores (70.333 and 75.333) is 5 points, but you will also see that there is a great deal of overlap of the ranges of the two sets of scores.

If you had pretest results for the twelve people in this experiment, you would be able to compute a before-and-after difference score for each individual. With this you can compare the size of the difference between the pretest and the posttest for the two groups. If the pretest scores were 60, 66, 69, 72, 75, 80 and 60, 66, 69, 72, 75, 80 and the posttest scores were 60, 66, 69, 72, 75, 80 and 65, 71, 74, 77, 80, 85, you would see change scores of 0, 0, 0, 0, 0, 0 and 5, 5, 5, 5, 5, 5. Now the picture is much clearer because the variability among individuals has been reduced.

Four-group Designs

Sometimes there is a concern that the pretest may influence the performance or behavior of the people you are studying. For example, the pretest may get people to thinking about the content of the experiment, or it may make them more aware of certain things than they would ordinarily be. To control for this, a two-group posttest only design might be added to the two-group pretest-posttest design. The result is what is known as the *Solomon four-group* design:

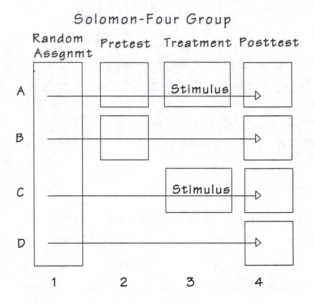

Experimental Controls and Comparisons

The discussion on experiments began with the statement that the experiment is the most highly controlled of the research designs. This control comes partly from the fact that the researcher structures the experimental situation and determines, to a greater or lesser extent, what experiences the experimental "subjects" will have. Another source of the control comes from the way experiments are set up, with various groups being subjected to different conditions. The division of subjects into conditions allows a number of comparisons to be drawn, each of which gives the researcher information about a facet of the research situation.

Two-Group PostTest Comparison

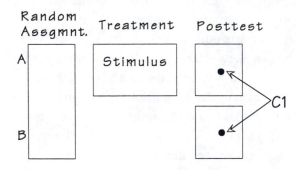

Only one comparison can be done with this simple design—the posttest of the experimental group (Group A) and the posttest of the control group (Group B). If there is a difference between these two measures, you would conclude that it must be due to the treatment that was received by members of Group A. You can only assume that the random assignment produced two groups that were equivalent before the treatment was administered.

Two-Group Pretest-Posttest Comparison

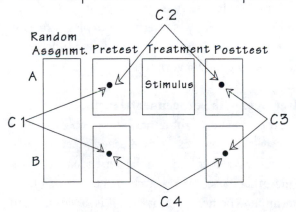

The two-group pretest-posttest design allows you to make four comparisons. Here you can see how the experimental approach introduces a high degree of control to the research situation.

- Comparison 1 puts the pretest measures of the two groups next to each other so you can determine whether or not the random assignment produced two equivalent groups.

- Comparisons 2 and 4 show how the two groups changed over the time spanned by the experiment.

You would probably hope that C 2 shows a bigger change than C

- Comparison 3 shows you how different the two groups were after the posttest. You would hope that any differences you see here would be due to the fact that Group A received the treatment and Group B didn't. But you won't be able to tell whether or not the difference you see in C 3 is due to the stimulus itself or to an interaction between the measurement procedure and the stimulus.

Solomon-Four Group Comparisons

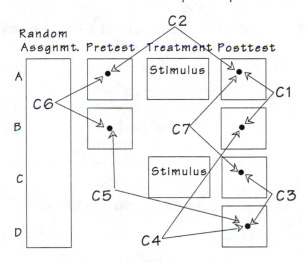

With the Solomon-four design, you have even more ability to narrow down the relation between the treatment and any changes you observe. For example, you can determine whether the pretest interacts with the treatment or with the posttest, and you can determine whether the passage of time or the occurrence of events external to the experiment are influencing your results.

- Comparison 1 shows differences between the posttest scores of Groups A and B, both pretested before the treatment

- Comparison 3 shows a similar comparison of Groups C and D, neither of which was pretested. You would hope C1 and C3 would show similar differences. If they don't, you would suspect that

the pretest somehow interacted with either the stimulus or the posttest itself.

- Comparison 4 will let you determine whether the pretest interacts with the posttest, as the only difference between group B and D is that group B took a pretest and D didn't.

- Comparison 5 should give you a result similar to that of Comparison 6, which is a check on the random assignment. If it doesn't, you would suspect that something is happening between the time of the pretest and the posttest, and this could make any other differences you see difficult to interpret.

- Comparison 7 will test the effect of the pretest on the posttest in groups that were exposed to the treatment. You would hope that there is no difference between the posttests of groups A and C. If there is a difference, you would suspect that the pretest is causing problems; it may be interacting with the stimulus.

The Experimental Method Reviewed

The experimental method derives its strength from the four types of control it gives the researcher:

1. Control over the composition of experimental and control groups. Because people are randomly assigned to groups, the researcher knows that there are no systematic differences between groups that may cause apparent changes in the dependent variable. Random assignment eliminates self-selection, in which people choose which group they want to be in. Self-selection can be expected to result in groups that differ in ways that are related to either the independent or dependent variables, thus introducing bias and reducing the validity of conclusions that may be drawn from the results. *Random assignment to conditions is the most important aspect of experimental design; it is what gives the experiment its unique ability to determine causal relationships.*

2. Control over the environment. The researcher has control over all aspects of the environment in which the experiment takes place—the presence or absence of other people, the type of furniture in the area, the appearance and behavior of any other people who may be in the area where the experiment takes place, the time of day, and so on. This control allows the researcher to rule out other factors as possible causes for whatever changes in the dependent variable might be observed.

3. Control over the independent variable. Since the goal of experimental research is to determine what effect a change in the independent variable has on the dependent variable, it is important for the researcher to have complete control over the independent variable. Without this control, the researcher will not know what is causing the variations seen in the dependent variable.

4. Control over the measurement of the dependent variable. The researcher can measure the dependent variable both before and after the experimental manipulation, which makes it possible to eliminate a variety of alternative explanations for the apparent relationship between the independent and dependent variables.

Advantages of the experimental method

The experimental method makes it possible to determine whether changes in the independent variable cause subsequent changes in the dependent variable. While other types of research make it possible to determine whether or not there is a correlation between a pair of variables, only the experiment can tell whether there is a causal relationship.

The four types of control built into the experimental method make it possible to rule out a wide range of alternative explanations for any apparent relationship that is identified between independent and dependent variables. To an extent, this can be accomplished with survey data by means of advanced statistical methods, but the experimental method provides a simpler and more direct way of achieving this goal.

Experiments, by their very nature, require a particular sequence of events to take place in a particular temporal order. They focus on change over time, while survey methods are much better at identifying static correlational patterns.

Disadvantages of the experimental method

The main weakness of the experimental method is their dependence on what many see as an "artificial" environment. The stereotypical "laboratory experiment" brings undergraduate students to a special room on a campus and presents them with conditions not often experienced in day-to-day life. While it is true that this allows the unpredictable complexities of ordinary life to be "controlled," it tends to remove the participants from the ordinary context in which they live and place them instead in an artificial environment that has little or no resemblance to the "real world." People may behave differently in the experimental setting than they would under more ordinary conditions. Consider, for example, the experimental conditions that would be used by a researcher who wishes to determine whether a particular factor influences how people behave in riots.

Researchers generally *want* to see changes in their dependent variables. They want to see differences between their experimental and control groups. The desire to find a difference may be subtly communicated to the people participating in the experiment in such a way as to affect their behavior in precisely the way the experimenter wants. The only problem is that the apparent changes in the dependent variable may be caused by the experimenter's subtle cues and not by the independent variable. This "experimenter effect" is often controlled by the use of "double-blind" designs, in which neither the people participating in the experiment nor the researchers with whom

they interact know which condition the people have been assigned to until after all measurements have been taken. Since the researchers don't know whether the people are in the experimental group or the control group, it is less likely that the researchers will unconsciously influence the results.

Due to the costs involved or the structure of the experimental situation, it is often difficult to obtain experimental samples large enough to obtain results that are stable enough to allow generalizations to larger populations. This is a most distressing situation for researchers to find themselves in, after all the time, money, and effort have been spent to create an elaborate experimental design.

One last problem with experimental methods is that they require the researcher to identify and control all relevant variables that might distort the apparent relation between independent and dependent variables. In the natural sciences where all the complexities of the social world do not have to be considered, this may be accomplished. But in the social sciences where the subject of inquiry is a social situation that takes place in a social context, it may not be possible to identify all relevant variables or potential "disturbances." This is one of the reasons that very few social experiments are considered conclusive. Someone will come along with a slightly revised experimental design that produces results that conflict with those produced by earlier researchers, thus creating a need for further research that may produce even more contradictory results that require still more research to sort out.

Important Terms and Concepts

causal relationships
control group
double-blind methods
experiment
experimental group
external validity
one-group pretest-posttest design
one-shot case study
posttest
posttest-only design
pre-experimental design
pretest
pretest-posttest design
random assignment to conditions
self-selection
solomon four group design
static group design
stimulus
test sensitization
two-group posttest design
two-group pretest-posttest design
validity of randomization

Chapter 21

Survey Research

The Nature of Survey Research

Survey research methods are well suited for the task of using a sample to learn about a large population. For example, television viewing preferences and voting intentions of entire nations are regularly studied by surveys. You've probably heard of more than one of the big polling and market research outfits—Angus Reid, Asia Market Intelligence, Deloitte & Touche, Dun & Bradstreet, Environics, Gallup, Harris, Marktrend Research, NORC (National Opinion Research Center), Research International Qualitatif, Roper, Strategic Research Associates, Yankelovich. Even if you haven't heard of any of these companies, you've heard the words they always use: "Nineteen times out of twenty, these results are accurate to within three percent."

Survey researchers conduct surveys—they collect information from samples that may contain as few as thirty (a small sample) or as many as thirty thousand or more (a very large sample) people. They may call their respondents on the telephone; they may mail a questionnaire to them; they may visit them door-to-door; they may send a questionnaire by e-mail; or they may invite television viewers or radio listeners to call a special telephone number. Respondents may be asked questions about facts, beliefs, opinions, moti-vations, fears, habits, or intentions. In any case, the goal is to obtain information that can be generalized to the population the respondents represent. Kerlinger (1964, p. 394) suggests that the variables of survey research can be classified as either sociological or psychological. Sociological facts are attributes of individuals associated with their membership in various social groupings based on political, religious, professional, racial, educational factors. Psychological variables include opinions, attitudes, and behaviors—what people think and do. Many survey researchers are interested in relating sociological variables to psychological ones; other researchers may only be interested in psychological variables.

Because the goal of most survey research is to learn about a population, you can see that it is important to have a representative sample, which means that you want to use probability sampling methods whenever possible. Sampling methods thus play a particularly important role in survey research.

Because surveys are expensive and time-consuming to conduct, they are usually done by or for organizations that have a question they want answered and the money it will cost to get the answer. Some large surveys, however, don't have a clearly pragmatic and applied goal; there are organizations that conduct surveys of national or international populations and

provide the data used by researchers studying a very wide range of social issues.

The main goal of survey research is to produce an accurate picture of the population from which the sample is drawn. Where experiments are used to determine causal relationships between variables, surveys produce correlational results. While they may indicate that a pair of variables are strongly related to one another, they ordinarily are not able to determine cause-and-effect relationships. However, because surveys methods can provide the data used to test hypotheses implied by theoretical explanations, they are not limited to purely descriptive applications.

Surveys and Time

There are two ways to deal with the passage of time in survey research. The first is the cross-sectional design in which you collect all your data at a single point in time. To deal with time you include in your sample people at various stages of the process you are studying. This way you get some people in the beginning, some in the middle stages, some later on, and others even later. For example, you may be interested in how people's attitudes and beliefs about alcohol and tobacco change between the ages of 15 and 20. A *cross-sectional survey* in which you interviewed a mix of people spanning this range of ages would do the trick. Although you wouldn't know how any one person's attitudes and beliefs changed, you would know how the attitudes and beliefs of those who are 15 years old differed from those who are 16, 17, 18, 19, and 20 years old.

The main problem with cross-sectional surveys is that you cannot be certain that the people in different age groups are comparable to one another. One group may have suffered through a war, a depression, a viral epidemic, or a period of extremely harsh weather conditions while another group didn't experience any of these problems. Perhaps laws changed in a way that increased or decreased the availability or cost of alcohol and tobacco. In other words, the data from a cross-sectional survey may give a valid and accurate picture of the attitudes and

beliefs of people of different ages. However, because they remove people from their historical context, they may tell you nothing about how people's attitudes and beliefs change as they grow older.

The second approach is the longitudinal design in which you follow a single group of people as they go through the process you are studying. To determine how people's attitudes and beliefs about alcohol and tobacco change between the ages of 15 and 20, you would start with a group of fifteen year-olds and interview them several times over the next five years. This *panel study* would allow you to track the attitudes and beliefs for each individual over the whole time period and, perhaps, to determine what factors might be related to the changes you see.

There are three problems with panel studies.

- The first is that, compared to cross-sectional ones, they take a long time to conduct and they involve repeated measurements.

- The second problem is that it may be difficult or impossible to follow the entire set of individuals over the entire time period. People move; they die; they get tired of participating in the research project. If you lose half of your respondents over a five year period, you may have some doubts about the reliability and validity of your results.

- The third problem is that things happen and have an effect on the people in the study. For example, in the study of attitudes towards alcohol and tobacco, the media coverage of the death of a popular public figure as a result of an accident in which alcohol played a central may lead to a shift in public opinion that influences the attitudes of the people in your study. You may not be able to determine whether the changes in attitudes are due to events like this or to the normal maturation process.

Selecting a Representative Sample

Since the main goal of survey research is to produce an accurate picture of the population from which the

sample is drawn, the way you select your sample is an important issue. There are four things to do here:

Define your population

Let's say the goal of your research is to determine the attitudes that people who drive across the Lion's Gate bridge have about a proposed new rapid transit link between the downtown core and the suburbs on the north shore of the Inlet. You have to decide who your population is. The population is the entire set of people, stories, organizations, neighborhoods, etc. that are addressed by your research question. In this case, the population could be the people who live in the suburbs and work downtown, the people who have cottages on the north shore, or the taxpayers who will pay a major portion of the cost of the new link. It could also be the people who drive across the bridge, regardless of where they live or work.

The choice you make here will depend on the context in which the study was designed and the intended application of the results. If the study was commissioned by a group of residents of the north shore community who were concerned about the effect increased traffic might have on their neighborhood, the population might be the residents of the north shore. If the study was commissioned by a government agency concerned about the increased levels of air pollution due to vehicular exhaust, the population might be people who live on the north shore and commute to work in the downtown core.

For some research situations you may have to deal with two populations. This would be the case if the goal of the research is to determine how upsetting people find televised stories about violent crime in the evening news. One population here is the people who watch the newscasts and the other is the televised stories. Since you can't get *all* viewers to tell you how they feel about *all* televised stories, you will have to sample both.

In any case, you must decide what your population is and develop a clear, complete specification of who or what is included or excluded from the population.

Specify your sampling elements

Sampling elements are the units that are selected or not selected to be in your sample. If you are studying the attitudes, opinions, beliefs, or habits of people, your sampling elements are very likely to be people. However, if you are studying organizations or social systems like neighborhoods, school districts, manufacturing companies, etc., you may sample social units and not individual people. For example, you might be studying take a sample of school districts. You would choose a number of school districts to be included in your sample and interview the members of the school board from each district. In this case, your sampling element would be the school district.

Not all samples involve people. For example, in the study of people's response to televised stories about violent crime, there were two populations—the people who watch the stories in the evening news and the stories themselves. Since you would have to sample both people and stories, it would appear that you would have two sampling elements—people and stories. However, since people ordinarily watch an entire newscast rather than an individual news story, you would probably take newscasts as your sampling element rather than individual stories. For each newscast that is selected, you would take all stories that fit the criteria for the study (stories about violent crime). For a particular newscast, this may be one story, several stories, or no stories at all.

Secure a sampling frame

A *sampling frame* is a list of the elements in the population that may be selected in the sample. The only members of the population that can be included in the sample are the ones on the list. For example, you may use a telephone directory as a sampling frame for a study of opinions about the accessibility and convenience of an urban recycling depot. A sample based on a random selection of people listed in the phone book will systematically exclude the people who aren't listed—people with very low income and people who live on the streets or under a bridge (they don't have telephones), single women and very

wealthy people (they have unlisted numbers), and people who moved into the city after the directory was printed. Other lists that might be used as sampling frames for studies of the residents of a city include voters' lists, city directories, lists of subscribers to utility services (gas, electric, water), etc. Since none of these lists were designed to be used as sampling frames, none of them are ideal; they will all provide biased samples that systematically over- or under-represent certain segments of the population.

With most sampling frames you will have to deal with one or more of these problems:

- missing elements: legitimate members of the population not included in the sampling frame. This is what happens when you use a phone book and some people don't have phones or have unlisted numbers.

- foreign elements: listings in the sampling frame for individuals no longer in the population. I once worked with a government agency whose payroll list included several people who had died in the past ten years.

- duplicate elements: population members listed more than once in the sampling frame. A friend of mine uses four different names, more than one of which appear on some lists. Another example here is telephone listings which show more than one telephone number for a name (main listing, fax number, teenager's number).

In all of these situations you should try to determine how many missing, foreign, and duplicate elements are in the sampling frame and what impact they will have on the quality of your sample. How is the set of individuals in the sampling frame different from the set of individuals in the population? How large is the difference? If the sampling frame will provide a sample that is biased in a way that any conclusions you draw about the population would be invalid, you should consider the possibility of using a different sampling frame. Alternatively, consider what remedial steps you could take to compensate for the problems with the sampling frame. In practice, it will probably be easier to simply redefine your population as the people listed in the sampling frame. Before you do this, though, you should ask yourself how this will affect the value of your research.

Choose a sampling method

While you are thinking about your sampling frame, you should also be thinking about how you will draw your sample. You have several decisions to make:

Probability *vs.* non-probability. The single thing that will have the largest impact on how you conduct your study is whether or not you intend to draw conclusions about the population on the basis of the data you collect. If you do, you must use a probability sampling method. If the goal of your study is to learn something about the people who answer your questions and you do not intend to make inferences about the population they represent, probability sampling methods are not necessary.

Remember that the main difference between probability and non-probability sampling methods is that with probability methods you must be able to specify the probability of being included in the sample for every member of the population, while for non-probability methods you don't need to know the probability of being selected for anyone. With probability methods you know who or what belongs to the population being sampled and you know how fairly the various members of the population are represented in the sample. Because of this, you can make inferences about the population on the basis of your sample data. You cannot do this with non-probability sampling methods.

Random *vs.* systematic. If your choice is to use a probability sample, you must decide whether random or systematic methods are more appropriate for your study. Random methods require a list of the members of the population or something that can be used like a list. You use a procedure or a device that produces random numbers which indicate which member of the list you will include in the sample.

For samples with fewer than two or three hundred members, you can use a table of random numbers

(Table 7).   For larger samples this becomes very tedious and time-consuming, so you will probably want to use a device like a computer program that can generate a list of random numbers, select the appropriate members of the population from the sampling frame, and print a list of the individuals to be included in the sample. An example of this approach is a *computer assisted telephone interviewing* (CATI) system in which the computer randomly selects telephone numbers from the sampling frame, dials the number for you, and then displays the questions of the survey on a screen one at a time and waits for you to enter the respondent's answer before it displays either the next question or instructions for the interviewer.

In many situations it is not possible or feasible to construct a list or quasi-list of the members of the population. You can still conduct a probability sample, though, if it is possible somehow to line up the members of the population so you can use a systematic selection procedure in which you obtain data from the driver of every 20th car, every 50th customer in a store or passenger on a rapid transit system, or the residents in every 10th house in a neighborhood.

To stratify or not to stratify.   When you need to make precise estimates of population parameters with a high degree of confidence and relatively small samples, you will be concerned about the efficiency of your sampling procedure. For example, you may be required to make very precise estimates with a high degree of confidence with a study that uses an expensive or time-consuming measurement. In situations like this, you should consider the possible benefits of stratified sampling. These methods effectively reduce the heterogeneity of the population, thereby reducing the size of the sample while maintaining the accuracy of your estimates and the confidence you can place in them. You can find additional discussion of these methods in Chapter 5.

Clusters or individuals? If the population you are studying is organized into groups of individuals so that it is easier to get access to the groups than to

individuals taken one at a time, you may want to use a form of cluster sampling. For example, in a study of the beliefs children in first grade have about science and religion, it is easier, less expensive, and less disruptive to randomly select classrooms and to survey all of the children in the selected classrooms than it is to randomly select individual children.

The Survey Questionnaire

Surveys can ask questions about facts, beliefs, and opinions. Questions about **facts** are the easiest to answer because they are more concrete and they have real, definite answers. Examples include questions like:

Do you own a car?

Do you subscribe to a newspaper?

Do you rent videos?

How old are you?

Questions about **beliefs** are more complicated than questions about facts for several reasons. A belief is what you think is true rather than what you know is true. A belief might be incorrect, and you may not be able to tell whether it is or not because you may not have the necessary information or because the required information does not exist. When you ask a question about what a person believes, you should phrase it so it is clear that you are asking about a belief and not a fact. Here are some examples of questions about beliefs:

Do you believe that Elvis is really dead?

Do you think the oil companies are colluding to keep prices high?

Do you think smoking cigarettes causes lung cancer?

Questions about **opinions** generally have to do with preferences or personal values. While it may be easy to ask questions about opinions, you may find it difficult to interpret the answers. One reason for this is that people don't always answer truthfully. Answers to questions about sensitive personal opinions

may be distorted by the respondent's desire to appear to be good, responsible, considerate, honest, etc. This is known as the *social desirability bias*. Here are a few examples of questions about opinions:

> Which would you rather live next to: a French family or an Irish family?

> If a clerk at a large supermarket gave you $10 too much change, would it be okay to quietly keep it?

> Is it okay to cooperate with a very ill person when they ask you to help them commit suicide?

> Which are better: American or Canadian movies?

Types of Questions

There are three ways to structure questions on a survey: closed or multiple-choice questions, fill-in-the-blank questions, and open or free-response questions.

1. Closed questions

Closed questions can take many different formats, each of which has particular advantages and drawbacks.

Rating questions. With these you ask the respondent to use a scale against which to judge something. You are no doubt familiar with the famous "1 to 10" scale.

Rate the how uncomfortable you would be in the following situations on a 1 to 10 scale where "1" means "not at all uncomfortable" and "10" means "more uncomfortable than I have ever been."

Rating	Situation
___	Flying in a small plane
___	Speaking in front of a large crowd
___	Being interviewed for the evening news on television

Ranking questions. Here you ask the respondent to rank a set of options according to a specified criterion. These questions are more difficult to answer because each of the options must be compared to all of the others before a ranking can be made. It is likely that the answers your respondents provide to these questions are less reliable than the answers would be if a rating format was used instead of a ranking format.

Please rank the following issues from 1 to 8, according to how important they were in influencing your decision of which computer to purchase.

rank	Issue	rank	Issue
___	quality	___	appearance
___	dependability	___	ease of use
___	performance	___	reputation
___	brand name	___	price

Checklist or inventory questions. Sometimes you want the respondents to indicate which of the items on a list of several items applies to them. An easy way to do this is to present the list and ask the respondents to check the items that apply. For example, in a study of the media consumption habits of high school students, you might use a checklist like this:

Please indicate which of the following sources you have used in the last month to get information about music and movies. Check all the ones you have used.

	Source		Source
___	radio reviews	___	television ads
___	television reviews	___	newspaper ads
___	magazine reviews	___	other advertising
___	newspaper reviews	___	friends
___	magazine advertising	___	other (please specify)

Composite measures

All of the examples presented above are *simple* measures in the sense that each issue in the examples was addressed by a single question. The *composite* approach uses of several questions to address each issue. To analyze the results, the answers to the set of questions are combined into a *scale* or an *index*. Two types of composite measures are described here.

Likert scales. Likert scales (named after Rensis Likert who developed them) are used for measurement of attitudes and opinions. A Likert scale contains several items, each of which consists of a statement and a request for the respondent to indicate whether they strongly agree, agree, disagree, or strongly disagree with the statement. Often a "neutral" option is included between "agree" and "disagree." An example of a Likert scale designed to measure opinions about Netscape and Microsoft Internet Explorer is in the box on the right.

For each respondent, you would add the numbers associated with the answers to all four of the items. If a respondent felt that Internet Explorer was far superior to Netscape, her answers would probably be "strongly disagree," "strongly agree," "strongly disagree," and "strongly disagree," and her score for the scale would be 5+5+5+5=20. A respondent who felt Netscape was far superior to the Microsoft program would probably get a score closer to 4.

Likert items are ordinally scaled. It is not assumed that the difference between "strongly agree" and "agree" is the same size as the difference between "agree" and "neutral." However, the fact that the item scores are added together to calculate the score for the scale means that the item scores are treated as if they were interval scaled. For analytic purposes, the ordinal level data from Likert items is treated as if it were interval data.

Notice that the questions were stated so that a person who felt strongly that one program was better than the other would have to choose "strongly agree" for some items and "strongly disagree" for others. Some of the statements were in favor of Netscape Navigator while others were in favor of Microsoft

a. Netscape Navigator is easier to use than Microsoft Internet Explorer.

   1. Strongly agree
   2. Agree
   3. Neutral
   4. Disagree
   5. Strongly disagree

b. Images display on the screen faster with Microsoft Internet Explorer than with Netscape Navigator.

   1. Strongly disagree
   2. Disagree
   3. Neutral
   4. Agree
   5. Strongly agree

c. The control bars in Netscape Navigator are more flexible than those in Microsoft Internet Explorer.

   1. Strongly agree
   2. Agree
   3. Neutral
   4. Disagree
   5. Strongly disagree

d. Microsoft's Internet Explorer is less intuitive than Netscape Navigator.

   1. Strongly agree
   2. Agree
   3. Neutral
   4. Disagree
   5. Strongly disagree

Internet Explorer. Also, the order of the options for the answers was varied so that "1" meant "strongly agree" for some items and "strongly disagree" for others. This is done in order to prevent a bias called *response set* in which respondents read the first few items carefully and see that their responses are on the "strongly disagree" end, and then skim the rest of the items, selecting "strongly disagree" for each without actually reading and understanding the statements.

There are three things to note about the items in a Likert scale:

- The statements are simple, clearly worded, and unambiguous. They are stated positively. Statements like the following should **not** be used:

I don't feel that statistics and research methods are not too important.

Although tuition is already too high and the government is cutting back on money for student aid, a study of the financial impact of tuition increases could be too expensive for what good it might do.

Considering the state of affairs, one might argue that it is good to eat a lot of green vegetables when it is appropriate.

● It is important that each statement says only one thing; it cannot be broken into two or more sentences without adding more information. Statements like the following are problematic because the respondent may agree with one part of the statement and disagree with the other, making it impossible for you to know the meaning of the responses.

The government is doing a good job with the environment and its focus on the new job creation program.

The way popular media objectify women is making it difficult for both young men and women, who should be getting a less biased view of the world in that stage of their lives.

● The list of possible answers should be the same from one item to another. You should not use "strongly agree, agree, neutral, disagree, strongly disagree" for some items and "very favorable, favorable, undecided, unfavorable, extremely unfavorable" or "extremely desirable, very desirable, considerably desirable, somewhat desirable, slightly desirable, not desirable" for others. These variations all require the respondent to make different kinds of decisions. To strongly agree with a statement is not the same as to find the statement very favorable or extremely desirable. Since Likert scales are composite measures and require you to combine the responses to several items into a single measurement, it is important that the items to be combined be compatible, so you should use a consistent set of answers for the items that make up the composite scale.

Semantic differential scales. This approach to measurement is very useful when you are dealing with a complex multidimensional issue and you want to determine the structure of the concept. When semantic differential scales were used to measure the characteristics of information sources that were associated with how credible the sources were seen by the audience, three underlying dimensions were uncovered: "competence" or whether the source was perceived as knowing the truth; "trustworthiness" or whether the source was perceived to be telling the truth; and "dynamism" or how powerful or energetic the source was.

Respondents are presented with a list of several (10 to 30) adjective pairs and asked to rate a target person, object, idea, event, etc., in terms of which adjective of each pair more correctly describes the target. The name "semantic differential" comes from the fact that the adjectives in each pair are opposites, delineating a continuum of meaning. There are usually five or seven points between the words in each pair as shown in the example below.

Please rate the person on each of the following scales. If the word on the left best describes the person, circle the "1". If the word on the right best describes the person, circle the "5". If the person is in between the word on the left and the word on the right, circle the appropriate number between the "1" and the "5".

strong	1	2	3	4	5	weak
authoritarian	1	2	3	4	5	tolerant
aware	1	2	3	4	5	oblivious
feeble	1	2	3	4	5	robust
flexible	1	2	3	4	5	rigid

Note that some adjective-pairs have been reversed so their "positive" word is on the left while others have the "negative" word on the left. This is done to prevent response set bias in which respondents go down the list and circle only 1's or only 2's, etc.

To use the results of a semantic differential scale, the codes for the reversed pairs (the ones with the "negative" word on the left) are adjusted so that a "1"

always means that the "positive" end was chosen and that a "5" always means that the "negative" end was chosen. This would produce the following result:

strong	1	2	3	4	5	weak
authoritarian	5	4	3	2	1	tolerant
aware	1	2	3	4	5	oblivious
feeble	5	4	3	2	1	robust
flexible	1	2	3	4	5	rigid

Next take the word-pairs that measure similar things and group them together. For the example above, the first and third word-pairs would be in one group and the second and fourth in another.

Now add together the circled numbers for the word-pairs in each group and divide the sum by the number of word-pairs in the group. This produces an *index* for each group of word-pairs. Ordinarily, you will have at least five word-pairs for each group.

If there are a large number of word-pairs and you don't know how they should be grouped, you can use an analytic method known as "factor analysis." This procedure identifies the underlying dimensions or "factors" along which responses to the word-pairs vary. Each word-pair has a "loading" on each factor. These loadings are like correlations; they tell the extent to which the word-pairs are associated with the factors. A word-pair having a high loading on one factor will have low loadings on all the other factors. Word-pairs that don't have any high loadings are usually ignored. You have to examine the factors to determine which word-pairs have high loadings on them in order to determine what dimensions the factors are measuring.

2. Multiple-choice questions

Many survey questions can be answered by providing a number or a word or short phrase. If the list of all the answers that your respondents might give for a question is short (no more than ten or twelve possibilities), you might set the question up as a multiple-choice item.

Which department do you work in?

a. sales
b. marketing
c. manufacturing
d. research

When you construct this kind of question, you must be careful to make sure that the list of answers you offer to your respondents is *exhaustive*—it must include all possible answers they might want to make. When this is not possible, you should include "other" as an option. Also, you should make sure that the items on the list of answers are *mutually exclusive*. If it is possible for a respondent to choose two or more answers from the list, your question is a checklist rather than a multiple-choice.

3. Open-ended questions

When the list of possible answers is long, or when you do not know what the possible answers might be, the multiple-choice format is either impractical or impossible, so you will need to use an open-ended approach. A few examples are shown here:

What word best describes how you feel when you think about economics? _____

What is your favorite place to go for a long summer vacation? _____

What was the first language you learned to speak?

_____

Of all the movies you have seen in the last year, which one did you like the best?

_____

You may want to ask some questions that will require longer answers. You are probably familiar with the "short-answer essay" questions often used on exams. Here are a few examples:

What was it about the film you named in the last question that you liked so much?

If you seated in the no smoking section of a restaurant eating dinner and the person sitting next to you opens a pack of cigarettes and prepares to light up, what would you say?

A benefit of questions like these is that they allow your respondent to provide longer, more complex answers than are possible with other formats. The main disadvantage of this approach is that you must study and analyze the longer, more complex answers before you can do anything with them. You will probably want to read all the answers your respondents provide, taking note of the range of different kinds of answers and making lists of specific words or phrases that you see. Then you would develop a coding system that would allow you to reduce the large set of long answers into a much smaller set of categories or themes. Finally, you would go through the original answers and code each one according to the system you developed. What you have effectively done is transformed the open-ended question with long, complex answers into a multiple-choice question for which your respondents (indirectly) provided the list of possible answers.

Criteria for Evaluating Survey Questions

Survey questions should be

- clear and easily understandable, stated in a direct and straightforward way;

- specific and precisely stated so the respondent will know exactly what it is you are asking;

- unambiguous and unequivocal so there is only one way to understand or interpret what the question is asking;

- simple and brief rather than complicated, cluttered, and long-winded;

- stated in terms that your respondents are likely to be familiar and comfortable with, without using complex technical terminology, jargon, or overly sophisticated wording.

Survey questions should *not* be

- leading; they should not draw the respondent toward a specific answer or make some answers clearly unattractive or undesirable;

- double-barreled; they should not ask about two or more things connected by words like "and," "or," "but," etc.;

- threatening; they should not make the respondent uncomfortable, put the respondent in a difficult or compromising position.

Don't you think that it's a good idea to consider the implications of how you dress when you go to a job interview? (leading)

What priority should the government place on increasing funding for post-secondary education and job training? (double-barreled)

Have you recently submitted distorted information on a tax return? (threatening)

When you are having a conversation with someone who thinks they are smarter than you and expects you to do what they want, even though it makes you obviously uncomfortable, what do you say to them or how do you respond to the way they treat you? (too long and complicated, unclear, double-barreled)

Order of Questions in Surveys

Since you hope your respondents will complete the survey, you want to make the experience interesting and not tedious. You want your respondents to be focused on the questions and not distracted with thoughts of the day's activities. The order in which you ask the questions can have a large effect on the way your respondents approach your survey.

It's a good idea to begin with some questions that are easy to answer. These will probably be questions about simple facts. Here are a few examples:

Please indicate your sex:	M	F
Do you own a computer?	Yes	No
Do you use electronic mail?	Yes	No
Do you drink coffee?	Yes	No
Do you have a dog?	Yes	No

Save the more complicated questions that may require some careful thought or concentration for later when you have piqued your respondents' interest and they are warmed up to the task.

Use an organizational pattern that complements the survey's research objectives:

- "funnel pattern"—moves from broad to specific

- "inverted funnel"—moves from specific to general;

- a "tree pattern" branches out in different directions, depending on the respondent's answers to early questions.

Topically related questions should be grouped together. A survey on mass media use patterns might involve questions about use of and opinions about radio, television, film, video, newspapers, magazines, and the internet. It may also ask about purchases of CDs, magazines, books, computer games, etc. For such a survey, you would probably begin with questions about the respondent's sex, age, education level, and other demographics. Then you might group the questions about each medium and take one set at a time—first the questions about use of the medium and second the questions about opinions about the medium. After the media have been dealt with individually, you might have a set of questions that ask for comparative judgements or ratings:

Which is more important to you for news: television, radio, newspapers, or magazines?

Which of the following do you think does more to inform people about current events in the world: television, radio, newspapers, or magazines?

Administering the Survey Questionnaire

There are two ways to present questions to your respondents: you can give them a copy of the questionnaire and let them read the questions and write or mark their answers or you can read the questions to them and record their answers.

Self-administered methods

There are several variations on the self-administered approach, mostly different in terms of how you get the questionnaire in the hands of the respondents:

- The distribution method that involves the smallest amount of personal contact with your respondents is to mail them. This is also the least expensive way. The lack of personal contact may mean that confidentiality is less of a problem than for other methods. This and the low cost may be the only advantages of using this method.

The main disadvantage is that you are likely to get a lower response rate with mailed questionnaires than with most other methods of distribution. This is likely due to one of several factors. A mailed questionnaire is often seen as an unwanted intrusion on the recipient's time and effort. Since there is no personal contact with the researcher, it is easy for the recipient to discard the questionnaire. In many instances, the recipient may misplace the questionnaire and find it several days or weeks later, only to conclude that it is now too late to bother.

There are a number of other problems that make this method even less attractive. One is that you don't know who is actually filling out the questionnaire. It could be the intended person, a roommate, a spouse, a secretary or someone else. Another problem is that your respondents may take the questionnaire less seriously than they would in a situation where they had some personal contact with you. They may be less likely to answer all questions, especially if the questions take more than a small amount of effort to answer.

There are a few things you can do to reduce the effect of the problems mentioned above. Use regular postage stamps instead of a postage meter. Type the recipient's name and address on the envelope rather than using printed labels. Include a cover letter addressed to the recipient with each questionnaire rather than an impersonal form letter. Write your signature with a pen on the

cover letter. All of these actions counteract the impersonality of a mailed questionnaire.

- You can personally deliver your questionnaires. This is more costly in terms of time and effort, but it is likely to result in a higher response rate, a more rapid response, a higher percentage of completed questionnaires, and perhaps more valid and accurate responses. It is also likely that the person you give the questionnaire to will be the person who fills it out.

- In some situations, you can send your questionnaires via e-mail. This can be a very fast way to distribute a large number of questionnaires over a geographically-dispersed area, but it also requires your respondents to do more of work than other methods of distribution: the respondent either has to a) print the questionnaire, fill it out, address an envelope, and pay for postage, or b) save the questionnaire as a file, edit the file, and mail it back. Filling out long questionnaires in this manner may be a rather tedious task, but short ones that are laid out in a way that makes them easy to respond to work very well.

- Another substitute for regular mail is the fax machine. There is software available that makes the distribution of questionnaires to a large number of recipients almost as quick and easy as e-mail. The main problems you are likely to encounter here are that most ordinary people do not have fax machines and using this method requires the respondent to either pay for the postage or take the time to fax the completed form back to you. Note also that this approach does not provide the degree of anonymity that is available with regular mail.

Oral interview methods

The distribution methods described above all require the respondent to read the questions and to write answers on a piece of paper or to type them on a keyboard. They all remove the researcher from direct, immediate conversation with the respondent.

To avoid the problems associated with the self-administered methods, you may decide to use face-to-face or telephone interviews instead.

- Face-to-face interviews are the most expensive, in terms of both time and money (you must travel to respondents' location), and the most intrusive of all the methods. If your sample is going to be more than a few dozen people, you will probably want to hire some additional interviewers. Before you send them out, you'll have to train them and run through some rehearsals with them so you can be sure they understand the procedures you want them to use.

 A major strength of the face-to-face approach is the ability to deal with complex topics. Because you can see how the respondent reacts to the questions as you ask them, you will have a better idea of how well they understood the questions and how they felt about answering them. You will be more likely to find out that some questions are confusing or don't make sense and you'll have an opportunity to discuss them with your respondents to see how they might be improved.

 In some circumstances the face-to-face method can be problematic because the respondent's identity is known and due to the lack of anonymity.

- Telephone surveys solve many of the problems of the face-to-face approach. Because you don't have to travel, it takes a lot less time to administer the questionnaire to people who are scattered around a city and its suburbs or around a continent. This also means that it is easier to get a representative sample. It may be easier to deal with sensitive issues over the telephone than in a face-to-face setting, since your respondents are more anonymous when you can't see their faces and when you're not sitting in their living rooms or kitchens.

 There are some drawbacks. With telephone surveys, it is difficult to keep the respondents on the line for long questionnaires. The interviews must be done when respondents are home.

Because you are interrupting them at home, you may get more refusals to participate and more people who end the conversation before answering all of your questions. Compared to the face-to-face approach, telephone interviewers are less expensive and easier to train.

Many companies that conduct telephone surveys use computer assisted telephone interviewing (CATI) systems where the interviewers sit at a computer that dials the telephone and puts the questions to be asked on the screen so the interviewer can read them to the respondent. The software that manages this also takes care of the data entry and coding, as the interviewer uses the computer's keyboard or the mouse to indicate the respondent's answers to the questions.

Response Rate Problems

Regardless of the method you use to administer your survey, you are not likely to obtain a 100% response rate. You will almost certainly get no response from some individuals and incomplete responses from others.

Total nonresponse

There are a number of reasons you will get no response from some individuals who were selected to be in your sample:

- You will be unable to locate some individuals for questioning. Their telephones have been disconnected; they have moved; they have left town; you don't have the correct telephone number or address.

- Sometimes you will locate individual but they will be unwilling to participate in the study. They say they are busy; they say it is inconvenient; they say they aren't interested.

- Some individuals will be unable to respond due to illness or language problems.

- You may locate the individuals and conduct the survey, and misplace or lose the data. You may have a computer problem that erases a file or a research assistant may lose the diskette that contains the data. If you don't have a backup copy in a safe place, it may not be possible to recover the data.

Since you have no response from these individuals, you may think that there is nothing you can do with them and you might as well forget about them. This would be an incorrect judgement, though, because it is likely that you actually can do a lot with the information you didn't get from these individuals.

There is one question whose answer is particularly important: Are the people who didn't respond different from the ones who did in any way that would have an adverse affect on the validity of your results? Here are some ways the nonrespondents may be different from the respondents:

- The nonrespondents may be concentrated in a particular neighborhood or area of the city that is different from the surrounding area in some relevant social or economic way. The residents may be unemployed, transient, extremely wealthy, or members of a religious or ethnic group that discourages or prevents them from participating.

- The nonrespondents may work in a particular organizational unit or department in which the morale is particularly poor or in which there is a high level of anxiety due to fear of layoffs or downscaling of work assignments.

- The nonrespondents may be mostly elderly, mostly young, mostly single parents, mostly apartment dwellers, or mostly people who speak a different language.

You probably have access to some of these kinds of information about your nonrespondents, even though they didn't fill our your questionnaire or answer your questions. Do as much as you can to see how the nonrespondents differ from the respondents. You may be able to get a reasonably accurate under-

standing of how your sample is biased—how it systematically under-represents certain segments of the population.

Item nonresponse

There are many reasons why some people don't answer some questions. Here are a few of them:

- Respondents may be unwilling to answer sensitive questions – questions about things that they feel are personal or questions about things they are not comfortable talking about. They may feel embarrassed about the answers they would have to give if they were being truthful, so they may simply refuse to answer.

- Your respondents may be unable to answer some questions because they don't have the required information. They may not know the answer. When this happens, some respondents may be unwilling to tell you they don't know, so they may just say they don't want to answer the question.

- Your respondents may be unable or unwilling to answer questions they don't understand or questions that are poorly constructed, obscure, vague, or that don't make sense.

- Sometimes, questions don't apply to the individual's circumstances and thus can't be answered. For example, it is hard for unemployed people to say whether or not they trust their supervisor or the people they have to deal with in the workplace.

You should examine all of the questions in your survey and determine whether some of them are left unanswered more often than others. If some questions are frequently not responded to, you should try to determine whether there are certain types of people in your sample who don't answer them. If you are able to identify a number of problematic survey questions, it is a good idea to try to talk to a few of the people who didn't answer them to see what the problem was.

It is important for you to remind yourself that the questions in your survey that make perfect sense to you will probably be somewhat confusing, completely nonsensical, or even insulting to some of your respondents. The reason this happens is that the experiences, families, and employment situations of your respondents are probably very different from yours. You may be amazed at the way some of your "perfectly clear and obvious" questions are completely misunderstood and interpreted in ways that you would never imagine. A thorough pre-test of your questionnaire will do a lot to reduce the severity of these kinds of problems.

Important Terms and Concepts

adjective pairs
checklist or inventory questions
closed questions
composite measures
computer assisted telephone interviewing (CATI)
cross-sectional survey
double-barreled questions
duplicate elements
exhaustive
face-to-face interviews
factor analysis
factor loading
foreign elements
funnel pattern
inverted funnel pattern
item nonresponse
leading questions
Likert scales
missing elements
multiple-choice questions

mutually exclusive
open-ended questions
oral interview methods
panel studies
questions about beliefs
questions about facts
questions about opinions
ranking questions
rating questions
response rate problems
sampling elements
sampling frame
self-administered methods
semantic differential scales
short-answer essay questions
simple measures
telephone surveys
total nonresponse
tree pattern
underlying dimensions

Notes

VI

Appendices

Symbols and Equations

name	symbol	equation	use
i[th] person's *score* on variable X	X_i	X_i	raw data
sample *mean*	$\bar{X}$	$\dfrac{\sum X_i}{n}$	Most common measure of central tendency for interval or ratio data.
population *mean*	μ_x	estimated by: $\bar{X}$	The most often used population *parameter* for central tendency.
i[th] person's deviation score	d_i	$X_i - \bar{X}$	Difference between person *i*'s score and the mean. Used in calculation of standard deviation, z-scores, covariance, correlation, and analysis of variance.
i[th] person's z-score	z_i	$\dfrac{X_i - \bar{X}}{s}$ or $\dfrac{d_i}{s}$	Standard score. Tells where the person is located in the distribution relative to the rest of the sample. Can be compared to z-scores for other variables.
sample *standard deviation*	*s* or sd	$\sqrt{\dfrac{\sum d_i^2}{n}}$	Most common measure of dispersion for interval or ratio data; used in the calculation of z-scores and other statistics and parameters
population *standard deviation*	σ	estimated by: $\sqrt{\dfrac{\sum d_i^2}{n-1}}$	Most used population parameter for dispersion. Note "n-1" in denominator – this gives an unbiased estimate
sample *variance*	s^2	$\dfrac{\sum d_i^2}{n}$	Fundamental measure of dispersion for an interval or ratio scaled variable.
population *variance*	σ^2	estimated by: $\dfrac{\sum d_i^2}{n-1}$	Fundamental population measure of variability of an interval or ratio scaled variable. Note "n-1" in denominator – this gives an unbiased estimate
standard error of the mean	$\sigma_{\bar{x}}$	estimated by: $\dfrac{s}{\sqrt{n}}$	Standard deviation of the sampling distribution of means. Used to tell how good an estimate of population mean the sample mean is (confidence estimates/intervals).

standard error of the difference between two means	$\sigma_{\bar{x}_1 - \bar{x}_2}$	estimated by: $\sqrt{\dfrac{s_1^2}{n_1} + \dfrac{s_2^2}{n_2}}$	Standard deviation of the sampling distribution of differences between means. **Used in z-test** to determine whether the difference between two sample means could be due to sampling variability.
z-test for a single mean	z	$\dfrac{\bar{x} - \mu}{\sigma_{\bar{x}_1 - \bar{x}_2}}$	Critical ratio used to test the significance of the difference between a sample mean and a hypothetical population mean. Used for samples with more than 30 members.
z-test for significance of difference between sample means	z	$\dfrac{\bar{x}_1 - \bar{x}_2}{\sigma_{\bar{x}_1 - \bar{x}_2}}$	Critical ratio used to test the significance of the difference between two sample means. Used for samples with more than 30 members.
corrected standard error of the difference between means (takes sample size into account;)	$SE_{\bar{x}_1 - \bar{x}_2}$	$\sqrt{\left(\dfrac{\Sigma d_1^2 + \Sigma d_2^2}{n_1 + n_2 - 2}\right)\left(\dfrac{n_1 + n_2}{n_1 n_2}\right)}$	Standard deviation of the sampling distribution of differences between means corrected for sample size. **Used in t-test** to determine whether the difference between two sample means could be due to sampling variability.
t-test for significance of difference between sample means	t	$\dfrac{\bar{x}_1 - \bar{x}_2}{SE_{\bar{x}_1 - \bar{x}_2}}$	Critical ratio used to test the significance of the difference between two sample means. Used for samples with less than 30 members.
t-test for a single mean	t	$\dfrac{\bar{x} - \mu}{\sigma_{\bar{x}_1 - \bar{x}_2}}$	Critical ratio used to test the significance of the difference between a sample mean and a hypothetical population mean. Used for samples with less than 30 members.
covariance for a pair of continuous variables	cov_{xy}	$\dfrac{\sum d_{x_i} d_{y_i}}{n}$	Relatively crude measure, based on deviation scores, of the strength of the relationship between a pair of continuous variables.
Pearson product-moment correlation (Pearson's r)	r_{xy}	$\dfrac{\sum z_x z_y}{n}$	Extremely useful measure, based on standard scores, of the strength of the relationship between a pair of continuous variables.
Spearman rank correlation (Spearman's rho)	r_s	$1 - \dfrac{6 \sum d_i^2}{n^3 - n}$	Useful measure of the strength of the relationship between a pair of ordinal variables. Based on squared differences in ranks of values in each pair (d_i^2). May also be used for continuous data.

APPENDIX A

Fisher's r to Z	Z	$\ln\left[\dfrac{1+r}{1-r}\right]$	Used to transform Pearson's r or Spearman's rho into Z which has a normally-distributed sampling distribution so it can be tested for significance.
standard error of the difference between two Zs (for Z from Fisher's r to Z)	$\sigma_{\bar{x}_1-\bar{x}_2}$	estimated by: $\sqrt{\dfrac{1}{n_1-3}+\dfrac{1}{n_2-3}}$	Standard deviation of the sampling distribution of differences between two Zs from Fisher's r to Z. Used to determine whether the difference between a pair of sample correlations could be due to sampling variability. Used for Pearson's r and Spearman's rho.
z-test for significance of difference between correlations	z	$\dfrac{Z_1-Z_2}{\sigma_{Z_1-Z_2}}$	Critical ratio used to test the significance of the difference between a pair of Pearson's r or Spearman's rho correlations.
standard error of the difference between two Zs (for Z from Fisher's r to Z)	$\sigma_{Z_1-Z_2}$	$\sigma_{Z_1-Z_2}=\sqrt{\dfrac{1}{n_1-3}+\dfrac{1}{n_2-3}}$	Standard deviation of the sampling distribution of differences between two Zs from Fisher's r to Z. Used to determine whether the difference between a pair of sample correlations could be due to sampling variability.
standard error of Z (for Z from Fisher's r to Z)	σ_Z	estimated by: $\dfrac{1}{\sqrt{n-3}}$	Standard deviation of the sampling distribution of Z from Fisher's r to Z. Can be used for estimating confidence intervals of Pearson's r or Spearman's rho.
t- test for significance of correlation	t	$r\sqrt{(n-2)/(1-r^2)}$	Critical ratio used to test the significance of Pearson's r or Spearman's rho.
between-groups Sum of Squares	SS_b	$n_1(\bar{x}_1-\bar{X}_T)^2+n_2(\bar{x}_2-\bar{X}_T)^2$	Measure of variability between groups. Used as the numerator in the F-ratio for ANOVA.
within-groups Sum of Squares	SS_w	$\sum(x_{i,1}-\bar{x}_1)^2+\sum(x_{i,2}-\bar{x}_2)^2+\ldots$	Measure of variability within groups. Used as the denominator in the F-ratio for ANOVA.
F-ratio	F	$\dfrac{MS_b}{MS_w}=\dfrac{SS_b/df_b}{SS_w/df_w}$	Critical ratio used to test the significance of the difference between sample means in a one-way Analysis of variance (ANOVA).

There are two major classes of standard deviations: those that apply to samples and those that apply to populations. You directly *calculate* the ones that apply to *samples* and you *estimate* the ones that apply to *populations*.

Statistical tests: their variables and their uses

	variables	level of scaling	sample size	purpose	example
χ^2 chi-square	one or more categorical variables	nominal	no more than 20% of cells have expected frequency less than 5	are row and column variables independent?	compare men and women in terms of passing or failing a course. IV: male/female; DV: pass/fail
t-test	1 discrete IV; 1 continuous DV	IV -- nominal DV -- int/ratio	less than 30 cases	could the difference between means be due to sampling variability?	compare ages of samples of men and women. IV: male/female; DV: age
z-test mean differences	1 discrete IV; 1 continuous DV	IV -- nominal DV -- int/ratio	30 or more cases	could the difference between means be due to sampling variability?	compare ages of samples of men and women IV: male/female; DV: age
z-test of a single mean	1 continuous variable	sample mean; population mean	30 or more cases	could the difference between sample mean and population mean be due to sampling variability?	could this sample with $\bar{x} = 87.4$ come from that population with $\mu = 95.3$?
ANOVA	discrete IV(s); 1 continuous DV	IV(s) -- nominal DV -- int/ratio	30 or more cases	could the difference between means be due to sampling variability?	compare ages of samples of students majoring in CMNS, PSYC, MATH, ECON, HIST. IV: major; DV: age
regression	continuous IV(s); 1 continuous DV	all interval or ratio	30 or more cases	describe the linear contributions of a set of independent variables to one dependent variable.	examine factors (age, GPA, undergrad major, family income) that contribute to success in graduate school. IVs: age, CGPA, major, income; DV: graduate performance
t-test for significance of correlation	2 continuous or ordinal variables	both at least ordinal	20 or more cases	could sample correlation be due to sampling variability?	relation between age and amount of time spent sleeping at night. V1: age; V2: time sleeping
z-test for correlation differences	2 pairs of continuous or ordinal variables	all at least ordinal	30 or more cases	could difference between sample correlations be due to sampling variability?	compare r (age - GPA) to r (age - coffee consumption). V1: age; V2: GPA; V3: coffee consumption
z-test for proportion differences	1 discrete IV; 1"continuous " DV	IV -- nominal DV -- ratio only	30 or more cases	could difference between a pair of proportions be due to sampling variability?	compare proportion of men and women who study math. IV: male/female; DV: % who study math

Table 1: Areas under the normal curve

($z = 0.0$ to $z = 0.67$)

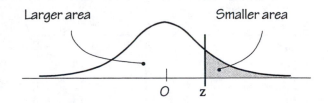

z	z to mean	smaller area	larger area	z	z to mean	smaller area	larger area
0.00	0.0000	0.5000	0.5000	0.34	0.1331	0.3669	0.6331
0.01	0.0040	0.4960	0.5040	0.35	0.1368	0.3632	0.6368
0.02	0.0080	0.4920	0.5080	0.36	0.1406	0.3594	0.6406
0.03	0.0120	0.4880	0.5120	0.37	0.1443	0.3557	0.6443
0.04	0.0160	0.4840	0.5160	0.38	0.1480	0.3520	0.6480
0.05	0.0199	0.4801	0.5199	0.39	0.1517	0.3483	0.6517
0.06	0.0239	0.4761	0.5239	0.40	0.1554	0.3446	0.6554
0.07	0.0279	0.4721	0.5279	0.41	0.1591	0.3409	0.6591
0.08	0.0319	0.4681	0.5319	0.42	0.1628	0.3372	0.6628
0.09	0.0359	0.4641	0.5359	0.43	0.1664	0.3336	0.6664
0.10	0.0398	0.4602	0.5398	0.44	0.1700	0.3300	0.6700
0.11	0.0438	0.4562	0.5438	0.45	0.1736	0.3264	0.6736
0.12	0.0478	0.4522	0.5478	0.46	0.1772	0.3228	0.6772
0.13	0.0517	0.4483	0.5517	0.47	0.1808	0.3192	0.6808
0.14	0.0557	0.4443	0.5557	0.48	0.1844	0.3156	0.6844
0.15	0.0596	0.4404	0.5596	0.49	0.1879	0.3121	0.6879
0.16	0.0636	0.4364	0.5636	0.50	0.1915	0.3085	0.6915
0.17	0.0675	0.4325	0.5675	0.51	0.1950	0.3050	0.6950
0.18	0.0714	0.4286	0.5714	0.52	0.1985	0.3015	0.6985
0.19	0.0753	0.4247	0.5753	0.53	0.2019	0.2981	0.7019
0.20	0.0793	0.4207	0.5793	0.54	0.2054	0.2946	0.7054
0.21	0.0832	0.4168	0.5832	0.55	0.2088	0.2912	0.7088
0.22	0.0871	0.4129	0.5871	0.56	0.2123	0.2877	0.7123
0.23	0.0910	0.4090	0.5910	0.57	0.2157	0.2843	0.7157
0.24	0.0948	0.4052	0.5948	0.58	0.2190	0.2810	0.7190
0.25	0.0987	0.4013	0.5987	0.59	0.2224	0.2776	0.7224
0.26	0.1026	0.3974	0.6026	0.60	0.2257	0.2743	0.7257
0.27	0.1064	0.3936	0.6064	0.61	0.2291	0.2709	0.7291
0.28	0.1103	0.3897	0.6103	0.62	0.2324	0.2676	0.7324
0.29	0.1141	0.3859	0.6141	0.63	0.2357	0.2643	0.7357
0.30	0.1179	0.3821	0.6179	0.64	0.2389	0.2611	0.7389
0.31	0.1217	0.3783	0.6217	0.65	0.2422	0.2578	0.7422
0.32	0.1255	0.3745	0.6255	0.66	0.2454	0.2546	0.7454
0.33	0.1293	0.3707	0.6293	0.67	0.2486	0.2514	0.7486

(more . . .)

Table 1: continued   ($z = 0.68$ to $z = 1.49$)

z	z to mean	smaller area	larger area	z	z to mean	smaller area	larger area
0.68	0.2517	0.2483	0.7517	1.09	0.3621	0.1379	0.8621
0.69	0.2549	0.2451	0.7549	1.10	0.3643	0.1357	0.8643
0.70	0.2580	0.2420	0.7580	1.11	0.3665	0.1335	0.8665
0.71	0.2611	0.2389	0.7611	1.12	0.3686	0.1314	0.8686
0.72	0.2642	0.2358	0.7642	1.13	0.3708	0.1292	0.8708
0.73	0.2673	0.2327	0.7673	1.14	0.3729	0.1271	0.8729
0.74	0.2704	0.2296	0.7704	1.15	0.3749	0.1251	0.8749
0.75	0.2734	0.2266	0.7734	1.16	0.3770	0.1230	0.8770
0.76	0.2764	0.2236	0.7764	1.17	0.3790	0.1210	0.8790
0.77	0.2794	0.2206	0.7794	1.18	0.3810	0.1190	0.8810
0.78	0.2823	0.2177	0.7823	1.19	0.3830	0.1170	0.8830
0.79	0.2852	0.2148	0.7852	1.20	0.3849	0.1151	0.8849
0.80	0.2881	0.2119	0.7881	1.21	0.3869	0.1131	0.8869
0.81	0.2910	0.2090	0.7910	1.22	0.3888	0.1112	0.8888
0.82	0.2939	0.2061	0.7939	1.23	0.3907	0.1093	0.8907
0.83	0.2967	0.2033	0.7967	1.24	0.3925	0.1075	0.8925
0.84	0.2995	0.2005	0.7995	1.25	0.3944	0.1056	0.8944
0.85	0.3023	0.1977	0.8023	1.26	0.3962	0.1038	0.8962
0.86	0.3051	0.1949	0.8051	1.27	0.3980	0.1020	0.8980
0.87	0.3078	0.1922	0.8078	1.28	0.3997	0.1003	0.8997
0.88	0.3106	0.1894	0.8106	1.29	0.4015	0.0985	0.9015
0.89	0.3133	0.1867	0.8133	1.30	0.4032	0.0968	0.9032
0.90	0.3159	0.1841	0.8159	1.31	0.4049	0.0951	0.9049
0.91	0.3186	0.1814	0.8186	1.32	0.4066	0.0934	0.9066
0.92	0.3212	0.1788	0.8212	1.33	0.4082	0.0918	0.9082
0.93	0.3238	0.1762	0.8238	1.34	0.4099	0.0901	0.9099
0.94	0.3264	0.1736	0.8264	1.35	0.4115	0.0885	0.9115
0.95	0.3289	0.1711	0.8289	1.36	0.4131	0.0869	0.9131
0.96	0.3315	0.1685	0.8315	1.37	0.4147	0.0853	0.9147
0.97	0.3340	0.1660	0.8340	1.38	0.4162	0.0838	0.9162
0.98	0.3365	0.1635	0.8365	1.39	0.4177	0.0823	0.9177
0.99	0.3389	0.1611	0.8389	1.40	0.4192	0.0808	0.9192
1.00	0.3413	0.1587	0.8413	1.41	0.4207	0.0793	0.9207
1.01	0.3438	0.1562	0.8438	1.42	0.4222	0.0778	0.9222
1.02	0.3461	0.1539	0.8461	1.43	0.4236	0.0764	0.9236
1.03	0.3485	0.1515	0.8485	1.44	0.4251	0.0749	0.9251
1.04	0.3508	0.1492	0.8508	1.45	0.4265	0.0735	0.9265
1.05	0.3531	0.1469	0.8531	1.46	0.4279	0.0721	0.9279
1.06	0.3554	0.1446	0.8554	1.47	0.4292	0.0708	0.9292
1.07	0.3577	0.1423	0.8577	1.48	0.4306	0.0694	0.9306
1.08	0.3599	0.1401	0.8599	1.49	0.4319	0.0681	0.9319

(more . . .)

Table 1: continued

z	z to mean	smaller area	larger area	z	z to mean	smaller area	larger area
1.50	0.4332	0.0668	0.9332	1.91	0.4719	0.0281	0.9719
1.51	0.4345	0.0655	0.9345	1.92	0.4726	0.0274	0.9726
1.52	0.4357	0.0643	0.9357	1.93	0.4732	0.0268	0.9732
1.53	0.4370	0.0630	0.9370	1.94	0.4738	0.0262	0.9738
1.54	0.4382	0.0618	0.9382	1.95	0.4744	0.0256	0.9744
1.55	0.4394	0.0606	0.9394	1.96	0.4750	0.0250	0.9750
1.56	0.4406	0.0594	0.9406	1.97	0.4756	0.0244	0.9756
1.57	0.4418	0.0582	0.9418	1.98	0.4761	0.0239	0.9761
1.58	0.4429	0.0571	0.9429	1.99	0.4767	0.0233	0.9767
1.59	0.4441	0.0559	0.9441	2.00	0.4772	0.0228	0.9772
1.60	0.4452	0.0548	0.9452	2.01	0.4778	0.0222	0.9778
1.61	0.4463	0.0537	0.9463	2.02	0.4783	0.0217	0.9783
1.62	0.4474	0.0526	0.9474	2.03	0.4788	0.0212	0.9788
1.63	0.4484	0.0516	0.9484	2.04	0.4793	0.0207	0.9793
1.64	0.4495	0.0505	0.9495	2.05	0.4798	0.0202	0.9798
1.65	0.4505	0.0495	0.9505	2.06	0.4803	0.0197	0.9803
1.66	0.4515	0.0485	0.9515	2.07	0.4808	0.0192	0.9808
1.67	0.4525	0.0475	0.9525	2.08	0.4812	0.0188	0.9812
1.68	0.4535	0.0465	0.9535	2.09	0.4817	0.0183	0.9817
1.69	0.4545	0.0455	0.9545	2.10	0.4821	0.0179	0.9821
1.70	0.4554	0.0446	0.9554	2.11	0.4826	0.0174	0.9826
1.71	0.4564	0.0436	0.9564	2.12	0.4830	0.0170	0.9830
1.72	0.4573	0.0427	0.9573	2.13	0.4834	0.0166	0.9834
1.73	0.4582	0.0418	0.9582	2.14	0.4838	0.0162	0.9838
1.74	0.4591	0.0409	0.9591	2.15	0.4842	0.0158	0.9842
1.75	0.4599	0.0401	0.9599	2.16	0.4846	0.0154	0.9846
1.76	0.4608	0.0392	0.9608	2.17	0.4850	0.0150	0.9850
1.77	0.4616	0.0384	0.9616	2.18	0.4854	0.0146	0.9854
1.78	0.4625	0.0375	0.9625	2.19	0.4857	0.0143	0.9857
1.79	0.4633	0.0367	0.9633	2.20	0.4861	0.0139	0.9861
1.80	0.4641	0.0359	0.9641	2.21	0.4864	0.0136	0.9864
1.81	0.4649	0.0351	0.9649	2.22	0.4868	0.0132	0.9868
1.82	0.4656	0.0344	0.9656	2.23	0.4871	0.0129	0.9871
1.83	0.4664	0.0336	0.9664	2.24	0.4875	0.0125	0.9875
1.84	0.4671	0.0329	0.9671	2.25	0.4878	0.0122	0.9878
1.85	0.4678	0.0322	0.9678	2.26	0.4881	0.0119	0.9881
1.86	0.4686	0.0314	0.9686	2.27	0.4884	0.0116	0.9884
1.87	0.4693	0.0307	0.9693	2.28	0.4887	0.0113	0.9887
1.88	0.4699	0.0301	0.9699	2.29	0.4890	0.0110	0.9890
1.89	0.4706	0.0294	0.9706	2.30	0.4893	0.0107	0.9893
1.90	0.4713	0.0287	0.9713	2.31	0.4896	0.0104	0.9896

(more . . .)

Table 1: continued   (z = 2.32 to z = 3.90)

z	z to mean	smaller area	larger area	z	z to mean	smaller area	larger area
2.32	0.4898	0.0102	0.9898	2.73	0.4968	0.0032	0.9968
2.33	0.4901	0.0099	0.9901	2.74	0.4969	0.0031	0.9969
2.34	0.4904	0.0096	0.9904	2.75	0.4970	0.0030	0.9970
2.35	0.4906	0.0094	0.9906	2.76	0.4971	0.0029	0.9971
2.36	0.4909	0.0091	0.9909	2.77	0.4972	0.0028	0.9972
2.37	0.4911	0.0089	0.9911	2.78	0.4973	0.0027	0.9973
2.38	0.4913	0.0087	0.9913	2.79	0.4974	0.0026	0.9974
2.39	0.4916	0.0084	0.9916	2.80	0.4974	0.0026	0.9974
2.40	0.4918	0.0082	0.9918	2.81	0.4975	0.0025	0.9975
2.41	0.4920	0.0080	0.9920	2.82	0.4976	0.0024	0.9976
2.42	0.4922	0.0078	0.9922	2.83	0.4977	0.0023	0.9977
2.43	0.4925	0.0075	0.9925	2.84	0.4977	0.0023	0.9977
2.44	0.4927	0.0073	0.9927	2.85	0.4978	0.0022	0.9978
2.45	0.4929	0.0071	0.9929	2.86	0.4979	0.0021	0.9979
2.46	0.4931	0.0069	0.9931	2.87	0.4979	0.0021	0.9979
2.47	0.4932	0.0068	0.9932	2.88	0.4980	0.0020	0.9980
2.48	0.4934	0.0066	0.9934	2.89	0.4981	0.0019	0.9981
2.49	0.4936	0.0064	0.9936	2.90	0.4981	0.0019	0.9981
2.50	0.4938	0.0062	0.9938	2.91	0.4982	0.0018	0.9982
2.51	0.4940	0.0060	0.9940	2.92	0.4982	0.0018	0.9982
2.52	0.4941	0.0059	0.9941	2.93	0.4983	0.0017	0.9983
2.53	0.4943	0.0057	0.9943	2.94	0.4984	0.0016	0.9984
2.54	0.4945	0.0055	0.9945	2.95	0.4984	0.0016	0.9984
2.55	0.4946	0.0054	0.9946	2.96	0.4985	0.0015	0.9985
2.56	0.4948	0.0052	0.9948	2.98	0.4986	0.0014	0.9986
2.57	0.4949	0.0051	0.9949	3.00	0.4987	0.0013	0.9987
2.58	0.4951	0.0049	0.9951	3.02	0.4987	0.0013	0.9987
2.59	0.4952	0.0048	0.9952	3.04	0.4988	0.0012	0.9988
2.60	0.4953	0.0047	0.9953	3.06	0.4989	0.0011	0.9989
2.61	0.4955	0.0045	0.9955	3.08	0.4990	0.0010	0.9990
2.62	0.4956	0.0044	0.9956	3.10	0.4990	0.0010	0.9990
2.63	0.4957	0.0043	0.9957	3.15	0.4992	0.0008	0.9992
2.64	0.4959	0.0041	0.9959	3.20	0.4993	0.0007	0.9993
2.65	0.4960	0.0040	0.9960	3.25	0.4994	0.0006	0.9994
2.66	0.4961	0.0039	0.9961	3.30	0.4995	0.0005	0.9995
2.67	0.4962	0.0038	0.9962	3.40	0.4997	0.0003	0.9997
2.68	0.4963	0.0037	0.9963	3.50	0.4998	0.0002	0.9998
2.69	0.4964	0.0036	0.9964	3.60	0.49984	0.00016	0.99984
2.70	0.4965	0.0035	0.9965	3.70	0.49989	0.00011	0.99989
2.71	0.4966	0.0034	0.9966	3.80	0.49993	0.00007	0.99993
2.72	0.4967	0.0033	0.9967	3.90	0.49995	0.00005	0.99995

Table 2: Critical values of t

	Level of significance for one-tailed test							
	.1	.05	.025	.01	.005	.0025	.001	.0005
	Level of significance for two-tailed test							
df	.2	.1	.05	.02	.01	.005	.002	.001
1	3.078	6.314	12.706	31.821	63.657	127.321	318.309	636.619
2	1.886	2.920	4.303	6.965	9.925	14.089	22.327	31.599
3	1.638	2.353	3.182	4.541	5.841	7.453	10.215	12.924
4	1.533	2.132	2.776	3.747	4.604	5.598	7.173	8.610
5	1.476	2.015	2.571	3.365	4.032	4.773	5.893	6.869
6	1.440	1.943	2.447	3.143	3.707	4.317	5.208	5.959
7	1.415	1.895	2.365	2.998	3.499	4.029	4.785	5.408
8	1.397	1.860	2.306	2.896	3.355	3.833	4.501	5.041
9	1.383	1.833	2.262	2.821	3.250	3.690	4.297	4.781
10	1.372	1.812	2.228	2.764	3.169	3.581	4.144	4.587
11	1.363	1.796	2.201	2.718	3.106	3.497	4.025	4.437
12	1.356	1.782	2.179	2.681	3.055	3.428	3.930	4.318
13	1.350	1.771	2.160	2.650	3.012	3.372	3.852	4.221
14	1.345	1.761	2.145	2.624	2.977	3.326	3.787	4.140
15	1.341	1.753	2.131	2.602	2.947	3.286	3.733	4.073
16	1.337	1.746	2.120	2.583	2.921	3.252	3.686	4.015
17	1.333	1.740	2.110	2.567	2.898	3.222	3.646	3.965
18	1.330	1.734	2.101	2.552	2.878	3.197	3.610	3.922
19	1.328	1.729	2.093	2.539	2.861	3.174	3.579	3.883
20	1.325	1.725	2.086	2.528	2.845	3.153	3.552	3.850
21	1.323	1.721	2.080	2.518	2.831	3.135	3.527	3.819
22	1.321	1.717	2.074	2.508	2.819	3.119	3.505	3.792
23	1.319	1.714	2.069	2.500	2.807	3.104	3.485	3.768
24	1.318	1.711	2.064	2.492	2.797	3.091	3.467	3.745
25	1.316	1.708	2.060	2.485	2.787	3.078	3.450	3.725
26	1.315	1.706	2.056	2.479	2.779	3.067	3.435	3.707
27	1.314	1.703	2.052	2.473	2.771	3.057	3.421	3.690
28	1.313	1.701	2.048	2.467	2.763	3.047	3.408	3.674
29	1.311	1.699	2.045	2.462	2.756	3.038	3.396	3.659
30	1.310	1.697	2.042	2.457	2.750	3.030	3.385	3.646
40	1.303	1.684	2.021	2.423	2.704	2.971	3.307	3.551
50	1.299	1.676	2.009	2.403	2.678	2.937	3.261	3.496
60	1.296	1.671	2.000	2.390	2.660	2.915	3.232	3.460
70	1.294	1.667	1.994	2.381	2.648	2.899	3.211	3.435
80	1.292	1.664	1.990	2.374	2.639	2.887	3.195	3.416
90	1.291	1.662	1.987	2.368	2.632	2.878	3.183	3.402
100	1.290	1.660	1.984	2.364	2.626	2.871	3.174	3.390
110	1.289	1.659	1.982	2.361	2.621	2.865	3.166	3.381
120	1.289	1.658	1.980	2.358	2.617	2.860	3.160	3.373
∞	1.282	1.645	1.960	2.327	2.576	2.808	3.091	3.291

Table 3: Critical values of χ^2

df	Probability								
	.5	.3	.2	.1	.05	.02	.01	.005	.001
1	0.455	1.074	1.642	2.706	3.841	5.412	6.635	7.879	10.828
2	1.386	2.408	3.219	4.605	5.991	7.824	9.210	10.597	13.816
3	2.366	3.665	4.642	6.251	7.815	9.837	11.345	12.838	16.266
4	3.357	4.878	5.989	7.779	9.488	11.668	13.277	14.860	18.467
5	4.351	6.064	7.289	9.236	11.070	13.388	15.086	16.750	20.515
6	5.348	7.231	8.558	10.645	12.592	15.033	16.812	18.548	22.458
7	6.346	8.383	9.803	12.017	14.067	16.622	18.475	20.278	24.322
8	7.344	9.524	11.030	13.362	15.507	18.168	20.090	21.955	26.124
9	8.343	10.656	12.242	14.684	16.919	19.679	21.666	23.589	27.877
10	9.342	11.781	13.442	15.987	18.307	21.161	23.209	25.188	29.588
11	10.341	12.899	14.631	17.275	19.675	22.618	24.725	26.757	31.264
12	11.340	14.011	15.812	18.549	21.026	24.054	26.217	28.300	32.909
13	12.340	15.119	16.985	19.812	22.362	25.472	27.688	29.819	34.528
14	13.339	16.222	18.151	21.064	23.685	26.873	29.141	31.319	36.123
15	14.339	17.322	19.311	22.307	24.996	28.259	30.578	32.801	37.697
16	15.338	18.418	20.465	23.542	26.296	29.633	32.000	34.267	39.252
17	16.338	19.511	21.615	24.769	27.587	30.995	33.409	35.718	40.790
18	17.338	20.601	22.760	25.989	28.869	32.346	34.805	37.156	42.312
19	18.338	21.689	23.900	27.204	30.144	33.687	36.191	38.582	43.820
20	19.337	22.775	25.038	28.412	31.410	35.020	37.566	39.997	45.315
21	20.337	23.858	26.171	29.615	32.671	36.343	38.932	41.401	46.797
22	21.337	24.939	27.301	30.813	33.924	37.659	40.289	42.796	48.268
23	22.337	26.018	28.429	32.007	35.172	38.968	41.638	44.181	49.728
24	23.337	27.096	29.553	33.196	36.415	40.270	42.980	45.559	51.179
25	24.337	28.172	30.675	34.382	37.652	41.566	44.314	46.928	52.620
26	25.336	29.246	31.795	35.563	38.885	42.856	45.642	48.290	54.052
27	26.336	30.319	32.912	36.741	40.113	44.140	46.963	49.645	55.476
28	27.336	31.391	34.027	37.916	41.337	45.419	48.278	50.993	56.892
29	28.336	32.461	35.139	39.087	42.557	46.693	49.588	52.336	58.301
30	29.336	33.530	36.250	40.256	43.773	47.962	50.892	53.672	59.703
32	31.336	35.665	38.466	42.585	46.194	50.487	53.486	56.328	62.487
33	32.336	36.731	39.572	43.745	47.400	51.743	54.776	57.648	63.870
34	33.336	37.795	40.676	44.903	48.602	52.995	56.061	58.964	65.247
35	34.336	38.859	41.778	46.059	49.802	54.244	57.342	60.275	66.619
37	36.336	40.984	43.978	48.363	52.192	56.730	59.893	62.883	69.346
38	37.335	42.045	45.076	49.513	53.384	57.969	61.162	64.181	70.703
40	39.335	44.165	47.269	51.805	55.758	60.436	63.691	66.766	73.402
42	41.335	46.282	49.456	54.090	58.124	62.892	66.206	69.336	76.084
44	43.335	48.396	51.639	56.369	60.481	65.337	68.710	71.893	78.750
46	45.335	50.507	53.818	58.641	62.830	67.771	71.201	74.437	81.400

(more . . .)

Table 3: continued

df	Probability								
	.5	.3	.2	.1	.05	.02	.01	.005	.001
48	47.335	52.616	55.993	60.907	65.171	70.197	73.683	76.969	84.037
49	48.335	53.670	57.079	62.038	66.339	71.406	74.919	78.231	85.351
50	49.335	54.723	58.164	63.167	67.505	72.613	76.154	79.490	86.661
52	51.335	56.827	60.332	65.422	69.832	75.021	78.616	82.001	89.272
54	53.335	58.930	62.496	67.673	72.153	77.422	81.069	84.502	91.872
56	55.335	61.031	64.658	69.919	74.468	79.815	83.513	86.994	94.461
58	57.335	63.129	66.816	72.160	76.778	82.201	85.950	89.477	97.039
60	59.335	65.227	68.972	74.397	79.082	84.580	88.379	91.952	99.607
62	61.335	67.322	71.125	76.630	81.381	86.953	90.802	94.419	102.166
64	63.335	69.416	73.276	78.860	83.675	89.320	93.217	96.878	104.716
66	65.335	71.508	75.424	81.085	85.965	91.681	95.626	99.330	107.258
68	67.335	73.600	77.571	83.308	88.250	94.037	98.028	101.776	109.791
70	69.334	75.689	79.715	85.527	90.531	96.388	100.425	104.215	112.317
72	71.334	77.778	81.857	87.743	92.808	98.733	102.816	106.648	114.835
74	73.334	79.865	83.997	89.956	95.081	101.074	105.202	109.074	117.346
75	74.334	80.908	85.066	91.061	96.217	102.243	106.393	110.286	118.599
76	75.334	81.951	86.135	92.166	97.351	103.410	107.583	111.495	119.850
78	77.334	84.036	88.271	94.374	99.617	105.742	109.958	113.911	122.348
80	79.334	86.120	90.405	96.578	101.879	108.069	112.329	116.321	124.839
81	80.334	87.161	91.472	97.680	103.010	109.232	113.512	117.524	126.083
82	81.334	88.202	92.538	98.780	104.139	110.393	114.695	118.726	127.324
84	83.334	90.284	94.669	100.980	106.395	112.712	117.057	121.126	129.804
86	85.334	92.365	96.799	103.177	108.648	115.028	119.414	123.522	132.277
88	87.334	94.445	98.927	105.372	110.898	117.340	121.767	125.913	134.745
90	89.334	96.524	101.054	107.565	113.145	119.648	124.116	128.299	137.208
92	91.334	98.602	103.179	109.756	115.390	121.954	126.462	130.681	139.666
94	93.334	100.679	105.303	111.944	117.632	124.255	128.803	133.059	142.119
96	95.334	102.755	107.425	114.131	119.871	126.554	131.141	135.433	144.567
98	97.334	104.831	109.547	116.315	122.108	128.849	133.476	137.803	147.010
100	99.334	106.906	111.667	118.498	124.342	131.142	135.807	140.169	149.449
102	101.334	108.980	113.786	120.679	126.574	133.431	138.134	142.532	151.884
104	103.334	111.053	115.903	122.858	128.804	135.718	140.459	144.891	154.314
106	105.334	113.126	118.020	125.035	131.031	138.002	142.780	147.247	156.740
108	107.334	115.198	120.135	127.211	133.257	140.283	145.099	149.599	159.162
110	109.334	117.269	122.250	129.385	135.480	142.562	147.414	151.948	161.581
112	111.334	119.340	124.363	131.558	137.701	144.838	149.727	154.294	163.995
114	113.334	121.410	126.475	133.729	139.921	147.111	152.037	156.637	166.406
115	114.334	122.444	127.531	134.813	141.030	148.247	153.191	157.808	167.610
116	115.334	123.479	128.587	135.898	142.138	149.383	154.344	158.977	168.813
118	117.334	125.548	130.697	138.066	144.354	151.652	156.648	161.314	171.217

(more...)

Table 3: continued

df	.5	.3	.2	.1	.05	.02	.01	.005	.001
				Probability					
120	119.334	127.616	132.806	140.233	146.567	153.918	158.950	163.648	173.617
122	121.334	129.684	134.915	142.398	148.779	156.183	161.250	165.980	176.014
124	123.334	131.751	137.022	144.562	150.989	158.445	163.546	168.308	178.408
125	124.334	132.784	138.076	145.643	152.094	159.575	164.694	169.471	179.604
126	125.334	133.817	139.129	146.724	153.198	160.705	165.841	170.634	180.799
128	127.334	135.883	141.235	148.885	155.405	162.963	168.133	172.957	183.186
130	129.334	137.949	143.340	151.045	157.610	165.219	170.423	175.278	185.571
132	131.334	140.014	145.444	153.204	159.814	167.473	172.711	177.597	187.953
134	133.334	142.078	147.548	155.361	162.016	169.725	174.996	179.913	190.331
136	135.334	144.142	149.651	157.518	164.216	171.976	177.280	182.226	192.707
138	137.334	146.206	151.753	159.673	166.415	174.224	179.561	184.538	195.080
140	139.334	148.269	153.854	161.827	168.613	176.471	181.840	186.847	197.451
142	141.334	150.331	155.954	163.980	170.809	178.716	184.118	189.154	199.819
144	143.334	152.393	158.054	166.132	173.004	180.959	186.393	191.458	202.184
146	145.334	154.455	160.153	168.283	175.198	183.200	188.666	193.761	204.547
148	147.334	156.516	162.251	170.432	177.390	185.440	190.938	196.062	206.907
150	149.334	158.577	164.349	172.581	179.581	187.678	193.208	198.360	209.265
160	159.334	168.876	174.828	183.311	190.516	198.846	204.530	209.824	221.019
180	179.334	189.446	195.743	204.704	212.304	221.077	227.056	232.620	244.370
200	199.334	209.985	216.609	226.021	233.994	243.187	249.445	255.264	267.541
300	299.334	312.346	320.397	331.789	341.395	352.425	359.906	366.844	381.425
400	399.334	414.335	423.590	436.649	447.632	460.211	468.724	476.606	493.132
500	499.333	516.087	526.401	540.930	553.127	567.070	576.493	585.207	603.446
600	599.333	617.671	628.943	644.800	658.094	673.270	683.516	692.982	712.771
700	702.000	719.128	731.280	748.359	762.661	778.972	789.974	800.131	821.347
800	802.000	820.483	833.456	851.671	866.911	884.279	895.984	906.786	929.329
900	902.000	921.756	935.499	954.782	970.904	989.263	1001.630	1013.036	1036.826
∞	1002.000	1022.960	1037.431	1057.724	1074.679	1093.977	1106.969	1118.948	1143.917

Table 4: Critical values of *F*

		Numerator degrees of freedom											(p = .05 p = .01)	
	1	**2**	**3**	**4**	**5**	**6**	**7**	**8**	**9**	**10**	**12**	**14**	**16**
1	161.45	199.50	215.71	224.58	230.16	233.99	236.77	238.88	240.54	241.88	243.91	245.36	246.46
	4052.2	**4999.5**	**5403.4**	**5624.6**	**5763.7**	**5859.0**	**5928.4**	**5981.1**	**6022.5**	**6055.9**	**6106.3**	**6142.7**	**6170.1**
2	18.51	19.00	19.16	19.25	19.30	19.33	19.35	19.37	19.38	19.40	19.41	19.42	19.43
	98.50	**99.00**	**99.17**	**99.25**	**99.30**	**99.33**	**99.36**	**99.37**	**99.39**	**99.40**	**99.42**	**99.43**	**99.44**
3	10.13	9.55	9.28	9.12	9.01	8.94	8.89	8.85	8.81	8.79	8.74	8.71	8.69
	34.12	**30.82**	**29.46**	**28.71**	**28.24**	**27.91**	**27.67**	**27.49**	**27.35**	**27.23**	**27.05**	**26.92**	**26.83**
4	7.71	6.94	6.59	6.39	6.26	6.16	6.09	6.04	6.00	5.96	5.91	5.87	5.84
	21.20	**18.00**	**16.69**	**15.98**	**15.52**	**15.21**	**14.98**	**14.80**	**14.66**	**14.55**	**14.37**	**14.25**	**14.15**
5	6.61	5.79	5.41	5.19	5.05	4.95	4.88	4.82	4.77	4.74	4.68	4.64	4.60
	16.26	**13.27**	**12.06**	**11.39**	**10.97**	**10.67**	**10.46**	**10.29**	**10.16**	**10.05**	**9.89**	**9.77**	**9.68**
6	5.99	5.14	4.76	4.53	4.39	4.28	4.21	4.15	4.10	4.06	4.00	3.96	3.92
	13.75	**10.92**	**9.78**	**9.15**	**8.75**	**8.47**	**8.26**	**8.10**	**7.98**	**7.87**	**7.72**	**7.60**	**7.52**
7	5.59	4.74	4.35	4.12	3.97	3.87	3.79	3.73	3.68	3.64	3.57	3.53	3.49
	12.25	**9.55**	**8.45**	**7.85**	**7.46**	**7.19**	**6.99**	**6.84**	**6.72**	**6.62**	**6.47**	**6.36**	**6.28**
8	5.32	4.46	4.07	3.84	3.69	3.58	3.50	3.44	3.39	3.35	3.28	3.24	3.20
	11.26	**8.65**	**7.59**	**7.01**	**6.63**	**6.37**	**6.18**	**6.03**	**5.91**	**5.81**	**5.67**	**5.56**	**5.48**
9	5.12	4.26	3.86	3.63	3.48	3.37	3.29	3.23	3.18	3.14	3.07	3.03	2.99
	10.56	**8.02**	**6.99**	**6.42**	**6.06**	**5.80**	**5.61**	**5.47**	**5.35**	**5.26**	**5.11**	**5.01**	**4.92**
10	4.96	4.10	3.71	3.48	3.33	3.22	3.14	3.07	3.02	2.98	2.91	2.86	2.83
	10.04	**7.56**	**6.55**	**5.99**	**5.64**	**5.39**	**5.20**	**5.06**	**4.94**	**4.85**	**4.71**	**4.60**	**4.52**
11	4.84	3.98	3.59	3.36	3.20	3.09	3.01	2.95	2.90	2.85	2.79	2.74	2.70
	9.65	**7.21**	**6.22**	**5.67**	**5.32**	**5.07**	**4.89**	**4.74**	**4.63**	**4.54**	**4.40**	**4.29**	**4.21**
12	4.75	3.89	3.49	3.26	3.11	3.00	2.91	2.85	2.80	2.75	2.69	2.64	2.60
	9.33	**6.93**	**5.95**	**5.41**	**5.06**	**4.82**	**4.64**	**4.50**	**4.39**	**4.30**	**4.16**	**4.05**	**3.97**
13	4.67	3.81	3.41	3.18	3.03	2.92	2.83	2.77	2.71	2.67	2.60	2.55	2.51
	9.07	**6.70**	**5.74**	**5.21**	**4.86**	**4.62**	**4.44**	**4.30**	**4.19**	**4.10**	**3.96**	**3.86**	**3.78**
14	4.60	3.74	3.34	3.11	2.96	2.85	2.76	2.70	2.65	2.60	2.53	2.48	2.44
	8.86	**6.51**	**5.56**	**5.04**	**4.69**	**4.46**	**4.28**	**4.14**	**4.03**	**3.94**	**3.80**	**3.70**	**3.62**
15	4.54	3.68	3.29	3.06	2.90	2.79	2.71	2.64	2.59	2.54	2.48	2.42	2.38
	8.68	**6.36**	**5.42**	**4.89**	**4.56**	**4.32**	**4.14**	**4.00**	**3.89**	**3.80**	**3.67**	**3.56**	**3.49**
16	4.49	3.63	3.24	3.01	2.85	2.74	2.66	2.59	2.54	2.49	2.42	2.37	2.33
	8.53	**6.23**	**5.29**	**4.77**	**4.44**	**4.20**	**4.03**	**3.89**	**3.78**	**3.69**	**3.55**	**3.45**	**3.37**
17	4.45	3.59	3.20	2.96	2.81	2.70	2.61	2.55	2.49	2.45	2.38	2.33	2.29
	8.40	**6.11**	**5.18**	**4.67**	**4.34**	**4.10**	**3.93**	**3.79**	**3.68**	**3.59**	**3.46**	**3.35**	**3.27**

Denominator degrees of freedom

(more...)

Table 4: continued

Numerator degrees of freedom   (p = .05 p = .01)

	18	20	24	30	40	50	60	75	100	150	200	500	∞
1	247.32	248.01	249.05	250.10	251.14	251.77	252.20	252.62	253.04	253.46	253.68	254.06	254.32
	6191.5	**6208.7**	**6234.6**	**6260.6**	**6286.78**	**6302.5**	**6313.0**	**6323.6**	**6334.1**	**6344.7**	**6340.0**	**6359.5**	**6366.0**
2	19.44	19.45	19.45	19.46	19.47	19.48	19.48	19.48	19.49	19.49	19.49	19.49	19.50
	99.44	**99.45**	**99.46**	**99.47**	**99.47**	**99.48**	**99.48**	**99.49**	**99.49**	**99.49**	**99.49**	**99.50**	**99.50**
3	8.67	8.66	8.64	8.62	8.59	8.58	8.57	8.56	8.55	8.54	8.54	8.53	8.53
	26.75	**26.69**	**26.60**	**26.50**	**26.41**	**26.35**	**26.32**	**26.28**	**26.24**	**26.20**	**26.18**	**26.15**	**26.13**
4	5.82	5.80	5.77	5.75	5.72	5.70	5.69	5.68	5.66	5.65	5.65	5.64	5.63
	14.08	**14.02**	**13.93**	**13.84**	**13.75**	**13.69**	**13.65**	**13.61**	**13.58**	**13.54**	**13.52**	**13.49**	**13.46**
5	4.58	4.56	4.53	4.50	4.46	4.44	4.43	4.42	4.41	4.39	4.39	4.37	4.37
	9.61	**9.55**	**9.47**	**9.38**	**9.29**	**9.24**	**9.20**	**9.17**	**9.13**	**9.09**	**9.08**	**9.04**	**9.02**
6	3.90	3.87	3.84	3.81	3.77	3.75	3.74	3.73	3.71	3.70	3.69	3.68	3.67
	7.45	**7.40**	**7.31**	**7.23**	**7.14**	**7.09**	**7.06**	**7.02**	**6.99**	**6.95**	**6.93**	**6.90**	**6.88**
7	3.47	3.44	3.41	3.38	3.34	3.32	3.30	3.29	3.27	3.26	3.25	3.24	3.23
	6.21	**6.16**	**6.07**	**5.99**	**5.91**	**5.86**	**5.82**	**5.79**	**5.75**	**5.72**	**5.70**	**5.67**	**5.65**
8	3.17	3.15	3.12	3.08	3.04	3.02	3.01	2.99	2.97	2.96	2.95	2.94	2.93
	5.41	**5.36**	**5.28**	**5.20**	**5.12**	**5.07**	**5.03**	**5.00**	**4.96**	**4.93**	**4.91**	**4.88**	**4.86**
9	2.96	2.94	2.90	2.86	2.83	2.80	2.79	2.77	2.76	2.74	2.73	2.72	2.71
	4.86	**4.81**	**4.73**	**4.65**	**4.57**	**4.52**	**4.48**	**4.45**	**4.41**	**4.38**	**4.36**	**4.33**	**4.31**
10	2.80	2.77	2.74	2.70	2.66	2.64	2.62	2.60	2.59	2.57	2.56	2.55	2.54
	4.46	**4.41**	**4.33**	**4.25**	**4.17**	**4.12**	**4.08**	**4.05**	**4.01**	**3.98**	**3.96**	**3.93**	**3.91**
11	2.67	2.65	2.61	2.57	2.53	2.51	2.49	2.47	2.46	2.44	2.43	2.42	2.41
	4.15	**4.10**	**4.02**	**3.94**	**3.86**	**3.81**	**3.78**	**3.74**	**3.71**	**3.67**	**3.66**	**3.62**	**3.60**
12	2.57	2.54	2.51	2.47	2.43	2.40	2.38	2.37	2.35	2.33	2.32	2.31	2.30
	3.91	**3.86**	**3.78**	**3.70**	**3.62**	**3.57**	**3.54**	**3.50**	**3.47**	**3.43**	**3.41**	**3.38**	**3.36**
13	2.48	2.46	2.42	2.38	2.34	2.31	2.30	2.28	2.26	2.24	2.23	2.22	2.21
	3.72	**3.66**	**3.59**	**3.51**	**3.43**	**3.38**	**3.34**	**3.31**	**3.27**	**3.24**	**3.22**	**3.19**	**3.17**
14	2.41	2.39	2.35	2.31	2.27	2.24	2.22	2.21	2.19	2.17	2.16	2.14	2.13
	3.56	**3.51**	**3.43**	**3.35**	**3.27**	**3.22**	**3.18**	**3.15**	**3.11**	**3.08**	**3.06**	**3.03**	**3.01**
15	2.35	2.33	2.29	2.25	2.20	2.18	2.16	2.14	2.12	2.10	2.10	2.08	2.07
	3.42	**3.37**	**3.29**	**3.21**	**3.13**	**3.08**	**3.05**	**3.01**	**2.98**	**2.94**	**2.92**	**2.89**	**2.87**
16	2.30	2.28	2.24	2.19	2.15	2.12	2.11	2.09	2.07	2.05	2.04	2.02	2.01
	3.31	**3.26**	**3.18**	**3.10**	**3.02**	**2.97**	**2.93**	**2.90**	**2.86**	**2.83**	**2.81**	**2.78**	**2.75**
17	2.26	2.23	2.19	2.15	2.10	2.08	2.06	2.04	2.02	2.00	1.99	1.97	1.96
	3.21	**3.16**	**3.08**	**3.00**	**2.92**	**2.87**	**2.83**	**2.80**	**2.76**	**2.73**	**2.71**	**2.68**	**2.65**

Denominator degrees of freedom

(more . . .)

Table 4: continued

					Numerator degrees of freedom								(p = .05 p = .01)
	1	2	3	4	5	6	7	8	9	10	12	14	16
18	4.41	3.55	3.16	2.93	2.77	2.66	2.58	2.51	2.46	2.41	2.34	2.29	2.25
	8.29	6.01	5.09	4.58	4.25	4.01	3.84	3.71	3.60	3.51	3.37	3.27	3.19
19	4.38	3.52	3.13	2.90	2.74	2.63	2.54	2.48	2.42	2.38	2.31	2.26	2.21
	8.18	5.93	5.01	4.50	4.17	3.94	3.77	3.63	3.52	3.43	3.30	3.19	3.12
20	4.35	3.49	3.10	2.87	2.71	2.60	2.51	2.45	2.39	2.35	2.28	2.22	2.18
	8.10	5.85	4.94	4.43	4.10	3.87	3.70	3.56	3.46	3.37	3.23	3.13	3.05
21	4.32	3.47	3.07	2.84	2.68	2.57	2.49	2.42	2.37	2.32	2.25	2.20	2.16
	8.02	5.78	4.87	4.37	4.04	3.81	3.64	3.51	3.40	3.31	3.17	3.07	2.99
22	4.30	3.44	3.05	2.82	2.66	2.55	2.46	2.40	2.34	2.30	2.23	2.17	2.13
	7.95	5.72	4.82	4.31	3.99	3.76	3.59	3.45	3.35	3.26	3.12	3.02	2.94
23	4.28	3.42	3.03	2.80	2.64	2.53	2.44	2.37	2.32	2.27	2.20	2.15	2.11
	7.88	5.66	4.76	4.26	3.94	3.71	3.54	3.41	3.30	3.21	3.07	2.97	2.89
24	4.26	3.40	3.01	2.78	2.62	2.51	2.42	2.36	2.30	2.25	2.18	2.13	2.09
	7.82	5.61	4.72	4.22	3.90	3.67	3.50	3.36	3.26	3.17	3.03	2.93	2.85
25	4.24	3.39	2.99	2.76	2.60	2.49	2.40	2.34	2.28	2.24	2.16	2.11	2.07
	7.77	5.57	4.68	4.18	3.85	3.63	3.46	3.32	3.22	3.13	2.99	2.89	2.81
26	4.23	3.37	2.98	2.74	2.59	2.47	2.39	2.32	2.27	2.22	2.15	2.09	2.05
	7.72	5.53	4.64	4.14	3.82	3.59	3.42	3.29	3.18	3.09	2.96	2.86	2.78
27	4.21	3.35	2.96	2.73	2.57	2.46	2.37	2.31	2.25	2.20	2.13	2.08	2.04
	7.68	5.49	4.60	4.11	3.78	3.56	3.39	3.26	3.15	3.06	2.93	2.82	2.75
28	4.20	3.34	2.95	2.71	2.56	2.45	2.36	2.29	2.24	2.19	2.12	2.06	2.02
	7.64	5.45	4.57	4.07	3.75	3.53	3.36	3.23	3.12	3.03	2.90	2.79	2.72
29	4.18	3.33	2.93	2.70	2.55	2.43	2.35	2.28	2.22	2.18	2.10	2.05	2.01
	7.60	5.42	4.54	4.04	3.73	3.50	3.33	3.20	3.09	3.00	2.87	2.77	2.69
30	4.17	3.32	2.92	2.69	2.53	2.42	2.33	2.27	2.21	2.16	2.09	2.04	1.99
	7.56	5.39	4.51	4.02	3.70	3.47	3.30	3.17	3.07	2.98	2.84	2.74	2.66
35	4.12	3.27	2.87	2.64	2.49	2.37	2.29	2.22	2.16	2.11	2.04	1.99	1.94
	7.42	5.27	4.40	3.91	3.59	3.37	3.20	3.07	2.96	2.88	2.74	2.64	2.56
40	4.08	3.23	2.84	2.61	2.45	2.34	2.25	2.18	2.12	2.08	2.00	1.95	1.90
	7.31	5.18	4.31	3.83	3.51	3.29	3.12	2.99	2.89	2.80	2.66	2.56	2.48
50	4.03	3.18	2.79	2.56	2.40	2.29	2.20	2.13	2.07	2.03	1.95	1.89	1.85
	7.17	5.06	4.20	3.72	3.41	3.19	3.02	2.89	2.78	2.70	2.56	2.46	2.38
60	4.00	3.15	2.76	2.53	2.37	2.25	2.17	2.10	2.04	1.99	1.92	1.86	1.82
	7.08	4.98	4.13	3.65	3.34	3.12	2.95	2.82	2.72	2.63	2.50	2.39	2.31

Denominator degrees of freedom

(more . . .)

Table 4: continued

Numerator degrees of freedom   (p = .05 p = .01)

	18	20	24	30	40	50	60	75	100	150	200	500	∞
18	2.22	2.19	2.15	2.11	2.06	2.04	2.02	2.00	1.98	1.96	1.95	1.93	1.92
	3.13	**3.08**	**3.00**	**2.92**	**2.84**	**2.78**	**2.75**	**2.71**	**2.68**	**2.64**	**2.62**	**2.59**	**2.57**
19	2.18	2.16	2.11	2.07	2.03	2.00	1.98	1.96	1.94	1.92	1.91	1.89	1.88
	3.05	**3.00**	**2.92**	**2.84**	**2.76**	**2.71**	**2.67**	**2.64**	**2.60**	**2.57**	**2.55**	**2.51**	**2.49**
20	2.15	2.12	2.08	2.04	1.99	1.97	1.95	1.93	1.91	1.89	1.88	1.86	1.84
	2.99	**2.94**	**2.86**	**2.78**	**2.69**	**2.64**	**2.61**	**2.57**	**2.54**	**2.50**	**2.48**	**2.44**	**2.42**
21	2.12	2.10	2.05	2.01	1.96	1.94	1.92	1.90	1.88	1.86	1.84	1.83	1.81
	2.93	**2.88**	**2.80**	**2.72**	**2.64**	**2.58**	**2.55**	**2.51**	**2.48**	**2.44**	**2.42**	**2.38**	**2.36**
22	2.10	2.07	2.03	1.98	1.94	1.91	1.89	1.87	1.85	1.83	1.82	1.80	1.78
	2.88	**2.83**	**2.75**	**2.67**	**2.58**	**2.53**	**2.50**	**2.46**	**2.42**	**2.38**	**2.36**	**2.33**	**2.31**
23	2.08	2.05	2.01	1.96	1.91	1.88	1.86	1.84	1.82	1.80	1.79	1.77	1.76
	2.83	**2.78**	**2.70**	**2.62**	**2.54**	**2.48**	**2.45**	**2.41**	**2.37**	**2.34**	**2.32**	**2.28**	**2.26**
24	2.05	2.03	1.98	1.94	1.89	1.86	1.84	1.82	1.80	1.78	1.77	1.75	1.73
	2.79	**2.74**	**2.66**	**2.58**	**2.49**	**2.44**	**2.40**	**2.37**	**2.33**	**2.29**	**2.27**	**2.24**	**2.21**
25	2.04	2.01	1.96	1.92	1.87	1.84	1.82	1.80	1.78	1.76	1.75	1.73	1.71
	2.75	**2.70**	**2.62**	**2.54**	**2.45**	**2.40**	**2.36**	**2.33**	**2.29**	**2.25**	**2.23**	**2.19**	**2.17**
26	2.02	1.99	1.95	1.90	1.85	1.82	1.80	1.78	1.76	1.74	1.73	1.71	1.69
	2.72	**2.66**	**2.58**	**2.50**	**2.42**	**2.36**	**2.33**	**2.29**	**2.25**	**2.21**	**2.19**	**2.16**	**2.13**
27	2.00	1.97	1.93	1.88	1.84	1.81	1.79	1.76	1.74	1.72	1.71	1.69	1.67
	2.68	**2.63**	**2.55**	**2.47**	**2.38**	**2.33**	**2.29**	**2.26**	**2.22**	**2.18**	**2.16**	**2.12**	**2.10**
28	1.99	1.96	1.91	1.87	1.82	1.79	1.77	1.75	1.73	1.70	1.69	1.67	1.65
	2.65	**2.60**	**2.52**	**2.44**	**2.35**	**2.30**	**2.26**	**2.23**	**2.19**	**2.15**	**2.13**	**2.09**	**2.07**
29	1.97	1.94	1.90	1.85	1.81	1.77	1.75	1.73	1.71	1.69	1.67	1.65	1.64
	2.63	**2.57**	**2.49**	**2.41**	**2.33**	**2.27**	**2.23**	**2.20**	**2.16**	**2.12**	**2.10**	**2.06**	**2.04**
30	1.96	1.93	1.89	1.84	1.79	1.76	1.74	1.72	1.70	1.67	1.66	1.64	1.62
	2.60	**2.55**	**2.47**	**2.39**	**2.30**	**2.25**	**2.21**	**2.17**	**2.13**	**2.09**	**2.07**	**2.03**	**2.01**
35	1.91	1.88	1.83	1.79	1.74	1.70	1.68	1.66	1.63	1.61	1.60	1.57	1.56
	2.50	**2.44**	**2.36**	**2.28**	**2.19**	**2.14**	**2.10**	**2.06**	**2.02**	**1.98**	**1.96**	**1.92**	**1.89**
40	1.87	1.84	1.79	1.74	1.69	1.66	1.64	1.61	1.59	1.56	1.55	1.53	1.51
	2.42	**2.37**	**2.29**	**2.20**	**2.11**	**2.06**	**2.02**	**1.98**	**1.94**	**1.90**	**1.87**	**1.83**	**1.81**
50	1.81	1.78	1.74	1.69	1.63	1.60	1.58	1.55	1.52	1.50	1.48	1.46	1.44
	2.32	**2.27**	**2.18**	**2.10**	**2.01**	**1.95**	**1.91**	**1.87**	**1.82**	**1.78**	**1.76**	**1.71**	**1.68**
60	1.78	1.75	1.70	1.65	1.59	1.56	1.53	1.51	1.48	1.45	1.44	1.41	1.39
	2.25	**2.20**	**2.12**	**2.03**	**1.94**	**1.88**	**1.84**	**1.79**	**1.75**	**1.70**	**1.68**	**1.63**	**1.60**

(more . . .)

Table 4: continued

	Numerator degrees of freedom												(p = .05	p = .01)
	1	2	3	4	5	6	7	8	9	10	12	14	16
75	3.97	3.12	2.73	2.49	2.34	2.22	2.13	2.06	2.01	1.96	1.88	1.83	1.78
	6.99	**4.90**	**4.05**	**3.58**	**3.27**	**3.05**	**2.89**	**2.76**	**2.65**	**2.57**	**2.43**	**2.33**	**2.25**
100	3.94	3.09	2.70	2.46	2.31	2.19	2.10	2.03	1.97	1.93	1.85	1.79	1.75
	6.90	**4.82**	**3.98**	**3.51**	**3.21**	**2.99**	**2.82**	**2.69**	**2.59**	**2.50**	**2.37**	**2.27**	**2.19**
125	3.92	3.07	2.68	2.44	2.29	2.17	2.08	2.01	1.96	1.91	1.83	1.77	1.73
	6.84	**4.78**	**3.94**	**3.47**	**3.17**	**2.95**	**2.79**	**2.66**	**2.55**	**2.47**	**2.33**	**2.23**	**2.15**
150	3.90	3.06	2.66	2.43	2.27	2.16	2.07	2.00	1.94	1.89	1.82	1.76	1.71
	6.81	**4.75**	**3.91**	**3.45**	**3.14**	**2.92**	**2.76**	**2.63**	**2.53**	**2.44**	**2.31**	**2.20**	**2.12**
200	3.89	3.04	2.65	2.42	2.26	2.14	2.06	1.98	1.93	1.88	1.80	1.74	1.69
	6.76	**4.71**	**3.88**	**3.41**	**3.11**	**2.89**	**2.73**	**2.60**	**2.50**	**2.41**	**2.27**	**2.17**	**2.09**
300	3.87	3.03	2.63	2.40	2.24	2.13	2.04	1.97	1.91	1.86	1.78	1.72	1.68
	6.72	**4.68**	**3.85**	**3.38**	**3.08**	**2.86**	**2.70**	**2.57**	**2.47**	**2.38**	**2.24**	**2.14**	**2.06**
400	3.86	3.02	2.63	2.39	2.24	2.12	2.03	1.96	1.90	1.85	1.78	1.72	1.67
	6.70	**4.66**	**3.83**	**3.37**	**3.06**	**2.85**	**2.68**	**2.56**	**2.45**	**2.37**	**2.23**	**2.13**	**2.05**
500	3.86	3.01	2.62	2.39	2.23	2.12	2.03	1.96	1.90	1.85	1.77	1.71	1.66
	6.69	**4.65**	**3.82**	**3.36**	**3.05**	**2.84**	**2.68**	**2.55**	**2.44**	**2.36**	**2.22**	**2.12**	**2.04**
600	3.86	3.01	2.62	2.39	2.23	2.11	2.02	1.95	1.90	1.85	1.77	1.71	1.66
	6.68	**4.64**	**3.81**	**3.35**	**3.05**	**2.83**	**2.67**	**2.54**	**2.44**	**2.35**	**2.21**	**2.11**	**2.03**
700	3.85	3.01	2.62	2.38	2.23	2.11	2.02	1.95	1.89	1.84	1.77	1.71	1.66
	6.67	**4.64**	**3.81**	**3.35**	**3.04**	**2.83**	**2.66**	**2.54**	**2.43**	**2.35**	**2.21**	**2.11**	**2.03**
800	3.85	3.01	2.62	2.38	2.23	2.11	2.02	1.95	1.89	1.84	1.76	1.70	1.66
	6.67	**4.63**	**3.81**	**3.34**	**3.04**	**2.82**	**2.66**	**2.53**	**2.43**	**2.34**	**2.21**	**2.10**	**2.02**
900	3.85	3.01	2.61	2.38	2.22	2.11	2.02	1.95	1.89	1.84	1.76	1.70	1.65
	6.66	**4.63**	**3.80**	**3.34**	**3.04**	**2.82**	**2.66**	**2.53**	**2.43**	**2.34**	**2.20**	**2.10**	**2.02**
∞	3.84	3.99	2.60	2.37	2.21	2.09	2.01	1.94	1.88	1.83	1.75	1.69	1.64
	6.64	**4.60**	**3.78**	**3.32**	**3.02**	**2.80**	**2.64**	**2.51**	**2.41**	**2.32**	**2.18**	**2.07**	**1.99**

Denominator degrees of freedom

(more . . .)

Table 4: continued

Numerator degrees of freedom   (p = .05   p = .01)

		18	20	24	30	40	50	60	75	100	150	200	500	∞
	75	1.74	1.71	1.66	1.61	1.55	1.52	1.49	1.47	1.44	1.41	1.39	1.36	1.34
		2.18	**2.13**	**2.05**	**1.96**	**1.87**	**1.81**	**1.76**	**1.72**	**1.67**	**1.62**	**1.60**	**1.55**	**1.52**
	100	1.71	1.68	1.63	1.57	1.52	1.48	1.45	1.42	1.39	1.36	1.34	1.30	1.28
		2.12	**2.07**	**1.98**	**1.89**	**1.80**	**1.74**	**1.69**	**1.65**	**1.60**	**1.55**	**1.52**	**1.47**	**1.43**
	125	1.69	1.66	1.60	1.55	1.49	1.45	1.42	1.40	1.36	1.33	1.31	1.27	1.25
		2.08	**2.03**	**1.94**	**1.85**	**1.76**	**1.69**	**1.65**	**1.60**	**1.55**	**1.50**	**1.47**	**1.41**	**1.37**
	150	1.67	1.64	1.59	1.54	1.48	1.44	1.41	1.38	1.34	1.31	1.29	1.25	1.22
		2.06	**2.00**	**1.92**	**1.83**	**1.73**	**1.66**	**1.62**	**1.57**	**1.52**	**1.46**	**1.43**	**1.38**	**1.33**
Denominator degrees of freedom	200	1.66	1.62	1.57	1.52	1.46	1.41	1.39	1.35	1.32	1.28	1.26	1.22	1.19
		2.03	**1.97**	**1.89**	**1.79**	**1.69**	**1.63**	**1.58**	**1.53**	**1.48**	**1.42**	**1.39**	**1.33**	**1.28**
	300	1.64	1.61	1.55	1.50	1.43	1.39	1.36	1.33	1.30	1.26	1.23	1.19	1.15
		1.99	**1.94**	**1.85**	**1.76**	**1.66**	**1.59**	**1.55**	**1.50**	**1.44**	**1.38**	**1.35**	**1.28**	**1.22**
	400	1.63	1.60	1.54	1.49	1.42	1.38	1.35	1.32	1.28	1.24	1.22	1.17	1.13
		1.98	**1.92**	**1.84**	**1.75**	**1.64**	**1.58**	**1.53**	**1.48**	**1.42**	**1.36**	**1.32**	**1.25**	**1.19**
	500	1.62	1.59	1.54	1.48	1.42	1.38	1.35	1.31	1.28	1.23	1.21	1.16	1.12
		1.97	**1.92**	**1.83**	**1.74**	**1.63**	**1.57**	**1.52**	**1.47**	**1.41**	**1.34**	**1.31**	**1.23**	**1.17**
	600	1.62	1.59	1.54	1.48	1.41	1.37	1.34	1.31	1.27	1.23	1.20	1.15	1.11
		1.96	**1.91**	**1.82**	**1.73**	**1.63**	**1.56**	**1.51**	**1.46**	**1.40**	**1.34**	**1.30**	**1.22**	**1.15**
	700	1.62	1.59	1.53	1.48	1.41	1.37	1.34	1.30	1.27	1.22	1.20	1.15	1.10
		1.96	**1.90**	**1.82**	**1.72**	**1.62**	**1.55**	**1.50**	**1.45**	**1.39**	**1.33**	**1.29**	**1.21**	**1.14**
	800	1.62	1.58	1.53	1.47	1.41	1.37	1.34	1.30	1.26	1.22	1.20	1.14	1.09
		1.96	**1.90**	**1.81**	**1.72**	**1.62**	**1.55**	**1.50**	**1.45**	**1.39**	**1.32**	**1.29**	**1.20**	**1.13**
	900	1.62	1.58	1.53	1.47	1.41	1.36	1.33	1.30	1.26	1.22	1.19	1.14	1.09
		1.95	**1.90**	**1.81**	**1.72**	**1.61**	**1.55**	**1.50**	**1.44**	**1.39**	**1.32**	**1.28**	**1.20**	**1.12**
	∞	1.60	1.57	1.52	1.46	1.39	1.36	1.32	1.30	1.24	1.20	1.17	1.11	1.00
		1.93	**1.87**	**1.79**	**1.70**	**1.59**	**1.53**	**1.47**	**1.44**	**1.36**	**1.29**	**1.25**	**1.14**	**1.00**

Table 5: Fisher's *r* to *Z*[*]

r	Z	r	Z	r	Z	r	Z	r	Z
0.000	0.000	0.200	0.203	0.400	0.424	0.600	0.693	0.800	1.099
0.005	0.005	0.205	0.208	0.405	0.430	0.605	0.701	0.805	1.113
0.010	0.010	0.210	0.213	0.410	0.436	0.610	0.709	0.810	1.127
0.015	0.015	0.215	0.218	0.415	0.442	0.615	0.717	0.815	1.142
0.020	0.020	0.220	0.224	0.420	0.448	0.620	0.725	0.820	1.157
0.025	0.025	0.225	0.229	0.425	0.454	0.625	0.733	0.825	1.172
0.030	0.030	0.230	0.234	0.430	0.460	0.630	0.741	0.830	1.188
0.035	0.035	0.235	0.239	0.435	0.466	0.635	0.750	0.835	1.204
0.040	0.040	0.240	0.245	0.440	0.472	0.640	0.758	0.840	1.221
0.045	0.045	0.245	0.250	0.445	0.478	0.645	0.767	0.845	1.238
0.050	0.050	0.250	0.255	0.450	0.485	0.650	0.775	0.850	1.256
0.055	0.055	0.255	0.261	0.455	0.491	0.655	0.784	0.855	1.274
0.060	0.060	0.260	0.266	0.460	0.497	0.660	0.793	0.860	1.293
0.065	0.065	0.265	0.271	0.465	0.504	0.665	0.802	0.865	1.313
0.070	0.070	0.270	0.277	0.470	0.510	0.670	0.811	0.870	1.333
0.075	0.075	0.275	0.282	0.475	0.517	0.675	0.820	0.875	1.354
0.080	0.080	0.280	0.288	0.480	0.523	0.680	0.829	0.880	1.376
0.085	0.085	0.285	0.293	0.485	0.530	0.685	0.838	0.885	1.398
0.090	0.090	0.290	0.299	0.490	0.536	0.690	0.848	0.890	1.422
0.095	0.095	0.295	0.304	0.495	0.543	0.695	0.858	0.895	1.447
0.100	0.100	0.300	0.310	0.500	0.549	0.700	0.867	0.900	1.472
0.105	0.105	0.305	0.315	0.505	0.556	0.705	0.877	0.905	1.499
0.110	0.110	0.310	0.321	0.510	0.563	0.710	0.887	0.910	1.528
0.115	0.116	0.315	0.326	0.515	0.570	0.715	0.897	0.915	1.557
0.120	0.121	0.320	0.332	0.520	0.576	0.720	0.908	0.920	1.589
0.125	0.126	0.325	0.337	0.525	0.583	0.725	0.918	0.925	1.623
0.130	0.131	0.330	0.343	0.530	0.590	0.730	0.929	0.930	1.658
0.135	0.136	0.335	0.348	0.535	0.597	0.735	0.940	0.935	1.697
0.140	0.141	0.340	0.354	0.540	0.604	0.740	0.950	0.940	1.738
0.145	0.146	0.345	0.360	0.545	0.611	0.745	0.962	0.945	1.783
0.150	0.151	0.350	0.365	0.550	0.618	0.750	0.973	0.950	1.832
0.155	0.156	0.355	0.371	0.555	0.626	0.755	0.984	0.955	1.886
0.160	0.161	0.360	0.377	0.560	0.633	0.760	0.996	0.960	1.946
0.165	0.167	0.365	0.383	0.565	0.640	0.765	1.008	0.965	2.014
0.170	0.172	0.370	0.388	0.570	0.648	0.770	1.020	0.970	2.092
0.175	0.177	0.375	0.394	0.575	0.655	0.775	1.033	0.975	2.185
0.180	0.182	0.380	0.400	0.580	0.662	0.780	1.045	0.980	2.298
0.185	0.187	0.385	0.406	0.585	0.670	0.785	1.058	0.985	2.443
0.190	0.192	0.390	0.412	0.590	0.678	0.790	1.071	0.990	2.647
0.195	0.198	0.395	0.418	0.595	0.685	0.795	1.085	0.995	2.994

[*]Calculated as: $Z = 1/2 [\log_e(1+r) - \log_e(1-r)]$

Table 6: Critical values of *r* (two-tailed)

df	Probability				
	0.1	0.05	0.02	0.01	0.001
5	0.6695	0.7545	0.8329	0.8745	0.9509
6	0.6215	0.7068	0.7887	0.8344	0.9249
7	0.5823	0.6665	0.7499	0.7977	0.8983
8	0.5494	0.6319	0.7155	0.7646	0.8721
9	0.5215	0.6021	0.6851	0.7348	0.8471
10	0.4973	0.5760	0.6581	0.7079	0.8233
11	0.4762	0.5530	0.6339	0.6836	0.8010
12	0.4576	0.5325	0.6121	0.6614	0.7800
13	0.4409	0.5140	0.5923	0.6412	0.7604
14	0.4259	0.4974	0.5743	0.6226	0.7420
15	0.4124	0.4822	0.5578	0.6056	0.7247
16	0.4001	0.4684	0.5426	0.5898	0.7085
17	0.3888	0.4556	0.5286	0.5751	0.6932
18	0.3784	0.4438	0.5156	0.5615	0.6789
19	0.3688	0.4329	0.5034	0.5488	0.6653
20	0.3599	0.4228	0.4922	0.5369	0.6524
21	0.3516	0.4133	0.4816	0.5257	0.6403
22	0.3438	0.4044	0.4716	0.5152	0.6288
23	0.3366	0.3961	0.4623	0.5052	0.6178
24	0.3298	0.3883	0.4535	0.4958	0.6074
26	0.3173	0.3739	0.4372	0.4786	0.5880
28	0.3061	0.3610	0.4226	0.4630	0.5704
30	0.2960	0.3494	0.4094	0.4488	0.5542
32	0.2869	0.3388	0.3973	0.4358	0.5392
34	0.2786	0.3292	0.3862	0.4239	0.5255
36	0.2709	0.3203	0.3760	0.4129	0.5127
38	0.2639	0.3121	0.3666	0.4027	0.5007
40	0.2573	0.3045	0.3578	0.3932	0.4896
45	0.2429	0.2876	0.3384	0.3722	0.4647
50	0.2307	0.2733	0.3218	0.3542	0.4432
55	0.2201	0.2609	0.3075	0.3386	0.4245
60	0.2109	0.2501	0.2949	0.3249	0.4079
65	0.2027	0.2405	0.2837	0.3127	0.3931
70	0.1954	0.2319	0.2738	0.3018	0.3799
75	0.1889	0.2242	0.2647	0.2920	0.3678
80	0.1830	0.2172	0.2566	0.2830	0.3569
85	0.1776	0.2109	0.2491	0.2748	0.3468
90	0.1726	0.2050	0.2423	0.2674	0.3376
95	0.1681	0.1996	0.2360	0.2604	0.3291
100	0.1638	0.1947	0.2301	0.2540	0.3212
110	0.1563	0.1857	0.2196	0.2425	0.3069
120	0.1497	0.1779	0.2105	0.2324	0.2944
130	0.1438	0.1710	0.2024	0.2235	0.2833
140	0.1386	0.1649	0.1951	0.2156	0.2733

(more...)

Table 6: continued

df	Probability				
	0.1	0.05	0.02	0.01	0.001
150	0.1340	0.1593	0.1886	0.2084	0.2644
160	0.1297	0.1543	0.1827	0.2019	0.2562
170	0.1259	0.1497	0.1773	0.1960	0.2488
180	0.1224	0.1456	0.1724	0.1905	0.2420
190	0.1191	0.1417	0.1678	0.1855	0.2357
200	0.1161	0.1381	0.1636	0.1809	0.2299
225	0.1095	0.1303	0.1544	0.1707	0.2170
250	0.1039	0.1237	0.1465	0.1620	0.2061
275	0.0991	0.1179	0.1398	0.1546	0.1967
300	0.0949	0.1129	0.1339	0.1481	0.1885
325	0.0912	0.1085	0.1287	0.1423	0.1812
350	0.0879	0.1046	0.1240	0.1372	0.1747
375	0.0849	0.1011	0.1198	0.1326	0.1689
400	0.0822	0.0979	0.1160	0.1284	0.1636
425	0.0798	0.0950	0.1126	0.1246	0.1587
450	0.0775	0.0923	0.1094	0.1211	0.1543
475	0.0755	0.0898	0.1065	0.1179	0.1503
500	0.0735	0.0876	0.1039	0.1149	0.1465
550	0.0701	0.0835	0.0990	0.1096	0.1397
600	0.0672	0.0800	0.0948	0.1050	0.1338
650	0.0645	0.0768	0.0911	0.1009	0.1286
700	0.0622	0.0741	0.0878	0.0972	0.1240
750	0.0601	0.0715	0.0849	0.0939	0.1198
800	0.0582	0.0693	0.0822	0.0910	0.1160
850	0.0564	0.0672	0.0797	0.0883	0.1126
900	0.0549	0.0653	0.0775	0.0858	0.1094
950	0.0534	0.0636	0.0754	0.0835	0.1065
1000	0.0520	0.0620	0.0735	0.0814	0.1038
1100	0.0496	0.0591	0.0701	0.0776	0.0990
1200	0.0475	0.0566	0.0671	0.0743	0.0948
1300	0.0457	0.0544	0.0645	0.0714	0.0911
1400	0.0440	0.0524	0.0622	0.0688	0.0878
1500	0.0425	0.0506	0.0601	0.0665	0.0849
1700	0.0399	0.0476	0.0564	0.0625	0.0797
1800	0.0388	0.0462	0.0548	0.0607	0.0775
1900	0.0378	0.0450	0.0534	0.0591	0.0754
2000	0.0368	0.0439	0.0520	0.0576	0.0735
2500	0.0329	0.0392	0.0466	0.0515	0.0658
3000	0.0301	0.0358	0.0425	0.0471	0.0601
4000	0.0261	0.0310	0.0368	0.0408	0.0520
5000	0.0233	0.0278	0.0329	0.0365	0.0466
6000	0.0213	0.0254	0.0301	0.0333	0.0425
7000	0.0197	0.0235	0.0279	0.0308	0.0394
9999	0.0165	0.0196	0.0233	0.0258	0.0329

Table 7:   Random numbers   (200 x 12)

	1	2	3	4	5	6	7	8	9	10	11	12
1	77073	51849	15761	85622	38905	72276	35466	67759	18843	82458	65979	97912
2	20837	95047	50724	16922	04405	30858	15787	23800	97665	49692	63862	20187
3	37504	15645	36630	28216	10056	97628	28670	53527	13431	32288	61192	46889
4	40392	58557	60446	11553	60013	38037	74917	24680	96583	58366	43385	64432
5	53408	14205	33152	70651	17314	93033	91498	05156	45630	89927	96910	64613
6	83662	06446	26077	60963	94985	11875	72384	45193	42431	37718	16388	31738
7	20781	65283	06185	35811	73248	69097	05306	75143	16052	83905	75986	95233
8	54068	15347	28066	92162	52503	13337	54139	10748	36134	00195	65383	87733
9	69082	45248	71749	84604	27996	19838	09911	58718	62903	07105	11175	16565
10	63397	11265	23439	36954	73244	98094	55031	96978	04461	59697	12560	92362
11	08171	14195	61156	43603	32512	14273	85582	70493	74326	87363	07377	79655
12	13133	12169	22748	13639	16566	16168	20635	06423	50596	51424	71806	29686
13	52516	20303	31485	66812	01278	69958	75378	68496	97829	04501	41987	66470
14	04896	82541	54028	34943	74763	30024	02524	14912	11774	74130	02698	36842
15	48157	59360	53531	87660	89286	24310	68200	29498	64755	24714	64913	77389
16	45765	70642	76212	85096	07584	56062	31830	52861	24820	44746	43479	46095
17	22039	95799	77230	92514	81015	06084	37047	41336	22480	12946	83275	01425
18	12180	00465	07963	24420	14038	32679	22147	16218	71982	94941	68620	91719
19	00381	98626	91451	07841	80847	95486	31261	89195	91619	28691	01136	90599
20	67964	64286	46929	26116	30469	81918	93602	52054	65240	84130	64708	30706
21	17396	68218	33021	76408	85880	80194	09667	58809	87667	11989	86906	24002
22	35110	86306	38729	07348	96574	07588	28435	01218	61957	00185	03221	24763
23	34741	80800	94816	63075	91192	56792	02681	56746	28773	82027	23169	01327
24	54007	80665	27399	92783	95272	33822	42494	96079	97787	90580	64953	48980
25	95005	43068	35887	48975	15254	68564	43652	46989	41425	22494	55882	08296
26	41335	09999	36482	43908	46195	86975	80459	68166	58730	58557	59732	15307
27	55603	06114	45903	91553	20440	18954	50071	33594	00431	38504	24494	61827
28	30435	11958	75257	41102	94193	90405	30588	78304	44521	57864	04817	48502
29	10231	45794	53082	33779	12851	85936	20325	89161	14729	46789	77232	30725
30	70819	46915	98876	04483	30267	95291	48762	41473	34289	91880	23704	79674
31	60075	63755	25355	29284	61818	59564	81074	98901	28931	32286	14290	67232
32	61780	29581	59971	24052	32427	86787	16483	15554	12839	73479	56066	00403
33	43460	22694	13926	50825	08373	14254	64301	99599	44684	94933	26237	64201
34	41592	30036	09316	72119	93400	57241	45029	85943	31584	17203	24429	71200
35	70877	14362	71558	74099	70080	24746	03933	00549	13741	34002	70935	90430
36	50590	64544	83973	30564	89045	75860	67075	14935	10968	30014	34443	83066
37	25565	55625	79789	09675	96585	92043	63641	09694	11726	71543	20908	91096
38	65104	93623	18479	72405	96391	42829	19825	90678	22196	46618	99610	35321
39	22208	45996	51070	32025	35678	39284	30773	93215	60431	62868	20488	27803
40	06277	81234	85277	40636	65631	58528	63342	78478	79006	41067	11405	81626

(more . . .)

Table 7: continued

	1	2	3	4	5	6	7	8	9	10	11	12
41	49637	46288	58906	24130	50492	12916	77852	43682	54700	34510	99835	15511
42	20696	21915	20605	06552	18913	63935	42015	32955	73168	27343	53753	23145
43	61525	45801	75401	64177	19553	20578	46032	46076	84445	59222	36618	32934
44	05249	09502	89138	32436	46759	75180	39461	13265	42365	25627	01767	91239
45	97223	11794	11679	74885	92146	91941	52064	37269	63636	23053	35796	18385
46	10796	43690	82173	69388	97081	25399	77624	15737	78140	97658	30055	24617
47	38722	94682	18037	40052	38731	43898	91198	60003	70416	77493	23253	03247
48	77156	58002	26004	36013	65998	15948	25931	08092	92112	16680	30022	79271
49	97959	87204	20952	39261	57594	82093	36337	15548	06520	72089	84446	75956
50	69941	84810	91343	90153	92783	99317	12551	39325	26468	31895	48687	77610
51	13589	90000	28902	51303	35906	57627	36774	53458	58230	54915	44336	44546
52	28496	27729	37172	47607	29714	95282	00029	84194	35186	58908	61847	57401
53	62811	51924	84678	80750	49972	69305	05630	08892	31830	62917	37724	22025
54	21576	22399	49991	82701	39049	90611	88388	27788	29902	53114	82324	04346
55	10828	71008	30032	40303	58749	90108	34513	50252	81942	87453	20243	20793
56	33999	10549	84318	22284	11715	86704	27196	82399	67477	83286	79068	88881
57	36076	26662	95763	83858	92031	52302	29031	23408	12706	40812	26708	67674
58	95274	58476	99681	28405	91567	60654	08285	44225	82093	25249	52810	64899
59	24751	77143	31327	97046	39066	82227	78451	11017	54872	33317	54878	19677
60	66686	88623	80504	21341	76694	90102	30368	90059	17480	76013	39892	52796
61	69102	86754	62596	49519	64097	78073	59694	64660	28483	09563	16098	44767
62	77881	38111	28158	49619	30189	79181	80772	30314	76965	35275	58678	87650
63	70116	36729	01277	58718	60807	68132	84510	44195	72804	00992	69876	95540
64	21598	82478	93163	74606	97779	58777	50216	75309	09341	93873	06957	21328
65	95117	29383	39354	21533	99375	94509	96220	63912	54917	81877	05009	70763
66	91344	15446	96607	64597	78048	36483	58766	70686	03679	27735	26766	52745
67	63271	87839	98528	43312	41266	42818	27370	97545	33960	64684	33582	97554
68	63081	99810	90831	95585	86737	85601	85199	27171	57414	41967	29762	97199
69	54739	86436	13434	81002	91847	61096	27928	71364	02420	60197	16214	05065
70	52521	11868	57838	71279	78496	80252	88378	66983	75584	32801	81523	49026
71	79295	09953	66247	99872	46169	50782	79682	12260	44007	15901	32234	40075
72	27516	57916	89496	56459	00364	14319	44529	84423	89235	66606	44691	08831
73	87331	59130	86596	16147	77840	51303	37483	75646	66807	17324	64105	97087
74	94389	84652	42837	50343	06910	25473	17273	98998	51984	80789	10581	24081
75	91813	84394	02933	81987	50149	40773	70651	28430	16153	77738	25938	34937
76	50995	62106	03714	10736	26527	28845	92523	28170	45345	06118	10441	78461
77	14836	39745	92732	38516	26385	50071	36813	01923	18973	67293	88992	73153
78	51146	09662	77056	70240	09914	19358	43993	88263	24128	03674	40714	71254
79	74236	78888	58938	69721	86472	20016	04118	06783	93705	99387	81204	90695
80	10711	05970	27415	60490	50546	18352	37177	25649	71922	89313	75685	25978

(more...)

Table 7: continued

	1	2	3	4	5	6	7	8	9	10	11	12
81	29441	09766	33883	67848	16856	91182	82718	39197	83170	32539	73133	32947
82	62576	00799	21717	96171	39901	01586	42122	37894	73022	66882	85533	41909
83	32740	45134	59968	70328	91280	34053	12652	34853	67504	35711	89218	70225
84	81842	02442	26533	23848	03426	70055	07566	61059	12212	43649	96073	82883
85	14875	02451	86481	74778	84956	48666	24874	51846	67738	69754	44648	95067
86	68555	03233	22302	21855	13558	52662	86367	54455	10338	44302	68335	92425
87	89011	05530	40147	39412	91634	89675	65450	10157	08014	81044	98487	55372
88	97547	55794	28805	21309	39692	90537	48988	40582	59868	00923	97073	89681
89	74441	15013	14519	06162	50182	98659	52496	91491	81777	18169	49825	06906
90	52884	15473	40288	07576	21565	41787	99838	76438	86495	07966	79661	60362
91	73503	54660	67338	37470	55291	67767	47236	86180	22411	45056	43686	21660
92	74621	45204	33872	83554	78175	72615	35277	89568	54146	30621	34666	29112
93	73702	00198	12482	68989	81319	25467	08720	43569	55044	11729	22445	16374
94	14407	33879	93969	26444	28061	17203	23030	52243	40771	25978	10735	20974
95	46990	54575	32286	23945	32247	75062	60540	88920	69832	63820	07486	04098
96	94405	60994	23752	94225	30283	57136	69079	02056	54158	25512	75513	37285
97	74030	21491	83650	98014	11703	80022	24672	54808	51333	52974	17292	15838
98	59813	71342	30517	89734	55788	17716	47637	26627	18835	44267	90100	99177
99	49344	12855	46157	50989	69873	44034	77574	80587	20229	80408	12072	92543
100	23044	96164	26399	74813	75937	64356	16161	11283	20986	06352	54186	88134
101	70592	29386	85959	02754	77948	64314	18566	22074	96198	85493	79246	80020
102	61348	68791	55318	24950	19207	00000	90922	16166	97827	65847	90005	07344
103	56241	37591	77009	80199	96352	84504	47776	66715	70104	37846	63005	16270
104	46408	62619	20727	54004	40747	18911	27837	50274	54528	41165	45014	48298
105	07142	34893	41668	13936	07232	38454	84376	03728	39731	56439	62770	66058
106	52625	51648	39836	18708	18603	45381	02413	53443	01323	21789	95151	87046
107	51073	79771	95109	85112	71768	93024	42844	63254	02579	43456	62726	31932
108	33328	29636	79564	22082	28861	56233	93942	66676	22313	02506	08245	61391
109	42246	27389	15853	33650	39864	84827	80420	09357	57645	38185	63062	81519
110	74823	34050	69674	08243	36438	04377	51210	77749	20463	19815	23503	09273
111	54138	90832	11925	11331	38393	54944	38609	00403	61717	63518	32236	74013
112	66088	30636	89066	17531	33369	23123	24587	29637	04265	81649	70379	47779
113	35325	03561	39109	95564	29612	84790	58742	63001	55603	15336	36879	21304
114	66265	06727	53459	73133	42325	43551	51993	31804	24280	57696	90577	11875
115	02591	35699	91185	43264	28680	21503	95824	13758	23109	76829	51032	82141
116	27185	93205	86141	55788	16644	26960	08698	83766	55156	92691	54065	54892
117	52812	03905	14610	45629	75108	30109	25936	92285	23022	16494	04682	76104
118	96974	39501	82901	12826	50402	95030	55223	18348	63134	86097	16651	38010
119	33576	09751	80361	11662	91412	53998	40490	06691	48099	96220	52940	52092
120	54371	96670	31475	85713	69475	65045	94785	47729	69841	10900	83985	19358

(more . . .)

Table 7: continued

	1	2	3	4	5	6	7	8	9	10	11	12
121	99173	97732	73177	84349	46475	97074	17732	12272	53319	28276	18773	08529
122	24937	00642	83652	27771	31527	67018	58339	89121	56056	21309	28832	68702
123	73156	17963	97000	62839	32861	86990	32283	67499	42258	22797	38194	11774
124	14630	84010	42916	81819	23040	16562	42402	37521	99580	35507	60381	15787
125	50154	30385	65172	33809	14299	09329	86726	91088	10781	90296	96360	11432
126	56902	43089	85856	71632	16205	43053	83100	57341	16710	44493	81544	96646
127	88573	32548	28147	62456	82908	31264	38057	21492	99399	91505	16293	21683
128	32443	65449	98352	96414	25976	70628	29271	52190	46216	43640	46848	65030
129	41966	07458	40811	98138	88978	52905	64850	18688	84764	22105	04032	56875
130	05229	76603	63550	82254	34073	54353	00991	46992	92201	13356	72092	38622
131	79845	49220	37052	28686	15733	23948	77398	16562	47644	41531	04025	39366
132	18266	92004	07456	00076	70258	14398	70698	17932	79915	26946	67026	02099
133	70386	64308	19485	79984	83940	66553	52574	00513	15993	77588	07726	36224
134	43202	86393	92414	99194	40329	00392	80647	18405	23062	90426	76234	52641
135	27694	51816	68126	91972	67695	46595	13563	36614	65912	81625	58573	31904
136	06547	24058	39096	81070	39222	87527	63901	77709	50663	87061	31016	84357
137	14507	06180	57158	44785	86730	63211	70960	20022	94921	21355	02214	04082
138	72551	49326	11159	35423	48106	03532	59630	85588	71790	67918	87049	16035
139	34911	46513	42322	90137	19742	01041	82994	74578	16026	37074	89048	20573
140	35795	92067	58367	70654	68393	74407	49634	85242	51005	27057	33598	75188
141	54615	01777	60956	78324	83297	68330	14596	07437	88295	59930	38496	87798
142	29641	67391	25987	56226	82148	54603	04769	52291	54472	04581	91600	08270
143	68511	58453	04923	28140	36918	77325	95214	52346	75173	28363	81748	22575
144	24782	99002	18425	57688	46403	88511	89411	27208	82647	45940	03302	84804
145	67126	85635	52974	33319	78920	03763	28151	19810	44435	09307	09684	52914
146	77463	15603	23003	10156	78886	23704	86598	51311	77122	86015	52526	98843
147	75838	03712	78507	67069	21689	17145	45963	93312	81093	13424	03792	21171
148	75251	43065	86090	00337	49710	69504	52274	53479	05941	42074	28711	44338
149	65910	44307	60092	54607	64176	89872	76670	88408	61315	17974	78404	24616
150	34895	70599	56523	77866	84531	11746	08256	44860	47751	49864	51817	84933
151	77928	29571	89521	75718	79675	91429	32096	25331	32847	46697	27573	17291
152	00922	87091	26386	55504	50345	43138	13894	14309	90459	31526	42862	80109
153	33199	70199	22981	37232	55896	32344	91272	05555	59477	28871	20313	96824
154	09482	56474	52982	64737	21997	01651	43571	87431	41404	68389	02350	94372
155	98266	40111	34741	76892	17998	89338	87181	46111	76360	67370	71620	09332
156	86877	40112	60612	01358	22512	49079	55838	59493	91747	90464	21749	23638
157	71903	68239	90541	19877	70406	06195	16222	42879	56303	70552	65669	97528
158	40977	93987	38111	17937	61267	09638	82108	86760	69617	36696	37955	97572
159	09361	18940	15834	12825	37622	06975	27292	88547	07512	47641	97497	19814
160	78582	26438	27561	14158	43966	34169	70122	27275	01410	83372	21778	12132

(more . . .)

Table 7: continued

	1	2	3	4	5	6	7	8	9	10	11	12
161	84900	12397	46125	11591	06591	71866	35292	42924	21732	37232	48467	76675
162	92811	65564	18434	19668	57697	00743	79462	04168	37135	18953	30574	46656
163	90702	17692	37743	32280	23493	31583	05191	40232	68151	06780	41466	10958
164	07442	71091	24499	38320	39273	60823	50146	90860	75254	79927	29072	01404
165	33621	58757	28145	32251	39123	23644	69603	12892	70211	32218	73691	13064
166	87883	41303	73864	24458	59158	61018	13250	87943	42595	81711	09290	31466
167	72514	41140	35950	96956	38084	68066	85052	57871	30415	80080	89044	46293
168	41944	50429	57915	65626	66205	04132	31416	04455	58905	03156	29220	90653
169	54938	42394	01143	01007	10526	98372	33568	68659	43423	10034	38564	32796
170	76474	96350	53339	64304	46322	25279	58706	67525	84608	04352	28807	46555
171	87860	56516	52741	10990	96097	93407	75375	15864	19358	34270	65715	60075
172	04497	66285	40907	11782	15907	36038	78375	34081	99281	04598	70788	29479
173	55773	71638	10195	32966	49657	70235	31571	12945	59158	54577	70804	00323
174	18451	04616	64410	32677	88655	13408	34566	47567	44504	77777	96224	23034
175	01028	74739	32958	11765	32253	72521	48001	39755	56465	01120	18649	31886
176	92375	45309	02821	06889	66640	01763	23899	64490	75891	85159	61358	43163
177	07326	23489	74920	71605	57699	41196	71981	76957	07937	86249	86816	10868
178	36240	77036	31424	28605	55992	45942	42128	30617	66967	00937	42971	01754
179	96908	19219	00831	55796	53218	27132	99373	57894	09832	39972	06140	83634
180	28213	64677	15225	77891	08332	22435	63134	87098	53487	55491	31899	13011
181	30301	52352	79678	39294	04054	31921	91189	97844	60061	37460	75980	79195
182	27346	95075	16359	36551	96412	95646	22237	31966	45334	13341	11105	34847
183	25963	47699	67452	63511	18263	41819	47697	32069	68017	51041	38708	53740
184	71727	13688	44449	41243	58343	67758	08290	16905	07762	54074	07260	07850
185	10824	02721	23369	57185	98753	36131	49924	71862	83628	22524	44318	50116
186	65195	17452	04597	53299	95138	68129	36824	84452	69575	45739	19098	77217
187	37783	04319	89208	02752	49909	17034	86938	62112	04293	42312	37204	79286
188	00254	52342	97275	93296	15294	40217	11400	91256	28827	80595	58086	39624
189	82824	07516	17713	94775	80945	33807	83681	20348	83145	05907	72072	00063
190	61752	59467	48113	23558	36302	24370	76078	39548	67026	96973	23193	97612
191	09966	91481	12724	36176	97063	34731	16787	36312	95701	35567	73458	06389
192	24965	78390	97469	45695	94990	90598	71533	52447	66513	83529	61156	39419
193	53128	18745	37312	86300	27796	64432	95616	08888	79059	29919	42158	35915
194	72563	62594	02732	04892	18336	57475	75561	46676	67438	27047	74994	09296
195	59120	23812	95923	64941	57884	45329	34050	62312	70646	38511	52198	77070
196	09374	43666	78729	88486	71645	32154	99472	22953	61106	96709	75842	60117
197	70625	84819	43861	59107	02621	35493	20644	50260	17835	43838	73255	92358
198	01510	73691	24417	60606	97891	53491	20038	63499	16784	85616	46524	26532
199	32015	60738	14567	11688	24411	74204	33864	46295	68446	66475	29263	17758
200	28747	36120	57690	88095	03462	74523	02326	86998	63421	14677	65037	64407

Glossary

absolute zero *vs.* arbitrary zero

When the number "0" means "none," it is an *absolute* zero. On the other hand, when "0" doesn't mean "none" — when it simply means the number halfway between "1" and "-1" (as in the Fahrenheit temperature scale), or the number one unit below "1" (as in the cumulative grade point scale used in most universities), it is an *arbitrary* zero. Absolute zero is a characteristic of *ratio scaling*, whereas an arbitrary zero is usually associated with *interval scaling*.

abstract concept

Concepts are abstract ideas. Examples include "truth," "love," "compassion," "alienation," "prejudiced," "exciting." They have no physical existence. They are like the names you put on the mental file folders in which you sort your experiences so you can make sense of them. Because your experiences are different from the experiences of other people, the contents of your mental file folders are different from the contents of theirs. Even though you may use the same label that other people use, because your mental file folder contains different experiences, your labels mean something different for you than the same labels mean for other people.

Accidental sample

Also known as *convenience sample.* A non-probability sample in which you select whoever happens to be available.

accuracy

When you estimate the amount of time it will take you to do something, your estimate may be more or less accurate. The closer your estimate is to the actual amount of time it takes, the more accurate it is. Accuracy is an issue in research when you use a sample statistic to estimate a population parameter.

alternate hypothesis

While the null hypothesis says that the pattern you see in your sample data is due to sampling variability and does *not* reflect a pattern that exists in the population your sample represents, the *alternate hypothesis* says that the pattern you see in your sample data is *not* due to sampling variability and that it *does* reflect a pattern that exists in the population. The alternate hypothesis is sometimes called the *research* hypothesis.

alternative explanation

If you are interested in the validity of a theory and you test a *hypothesis* that is logically implied by the theory, you will probably feel that your theory is supported by your data. It is usually possible, however, to come up with a different theory that also implies the same hypothesis. This different theory provides an *alternative explanation* for your data.

amount

When you are counting discrete objects (books, people, cars), you talk about the number of things you see. When you are measuring a continuous quantity (sand, fear, anxiety), you talk about the *amount.*

analysis of variance

Also known as ANOVA. An analytic procedure that tests the size of the differences among the means of two or more groups by means of comparing the between-groups variance (differences between groups) to the within-groups variance (differences between members of groups and other members of the same groups).

antecedent condition

A condition or event that happens *before* something else happens. Possibly, something that caused something else to happen.

applied research

Research that is intended to address a specific problem or issue where the result of the research has an immediate application. For example, a study of the relative efficiency of a company's internal communication systems. Applied research is usually contrasted with *basic* research.

arithmetical operations

Things you normally do with numbers, including addition, subtraction, multiplication, division, square root.

assumptions behind inferential statistics

Most inferential statistics make assumptions about the sample or the population the sample comes from. The most common one is that the sample is randomly selected from the population.

average

An informal somewhat vague word meaning common, not too good and not too bad, ordinary, or typical. If you mean the result you get when you add up all the numbers and divide by how many there are, you're talking about the *mean*.

average deviation

A useless measure of dispersion for interval or ratio data. The mean of the absolute values of the deviation scores for a set of data. If you don't take the absolute values, the sum of the deviation scores will be zero which would give a mean of zero, resulting in a misleading estimate of the spread of the data.

basic research

Also called *pure* research. Sometimes described as *curiosity-driven* research. Research that is not done in order to produce results that can directly address a specific problem or situation.

bell-shaped curve

This is a descriptive name for the *normal* curve, which has the shape of a cross-section of a bell. SEE ALSO *normal curve*.

between-groups degrees of freedom

ANOVA (*analysis of variance*) requires two *degrees of freedom*. The one for the numerator is the number of groups minus one. Also known as *numerator* degrees of freedom.

between-groups sum of squares ($_{Ssb}$)

Used in ANOVA (*analysis of variance*), this is a measure of the differences between group means and the grand mean. It is calculated as the sum of the squared differences between the means of each group and the grand mean, weighted according to the number of cases in each group.

between-groups mean square (MS_b)

Used in ANOVA (*analysis of variance*), this is also a measure of the extent to which group means differ from one another and from the grand mean. It is calculated as the *between-groups sum of squares* divided by the *between-groups degrees of freedom*.

between-groups variance

Same as *between-groups mean square*.

bias

Systematic distortion or error. When a measurement is biased, it is consistently distorted in a particular direction. CONTRAST WITH *random error*.

biased variance

Also known as *systematic* variance. The portion of variance in one variable that can be explained or accounted for by another variable is biased variance. This means that the value of the variable being explained is determined at least in part by the second variable rather than being random or *unbiased*. CONTRAST WITH *random variance*.

bins

When you make a frequency histogram for a variable for which there are many values, like Age, or a continuous variable like Height, you will probably want to somehow collapse the values into a smaller set of *bins* and have one vertical bar on the histogram for each bin. Ex: for Age you might use UNDER 20, 21-30, 31-45, 46-60, OVER 60.

boundary conditions

The circumstances or conditions in which the generative force in a theory is likely to explain its effects.

categorical variable

A variable that can take only a small number of values is *categorical* or *discrete*. Family size, profession, and gender are usually considered to be categorical. CONTRAST WITH *continuous variable*.

causal explanation

A theory that explains patterns by reference to uncontrollable antecedents employs *causal explanation* and is called a *law*.

causal relationship

A situation in which a change in one thing causes a subsequent change in another thing. SEE *cause*.

cause

An antecedent condition (something that happens first) that produces a consequent *effect* (something that happens later as a result of what happened earlier) over which the people or objects involved have no control. The effect happens whether or not the people or objects involved want it to; it is an unavoidable consequence of the cause. SEE ALSO *necessary cause*, *sufficient cause*, *probabilistic cause*.

cell's contribution to chi-squared

When you calculate chi-squared, in each cell of the table, you subtract the expected value from the observed value, square the difference, and divide the result by the expected value. The result of this is the cell's contribution to chi-squared. The sum of these contributions is chi-squared.

census

A sample that includes the entire population.

central tendency

This is an unfortunate name for a way of summarizing the data in your sample that tells you what the typical value, the value seen most often, or the central value is. Measures of central tendency include the mode, the median, and the mean.

Chi-squared — χ^2

Chi-squared is a measure of the extent to which the values in your data differ from the values you would expect to see if a certain assumption about your data is true. For bivariate data, the assumption is that the two variables are not related to one another. For a single variable, the assumption is that the frequency distribution of your data matches a pre-defined set of probabilities.

circular definition

A definition that uses the term it is trying to define as part of the definition. EX: *negative advertising is advertising that contains negative terms.* Also, a definition so complicated and hard to understand that it makes your head spin.

closed question

A question for which the answer is selected from a short list of possibilities. Multiple-choice exam questions are closed questions.

column percents

In a *crosstabulation*, these are the numbers that tell you what percent of the cases in a column fall in a given row. The sum of the column percents in a column should be 100%. SEE ALSO *row percents*.

computational formula

A formula that you can use to calculate a statistic that differs from the *definitional* formula in three ways: it looks more complicated; it is a lot less work to use; and the result is likely to be more accurate because there is less rounding error.

concept

A word that expresses an *abstraction* formed by *generalization from particulars*. For example, "prejudice." We group all the things we consider to be examples of prejudice together because we are interested in what it is that they have in common. So we can talk about it, we give the grouping a name, "prejudice." The name we give the grouping is thus an abstraction formed by generalization from all the particular examples.

conceptual definition

A definition that clearly explicates the meaning of a concept. It should include a specification of all essential qualities of the concept. It should be clear, complete, precise, and not circular.

conceptualizing

The process of developing conceptual definitions, of specifying the meaning of your concepts and the relationships between #or among them, and of relating your conceptual definitions to those of other researchers.

confidence estimate

How confident you can be that your estimate of a population parameter is accurate to within a specified range. SEE ALSO *confidence interval*, *confidence level*.

confidence level

The estimated probability that a population parameter lies within a given confidence interval. When a newspaper article says that the results show that 23% of the population supports the President and that these results are accurate within 3 percent 19 times out of 20, the confidence level is 95% (19 times out of 20). SEE ALSO *confidence estimate, confidence interval*.

confidence interval

The range of values within which a population parameter is estimated to lie at a specified level of confidence. The confidence interval in the example above is from 20% to 26%. Also, the minimal distance you want between yourself and an angry Doberman. SEE ALSO *confidence estimate, confidence level*.

confounded

Confused, mixed up, misunderstood.

consistency

The extent to which a measure's results do not change when the measurement is repeated. You get almost the same result every time.

construct

A concept created explicitly for a specific scientific purpose.

construct validity

The extent to which your construct or concept is a single unidimensional one, and your measuring instrument is able to measure the intended construct and nothing more. If the construct is solid and coherent and doesn't have a range of aspects that interact with your measurement approach, and if various operational definitions of the construct result in identical or similar measurements, then the construct and measurement approach together have construct validity.

contingency table

Another name for *crosstabulation table*.

continuous variable

A variable that can take any value in the range from its highest and lowest value. Age, water, income, and freedom are continuous. CONTRAST WITH *categorical variable*.

control group

In an experiment, the group to which the treatment (stimulus) is <u>not</u> administered. CONTRAST WITH *experimental group*.

convenience sample

Also known as *accidental sample*. A non-probability sample in which you select whoever happens to be conveniently available.

correlation

A measure of the strength of association between a pair of *continuous* variables, based on the sum of the *cross products* of the z-scores of the variables. Also known as *Pearson's r* or *Pearson product-moment correlation*. Ranges from -1.0 to 1.0.

counts

Also known as *frequencies*. In a crosstabulation, the *counts* tell how many cases fall into each cell.

covariance

A measure of the strength of association between a pair of continuous variables, based on the sum of the *cross products* of the *deviation* scores of the variables. Unlimited range.

criteria for assessing conceptual definitions

A conceptual definition should include a specification of all essential qualities of the concept; it should be clear, complete, precise, and not circular.

criteria for assessing problem statements

Problem statements should be clear and specific; *empirically verifiable*, phrased affirmatively, and stated simply.

criterion validity

The extent to which your measurement agrees with a second measure you know to be valid.

3333
333

critical region
The area beyond the *critical value* calculated in a test of *statistical significance*. If your *critical ratio* falls in the critical region, you usually reject the *null hypothesis*.

critical ratio
The ratio obtained by dividing a statistic by its *standard error*; used to compare with the *critical value* to determine whether or not you land in the *critical region*.

critical value
The boundary of the *critical region* for use in a test of *statistical significance*.

cross-product
Multiplication of each value in one set of values by the corresponding value in a second set of values. Used in *correlation* and *covariance*.

cross-sectional
An approach to measurement in which you obtain data from individuals representing all segments of a population. CONTRAST WITH *longitudinal*.

cross tabulation
A procedure by which you make a two-dimensional table with rows corresponding to the values of one variable and columns corresponding to the values of the other variable. Ordinarily used with *discrete* variables.

cumulative percentage
The percentage of cases encountered up to and including a specific point.

curvilinear
A type of relationship which must be plotted as a curve rather than a straight line. An equation that requires values to be raised to higher or lower powers (i.e. square, cube, square root) or that involves logarithms.

deduction
Reasoning from a general statement to a specific case. The logical procedure used to develop hypotheses from theories. CONTRAST WITH *induction*.

degrees of freedom
A number or pair of numbers used in performing chi-square, t-test, and ANOVA. Based on the number of cases in the data or the number of values a variable can take.

denominator degrees of freedom
ANOVA requires two degrees of freedom. The one for the denominator is the number of cases minus the number of groups. Also known as *within-groups* degrees of freedom.

dependent variable
A variable whose value depends on the value of another variable. In a cause-and-effect relationship, the dependent variable is the effect. CONTRAST WITH *independent variable*.

descriptive research
The goal of descriptive research is to obtain a complete and accurate *description* of events, conditions, circumstances, processes, and relationships surrounding the focus of the research. CONTRAST WITH *explanatory* and *exploratory research*.

descriptive statistics
Statistics that summarize the data in your sample, without any reference to the population from which the sample is drawn. CONTRAST WITH *inferential statistics*.

descriptive terms
These parts of problem statements represent classes of phenomena, including *constructs* and *variables*. CONTRAST WITH *operative terms*.

deviation scores
The difference between the original values of a variable and the mean of the set of values. An individual whose score on the variable is above the mean will have a positive deviation score. An individual whose score is below the mean will have a negative deviation score. COMPARE WITH *standard scores*.

direct or positive relationship
A relationship between a pair of variables such that individuals with high scores on one variable tend to have high scores on the other variable,

while individuals with low scores on one variable tend to have low scores on the other variable. CONTRAST WITH *negative* or *inverse relationship*.

directed hypothesis

A hypothesis in which the direction of a difference is predicted. Ex: men drink more coffee than women. For directed hypotheses, you use *one-tailed* significance tests. CONTRAST WITH *undirected hypothesis*.

dispersion

The spread of values in a set of data. The more spread out the values are, the greater the *dispersion*. Commonly measured by *variance*, *inter quartile range*, *range*.

double-blind methods

Experimental methods in which neither the person from whom data is collected nor the experimenter know which condition the person is in. Double-blind methods reduce or eliminate *experimenter bias*.

effect

Something that happens later as a result of something that happened earlier.

empirical

Something that can be either observed or *inferred* from observation.

empirical research

Research in which the questions are about things that exist or happen, and in which the answers are obtained by somehow observing things in the world

empirically verifiable

A theory that can be verified by observations of things that exist or happen. A theory whose truth would have real-world implications which can be tested or observed.

error variance

The fluctuation or varying of measures due to chance. Also called 'random' variance. The variance left over in a set of measures after all known sources of systematic variance have been removed from the measures.

essential qualities

The qualities that must be present; the necessary ingredients. Used in conceptual definitions.

estimating population parameters

Because you only have data from a sample (a subset of the population) you cannot measure aspects of the population — you only have access to the sample. So you must *estimate* characteristics of the population.

estimation of *standard error of the mean* (SEM)

Because the *SEM* is a population *parameter*, it must be estimated. You estimate the *SEM* by dividing an estimate of the population's *standard deviation* by the square root of the sample size.

estimation versus calculation

Because your data describes the whole sample, you can *calculate* summary statistics for the sample. However, because you only have data from a sample (a subset of the population) you cannot measure aspects of the population. So you must *estimate* characteristics of the population.

expected values

The values you would expect to see if a certain assumption is true. When calculating *chi-square*, the assumption, the null hypothesis, is that the row variable is not related to the column variable.

experiment

A study in which you randomly assign the participants to one of two conditions, administer a treatment (stimulus) to the members of one group, take measurements of both groups, and compare the results. Any differences you see are attributed to the treatment you administered to the group.

experimental group

In an experiment, the group to which the treatment (stimulus) is administered. CONTRAST WITH *control group*.

explained variance

If a pair of variables are related to one another, learning the value of one variable will allow you to narrow down the likely range of values of the other one. The stronger the relationship is, the

more variance in one variable is explained by the relationship with the other one. Also called *variance accounted for*.

explanatory research

The goal of explanatory research is to explain causal relationships between events and circumstances. CONTRAST WITH *descriptive* and *exploratory research*.

exponential

A mathematical statement that requires the use of powers higher or lower than 1.

external validity

The extent to which results based on a sample can be generalized to the population the sample came from. Depends on how representative the sample is or how natural is the setting in which the research was conducted.

extreme value

A value that is considerably higher or lower than the great majority of other values.

face validity

The extent to which a measurement seems like it should be a reasonable measure of that which it is supposed to measure.

fail to reject the null hypothesis

When a difference is so small that it could easily be due to *sampling variability* (i.e. the evidence is not sufficient for you to rule out sampling variability as a reasonable explanation for the difference), you *fail to reject* the *null hypothesis*.

field research

Research conducted in the natural setting where day-to-day life activities take place. CONTRAST WITH *laboratory study*.

Fisher's *r* to *Z* transformation

A transformation that you apply to Pearson's *r* or to Spearman's rho to allow you to perform tests of the significance of the difference between two correlations.

frequencies

Also known as *counts*. The number of times the various values of a variable occur in a set of data.

frequency distribution

A summary of the values for a variable which shows how many times each of the possible values of the variable occurred. Ordinarily used for *categorical* data, sometimes used for *continuous* data which has been collapsed into a set of *bins*.

gamma

A PRE measure of the strength of association between a pair of ordinal variables. This measure tells you the proportional reduction in errors made predicting the value of one variable when you know the value of the other one.

generalizability

The extent to which results based on a sample can be generalized to the population the sample came from. Also the extent to which a person has what it takes to be made a general.

generalization from a sample to a population

If you interview a random sample of 50 residents of a small town and almost all of them say they drink coffee, you are generalizing from the sample to the population if you conclude that almost everyone who lives in the town drinks coffee.

generative forces

Part of an explanation. The causes, rules, or reasons that explain why something happens.

grounded theory

When the scientist begins by making observations and then constructs a theoretical explanation that would account for the observed patterns. This is *grounded theory*. The logical approach is *data-to-theory* and the logical method used here is *inductive*. The logical pattern is to move from the specific to the general.

heterogeneity

The extent to which the members of a population (or sample) are different from one another. The greater the heterogeneity, the larger the sample is needed for a given level of confidence.

heuristic

A theory has *heuristic value* if it sets the stage for further conceptual developments and empirical research.

histogram

A graphic representation of a *frequency distribution* in which each frequency is represented by a vertical bar whose length is proportional to the frequency.

homogeneity

The extent to which the members of a population (or sample) are similar to one another. The greater the homogeneity, the more accuracy you can have at a given level of confidence.

hypothesis

A prediction based on a theory. A hypothesis states what you would expect to see happen if the theory is true. While theories are abstract and general, hypotheses are concrete and specific.

idiographic

An idiographic study is one that explores a single person or event or situation in detail. Although the researcher doing this kind of work would learn a great deal about the idiosyncratic thoughts or behaviors of the person or situation, this information would apply only to the specific situation that was studied. CONTRAST WITH *nomothetic*.

independent variable

A variable whose value determines or influences the value of another variable. The cause. CONTRAST WITH *dependent variable*.

indirect or inverse or negative relationship

A relationship between a pair of variables in which an increase in the value of one is associated with a decrease in the value of the other. The *correlation* between variables negatively related to one another will be negative. CONTRAST WITH *positive* or *direct relationship*.

induction

Reasoning from specific cases to a general statement. The logical procedure used to develop theories from data. CONTRAST WITH *deduction*.

inferential statistics

Statistics based on sample data and used to estimate population parameters. CONTRAST WITH *descriptive statistics*.

inflection points

The points on a curve in which the direction of curvature switches direction. On a *normal curve*, the points at which the *z-score* is -1.0 and 1.0.

information-theoretic uncertainty

A measure of *dispersion* for *nominal* level data, this measure is based on the relative probabilities of the possible outcomes.

intercept

Also called the *Y-intercept*. The point where the *regression line* crosses the Y axis (the vertical axis). The value of the dependent variable where the independent variable equals zero.

internal validity

The consistency of the set of operational and conceptual definitions and the logical relations among them.

interpretive research

An abstract and conceptual approach to research focusing on the deeper meanings underlying events or situations.

interquartile range (IQR)

The difference between the first and third *quartiles*. The range of values that includes the middle 50% of all cases. A measure of *dispersion* for *ordinal data*.

interval scaling

An approach to measurement in which the cases are ordered and placed onto a scale graduated in equal units. Ex: Fahrenheit and Celsius temperature scales. SEE ALSO *nominal, ordinal, ratio saling*.

intervening variable

A variable that stands between an independent variable and a dependent variable and alters the size or direction of the effect the independent variable has on the dependent variable.

inverse relationship

A relationship between a pair of variables in which an increase in the value of one is associated with a decrease in the value of the other. The

correlation between variables negatively related to one another will be negative. CONTRAST WITH *positive* or *direct relationship*.

inverted U-shaped relationship

A relationship between a pair of variables in which the value of the dependent variable is low when the value of the independent variable is low, the dependent variable increases as the independent variable increases up to a point beyond which further increases in the independent variable are paired with decreases in the dependent variable. When plotted, this relationship looks like an upside-down U. This is a curvilinear relationship. CONTRAST WITH *U-shaped relationship*.

kurtosis

A measure of the extent to which a distribution is flattened with a wide peak, or narrow, with a thin pointy peak.

laboratory study

Research conducted in an artificial environment, all aspects of which are controlled by the researcher. CONTRAST WITH *field research*.

lambda

A PRE measure of the strength of the association between a pair of nominal variables. The proportional reduction in errors made predicting the value of one variable when you know the value of the other one turns out to be *Yule's Q*.

law

A *theory* that explains patterns by reference to uncontrollable *antecedents* and employs *causal explanation*. A statement of a universally invariant relationship.

linear

A mathematical relationship that can be plotted as a straight line on ordinary graph paper and expressed in the form $y = b_1 x_1 + b_2 x_2 + \ldots + a$, where the b's and a are constants and the x's are variables.

linear regression

A type of analysis of the relationship between a pair of variables in which the relationship can be plotted best as a straight line. CONTRAST WITH *curvilinear regression*.

longitudinal

A study in which you collect data from the same individuals over a period of time so you can see how they change. Example: in a longitudinal study of friendship patterns of high school students, you might follow the same students over the four years of high school, collecting data in each of the four years. CONTRAST WITH *cross-sectional*.

magnitude

Size. Measured on a ratio level scale where "0" means "none."

mapping

In measurement, the procedure used to match numbers to the aspect of reality being measured.

marginal counts

The numbers in a *crosstabulation* that tell how many cases fall in each row or column.

marginal percentages

The percentages in a *crosstabulation* that tell what portion of the total are in each row or column. SEE ALSO *row* and *column percentages*.

marginals

The *marginal counts* and *percentages* in a *crosstabulation*.

mean absolute deviation

A measure of *dispersion* obtained by calculating the mean of the absolute values of the deviation scores. The *standard deviation* is almost always used instead of this measure.

mean

Known informally as the "average." A measure of *central tendency* calculated by dividing the sum of all the values by the number of values. Used for *interval* or *ratio scaled* data.

mean square

An alternate name for *variance*, which is the mean of the squared deviation scores. *Mean square* is the term ordinarily used when discussing *Analysis of Variance* (*ANOVA*). SEE ALSO *root mean square*, *between-groups mean square*, *within-groups mean square*, *variance*.

measurement

A procedure by which information concerning some aspect of reality is obtained. Includes sorting into categories, arranging in increasing or decreasing order, counting, assessing amounts and distances.

median

A measure of *central tendency* used for ordinal, interval, ratio data. If there are an odd number of cases, the middle value in a rank-ordered list of values; if there are an even number of cases, halfway between the two middle values.

midpoint of range

Halfway between the highest and lowest values a variable takes. A worthless, useless measure of central tendency.

modal value

The value that occurs more often than all other values.

mode

A measure of central tendency for nominal data. The value that occurs more often than other values.

multimodal distribution

A distribution in which there are two or more distinct *modes*.

multiple regression

A *regression analysis* that simultaneously examines the effects of a set of independent variables on a single dependent variable.

multiple methods, multiple measures

Also known as multi-methods multi-measures. An approach used to assess *construct validity* in which several measurement methods are used to perform several different measures of a *construct*.

necessary cause

An *antecedent condition* (something that happens first) that <u>must</u> happen before a consequent *effect* happens. The cause might not be enough by itself to produce the effect, but if the causal event does not happen, the effect will not happen. SEE ALSO *cause, sufficient cause, necessary and sufficient cause, probabilistic cause.*

necessary and sufficient cause

An *antecedent condition* (something that happens first) that must happen before a consequent *effect* happens and that is enough, by itself, to produce the effect. The effect happens whenever and only when the cause happens. SEE ALSO *cause, necessary cause, sufficient cause, probabilistic cause.*

negative finding

A research study in which the *null hypothesis* is not rejected.

nominal scaling

An approach to measurement in which the cases are sorted into a set of categories that have no *mathematical relationship* between them. SEE ALSO *ordinal, interval, ratio saling.*

nomothetic

Nomothetic research attempts to discover what systems of laws or principles govern different aspects of reality, while idiographic research is interested in describing only a single event, person, or situation.

non-probability sample

A type of sample in which the probability of being included in the sample is not known for all members of the population.

normal curve

A plot of a *normal distribution*. SEE *normal distribution*. Used for a variety of *descriptive* and *inferential statistics* for *interval* and *ratio scaled* data.

normal distribution

Also known as the bell-shape distribution or the bell curve. A symmetrical distribution in which most cases are clustered near the mean and the further away from the mean you go, the fewer cases there are. The shape of this distribution is described in Table 1. The distribution of large numbers of random events and the means of samples in a *sampling distribution* will be normally distributed.

null hypothesis

The hypothesis that the variables you are examining are not related to one another. Any apparent relationship must be due to *sampling variability*.

number

A symbol composed of one or more of the characters from 0 to 9, possibly including a decimal point or a leading minus sign, and indicating how many objects there are, how much of something there is, where something is located along a continuous scale or how many steps it is along a discrete scale. Numbers have *mathematical* meaning, whereas *numerals* do not and *ordinals* only specify ordering relationships.

numeral

A symbol which is used as a label, which has no mathematical meaning, and which is composed of one or more of the characters from 0 to 9. Example: Wayne Gretzky's "99".

numerator degrees of freedom

ANOVA (*analysis of variance*) requires two *degrees of freedom*. The one for the numerator is the number of groups minus one. Also known as *between-groups* degrees of freedom.

observed and expected

Used in the calculation of *chi-squared*. The *observeds* are the numbers of cases falling into the cells of the table. The *expecteds* are the numbers of cases you would expect to fall in the cells if the row variable is independent of the column variable (i.e. if the *null hypothesis* is true).

one-tailed test

The type of *significance test* you perform when your hypotheses are *directed*. Called "one-tailed" because the *critical region* occupies only one tail of the distribution. COMPARE WITH *two-tailed test*.

open-ended

A type of question that doesn't provide a list of possible answers to choose from.

operational definition

A specification of the operations or procedures that will be done in order to measure a concept.

operative terms

Words used in problem statements or hypotheses to clarify the relationship between the specified classes. Examples: "increasing," "decreasing," "is related to increasing," "immediately," "dimin-

ishes," etc. May also be used to specify the type of relationship you expect to observe. Examples: *linear, curvilinear, exponential, positive, negative, direct, inverse, inverted U-shaped*, and *U-shaped.*

ordinal

They look a bit like numbers, but they only tell what order things are. Examples are 1st, 2nd, 3rd. No mathematical operations can be performed on ordinals.

ordinal scaling

An approach to measurement in which the cases are ordered into a set of increasing (or decreasing) categories. SEE ALSO *nominal, interval, ratio scaling.*

parameter

A summary description of a given variable for the entire population. Example: the mean age of citizens in the country.

parsimony

A parsimonious theory has few concepts and relationships; it is not complex, complicated, and elaborate.

participant observation

An approach to data collection in which the researcher joins or participates in the social system being studied, thereby getting access to information that might otherwise not be available.

Pearson product-moment correlation

Also known as *Pearson's r*. A measure of the strength of a relationship between a pair of continuous interval- or ratio-scaled variables. Defined as the mean of the cross-products of the *z*-scores of the two variables.

percentage across, compare down

A method of interpreting crosstabulation tables in which you compare the row percents up and down within a single column. The appropriate method to use when the independent variable is the one that determines which row a case is in.

percentage down, compare across

A method of interpreting crosstabulation tables in which you compare the column percents back and forth within a single row. The appropriate

method to use when the independent variable is the one that determines which column a case is in.

perspicuity

The extent to which a statement is precisely stated, clear, lucid, readily understandable, unambiguous. An important characteristic of theories, conceptual definitions, problem statements, hypotheses.

phrased affirmatively

A problem statement is phrased affirmatively if it states or predicts what *is* or *will be* the case, rather than what is not or what will not be the case.

population

The entire set of individuals, events, units with specified characteristics. ex: citizens of Mexico; students; adults; women; newspaper articles.

population parameters vs. sample statistics

Parameters describe populations, can only be estimated, and use Greek letters for symbols. Statistics describe samples, can be calculated directly, and use roman letters for symbols.

positive research

Research about what *is* the case, rather than *normative* research, which is research about what *ought to be* the case.

posttest

A measurement taken after the application of the experimental manipulation/stimulus.

posttest-only design

An experiment in which all measurements are done after the application of the experimental manipulation/stimulus.

pre-experimental design

An experiment in which one or more of the necessary steps (usually random assignment to conditions) is left out.

predictive validity

A measurement whose predictions turn out to be accurate has predictive validity.

pretest

A measurement taken at the beginning of an experiment before the application of the experimental manipulation/stimulus.

pretest-posttest design

An experiment in which all measurements are done <u>both</u> before and after the application of the experimental manipulation/stimulus.

probabilistic cause

An antecedent condition (something that happens first) that is <u>usually</u> followed by a consequent *effect*. When the causal event happens, it is likely that the effect will occur. SEE ALSO *cause, sufficient cause, necessary cause.*

probability samples

A type of sample in which the probability that any individual will be included in the sample is known. The only kind of sample that can be used to make valid generalizations.

problem statements

A hypothesis that describes a relationship which is the subject of a research study or a question that a research study is designed to answer. SEE ALSO *research hypothesis, research question.*

proportionate reduction of error (PRE)

The percentage by which errors of prediction in the value of one variable can be reduced by knowledge of the value of a second variable.

quasi-experimental design

Almost an experiment. An *experiment* missing a critical piece — usually one in which cases are not randomly assigned to conditions.

quota sample

A type of *non-probability* sample in which you select cases in order to match the population's proportions on a number of characteristics. Because it is not possible to match a population on all relevant characteristics, quota samples are not likely to be representative of the population.

r-squared

Pearson's r squared. A measurement of percentage of *variance* in one variable accounted for or explained by the relationship to a second variable.

random variance

Variability in the value of a dependent variable that cannot be explained or accounted for by the independent variable(s).

random assignment to conditions

In experiments, individuals are randomly assigned to control or experimental groups which guarantees that there are no systematic differences between the groups.

random error

The fluctuation or varying of measures due to chance. Also called 'random' variance. The variance left over in a set of measures after all known sources of systematic variance have been removed from the measures.

random sample

A sample in which individuals are selected randomly from the population. Characterized by equal probability and independence of selection.

random selection

A process in which members are drawn from a population where each member of the population has the same chance of being selected as all other members, and where the selection of one person has no influence on anyone else's chances of being selected.

range

The difference between the highest and lowest values for a variable. The weakest measure of *dispersion*. A place where the skies are not cloudy all day.

rank-order correlation

See Spearman's rho.

ratio scaling

An approach to measurement in which the cases are ordered and placed onto a scale graduated in equal units where the value "0" indicates "none." SEE ALSO *nominal, ordinal, interval saling*.

reason

A type of generative force which refers to the preexisting goals, needs, and desires of a person that explain patterns of behavior.

regression

A method of analysis in which the relationship between independent and dependent variables are expressed as a regression equation. If the equation is *linear*, it is linear regression. If the equation is *curvilinear*, it is curvilinear regression. There may be several independent variables in a regression equation.

regression line

The line defined by a regression equation.

regression equation

An equation that uses independent variable(s) to predicts the value of a dependent variable. A *linear* regression equation is usually expressed in the form $y = b_1 x_1 + b_2 x_2 + b_3 x_3 + \ldots + a$, where the b's and a are constants and the x's are variables.

reject the null hypothesis

When a difference is so large that it could not be due to *sampling variability*, the *null hypothesis*, which says that the difference is due to sampling variability, is rejected.

reliability

A measure is reliable to the extent to which repetitions of the measurement give the same result.

representativeness

The extent to which a sample has the same distribution of characteristics as the population from which it was selected. A representative sample is necessary if you want to make statements or conclusions about the population with any degree of confidence.

research hypothesis

A problem statement expressed as a hypothesis. A hypothesis that describes a relationship whose validity is the subject of a research study.

research question

A question that a research study is designed to answer. May be a question requiring a description ("What is the non-verbal content of cigarette advertising in national magazines?") or a question requiring a causal explanation ("Are ads that attempt to use fear of cancer and heart disease to convince people to stop smoking more or less effective than ads that take other approaches?").

residuals

The variability in values of the dependent variable that is not accounted for (i.e. left over) after the effect of the independent variable(s) has been taken into consideration. Errors in predictions made with a *regression equation*.

root mean square

The square root of the mean of the squared differences between the individual values and the mean of the values. Also known as *standard deviation*.

row percents

In a *crosstabulation*, these are the numbers that tell you what percent of the cases in a row fall in a given column. The sum of the row percents in a row should be 100%. SEE ALSO *column percents*.

rule

A social norm, custom, or tradition that specifies expected or required behavior.

rule-based explanation

A theory that explains by reference to norms, social customs, or tradition.

sample

A subset of the population from which data is collected and used as a basis for making statements about the entire population.

sampling distribution

If you draw all possible samples of a given size from a population and calculate the value of a statistic (i.e. the mean) for each sample, the resulting list of values will be the *sampling distribution* of that statistic. Certain characteristics of the sampling distribution allow the calculation of things like confidence intervals or levels. Probability samples are generally required for these calculations and estimates to be made.

sampling distribution of differences between sample means

If you draw all possible pairs of samples of a given size from a population and calculate the difference between the means of each pair of samples, the resulting list of values will be the *sampling distribution of differences between sample means*.

sampling distribution of sample means

If you draw all possible samples of a given size from a population and calculate the mean for each sample, the resulting list of values will be the *sampling distribution of sample means*.

sampling frame

The list or quasi-list of the members of the population from which your sample is to be selected. If the sample is to be truly representative of the population, the sampling frame should include all members of the population.

sampling interval

In *systematic sampling*, one plus the number of individuals you skip before you select the next member of the sample. If you are taking every k^{th} person, you skip $k-1$ and take one, and the sampling interval is k. To determine the sampling interval, divide the population size by the desired sample size.

sampling ratio

The proportion of a population taken into the sample. The sample size divided by the population size.

sampling variability

If more than one sample were taken from a single population, each would have a different value for a given statistic. The differences between samples is *sampling variability*. The more heterogeneous the population is, the greater the sampling variability for samples of a given size.

sampling unit

An element or set of elements considered for selection in a sample. In a simple random sample, the *sampling unit* is the individual. In a cluster sample, the sampling unit will be a cluster of individuals.

self-selection

When individuals volunteer to participate in a research study or decide whether they will be in the experimental or control group, they are said to be self-selected. Self-selection generally is avoided because it leads to bias.

significance test

A test to determine the extent to which the apparent relationship you see in your data could be due to *sampling variability* alone.

skewness

The extent to which the majority of cases are clustered in the high or low end of the scale, rather than in the middle.

slope of the regression line

Indicates how large a change in the dependent variable is predicted for a given change in the independent variable. A positive slope indicates that an increase in the independent variable will be associated with an increase in the dependent variable. A negative slope indicates that an increase in the independent variable will be associated with an decrease in the dependent variable.

Solomon four group design

An experimental design in which there are four groups. Two *control groups* and two *experimental groups*, one of each with and one without a *pretest*. Equivalent to a combination of *posttest only* and *pretest-posttest* designs.

Somers' *d*

A measure of the strength of association between a pair of ordinal variables. Very similar to gamma, except Somers' *d* takes tied pairs, ignored by gamma, into account. *d* is a more conservative measure than gamma, and it does not have a PRE interpretation.

Spearman's rho (r_s)

A measure of the strength of a relationship between a pair of rank-ordered variables. With this measure, there will be a perfect relationship if the object having the highest score on one variable also has the highest score on the other variable; the one having the second-highest score on one variable has the second-highest score on the other variable, and so on. This measure does not have a PRE interpretation. It can be used in the same tests of significance as Pearson's *r*.

standard deviation

The most often used measure of dispersion for interval- or ratio-scaled data. Defined as the square root of the mean of the squared deviation scores. Also known as the *root mean square*.

standard deviation of sampling distribution

The standard deviation of a sampling distribution is a *standard error*.

standard errors

The standard deviation of a sampling distribution is a *standard error*. For example, the standard deviation of the sampling distribution of sample means is the *standard error of the mean*.

standard error as measure of sampling variability

Because standard errors are measures of the amount of dispersion of values in a sampling distribution, they are measures of the extent to which the value of a statistic varies from sample to sample—i.e. a measure of *sampling variability*.

standard error of the difference between means

The standard deviation of the sampling distribution of differences between sample means is the *standard error of the differences between means*, sometimes abbreviated SEDBM.

standard error of the mean

The standard deviation of the sampling distribution of sample means is the *standard error of the mean*, sometimes abbreviated SEM.

standard error of the proportion

The standard deviation of the sampling distribution of sample proportions is the *standard error of the proportion*.

standard error as SD of sampling distribution

All standard errors are standard deviations of sampling distributions.

standard scores

When *deviation scores* are divided by the *standard deviation*, you get standard scores. Also known as *z-scores*.

static group design

A two-group *quasi-experimental design* in which individuals are not randomly assigned to conditions.

statistic

A summary description of a given variable for the sample. Example: the mean age of people in the

sample. Statistics are the data upon which estimates of population parameters are based.

statistical significance

The extent to which the apparent relationship you see in your data is not likely to be due to *sampling variability* alone.

statistically significant difference

A difference so large that it could not have been caused by sampling variability.

stimulus

Something that is done to the individuals in the experimental group but not to the individuals in the control group.

stratified sample

A sampling procedure that divides the population into relatively homogeneous groups (strata) before samples are drawn from each group. May use random, systematic, or cluster methods to draw the samples from the strata.

stratum

A subset of a population. Used in stratified sampling methods. To be useful, a stratum must be comprised of individuals that are homogeneous in some way that is relevant to the study being conducted.

sufficient cause

An *antecedent condition* (something that happens first) that is always followed by a consequent *effect*. The cause by itself is enough to produce the effect, but other things may also produce the effect. SEE ALSO *cause, necessary cause, necessary and sufficient cause, probabilistic cause.*

sum of squares (SS)

The sum of the squared differences between the individual values and the mean of the values. Used in the calculation of *variance, standard deviation*, and *analysis of variance*.

systematic error

In measurement, bias or systematic distortion. When a measurement is biased, it is consistently distorted in a particular direction. CONTRAST WITH *random error.*

systematic variance

Variance in one variable that can be explained or accounted for by a relationship to other variables.

teleological explanation

An explanation that makes reference to goals or subjective reasons for acting.

theory

A set of statements about a number of concepts and the relations between them. A formal statement of definitions and propositions concerning the relations among a set of constructs created for the purposes of explanation, understanding, prediction, and control of phenomena.

tradeoff between precision and confidence

When you estimate a population parameter n the basis of a sample statistic, you can make a very precise prediction with low confidence or you can make a less precise prediction with higher confidence. When the precision is increased, the confidence goes down.

two-tailed test

The type of *significance test* you perform when your hypotheses are *not* directed. Called "two-tailed" because the *critical region* occupies both tails of the distribution. COMPARE WITH *one-tailed test.*

Type I error

The error you make if you reject a true *null hypothesis* — that is, if you conclude that the difference in your data indicates a real difference in the population, when in fact there is none (i.e., when the difference in your sample data was due to *sampling variability*).

Type II error

The error you commit if you fail to reject a false *null hypothesis*—that is, if you conclude that the pattern in your data is due to *sampling variability* when, in fact, it is because your sample came from a population in which the same pattern was present.

U-shaped relationship

A relationship between a pair of variables in which the value of the dependent variable is high

when the value of the independent variable is low, the dependent variable decreases as the independent variable increases up to a point beyond which further increases in the independent variable are paired with increases in the dependent variable. When plotted, this relationship looks like a U. This is a curvilinear relationship. CONTRAST WITH *inverted U-shaped relationship*.

undirected hypothesis

A hypothesis in which the direction of a difference is <u>not</u> specified. Ex: men and women drink different amounts of coffee. CONTRAST WITH *directed hypothesis*.

unexplained variance

SEE *Random variance, error variance, residuals*.

unit of analysis

The smallest unit or individual that is accepted in a sample. Usually our sampling unit will be the individual person, although you may use advertisements, movies, episodes of television programs, conversations, organizations, families, etc.

unobtrusive

An unobtrusive measurement method is one that can be carried out without disturbing or intruding on the people being measured, one that is not noticeable or drawing of attention.

validity

In measurement, the extent to which the measurement is sensitive only to differences in what it is supposed to be measuring.

variability or spread around the mean

If the values in a sample are not all the same, there will be some variability from case to case. The values will be spread out around the mean.

variable

Variables are empirical indicators, or symptoms, of *constructs*. A variable is something concrete that you can observe, and by its appearance you can tell whether the concept is present or absent or to what extent it is present.

variance

A measure of the extent to which a set of values are different from one another, calculated as the mean of the squared differences between the values and the mean of the set of values. Sometimes called the *mean square*.

variance accounted for

If a pair of variables are related to one another, learning the value of one variable will allow you to narrow down the likely range of values of the other one. The stronger the relationship is, the more variance in one variable is accounted for by the relationship with the other one. ALSO CALLED *explained variance*.

within-groups degrees of freedom

ANOVA (*analysis of variance*) requires two *degrees of freedom*. The one for the denominator is the number of cases minus the number of groups. Also known as *denominator degrees of freedom*.

within-groups mean square

(MS_w) Used in ANOVA (*analysis of variance*); a measure of the variability within the groups, calculated as the *within-groups sum of squares* divided by the *within-groups degrees of freedom*.

within-groups sum of squares ($_{Ssw}$)

Used in ANOVA (*analysis of variance*); a measure of the variability within the groups. Calculate the ordinary *sum of squares* for each group, and add them together: $SS_1 + SS_2 + \ldots + SS_k$

within-groups variance

Same as *within-groups mean square*.

Yule's Q

A measure of the strength of the association between a pair of nominal variables. Like lambda, Q also has a PRE interpretation. It is the proportional reduction in errors made predicting the value of one variable when you know the value of the other one. Q indicates to what degree the pairs tend to fall in one diagonal more than another. When the variables are independent, the pairs are equally likely to fall in each diagonal.

z-score

When *deviation scores* are divided by the *standard deviation*, you get *z*- scores. Also known as *standard scores*.

Notes

Exercises

Chapter 1. Science

1. What is the nomothetic-deductive approach to research?

2. What is the idiographic approach to research?

3. What are the advantages and disadvantages of the nomothetic-deductive and idiographic approaches to research?

4. What is the difference between description and explanation? Why is explanation more difficult to do?

5. Compare and contrast causal explanation, rule-based explanation, and teleological explanation?

6. What are generative forces and what do they?

7. What is the difference between deduction and induction?

8. What is grounded theory and how is it related to the theory used in nomothetic-deductive research?

9. Parsimony and perspicuity are important characteristics of a good theory. What is the difference between the two and how are they different from utility?

10. Which approach is better — quantitative or qualitative? Justify your answer?

11. Compare and contrast laboratory and field research methods and discuss their strengths and weaknesses?

12. What does it mean to say that empirical research is "positive"?

Chapter 2.   Conceptualizing

1. What are "essential qualities"?

2. What role do essential qualities play in conceptual definitions?

3. Why do you need a conceptual definition when you already have a perfectly good operational definition?

4. What is the difference between a variable and a concept?

5. What is the relation between an hypothesis and a theory?

6. What is empirical research?

7. A professor is studying learning and academic performance and uses GPA as a measure of how much her students have learned. Discuss why (or why not) this is an adequate conceptual definition of learning.

8. What is "reification," and how can it cause problems with the development of conceptual definitions?

9. Why do researchers test hypotheses when they are really interested in theories?

10. What does it mean to say that something is "empirically verifiable"? Give an example.

Chapter 3. Operationalizing

1. Why do you need an operational definition when you already have a perfectly good conceptual definition?

2. Why can't you skip the conceptual definition and use only an operational definition to define your concept? i.e. why is it also necessary to have a conceptual definition?

3. What is the difference between conceptual and operational definitions?

4. A professor is studying learning and academic performance and uses GPA as a measure of how much her students have learned. Discuss why (or why not) this is an adequate operational definition of learning.

5. What role should essential qualities play in operational definitions?

6. What is the difference between a *numeral* and a *number*?

7. What is the difference between a *number* and an *ordinal*?

8. In what way is ratio scaling "stronger" than interval or ordinal scaling?

9. How do you tell which level of scaling is appropriate for a particular situation? (What aspects of the situation do you consider? Why do these aspects matter?)

10. Under what conditions would you have to use a lower level of scaling than the one that matches the phenomenon you want to measure? Give an example.

11. What can you do with interval or ratio scaling that you can't do with nominal or ordinal scaling?

12. Under what conditions does "0" not mean "none"? What are the consequences of this?

13. If you have a ratio-scaled variable and want to compare two values, what kind of comparisons can you make?

14. If you have an ordinal-scaled variable and want to compare two values, what kind of comparisons can you make?

15. If you have an interval-scaled variable and want to compare two values, what kind of comparisons can you make?

Chapter 4. Validity and reliability

16. What is the difference between the reliability and validity of a measurement?

17. What is construct validity and how do you test for it? Give an example.

18. What are the consequences of a lack of construct validity? Give an example to illustrate your answer.

19. What is it about construct validity that makes it more difficult to assess than the other types of validity?

20. What is the difference between construct validity and predictive validity? What would the consequences be if you confused the two and thought you had construct validity when you only had predictive validity?

21. What is the difference between random error and systematic error?

22. What is the difference between the precision of a measurement and its accuracy?

23. Why does the multiple methods, multiple measures approach used to assess construct validity?

24. What is the difference between the precision and the validity of a measurement?

25. A professor is studying learning and academic performance and uses GPA as a measure of how much her students have learned. Discuss why (or why not) this is a valid measure how much her students have learned.

Chapter 5. Sampling

1. Distinguish between probability and non-probability sampling and discuss the advantages and disadvantages of each.

2. Discuss the main types of probability sampling methods and explain their strengths and weaknesses.

3. Explain how to select a sample with each of the probability sampling methods.

4. List all the *essential qualities* of a simple random sample. (***do not include non-essential qualities!***)

5. List all the *essential qualities* of a probability sample. (***do not include non-essential qualities!***)

6. Under what conditions would you use systematic sampling with a random start instead of simple random sampling?

7. What is stratified random sampling and under what conditions would you want to do it instead of simple random sampling?

8. Why are non-probability samples not likely to be representative of the populations from which they were drawn?

9. What factors affect the efficiency of a sampling method?

Chapter 6. Univariate descriptive statistics

1. Compute the mode, median, and mean for the following four sets of numbers:

   1. 2, 7, 6, 5, 3, 8, 6, 4, 9, 7
   2. 6, 2, 2, 5, 4, 2, 3, 4, 5, 6, 3
   3. 2, 5, 8, 2, 8, 4, 2, 8, 1, 9, 9
   4. 3, 5, 4, 8, 6, 9, 4, 43, 7, 2

2. Use this set of numbers for the following questions:

   4, 3, 5, 4, 1, 2, 5, 4, 3, 4, 1, 2, 4, 3, 5, 2, 3, 5, 7, 6, 4, 1, 2, 4

3. Assume the numbers in the data are the answers you get when you ask people "How many magazines do you subscribe to?" What are the proper measures of central tendency and dispersion for this data? Calculate their values.

4. Assume the numbers in the data are the answers you get when you ask people "Name your favorite television program." Then you classify each program according to its thematic content. You use a system that has seven different classes (eg. 1=science fiction, 2=comedy, 3=romance, 4=adventure, 5=news, ...). The numbers in the data indicate which category their favorite programs fall into. What are the proper measures of central tendency and dispersion for this data? Calculate their values.

5. Assume the numbers in the data are the answers you get when you ask people "What is your household's annual income? I'm going to read a list of possible ranges, and I want you to stop me when I read the range that describes your household's income." You then read the following list and record their answers:

   1) below $10,000
   2) between $10,000 and $15,000
   3) between $15,000 and $24,000
   4) between $24,000 and $35,000
   5) between $35,000 and $45,000
   6) between $45,000 and $60,000
   7) above $60,000

   What are the proper measures of central tendency and dispersion for this data? Calculate their values.

6. Below are the final exam scores in percentages for students in a course on postmodernist approaches to analysis of individual differences in skiing preferences. Calculate the modes, medians, and means for the males and for the females.

Males			Females		
64.10	76.56	95.31	69.74	85.53	88.16
75.00	75.00	53.13	92.11	76.32	77.63
64.06	46.88	98.44	61.84	52.63	96.05
78.13	85.94	93.75	84.21	88.16	80.26
67.19	87.50	92.19	61.84	75.00	90.79
71.88	76.56	70.31	72.37	73.68	82.89
78.13	71.88	93.75	68.42	96.05	88.16
32.81	79.69	50.00	64.47	90.79	63.16
71.88	57.81	60.94	80.26	46.05	64.47
59.38	68.75	75.00	78.95	76.32	63.20

   a. Which of the measures of central tendency are the most and least appropriate for this data?

   b. Which tell you more about the relative performance of males and females on the exam?

   c. Discuss the benefits and drawbacks of each measure of central tendency.

    d. Compute the range, interquartile range, and standard deviation.

    e. Discuss the benefits and drawbacks of each measure of dispersion.

7. Use the table of random numbers (Table 7 in Appendix B) for this question. Use the last two digits of the 5-digit numbers. Starting at the top of the second column, scan down and mark the numbers that are between 10 and 29, including 10 and 29. Do this until you get a total of 15 numbers. Write these 15 two-digit numbers on a piece of paper. Calculate the median, the mean, and the standard deviation for these numbers. Use the computational equation for standard deviation.

8. Analyze all four sets of numbers in Question 1 in terms of which of the measures of central tendency are the most and least appropriate. For each set of numbers, discuss the benefits and drawbacks of each measure of central tendency.

9. On a mid-term exam, the median score is 73 and the mean is 79. Which student's score is likely to be further away from the median – the one at the top of the class or the one at the bottom? Why?

    a. What is the variance?

10. If the standard deviation of a sample is 5.3,

    a. What is the sum of the squares?

    b. What is the root mean square?

11. Compute the standard deviation, range, and interquartile range for the following data:

81.13	75.42	92.04
87.25	63.89	85.90
74.89	77.76	88.53

    a. Remove the lowest score and repeat the calculations.

    b. Which of the three measures changed the most? Why?

    c. Which of the three measures changed the least? Why?

12. Multiply each of the nine numbers in Question 11 a by a constant, say 0.4, and calculate the standard deviation. What is the effect on the standard deviation of multiplying the numbers by a constant? Try it with a different constant, say 1.3. What is the effect? What is the general pattern here?

13. Subtract a constant, say 50.0, from each of the nine numbers in Question 11, and calculate the standard deviation. What is the effect on the standard deviation of subtracting a constant? Try it with a different constant, say 63.89. What is the effect? What is the general pattern here?

14. What is the nature of the sample data if $s = 0$ and $n = 75$?

Chapter 7. Distributions

1. Prepare a table showing the frequencies, percentages, and cumulative percentages for the following data. Make the bins 5 units wide and make the first bin have the lower limit of 41

    89, 69, 76, 88, 74, 41, 49, 68, 72, 83, 66, 69, 70, 77,
    56, 61, 58, 56, 63, 61, 66, 74, 69, 76, 68, 72, 83, 56

2. Draw a histogram for the results of #1. Make the bins 5 units wide and make the first bin have the lower limit of 41.

3. Draw histograms for the following types of distributions:

    1. symmetric single-peaked distribution
    2. symmetric bimodal distribution
    3. asymmetric single-peaked distribution
    4. asymmetric bimodal distribution
    5. rectangular (flat) distribution

4. Below are the final exam scores in percentages for students in a statistics course that uses a different text.

male		female	
81.61	56.66	66.76	93.92
83.68	75.30	65.19	87.65
59.51	84.02	73.22	90.34
70.79	60.25	69.50	89.62
63.45	89.66	89.24	44.35
64.99	77.15	74.92	72.00
62.88	86.19	83.21	54.10
84.59	66.80	83.23	90.46
82.94	88.48	82.79	77.64
38.82	73.54	89.03	62.54
75.39	64.06	72.34	82.96
69.35	51.72		

1. Construct separate frequency tables for males and females. Set them up so they have 12 bins.

2. Draw a histogram that shows both distributions, like the one on the right side of page 58.

3. Do women do better than men? What can you say about this by examining the table and histogram you made?

4. Draw the cumulative percentage curves for the two groups on the histograms, using red for males and blue for females.

5. Locate the medians for the two groups by examining the cumulative percentage curves. What do the medians tell you in response to question 4 c?

6. Are either of these distributions normal? How can you tell? If they aren't, what is it about them that makes them not normal?

5. Assume the mean is 72 and the standard deviation is 2.4.

   1. What percent of cases lie between the mean and 2.0 standard deviations above the mean?

   2. What percent of cases are more than 1.8 standard deviations away from the mean?

   3. What percent of cases are more than 1.2 and less than 1.8 standard deviations below the mean?

   4. If you want the top fifteen percent of scores, how far above the mean do you have to go?

6. If the scores on an exam are normally distributed, the mean exam score is 86.4, the standard deviation is 11.5, and the sample size is 500, how many people have scores above 95?

7. If the scores on an exam are normally distributed, the mean is 83.1, standard deviation is 13, and sample size is 600, how many people have scores between 95 and 105?

8. What is the z-score of the person in the 80th percentile?

9. Does the answer to question 8 depend on the mean and standard deviation? Why or why not?

10. If your z-score is 1.85, what percentile are you in? σ^2

Chapter 8. The normal curve and samples: sampling distributions

1. If you have a population with σ^2 of 144.0, what will $\sigma_{\bar{x}}$ be for samples of size 100?

2. If you have a sample of 32 people and the variance (calculated as $s^2 = \dfrac{\sum d_i^2}{n}$) is 7.75, what is your best estimate for the standard error of the mean? (Be careful: Make it the *best* estimate possible with the data you have.)

3. If you are drawing random samples of 50 cases from a population that is normally distributed, has a population mean of 247 and a population standard deviation of 60.5, is the sampling distribution of sample means normally distributed?

4. If you are drawing random samples of 50 cases from a population that has a distribution shaped like the drawing below, population mean of 247 and population standard deviation of 60.5, is the sampling distribution of sample means normally distributed? Why or why not?

5. It the mean of the sampling distribution is 193.482, the standard error of the mean is 100.0, and the sample size is 50, what is the mean of the population?

6. All standard errors are standard deviations.

   a. Standard deviations of what?

   b. How are they different from ordinary standard deviations of the data in a sample?

   c. Standard deviations measure the dispersion in your data. What dispersion do standard errors measure?

7. What is the probability that your sample mean is within one standard error of the population mean?

8. What is the probability that your sample mean is within 1.85 standard errors of the population mean?

9. What is the probability that your sample mean is more than 1.66 standard errors away from the population mean?

Chapter 9. Inferential statistics: from samples to populations

1. What is the relationship between sampling variability and standard errors?

2. Assume $\sigma_{\bar{x}}$ is 2.40 and the sample size is 36. What will $\sigma_{\bar{x}}$ be if you change the sample size to:

   a. 72

   b. 9

   c. 144

3. Assume $\sigma_{\bar{x}}$ is 3.60 and your estimate for σ 9.00. Assuming your sample size does not change, what will $\sigma_{\bar{x}}$ be if you could change σ to:

   a. 12.0

   b. 4.5

   c. 13.5

4. If the sample's standard deviation tells you how good the sample's mean is as a description of the typical person in the sample, the standard error of the mean tell you how good the sample's mean is as a description of what? In other words, if the sample's standard deviation tells you how far the sample's mean is from the typical person in the sample, the standard error of the mean tells you how far the sample's mean is likely to be from what?

5. Calculate $\sigma_{\bar{x}}$ for the following eleven samples:

	n	s	$\sigma_{\bar{x}}$
a.	36	6.0	
b.	36	8.0	
c.	36	12.0	
d.	49	6.0	
e.	49	8.0	
f.	72	12.0	
g.	98	6.0	
h.	98	8.0	
i.	98	12.0	
j.	144	12.0	
l.	144	8.0	

6. Examine the answers you obtained for question 5.

    a. What effect does doubling the sample size have on $\sigma_{\bar{x}}$ when s doesn't change?

    b. What effect does quadrupling the sample size have on $\sigma_{\bar{x}}$ when s doesn't change?

    c. What effect does doubling s have on $\sigma_{\bar{x}}$ when the sample size doesn't change?

    d. What effect does increasing s have on $\sigma_{\bar{x}}$ when the sample size doesn't change?

7. Overall, what is the relation between sample size and $\sigma_{\bar{x}_1 - \bar{x}_2}$?

8. Calculate $\sigma_{\bar{x}_1 - \bar{x}_2}$ for the following six pairs of samples:

	sample 1		sample 2		
	n	s	n	s	$\sigma_{\bar{x}_1 - \bar{x}_2}$
a.	45	5.50	45	5.50	
b.	60	5.50	60	5.50	
c.	60	8.50	60	8.50	
d.	45	5.50	60	5.50	
e.	45	11.00	45	11.00	
f.	180	5.50	180	5.50	

9. Examine the answers for question 7.

    a. What effect does increasing s have on $\sigma_{\bar{x}_1 - \bar{x}_2}$ when the sample size doesn't change?

    b. What effect does increasing the sample size have on $\sigma_{\bar{x}_1 - \bar{x}_2}$ when s doesn't change?

    c. What effect does increasing the size of one sample have on $\sigma_{\bar{x}_1 - \bar{x}_2}$ when s and the other sample size don't change?

    d. What effect does doubling the sample size have on $\sigma_{\bar{x}_1 - \bar{x}_2}$ when s doesn't change?

    e. What effect does quadrupling the sample size have on $\sigma_{\bar{x}_1 - \bar{x}_2}$ when s doesn't change?

    f. Overall, what is the relation between sample size and $\sigma_{\bar{x}_1 - \bar{x}_2}$?

10. How is the shape of the sampling distribution related to your ability to make confidence estimates?

Chapter 10. Univariate inferential statistics

1. Say you want to know how many hours of television the average student watches per night. Say you have taken a random sample of 100 students, and that the mean number of hours for the ones in your sample is 7.50 and the standard deviation is 5.00.

    a. What is your best estimate for the mean number of hours for all students?

    b. What is your best estimate for the standard error of the mean?

    c. If you want to be 95% certain about your answer, what is the range of error you must be willing to accept?

    d. How confident can you be that your estimate is accurate to within 1 hour?

2. Say you want to know how many movies the average Vancouver high school student watches per month. Say you have taken a random sample of 200 Vancouver high school students, and that the mean number of movies for the ones in your sample is 14.00 and the standard deviation is 4.50.

   a. What is your best estimate for the mean number of movies for all students?

   b. What is your best estimate for the standard error of the mean?

   c. If you want to be 95% certain about your answer, what is the range of error you must be willing to accept?

   d. If you want to be 99% certain about your answer, what is the range of error you must be willing to accept?

   e. How confident can you be that your estimate is accurate to within 1 movie per month?

3. Say you want to know how many speeding tickets the average professor has received. Say you have taken a random sample of 100 professors, and that the mean number of tickets for the ones in your sample is 12 and the standard deviation is 3.

   a. What is your best estimate for the mean number of tickets for all professors?

   b. What is your best estimate for the standard error of the mean?

   c. If you want to be 95% certain about your answer, what is the range of error you must be willing to accept?

   d. How confident can you be that your estimate is accurate to within 1 ticket?

   e. How confident can you be that your estimate is accurate to within 2 tickets?

   f. If your sample was 400 professors, what would be your best estimate for the standard error of the mean?

   g. If your sample was 400 professors, how confident could you be that your estimate is accurate to within 1 ticket?

4. If you quadruple the size of a sample, how would this affect the width of a 99 percent confidence interval? How would it affect the width of a 95 percent interval? Why?

5. Nationally, about 27 percent of households have a computer with a connection (by modem) to the internet. You think this number is too low for a description of your community, so you do a survey with the goal being to collect data that will allow you to determine whether your suspicion is accurate. What is your null hypothesis? What is the alternate hypothesis?

6. The Universal Anti-Smoking Institute (UASI) runs a highly regarded program that claims to be more effective at convincing young people to stop smoking than all other similar programs. They claim that the average graduate of their program smokes fewer than 10 cigarettes per week. You have been asked by the Federal Truth In Advertising Commission to test the accuracy of the claims of the UASI. You begin your assessment by administering a test to a sample of 36 graduates of the UASI program. Your results show that the mean number of cigarettes smoked per week is 16 with a standard deviation of 22 cigarettes.

   a. Could you get a sample with a mean smoking rate of 16 cigarettes per week from a population with a mean smoking rate of 10 cigarettes per week?

     1) Use the 95% confidence level to answer this question.

     2) Use the 90% confidence level to answer this question.

b. Assume the claims of the UASI are truthful and accurate.

1) What are the chances of getting a sample of 36 graduates of their program with a mean smoking rate of 16 cigarettes per week and a standard deviation of 22 cigarettes?

2) What are the chances of getting a sample of 36 graduates of their program with a mean smoking rate of 12 cigarettes per week and a standard deviation of 22 cigarettes?

Chapter 11. Crosstabulation

1. A study of Frozen Salmon University faculty and their use of personal stress management counselling sessions (PSMCS) was conducted. The answers to two questions produced the following data. Calculate the marginals, row percents, and column percents for the following table:

Faculty use of PSMCS

		Users	non-Users	Totals
Sex	male	29	37	66
	female	11	42	53
	Totals	40	79	119

a. What would it mean to "percentage across, compare down" on this table?

b. Which is more appropriate for this table -- "percentage across, compare down"; or "percentage down, compare across"? Why?

c. Interpret what this table tells you about the relation between sex and use of personal stress management counseling services.

2. Calculate the marginals, row percents, and column percents for the table shown below.

Preferred flavor of Ice Cream

		Chocolate	Vanilla	Strawberry
Sex	male	25	15	15
	female	35	20	10

a. Do "percentage across, compare down" on this table.

b. Do "percentage down, compare across" on this table.

c. Which is more appropriate for this table -- "percentage across, compare down"; or "percentage down, compare across"? Why?

d. Interpret what this table tells you about the relation between sex and preferred ice cream flavor. Make sure your interpretation is in terms of the variables. ("Compared to women, men were more likely to ....." or "Compared to Chocolate and Vanilla, Strawberry was more likely to ...")

3. A large study was conducted in the Los Angeles area, where there are serious problems with STD's (sexually-transmitted diseases) and drug addiction.

   Compute the rest of the counts, the row and column percentages, and row and column marginal counts and percentages for the table below.

		Drug user		
		yes	no	total
STD carrier	yes	.	60	150
	no	100	.	220
	total	.	.	

4. Using the "percentage down compare across" strategy, explain what the table shows.

Chapter 12. Strength of relationships: Discrete data

1. What does it mean to say that a measure has a PRE interpretation?

2. In a relationship between an ordinal-scale variable and a nominal-scale variable, which measures of association are appropriate?

3. What does it mean to say that the association between one pair of nominal-scale variables is stronger than the association between another pair of nominal-scale variables?

4. In a relationship between an interval-scale variable and a nominal-scale variable, which measures of association are appropriate?

5. In a relationship between an interval-scale variable and an ordinal-scale variable, which measures of association are appropriate?

6. For data in which you could use either lambda or gamma, why are you likely to get a higher result with gamma?

Support for proposed Free Beer Law by Age, Texas, 1995

	Age		
	Over 21 (+)	Under 21 (-)	
Support			Total
Favor (+)	371	663	1034
Oppose (-)	218	178	396
Total	589	841	1430

Calculate lambda and Yule's Q for the data in the above table.

7. Why does lambda give you different results when you starting with the second variable than with the first? Explain what the cause of the difference is and what it means.

8. Discuss what the two measures tell you about the relationship between Age and Support for the proposed law.

Support for proposed Free Beer Law by Education, Texas, 1995

Support	Education			Total
	less than High School	High School	Some college or more	
Favor (+)	427	258	169	854
Oppose (−)	111	188	235	434
Total	538	446	404	1288

Support for proposed Free Beer Law by Education, Alberta, 1995

Support	Education			Total
	less than High School	High School	Some college or more	
Favor (+)	282	238	278	798
Oppose (−)	186	268	330	784
Total	468	506	608	1582

9. Calculate lambda and Yule's Q for the data in the above tables.

10. Discuss what the two measures tell you about the relationship between Age and Support for the proposed law in Texas and in Alberta.

11. Using the data in the two tables above Question 9, calculate lambda and Yule's Q for the association between place of residence (Texas *vs*. Alberta) and support for the proposed Free Beer Law.

Chapter 13. Strength of relationships: Continuous data

1. Compare Pearson's *r* and covariance in terms of how they are calculated and discuss the difference between the two.

2. What are the consequences of the difference between how Pearson's *r* and covariance are calculated?

3. What useful properties are characteristic of Pearson's *r* but not of covariance?

Consider the following table which shows the scores twelve students received on two exams:

	Exam 1	Exam 2			Exam 3	Exam 4
a	42.66	81.68		a	83.68	45.51
b	85.62	49.51		b	45.51	92.99
c	75.30	75.39		c	68.39	55.88
d	43.46	77.61		d	75.61	75.61
e	85.74	31.82		e	35.82	83.68
f	41.72	84.59		f	87.59	63.45
g	85.53	61.88		g	55.88	72.35
h	85.39	63.45		h	63.45	87.59
i	43.25	79.94		i	79.94	66.79
l	85.48	70.79		l	66.79	68.39
k	84.02	74.35		k	72.35	79.94
l	41.54	96.99		l	92.99	35.82

4. Make a scatterplot for the exam scores with the X-axis for Exam 1 and the Y-axis for Exam 2. Do another one for Exam 3 and Exam 4.

5. Calculate the variance and standard deviation for the scores of the first two exams.

6. Calculate the covariance between the scores on the first two exams.

7. Calculate Pearson's r between the scores on the first two exams.

8. Calculate Spearman's rho between the scores on the first two exams.

9. Discuss the difference between the covariance and the Pearson's r.

10. Discuss the difference between the Pearson's r and the Spearman's rho.

11. Why is one higher than the other? (the scatterplot may help with this)

12. What does this show about situations in which Spearman's rho may be more useful than Pearson's r?

13. Subtract 30.0 from the scores for Exam 2 and recalculate covariance, Pearson's r, and Spearman's rho. What effect did this transformation on the data have on the results? Explain why this happened.

14. Multiply the scores for both exams by 0.5 and recalculate covariance, Pearson's r, and Spearman's rho. What effect did this transformation on the data have on the results? Explain why this happened.

15. What are the implications for the results you obtained in Questions 10 and 11? Are there particular situations in which you use take advantage of these results?

16. Calculate Pearson's r between the scores on the third and fourth exams.

17. Calculate Spearman's rho between the scores on third and fourth exams.

18. Compare the results from questions 16 and 17 to those from questions 7 and 8. Explain why the Pearson's r is almost the same while the Spearman's rho is different. The scatterplots may help you.

Chapter 14. Regression

Consider the following table which shows the scores of another twelve students on the final exams of four courses:

	Course 1	Course 2			Course 3	Course 4
a	83.68	87.59		a	42.66	81.68
b	45.51	35.82		b	85.62	49.51
c	68.39	83.68		c	75.30	75.39
d	75.61	66.79		d	43.46	77.61
e	35.82	55.88		e	85.74	31.82
f	87.59	79.94		f	41.72	84.59
g	55.88	68.39		g	85.53	61.88
h	63.45	45.51		h	85.39	63.45
i	79.94	75.61		i	43.25	79.94
j	66.79	72.35		l	85.48	70.79
k	72.35	63.45		k	84.02	74.35
l	92.99	92.99		l	41.54	96.99

Use the data for the first two courses for Questions 1 - 11. Use the data for the 3rd and 4th courses for Questions 12 - 16.

1. Calculate the means and standard deviations of the scores in the first two courses.

2. Calculate Pearson's r for the scores in the first two courses.

3. Calculate a regression equation, using the scores on the first course as the independent variable and the scores on the second course as the dependent variable.

4. Draw a scatterplot for the data for the first two courses and draw the regression line on the graph. Label the Y-intercept.

5. Locate the means of the first two courses on the graph and determine whether the regression line passes through the two means.

6. What is the coefficient of determination for the data for the first two courses? What does it mean?

7. What is the slope of the regression line? What does the slope tell you about your variables and how they are related to one another?

8. Calculate the residuals for students c, f, g, and k.

9. If the correlation between the scores in the first two courses was lower, what effect would this have on the residuals?

10. If a student received a score of 50 in the first course, what would you expect the student's score in the second course would be?

11. If a student received a score of 100 in the first course, what would you expect the student's score in the second course would be?

12. Calculate the means and standard deviations of the scores in the third and fourth courses.

13. Calculate Pearson's *r* for the scores in the third and fourth courses.

14. Calculate a regression equation, using the scores on the third course as the independent variable and the scores on the fourth course as the dependent variable.

15. Draw a scatterplot for the data for the third and fourth courses and draw the regression line on the graph. Label the Y-intercept.

16. After looking at the scatterplot from Question 15, discuss the appropriateness of the analysis you did in Question 14. What is the problem? What are the consequences of doing this kind of analysis on data like the data for the third and fourth courses?

Chapter 15. Statistical significance

1. You are doing some research and have collected some data from a sample of people who were randomly selected from a population in which you are interested. You have spent many nights pondering your data and, in a flash of insight, you have identified what seems to be an important pattern in the numbers.

   a. What would your null hypothesis be? (You can't answer this question in any detail with reference to means, frequencies, or percentages, but you should be able to answer it in a way that incorporates what you know about the role played by null hypotheses.)

   b. What would your alternate hypothesis be?

2. Because your insight has given you a burst of energy, you decide to forge ahead and test your hypotheses. Which one do you test? Why that one and not the other one?

3. The test will involve a critical value. What are critical values? What role do they play in the testing of hypotheses? What do you do with them? Where do you get them?

4. You have to do something with your data before the critical value comes into play, then you compare the result to the critical value. What do you look for when you do the comparison? How do you decide what the outcome of your test of the hypothesis is?

5. What is Type I error?

6. What is Type II error?

7. Which error is less desirable – Type I or Type II? Why?

8. Under what conditions do you fail to reject the null hypothesis?

9. Does a failure to reject the null hypothesis mean that you should give up your career as a researcher and go back to your part time job as a barista in a trendy espresso bar?

10. What are you left with when you do reject the null hypothesis?

11. What does it mean when you say that the pattern you see in your data is "statistically significant"?

Chapter 16. Chi-squared

1. Consider the following table:

Preferred flavor of Ice Cream

Sex	Chocolate	Vanilla	Strawberry	Coffee	Total
male	25	15	15	29	84
female	35	20	10	20	85
Total	60	35	25	49	169

2. If you were going to perform a chi-square test on this table, what would your *degrees of freedom* be?

3. What would the expected number be for the male vanilla cell? (How many men would you expect to prefer vanilla?)

4. What is the contribution of the female strawberry cell to the value of chi-square?

5. What is the value of chi-square for this table?

6. What is the null hypothesis?

7. Is the row variable independent of the column variable?

8. Do you reject the null hypothesis?

9. How certain are you of your answer?

10. How do you know that is how certain you are?

11. Which method would be more appropriate for interpreting this table – percentage down, compare across or percentage across, compare down? Why?

12. In a large survey done in the USA on a regular basis (the General Social Survey), people were asked "Taken all together, how would you say things are these days — would you say that you are very happy, pretty happy, or not too happy?" The results of this question are shown here:

Reported Happiness *vs.* Marital Status

Happiness	Marital Status			
	Married	Divorced	Single	Total
Very	347	97	58	502
Less than Very	467	256	220	943
Total	814	353	278	1445

13. What is the null hypothesis?

14. If you were going to perform a chi-square test on this table, what would your *degrees of freedom* be?

15. What is the null hypothesis?

16. What is the value of chi-square for this table?

17. Do you reject the null hypothesis?

18. How certain are you of your answer?

Chapter 17. z-test for differences between means

1. ***Earphones and earplugs, Inc.*** wants to focus its marketing for a new compact disc player on young affluent professionals. Their marketing department identified two magazines, *Wired Xers* and *Quiche & Volvo* as being especially popular among their target population. The advertising department of *Quiche & Volvo* claims that the age of its average subscriber is *not the same* as the average subscriber of *Wired Xers*. Formulate a pair of research and null hypotheses to test this claim.

    a. H_A:

    b. $H_\emptyset$:

2. Would you be doing a 1-tailed test or a 2-tailed test?

3. Determine the critical value for a 95% level of confidence ($p < 0.05$).

4. Draw a normal curve, mark it with *z* values and ages, and shade the critical region.

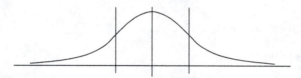

5. The advertising department of *Wired Xers* argued that, in fact, its readers were *younger than* those of *Quiche & Volvo*. Formulate the research and null hypotheses needed to test this contention. Then determine the critical region for a level of significance of $p < 0.05$.

    a. H_A

    b. $H_\emptyset$:

6. Would you be doing a 1-tailed test or a 2-tailed test?

7. Determine the critical value for a 95% level of confidence ($p < 0.05$).

8. Draw a normal curve, mark it with *z* values and ages, and shade the critical region.

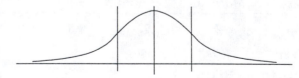

9. A random sample of size 24 was selected from individual subscribers to *Wired Xers*. The ages were as follows:

    23 43 27 45 30 32 26 42 43 25 38 35
    28 26 44 47 40 34 45 43 43 42 32 32

A similar sample was drawn for *Quiche & Volvo*:

29 28 49 45 47 35 34 45 49 53 36 44
30 36 34 42 43 26 33 46 37 47 48 35

Calculate the means and standard deviations. To help, I've calculated some sums for you. I've used "W" for *Wired Xers* and "Q" for *Quiche & Volvo*.

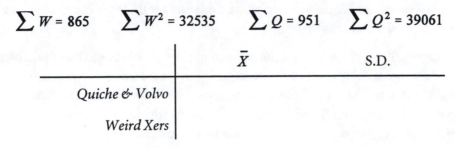

$$\sum W = 865 \qquad \sum W^2 = 32535 \qquad \sum Q = 951 \qquad \sum Q^2 = 39061$$

	$\bar{X}$	S.D.
Quiche & Volvo		
Weird Xers		

10. Estimate the standard error of the mean for the population from which the *Q&V* sample was drawn.

11. Calculate the .95 and .99 confidence intervals about the mean for the *Q&V* sample.

12. Can you conclude that the readers of *Q&V* are older than the readers of *W-Xers*? Determine whether the difference between the sample means is statistically significant. Use .05 as your probability level. Be careful here. Draw a normal curve and label it appropriately and shade the critical region. Don't be misled by the last two questions.

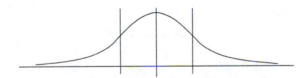

Chapter 18. Tests for correlations

1. You do a survey of a sample of 82 of your fellow students and ask about how much coffee they drink and how much sleep they get on a typical night. You calculate Pearson's *r* for the data and find a correlation of 0.22. You would like to know if this correlation could be due to sampling variability.

2. What are your null and alternate hypotheses?

3. What test do you perform?

4. Assume the 95% confidence level is okay. What is the critical value? How do you determine that?

5. What are the chances of getting a correlation as large as 0.22 in a sample of 82 students when the population correlation is zero?

6. What decision do you make about your hypotheses?

7. Your roommate doesn't believe your conclusion, so she does her own study with a random sample of 77 students. She finds Pearson's *r* of 0.2203. Still using the 95% confidence level, what is the critical value?

8. What are the chances of getting a correlation as large as 0.2203 in a sample of 77 students when the population correlation is zero?

9. What decision does she make about her hypotheses?

10. After she finishes her study she shows you her results and says that your results are wrong. You show her your calculations and the table you used to find the critical value and convince her that your calculations were correct. You check her calculations and see that they are also correct. How do you reconcile the contradictory results?

11. You don't sleep well at night, worrying about the contradiction you saw in the results of the two studies described in the first ten questions. You are so groggy in the morning that you knock your coffee cup off of the counter and it falls on the floor, spraying coffee all over the room. When you see the little brown spots scattered all over the white tile on the floor, you decide to do a scatterplot of your data and see what it looks like. You see something like the picture below.

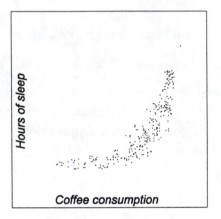

What do you conclude after studying the scatterplot?

12. Could you use Spearman's rho instead of Pearson's *r*? What would the effect be if you did this? Is it a good thing to do?

13. In an attempt to develop a better understanding of your results, you do another survey. This time you ask a random sample of 90 students how long they sleep in a typical night and how many credits they are carrying. You find a correlation of .48 between hours of sleep and number of credits carried. This seems like a big difference — it's more than twice as large as 0.22 – the correlation between coffee and sleep. What would the null and alternate hypotheses be for a test of the significance of the difference?

14. What statistical test do you use?

15. Using the 95% confidence level, what is the critical value?

16. Perform the test. What is the probability of getting a difference between Pearson's *r* as large as the one between .48 and .22 (with samples of 82 and 90) when there is no difference in the population correlations? Do you reject the null?

17. What do you conclude about the relative strength of associations between coffee and sleep and between credits and sleep?

Chapter 19. More mean differences: z, t, and F

1. Samples of students enrolled in two courses covering the same material received the following grades on their term project:

    Course A: 75.6, 55.9, 63.5, 66.8, 87.6, 93.0, 68.4, 79.9, 83.7, 35.8, 45.5, 72.4

    Course B: 55.4, 69.5, 72.7, 56.8, 46.4, 52.7, 62.8, 66.4, 60.1, 29.7, 37.8, 77.2

    Can you conclude from this data whether the mean grade given in Course A was *different* from the mean grade given in Course B? Which test is appropriate to do this?

2. Use the 95% level of confidence. What are your null and alternate hypotheses?

3. Is this a 1-tailed test or a 2-tailed test?

4. What are your degrees of freedom and the critical value?

5. Do you reject the null hypothesis?

6. What is your conclusion about the mean grades in the two courses?

7. Instead of determining whether the grades in the two courses were different, determine whether the mean grades in Course A were higher than the mean grades in Course B. Which test is appropriate?

8. Use the 95% level of confidence. What are your null and alternate hypotheses?

9. Is this a 1-tailed test or a 2-tailed test?

10. What are your degrees of freedom and the critical value?

11. Do you reject the null hypothesis?

12. What is your conclusion about the mean grades in the two courses?

13. A sample of a group of students in an evening offering of Course A received the following grades:

    Evening Course: 61.7, 12.8, 31.7, 45.5, 51.6, 54.5, 61.7, 67.6, 75.5, 82.3, 89.4, 99.2

    Determine whether which course the student was in is related to the mean grade awarded for the project. This requires an Analysis of Variance (ANOVA). What are your hypotheses?

14. What are the degrees of freedom?

15. Use the 95% confidence level. Make a summary ANOVA table on page 157. Compute the Sums of Squares, Mean Squares, and the F-ratio.

16. What is the critical value of F?

17. Do you reject the null hypotheses?

18. Interpret the results of the ANOVA. You will need to compare the three means and discuss the between-groups and within-groups variances.

19. When should you do a t-test instead of a z-test?

20. When should you do an F-test instead of a z-test? What can ANOVA do that the other tests for differences between means can't do?

Chapter 20. Experiments

1. Under what conditions are experimental research most appropriate?

2. What can you do with experiments that you cannot do with other approaches to research?

3. Why are control groups used in experiments? What do they do for you?

4. Why is random assignment to groups used in experiments? What does it do for you?

5. What are the main strengths and weaknesses of experiments?

6. Compare the two-group pretest-posttest design to the two-group posttest only design. What additional information does the pretest give you in the former? What potential sources of invalidity does the pretest allow you to rule out?

7. Compare the Solomon four-group design to the two-group pretest-posttest design. What additional information do the additional groups give you in the former? What potential sources of invalidity do they allow you to rule out?

8. How can you determine whether the pretest is influencing the way people respond to the experimental stimulus?

9. How can you determine whether the pretest is influencing the way people respond to the posttest?

10. How can you check the validity of the random assignment to conditions?

11. Many people believe that they can tell when someone is looking at them, even when they are looking in the other direction and cannot see the person who is looking at them. Design an experiment that will answer the following question:

    Can people tell when someone who they cannot see is looking at them?

    a. Describe the general setting in which you would conduct the experiment and how you would do it.

    b. What are your variables?

    c. What are your hypotheses?

    d. What are the experimental and control groups you would use in the experiment?

    e. How would you select the people who would participate in the experiment?

    f. How would you determine which people would be assigned to control and experimental groups? Be specific.

    g. What would the difference be between the experimental and control groups?

    h. What would you tell the people about the experiment before the actual measurements are done?

    i. How would you determine whether or not they could tell when someone was looking at them?

    j. Assume people can tell when someone is looking at them only most of the time. In other words, sometimes they think someone is looking when no one is looking and sometimes they think no one is looking when someone is looking, but that they are right about 70% of the time. How would you modify your experiment to take this into account?

12. Conduct the experiment you designed in Question 11. Use at least twenty people in each of the experimental and control groups. Use the appropriate statistical methods to analyze your results. Write a brief (4-8 pages) report describing your research. Include the following sections in your report: the research question, the research design, selection and assignment of participants, results, discussion, how the experiment could be improved.

Chapter 21. Survey research

1. What can you do with survey methods that you cannot do with other types of research?

2. What are the main strengths and weaknesses of survey methods?

3. Compare and contrast Likert scales and semantic differential scales in terms of how they are structured, the situations in which they are most appropriate and useful, and their strengths and weaknesses.

4. Compare and contrast Likert scales and short-answer essay questions in terms of how they are structured, the situations in which they are most appropriate and useful, and their strengths and weaknesses.

5. Discuss the strengths and weaknesses of ranking questions.

6. When are multiple-choice questions especially useful?

7. Design a five-item Likert scale that measures the extent to which people are afraid of mathematics.

8. Design an eight-item semantic differential questionnaire that measures students' opinion of their instructor's competence as a teacher.

9. Discuss the relative strengths and weaknesses of face-to-face interviews, telephone surveys, and self-administered questionnaires.

10. What factors would be the biggest threats to validity with telephone surveys?

11. What factors would be the biggest threats to validity with self-administered questionnaires?

12. What factors would be the biggest threats to validity with face-to-face interviews?

13. What is factor analysis, when would you use it, and what do you do with it?

14. What is the best way to determine whether your respondents' interpretations of the questions in your survey are in agreement with one another and with yours? What would you expect to see if they weren't?

15. What is wrong with the following survey questions?

    a. If you went to a record store and saw an expensive boxed CD set that you have wanted for a long time but haven't purchased because of the cost, would you steal it?

        Yes ____   No ____

    b. Where do you get most of your information about political events, economic issues, and investment opportunities?

        Newspaper ____   Television ____   Radio ____

c. How old were you the first time you rode a bicycle? ____

d. Do you agree or disagree with the new defense policy that says the government shouldn't get involved with military or political issues that aren't affected by the national interest?

   Agree ___   Disagree ___

e. How often do you pick your nose?

   Never ___   Once a week ___   Every day ___

f. How often do you talk to your best friend?

   Sometimes ___   Once a week ___   Every day ___   Whenever I can ___   Often ___

References

Babbie, E. (1989). *The Practice of Social Research, 5th Edition.* Belmont, California: Wadsworth Publishing Company.

Bowers, J.W. and Cartwright, J.A. (1984). *Communication Research Methods.* Glenview, Illinois: Scott, Foresman and Company.

Downie, N.M. and Starry, A.R. (1977). *Descriptive and Inferential Statistics.* New York: Harper & Row.

Frankfort-Nachmias, C. and Nachmais, D. (1992). *Research Methods in the Social Sciences, 4th Edition.* New York: St. Martin's Press.

Freeman, L. C. (1965). *Elementary applied statistics : for students in behavioral science.* New York : Wiley.

Johnson, A.G. (1988). *Statistics.* Orlando: Harcourt Brace Jovanovich.

Kerlinger, F. (1964). *Fundamentals of Behavioral Research.* New York: Holt, Rinehart and Winston.

Kenny, D.A. (1987). *Statistics for the Behavioral Sciences.* Toronto: Little, Brown and Company.

McNemar, Q. (1969). *Psychological Statistics, 4th Edition.* New York: John Wiley and Sons.

Nagel, E. (1961). *The Structure of Science: Problems in the Logic of Scientific Explanation.* New York: Harcourt, Brace & World.

Runyon, R.P. and Haber, A. (1976). *Fundamentals of Behavioral Statistics, 3rd Edition.* Menlo Park, California: Addison-Wesley.

Seigel, S. (1956). *Nonparametric Statistics for the Behavioral Sciences.* New York: McGraw-Hill Book Company.

Smith, M.J. (1988). *Contemporary Communication Research Methods.* Belmont, California: Wadsworth.

Index

italic — glossary
bold — definition

A

absolute zero 26
abstract concepts 8, 11, 17, 19, *215*
accuracy 76, 82, 90, 112, *215*
adjective pairs 178
alternate hypothesis **83**, 126, *215*
alternative explanations **11**, *215*
antecedent condition 9, *215*
applied research **14**, 15, *216*
area under the normal curve **62**, 64-67, 82
arithmetical operations 25, 46, *216*
assumptions behind inferential statistics *216*
assumptions of Science 6
average deviation **50**, *216*

B

basic science **14**, 15, *216*
bell-shaped curve **62**, *216*
between-groups sum of squares **158**, *216*
between-groups mean square **159**, *216*
bias **30**-32, 176-178, *216*
biased variance **152**, *216*
bins **61**, *216*, *221*
boundary conditions 9, 19, *216*

C

category 24-26, 92, 94
causal explanation **9**, *217*
causal relationships 4, 13, 168, 172, *221*
causes 9, 164, 165, 168, *217*
census *217*
central tendency **46**-59, 104, *217*
  mean **47**-55, 60-84, 135-143, 154-160, *223*
  median **47**-49, 51, 61, *224*
  mode **46**-48, 51, *224*
checklist or inventory questions 176
Chi-squared 104, **127-133**, 154, *217*
circularity 22
closed questions 19, 20, 176, *217*
coefficient of alienation **117**,
coefficient of determination **111**, 117
column percents **88**, *217*
comparisons of two values 26
composite measures **177**, 178
computational formulas **52**, 54, 109, 112-113, 118, *217*
computer assisted telephone interviewing 175, 183
concept **17**-23, 27, 29, *217*
concepts and constructs 17, *217*
conceptual definitions **21**-23, 30, 33, *217*
conceptualization 17-22, 217
concordant pairs **97**, 100
concrete reality 11
conditionally perfect association **98**
confidence intervals **40**, 41, **76**, 79, *218*
confidence level **76**, 125, 138-140, *218*
conservative measure 102, *229*
consistency **29**, 30, 32, *218*
construct validity **30**, 33, 34, *218*
constructs 17-23, 30, 32-34
continuous 46-51, 61, 104-107, *218*
continuous *vs* discrete 25, *218*
control group **165**-167, 169, *218*
correlation **99-103**, 110-113, 116-119, *218*
correlation matrix 101
counts **88**, 89, 92, 128, 130, *218*
covariance **107-111**, *218*
criteria for assessing conceptual definitions **21-22**, *218*
criteria for assessing problem statements **19-20**, *218*
criteria for evaluating theory **12**
criterion validity **30**, *218*
critical ratio **151**, 153, *219*
critical region 139, *219*
critical value **125**, 139, *219*
cross-products **98**, 108, 110, 112, 113, *219*
cross-sectional **14**, 15, 172, *219*
crosstabulation **87- 92**, 97-100, 132, 133, *219*
cumulative percentage **61**, *219*
curvilinear regression **118**, *223*, *227*

D

data reduction 93
data-to-theory **10**, *221*
deduction **7**, 10
degrees of freedom **50**, 130, 146, 154-156, 159, *219*
denominator degrees of freedom **159**, *219*
dependent variables 20, 21, 93, 94, 168, 169, *227*
descriptive statistics **45**, 46, 75, 93, 111, *219*, *222*
descriptive terms **20**, *219*
deviation scores **49**, **50**, 52, 53, 107-112, 154, *219*
differences between means 135-144, 151-159
direct or positive relationship 21, *220*
directed hypothesis **139**, *220*
discordant pairs **97**, 100
dispersion **48**-53, 59, 76, 104, 110, *220*
  heterogeneity 40, 54, 175, *221*
  interquartile range (IQR) **49**, *222*
  range **47**, 49, 53, 60, 61, *227*
  standard deviation **49-56**, 62-83, 107, *229*
displacement of the origin 27
distance between points 26
distribution **59-67**, 69-83, 123-125
double-blind methods **163**, 169, *220*
duplicate elements **174**

The Zen of Empirical Research by Dr. William D. Richards is a friendly, accessible introduction to quantitative research methods and statistics for students — especially for those with an Arts background or limited mathematical experience.

This text begins by providing students with a grounding in the principles of science and with a practical understanding of how to develop precise, empirically testable questions. It clearly explains the most common statistical methods used to answer these questions, and presents a detailed discussion of experimental design, survey research and sampling methods.

Developed through classroom use and student input, this text is, above all, a *student's* text book. Its unique first person conversational approach, informal humor and every day examples make abstract concepts clear and statistics fun. The emphasis is always on understanding the logic behind statistics rather than on math, formulae, or rote problem solving, which ensures that students are able to apply the skills they've learned to answer real research problems. *The Zen of Empirical Research* also features:

- a glossary of empirical, scientific, and statistical terms and concepts
- numerous Canadian, American, and international examples with detailed explanations
- step-by step guides for all major statistical tests
- a list of key concepts at the end of every chapter
- a large set of practice questions to help students master the material
- a summary table of statistical tests and the conditions for using them
- a web site (http://www.sfu.ca/~richards) with answers to exercises and supporting material

HAMPTON PRESS, INC.
CRESSKILL, NEW JERSEY

ISBN 1-57273-245-8